The Stanislavsky Heritage

CONSTANTIN STANISLAVSKY IN 1933.

The Stanislavsky Heritage

Its Contribution to the Russian and American Theatre

By CHRISTINE EDWARDS

Associate Professor, Speech-Theatre Department, Long Island University

New York University Press ❋ 1 9 6 5

Acknowledgments

For permission to quote the many passages from Stanislavsky's works acknowledgment is made to Theatre Arts Books, 333 Avenue of the Americas, New York, N. Y. 10014, as follows: *My Life in Art* (Copyright 1924 by Little, Brown & Co.; Copyright 1948 by Elizabeth Reynolds Hapgood for the Stanislavski Estate; also reproduced by permission of Geoffrey Bles, Ltd., 52 Doughty Street, London W. C. 1, England); *An Actor Prepares* (Copyright 1936 by Theatre Arts, Inc.; Copyright 1948 by Elizabeth Reynolds Hapgood; also reproduced by permission of Geoffrey Bles, Ltd.); *Building a Character* (Copyright 1949 by Elizabeth Reynolds Hapgood; also reproduced by permission of The Bodley Head Ltd., 10 Earlham Street, London W. C. 2, England); *The Seagull Produced by Stanislavsky* (translated by David Magarshack; All Rights Reserved; also reproduced by permission of Dennis Dobson, Ltd., 42 Great Russell Street, London W. C. 1, England); *Stanislavski's Legacy* (Copyright 1958 by Elizabeth Reynolds Hapgood); and *Creating a Role* (Copyright 1961 by Elizabeth Reynolds Hapgood; also reproduced by permission of Geoffrey Bles, Ltd.). Grateful acknowledgment is also made to Toby Cole for permission to quote from *Acting, A Handbook of the Stanislavski System* (Copyright 1955 by Crown Publishers); to Columbia University for the use of material in *Papers on Acting* (Copyright 1958 by Hill and Wang); to Grove Press, Inc., for the use of quotations from *On Actors and the*

v

vi *ACKNOWLEDGMENTS*

Art of Acting, by George Henry Lewes; to David Magarshack for permission to quote from his *Stanislavsky, A Life* (All Rights Reserved); to Columbia University Press for permission to quote from N. A. Gorchakov's *The Theatre in Soviet Russia;* and to Charles Scribner's Sons for permission to quote from *Richard Mansfield* by Paul Wilstach.

To

my brother, Leonard L. Hyams, M.D., F.A.C.S.,
whose constant interest, enthusiasm, and
valued criticism have encouraged and sustained me,

and

Vera Soloviova, who through her knowledge
and guidance inspired me and made the
Moscow Art Theatre come alive for me.

"When I look back over the roads that I have traveled during my long life in art, I want to compare myself to a gold-seeker who must first make his way through almost impassable jungles in order to find a place where he may discover a streak of gold, and later wash hundreds of tons of sand and stones in order to find at last several grains of the noble metal. And, like the gold-seeker, I cannot will to my heirs my labors, my quests, my losses, my joys and my disappointments, but only the few grains of gold that it has taken me all my life to find."

—Constantin Stanislavsky

"When I look back, does the result that I have devoted during my long life in it, I want to compare myself to a goldsearcher who must first make his way through almost impassable jungles, in order to find a place where he may discover a streak of gold, and must wash hundreds of tons of sand and stones in order to find at last several grains of the noble metal. And, like the gold seeker, I consign to my heirs my labors, my quests, my losses, my joys and my disappointments, but only the few grains of gold that it has taken me all my life to find."

—Constantin Stanislavski

Foreword

Just as the saturation point seems to have been reached in the argument pro and con the Stanislavsky System, up comes Christine Edwards (in private life Emmie E. Hyams) with this fine volume providing some new and useful clarity in two main areas of the discussion. First, she brings carefully documented and much needed truth to the history of the ideas embodied in Stanislavsky's work from their inception in prerevolutionary Russia right up to present day American theatre. Second, the popular misconception that the System is an acting style is laid to rest for all time.

For over thirty years we in the United States have been treated to much loose talk about the Stanislavsky System. Babblers range from movie gossip columnists who attribute a fancied rude brush-off from Marlon Brando to his training at the Actors Studio all the way to self-styled drama teachers who feel qualified to teach what has come to be known as "The Method" because they once went to a New Year's Eve party at the home of Lee Strasberg, head of the Studio. What a relief it is, therefore, to read a comprehensive résumé of Stanislavsky's influence on the American Theatre by someone who actually knows who he was!

It is a far cry, Miss Edwards wisely points out, from Stanislavsky's lifelong search for theatrical truth to the narrow confines of some of his "Method" disciples. These latter-day Method "hams" are recognizable by a certain stance, certain gestures, certain tones (or non-tones), based no doubt on early Brando characterizations. At least the old-time, cape-swinging actors were trying to make life larger, not art smaller. The lunatic fringe might not believe that in the first year of the Actors Studio Marlon Brando (in my class) worked on a long scene from *Reunion in Vienna,* playing the Alfred Lunt part. Hilarious he was, too, performing in high style, replete with pencil-thin moustache, long cigarette holder, sword, and Hapsburg accent.

My point is that a proper study of Stanislavsky's elements outlined in his writings on performing technique should not limit the actor to one style but free him to play in any and all styles. "The aim of techniques is to free the spirit," as Martha Graham has said. Other performing arts have well-known "methods," too. In the dance, many artists study the Cecchetti technique and it does not interfere with the development of a wide variety of dancers with individual styles. In the field of vocal art, there is the Marchesi Method. There were two famous Emmas in operatic history who studied personally with Mme. Mathilde Marchesi: Emma Calvé and Emma Eames. Calvé was the well-known fiery Carmen; Eames was an "iceberg"—She played the Countess in *The Marriage of Figaro* notably. It was also said that when she sang Schubert's "Who Is Sylvia?" it seemed as though that lady wasn't on her guest list. And yet both Emmas, hot and cold, studied the Marchesi Method.

Another canard still circulated by enemies as well as some friends of "The Method" is that the only important aim for the actor is to "feel truthfully inside," excluding any thought of the implements that must express that sense of truth. How little these people must know of Stanislavsky, who, over the decades, performed in or directed productions in every style, from farce to opera. And what blindness afflicts them when, in studying his books, they come upon such items as External Tempo and Rhythm, Diction, Rules of Speaking, the Sentiments of the Language, Movement, Dancing, Fencing, Sports, Acrobatics, Plastique, the Way of Walking?

In *Creating a Role,* Stanislavsky carefully synthesized the actor's "inner" preparation introduced in *An Actor Prepares* with the work on characterization he delineated in *Building a Character.* As proof of the contention of this present volume that Stanislavsky constantly emphasized the interrelation of inner and outer technique, the reader would do well to acquaint himself with all three of the above-mentioned books.

In addition to covering painstakingly the vast field of the Stanislavsky System itself, Miss Edwards gives us one of the most exhaustive histories of the entire Russian theatre. And for good measure we get a thorough historical documentation of the major acting theories in the rest of the world. This book is a monumental work of love and can take its place pridefully on the shelf next to the books of Stanislavsky himself.

Katonah, New York   ROBERT LEWIS
July, 1964

Preface

The subject of acting technique is extraordinarily complex. There is a strong temptation in writing about it to indulge in abstractions or fanciful theorizing that moves progressively further and further away from what the actor is actually doing.

My purpose has been to follow as closely as I could the technique of certain actors and their motivations. I have tried, insofar as possible, to convey the flavor of the personalities of my protagonists in the story of the development of the theatre in Russia and in America, and of the evolution, expansion, and interpretation of Stanislavsky's System. This accounts for my heavy reliance on actual quotations. Moreover, I feel that the exact words of the persons concerned with this entire subject are of greater value and interest to the reader than a paraphrase could possibly be.

The difficulty in rendering Russian names in English accounts for the variation between *y* and *i* in the spelling of Stanislavsky, Sergeyevich, and Alexeiev, as well as between *C* and *K* for Constantin. Variations also occur between the spellings used here and those used in other reference books on the subject for various other Russian names, such as Danchenko, Chekhov, Meyerhold, Shchepkin, as well as for the word Tsar (Czar). I have chosen to follow the spelling dictated by English usage rather than to attempt a phonetic transliteration, but in quoting other writers or the titles of their books I have followed their—or their publishers'—spelling.

I wish to acknowledge my special indebtedness to the late Dr. Dorothy I. Mulgrave for her constant encouragement and painstaking supervision of the original study from which this work is derived as well as to Professor William P. Sears, Jr. and Professor Fred C. Blanchard, all of New York University, and Dr. Francis D. Wormuth of the University of Utah.

Grateful appreciation is also expressed to John Gassner, Sterling Professor of Playwriting at Yale University, for the use of his library and for his ever ready counsel; to Elizabeth Reynolds Hapgood, without whose interest and valuable cooperation much of this work would have been impossible; to the members of the jury: Vincent J. Donehue, Mildred Dunnock, John Gassner, Norris Houghton, and Vera Soloviova, for their considered judgment; and to the following persons who have contributed their time, goodwill and other imponderables: Tamara Daykarhanova, Edythe Dineen, Kathryn Eames, Vallerie Freeman, Anita Grannis, Director of the State Theatre of North Carolina, Dr. Louise Gurren, Theresa Held, Phyllis M. Hofmann, Bill Knisely, Robert Lewis, James F. Macandrew, Mary T. McGrath, Marguerite McNeil, Carrie C. O'Gorman, Edward L. O'Gorman, Sydonia Presser, Dr. George J. Primavera, Dr. Letitia Raubicheck, Charles W. Raubicheck, Dr. James P. Romualdi, Professor Anaid Sarantchova of Columbia University, Beatrice Stillman, Daina Talborg; and to my friends of the Russian Theatre today who received me with open hearts and aided me in countless ways: Seraphima Ghermanovna Birman, former member of the Moscow Art Theatre and its First Studio, and presently actress, writer, and director in Moscow, Igor Constantinovich Alexeiev (Stanislavsky's son), Deema Kachalov (son of the famous actor of the Moscow Art Theatre), Fedya Mikhalsky, Director of the Moscow Art Theatre Museum who sent me the personal photographs of Stanislavsky, Mitya Sulerzhitsky (son of Stanislavsky's associate and dearest friend, Leopold Sulerzhitsky), and his wife, Masha; Natalya Vlasova, and Yuri Zavadsky, Director of the Mossoviet Theatre.

It would be graceless to try to define the debt which any student of the Russian Theatre owes to the following for their very excellent works: Nicolas Evreinoff, *Histoire du Théâtre Russe;* René Fülöp-Miller and Joseph Gregor, *The Russian Theatre;* Joseph Macleod, *Actors Cross the Volga;* B. V. Varneke, *History of the Russian Theatre;* Alexander Bakshy, *The Path of the Modern Russian Stage;* Nikolai M. Gorchakov, *Stanislavsky Directs;* and Oliver M. Sayler, *The Russian Theatre* and *Inside the Moscow Art Theatre.*

Contents

Illustrations

The Stanislavsky Heritage

Introduction

❂

On August 7, 1938, Constantin Sergeyevich Alexeiev, commonly known as Constantin Stanislavsky, died in Moscow at the age of seventy-five. In the twenty-seven years since his death there has been an increasing awareness of this man and of the system of acting which he developed. If articles in the newspapers and periodicals and discussions by well-known theatre people are any indication, the Stanislavsky System is still a vital force in the lives of today's actors, directors, and students of the theatre.

The Moscow Art Theatre was a unique and rewarding experience in the history of world theatre, and the system of acting which Stanislavsky developed has influenced acting in Russia and elsewhere.

It is the purpose of this volume to explore that influence and to investigate the contributions of the Stanislavsky System to American theatre art and practice. To do this, we must look first at the Moscow Art Theatre and understand its origins and its *raison d'être*.

Although there had been imperial theatres in St. Petersburg and Moscow since the days of Catherine the Great, literature on the theatre indicates that the actual staging had been haphazard and the acting anything but realistic. There were no dress rehearsals until 1894. In writing to a friend of the first performance of his *Sea Gull* in St. Petersburg on October 17, 1896, Chekhov himself says, "There were only two rehearsals, the actors did not know their parts—and the result was a general panic and utter depression; even Madame

1

Kommisarzhevsky's acting was not up to much, though at one of the rehearsals she acted marvellously, so that people sitting in the stall wept with bowed heads." Indeed, the author was so filled with shame and vexation that he went back to Melihovo the following day "full of doubts of all sorts," and feeling that he ought not to write any more plays. Fortunately, the second and third performances were successful and friends quickly wrote to Chekhov to tell him so.[1]

How different the public's reaction was only a little more than two years later when on December 17, 1898 the Moscow Art Theatre presented *The Sea Gull* and what a vastly significant experience it was for Anton Chekhov. So signal was its success, indeed, that a sea gull with spread wings became and still remains the emblem of that organization which continued to be the supreme interpreter of Chekhov. Speaking of Chekhov's influence in Russian drama and throughout the world, Freedley makes this comment:

> Whether this would have been true of Chekhov had his work not been combined with the complementary genius of Stanislavsky is debatable. The perfect combination of the ensemble work on stage refined the extraordinary character portrayal of the dramatist, and once seen, the effect is haunting.[2]

Just as Chekhov's work was combined with Stanislavsky's artistry, so the "complementary genius" of Nemirovich-Danchenko combined with Stanislavsky was responsible for the founding of the organization which came to be known as the Moscow Art Theatre. At the historic seventeen-hour meeting between the two men in June, 1897,[3] there began what was to become "the largest, busiest, most influential organization devoted to dramatic art in the world." [4] For the next forty years it was to be guided by the hand and mind of its cofounder, Constantin Sergeyevich Stanislavsky, winning acclaim not only in its own land but in many European countries and finally, also, in America.

In 1906, the Moscow Art Theatre played a season in Berlin and followed this "by a highly successful tour, which included Dresden, Leipzig, Prague and Vienna." [5] Much has been recorded of the two visits of the Moscow Art Theatre to the United States in 1923 and 1924. "A total of 380 performances of thirteen productions in twelve American cities in the course of two seasons" [6] was no mean accomplishment. Freedley says of this visit:

> It is not too much to say that the whole American theatre was affected by this visit, which left memories, methods and a number of the actors

who preferred life in America to the more restricted freedom of their native land.[7]

"Memories, methods and a number of actors" have been dealt with in this volume, for it was largely through these actors that the Stanislavsky System or method of acting came to be recognized in America. The effect was like a chain reaction emanating from the source, Stanislavsky, and from there to several of the younger and more gifted of his pupils, with whom he formed the First Studio as a testing ground for his new ideas. "The First Studio brought out the talents of Richard Boleslavsky and the brilliant Michael Chekhov." [8] These two and several others of its members were to become known in America as actors, directors, and teachers of the method which they had helped to create. Boleslavsky, Bulgakov, Bulgakova, Chekhov, Daykarhanova, Jilinsky, Ouspenskaya, and Soloviova have had an influence upon many young actors and actresses of a new generation.

Notes

1. *Letters of Anton P. Tchekov to his Family and Friends,* Translated from the Russian by Constance Garnett. (London, Chatto and Windus, 1920), pp. 341–42.
2. George Freedley and John A. Reeves, *A History of the Theatre* (New York: Crown Publishers, 1941), p. 401.
3. Constantin Stanislavski, *My Life in Art*, translated by J. J. Robbins (New York: Theatre Arts Books, 1948), p. 295.
4. Oliver M. Sayler, *Inside the Moscow Art Theatre* (New York: Brentano, 1925), p. viii.
5. Freedley, p. 539.
6. Sayler, p. 18.
7. Freedley, p. 540.
8. Freedley, p. 540.

one

The Origin and Development of the Russian Theatre

THE INFLUENCE OF THE COURT

By the end of the first decade of the twentieth century, the Moscow Art Theatre was making a distinctly favorable impression upon the theatre of the West. The far-reaching influence [1] which it exerted during the next two decades is all the more remarkable in view of the retarded and feeble beginnings of the Russian theatre. In France in the year 1673 the plays of Molière were being performed at the newly-founded Comédie Française, whereas in Russia at that time there was almost no native repertoire and there were virtually no native actors. [2] The first recorded performance of any play took place before Tsar Alexis Mikhailovich only one year before, on October 17, 1672, in the village of Preobrajenskoie just outside Moscow.

Under the influence of his second wife, Nathalie Narychkine, educated in European ways, Tsar Alexis Mikhailovich had overcome the traditional scruples dictated by the Orthodox Church against clowning, buffoonery, and other forms of entertainment. He even went so far as to authorize one Gregori, a German pastor in his employ, to make an adaptation of the Book of Esther and have it played before him in a special room in one of the summer palaces in the nearby village of Preobrajenskoie. [3] This first of Russian theatres was short lived, ending four years later with the death of the Tsar [4] and the exile of the noble, Matveyev, "the chief sponsor of these western customs." [5]

5

His son, Tsar Feodor III, showed little interest in theatre. However, the latter's sister, Sophia Alexeyevna, translated many works of literature from German and French and even wrote an original verse drama entitled *Catherine the Martyr*. It was she who introduced Molière to the Russian court. She gave dramatic performances in her own apartment for the entertainment of the younger nobility and her female servants.

The imperial influence was strengthened under Peter I (The Great), who had a theatre built in Moscow and encouraged attendance by exempting all who came from the customary toll for leaving the Kremlin after sundown. However, this venture met with little success, since the plays done in German could not be understood by most of the audience and those done in Russian failed to please them, either because of the subject matter or the acting.[6] Peter believed the theatre would have a civilizing effect upon his "backward subjects." He even commanded that the children of the nobility who attended the Sukarev School should be taught acting and encouraged to give regular performances.

After the victory over Charles XII of Sweden, according to Fülöp-Miller, Peter moved his court to St. Petersburg, where he had a theatre erected. Here regular performances were given, starting in 1724. Eleven years later in 1735, after Peter's death, under the regency of Peter's first wife, Anna, an Italian company was invited to court by the Empress. Thus the Russian people came under the influence of the Commedia dell' Arte, the opera, and the ballet. In fact, a school for ballet was established at court for twelve girls and twelve boys in the imperial service. This was followed by the first Russian chorus.

Elizabeth, the illegitimate daughter of Peter I, who overthrew the rule of her stepmother, did much to advance the state of the Russian theatre. In 1740, the year before she was crowned empress, she had a theatre accommodating 5,000 spectators built in Moscow for her coronation. She imported a French, a German, and an Italian company, but since she preferred the French, she installed it in the theatre in the Winter Palace, and by proclamation, all "decently clad" citizens were admitted free to their performances. She also had a theatre built in St. Petersburg, the first to be made of stone, for the French company.

It was also in her reign that the first provincial theatre was started in Russia by a member of the bourgeoisie. In 1746 Fydor Volkov, the son of a rich leather manufacturer, was much impressed by the

French company during a visit he made to St. Petersburg. On his return to Yaroslav, a town on the Volga, he assembled a company of players from among his friends and servants and members of church choirs, and began to give performances in an old shed. He was actor, director, scene designer, and musical director at the same time.

When the Empress Elizabeth heard of this, she sent for Volkov and his company to play before her at Court in St. Petersburg. So pleased was she with the performance that she gave him a ring and kept the company there, sending Volkov and his friend Dmitrevsky to the Cadet School to be educated.[7]

In 1756 Elizabeth had a theatre built especially for Volkov, and in the following year she sent him and his colleague, Shumsky, to Moscow "to establish a Russian theatre there and from that time performances in Russian were given regularly in both capitals." [8] Alexander Bakshy makes the following comment upon this:

> Thus the nucleus of the first trained company of Russian actors was formed, making possible the establishment of a permanent Court theatre. Exceptional intelligence and organizing gifts naturally placed Volkov at the head of the company, whilst his efforts to popularize the art he loved so much, in the country have earned him the name of "the father of the Russian theatre." [9]

After the death of Elizabeth and the brief incumbency of her nephew, Peter III, the latter's German wife, Sophie, seized power and became Catherine II (the Great). During her reign she brought about several advances in the development of the Russian theatre. She gave Volkov an estate in the country and made him a noble. She founded a theatre in St. Petersburg for the common people. The actors, who were clerks, bookbinders, and other tradesmen, had been performing in an open-air amphitheatre. Finally, in 1779, the first permanent dramatic school was founded in St. Petersburg to attract "a regular succession of actors drawn from the Russian people." [10]

By the first quarter of the nineteenth century the repertoire of the Russian stage included Shakespeare, Schiller, Corneille, Racine, and Molière. During the reign of Alexander I Russia was recognized as a world power, and with the conquest of Napoleon in 1812, the Russian language was finally accepted as a fitting expression of poetic feeling and the poet Pushkin received the appreciation which he deserved.[11]

Several important theatres were built in Moscow. The Bolshoi (Large) Theatre opened in 1824, the Maly (Little) Theatre in 1825, and the Alexander Theatre, in St. Petersburg, in 1831, after Alexander's death.[12] Thus the influence of the court brought about the gradual establishment of the imperial theatres. In the latter part of the eighteenth century, another influence which was of equal importance, but at the opposite pole from the imperial influence, had begun to show its effect upon the Russian theatre.

THE SERF THEATRE

The first mention of a serf in the role of entertainer had occurred in 1744 at the marriage of the Empress Elizabeth's nephew, Peter, to Sophie of Anhalt-Zerbst, the future Catherine II. The Empress had had a "Ballet of Flowers" presented in the theatre at the court, and the ballerinas were young serfs who had been directed by Jean-Baptiste Lande, the head dancing master of Russia, and, in fact, Elizabeth's own instructor.[13]

Following the example set by the court, the nobles constructed theatre auditoriums in their castles or in separate buildings on their estates. Evreinoff tells us that because of either natural indolence or the memory of the former ecclesiastic prohibitions, they were reluctant to "tread the boards" themselves. However, they found actors among their peasants who had a natural grace in speech, gesture, song, and dance gained through expressing their folklore.

The establishment of these "serf theatres" has been described as the most significant achievement of the nobility. An important factor in the development of this "unique form of theatrical organization" (as Fülöp-Miller calls it) was the winning of "imperial privilege" by the nobility in 1762. Previously the members of the ruling class had been themselves subject to corporal chastisement at the command of the Tsar. In addition they had been obliged to reside at court. After securing exemption from public service and compulsory residence in the capital, many of them returned to their estates in the country. Here they started to establish companies of actors, dancers, singers, and musicians from among the peasants who belonged to them, to provide entertainment at such seasons as Lent when the theatres at the capital were not open.

In this way many serf theatres developed and some of them became famous. A certain Count Peter Borrisovitch Chérémétiev brought the manorial theatre to its highest point of glory. He built three theatres, one in Moscow, the other two on his estates on the outskirts of Kouskovo and Ostankino.

In his memoirs the French ambassador at St. Petersburg has preserved an account of a presentation given at Kouskovo during a visit of Catherine II to Count Chérémétiev in 1787. He speaks of the magnificence of the theatre and of the production (grand opera), of the quality of the singing, the elegance of the costumes, and the beauty and art of the dancers. He remarks particularly upon the fact that the composers, both of words and of music, the architect of the theatre, the painter who decorated it, as well as the actors, actresses, and musicians, all belonged to Count Chérémétiev, "who takes great pains for their education and to whom they owe their talent." [14]

Another famous serf troupe belonged to the wealthy Prince Yussapov, who retired to his estate at Archangelskoie and developed a *corps de ballet* of thirty young girls chosen from the domestics in his castle. According to Fülöp-Miller, the Prince converted an old farm building into a dancing school and hired a staff of music and dancing instructors to train the girls in strict seclusion there as dancers and singers. He is reputed even to have taken the entire company to Moscow to see the actors of the Imperial Theatre perform, in order for them "to become familiar with the techniques of the stage and form themselves on the best models." [15]

In summer this company performed ballets, operas, comedies, and the national dances of various sections of Russia out-of-doors; in winter they played in a theatre especially built for them in the castle.

The singers of Yussapov's company later took part in a performance of Italian opera in Moscow. In fact they gave some performances at the Nobles' Club in Moscow, for which, ironically enough, the Prince received a sizable payment.

Prince Yussapov was noted for his concern for his dancing girls, buying them costly gifts, calling the best doctors to attend them if they became ill, giving them dowries when they married. He even had miniature snow hills built in the courtyard in winter so that they could go tobogganing. Nevertheless, he occasionally forced them to dance naked before the audiences of his invited guests.[16] However, according to the terms of his will, all adult singers and dancers of his company became enfranchised upon his death. Most of these were hired by other noblemen to develop new theatrical companies from their serfs.

Joseph Gregor maintains that the "social despotism" of the serf theatres stemmed from "an unabridged gulf between the aristocratic audience and the enslaved actor." His collaborator, Fülöp-Miller, speaking of the "degrading and humiliating factor which was essentially part of the whole system of serfdom," offers this explanation:

> . . . the condition of the artists, their good or bad treatment, their rise or fall, was dependent in the last resort on the arbitrary caprice of their masters, who could use them kindly or expose them to deepest humiliation according to the whim of the moment. In many country houses, the female players were looked upon as members of the family and in a few cases, raised by marriage to a position of actual equality.[17]

The best-known example of a marriage between an aristocratic theatre owner and a serf-actor is that of Count Nicolas Petrovitch Chérémétiev, son of the founder of the famous company, and Paracha Jemtchougova. The Count fell deeply in love with the beautiful young daughter of his blacksmith and raised her to eminence in his company. She won applause from the Emperor of Austria and from Tsar Paul I. For ten years she and the Count lived together in a new house built near the theatre. Finally, in 1800, they were married by the Metropolitan of Moscow in the cathedral there. Three years later, upon the birth of a son, Paracha died, leaving the Count inconsolable. He himself lived only six years longer, and the most famous of the serf theatres disappeared almost "when the voice of Paracha died away." [18]

In summing up the events of the eighteenth-century Russian theatre, Varneke declares: "Our young theatre gradually grew from an object of noblemen's entertainment into a theatre for the people and for their creative expression. Many talents developed to full artistry despite the adverse conditions which were prevalent in the serf theatres." [19]

By the beginning of the nineteenth century, Evreinoff maintains, "There was hardly a wealthy estate which did not have its orchestra, choral group and actors doing their best to entertain their masters." The "absolute ownership" which the nobles possessed over their serfs gave them the right not only to mistreat them but even to sell them to other masters. Sometimes they were even sold to the imperial theatres. However, such a change was desirable since it resulted in an improvement in status. In this regard Evreinoff says:

> At all events it must be admitted to the credit of the administration of the Imperial Theatres that a serf was never bought without his family and that above all, they were liberated from the moment they were bought. It can therefore be said that they were *redeemed* rather than *bought*.[20]

This hope of possible enfranchisement prompted the serf-actors of Alexis Stolypine to petition Tsar Alexander I to buy them after their master had put them at the disposal of the Imperial Theatre of Moscow in the hope of getting a good price for them. Stolypine had asked 42,000 rubles for the troupe of actors and the orchestra, which amounted to seventy-four persons, "children included." The Tsar's chamberlain struck a bargain and bought the entire company for 32,000 rubles.

The first quarter of the nineteenth century saw the so-called "Golden Age" of the serf theatres.[21] Two of the largest companies were those belonging to Count Kamenski and Prince Chakhovski (Shakhovsky), respectively.

The theatre of Count Kamenski, as described by Macleod, was located in the city of Oryol. The productions were mounted lavishly and directed by the Count, who took care of every detail himself, even the choice of the recipients of complimentary tickets. This may have been the best of the slave theatres. In addition to his household serfs, the Count had acquired another group of actors. For these he was reputed to have paid the "sum of 500 peasants, or in the elegant financial diction of the day, 'five hundred agricultural souls.' "

From accounts of the period, however, the acting seems to have left much to be desired. Macleod makes this reference to the strictness of Kamenski's discipline: "He tried to get the company to memorize their parts so well that they could dispense with a prompter. He came down heavily on any one who 'dried.' "[22] This tyrannical theatre owner and manager sat in his box during performances, making note of any mistakes made by the actors on stage. After each act he would go into the wings to punish the offenders, whose cries sometimes reached the ears of the audience.

The rigorous manner of living which prevailed at the Count's theatre is vividly described by Evreinoff:

> The theatre of the Count resembled a barracks; the musicians of the two orchestras, one of strings and one of wood winds, were dressed in military uniforms; the actors took their meals together; a roll of the drums announced the beginning and the end of the meal; they ate standing, the Count having declared that this way they would be satisfied without overeating; the actresses lived confined in cell-like rooms; corporal punishment was as frequent as in the Russian army of that time.[23]

Kamenski seems to have been as inordinate in the management of his productions as in his discipline of their personnel. For each production he insisted upon new costumes and decorations, spending more than 30,000 rubles on the *Caliph of Bagdad* for silks, brocades, velvets, and ostrich plumes. His extravagance forced him to sell thousands of his peasants and he was completely ruined when he died in 1835.

Prince Nicolas Chakhovski, on the other hand, was a somewhat more benevolent despot. His estate was in Nizhny-Novgorod, and every year from July until the beginning of autumn his company of serf actors played at the Great Fair there.[24] Actors, singers, and orchestra all belonged to the Prince and were equal in number to an imperial theatre company. The Prince exercised the strictest discipline, especially among the girls, as Macleod points out:

> The girls were kept almost under lock and key like jewels. They were guarded, rigorously, by old women, "Mamushki," selected by the Prince as "reliable." They were delivered, like private letters, in a carriage to the rehearsals in the mornings, and again to the performances in the evening; and again brought back in a carriage, like a confidential answer, after the show. And both at rehearsal and at performance the "Mamushki" watched them in the dressing room till the stage manager called them to the stage; and in the wings watched another "Mamushka," called a "watch woman," who never let them out of her sight, and stopped them saying a single word to any male actor beyond what was written in the script.[25]

The Prince himself gave the girls lessons in "elocution and deportment so they could impersonate great ladies on the stage"; and they were taught to read but not to write—at least, not until after they were married, for fear they might carry on an amorous correspondence before their marriage. Afterward, however, the Prince felt their morals were in their husbands' hands.[26]

Chakhovski was apparently a man of very high character. For one thing, he did not have his "favorites" among the girls, in the usual sense of the word, since he was the most perfect husband. He avoided, as far as possible, subjecting his actresses to corporal punishment. He seems to have been of a puritanical nature, deleting from the plays he produced all jokes with the slightest suggestion of double meaning. Moreover, in the large wooden house where the troupe was lodged the two sexes were strictly separated, and a chaperon was appointed to insure their good behavior. The slightest deviation was punished by the rod, and serious offenders were made to wear a collar with iron spikes. On the other hand, he played the part of a father, arranging marriages as soon as the girls reached the age of twenty-five, providing them with dowries, and increasing the salaries of the newly-wedded members of the troupe.[27]

To learn the conduct of high society, inexperienced actresses were assigned to the service of the Princess, where they learned to converse, to read, and to embroider; and the best members of the company were admitted to the balls given at the palace. Finally, as a preparation for his production of the comedy of Griboyedov, *Woe from Wisdom,* the Prince even took the leading players to Moscow to watch from the gallery the balls given at the Nobles' Club there. Chakhovski's artistic taste seems to have been rather high, judging from the repertoire of his company, which included among the comedies, tragedies, and vaudeville, selections from Shakespeare, Calderon, Schiller, Mozart, and Griboyedov.[28]

Speaking of Prince Chakhovski's company, Macleod remarks, "The standards of acting were not high." Referring to an account of the uninspired acting at a certain performance by the company of Count Kamenski, the same writer concludes, "The Count was in advance of his company."

EARLY NINETEENTH CENTURY THEATRE PRACTICE

There were few good Russian plays worthy of mention. Tsar Nicholas had little appreciation for the theatre except as it might affect the rising middle class whom he mistrusted. He therefore demanded a "patriotic repertoire," and insisted upon the expurgating of any passage that might "evoke applause for its independent views by the 'non-privileged' classes." [29]

In acting, the emphasis appears to have been upon the manner of speaking the lines. According to the memoirs of a writer of the period, Semyonova, one of the leading actresses of the period, "sang." Actors demanded dramatic exits which aroused the audiences to applause. Macleod ascribes the origin of the phrase "clap-trap" to this tendency:

> Vociferous applause leads to a return on stage and a bow, which renews the applause, which renews the bow, which renews the applause, and so forward with the action suspended till player and applauder are satisfied and quiet ensues for the next passage.[30]

There was a school in St. Petersburg for those who wished to go on the stage. Here everything seems to have been included in the curriculum, from opera singing to carpentry—except acting. Rehearsals were few and actors received little help from anyone in the creation of their parts. Before the first rehearsal, the stage manager read the play to the company, "alluding to each character by the tone of his voice if he was able." It was his business also to indicate entrances and exits as convenience or tradition dictated, and then, as now, to make sure at performances that each actor was ready for his entrance.

FAMOUS ACTORS

In spite of all the obstacles, at the imperial theatres in St. Petersburg and Moscow in the first half of the nineteenth century there were many fine actors who won the admiration of their audiences. Each city had its favorites.

KARATYGIN AND MOCHALOV

The idol of St. Petersburg theatregoers was Vassily Karatygin, whose theory of acting concurred with Diderot's as he expressed it in his "Paradox," namely, that of the absence of feeling or "sensibilité," or the elevation of intelligence. His interpretations were always planned in advance down to the smallest detail; he was skilled in the craftsmanship of his profession.

In Moscow, Paul Mochalov was equally popular, though he was a completely different kind of actor. Far from planning his role in advance, he left everything to the inspiration of the moment. Consequently his performances were uneven, not only from one night to another, but sometimes from scene to scene. However, one moment of inspiration in an evening's performance was often enough to win him the title of "genius" from his adoring public. Unfortunately, his lack of mastery was often caused by drink.[31] On the other hand, he realized the vast difference that existed between his conception of a role and his performance, except in his inspired moments. Nevertheless, concerning the art of acting, Mochalov wrote:

> In the first place, the actor must proceed with the analysis of the author's thinking and intentions, that is, with the discovery of what he meant to express by such and such words, and what his aim was. . . . Depth of soul and a lively imagination are the two faculties constituting the basis of talent, however. Only then does the actor possess the gift to convey to the audience what he feels in his soul, that is, to make his imagination picture vividly the action, whether described or taking place—in brief, only then can the actor make the spectator forget himself.[32]

SHCHEPKIN

The methods of both Karatygin and Mochalov were challenged by another actor in Moscow who subsequently became one of the brightest stars in the Russian theatre, and his rise to fame is as romantic as any piece in which he may ever have played. For Michael Semyonovich Shchepkin was born a serf in the year 1788 on the estate of Count Volkenstein, to whom his father acted as valet.[33]

As a boy he played small parts in the little village school and was adjudged better than the other children even then. At fourteen, he was entered in the private theatre of Count Volkenstein and played various roles in popular comedies. In 1805, when Shchepkin was only seventeen, he substituted for an actor who had been drinking too much. Shortly afterward, he came under the influence of Prince Metcherski, an amateur actor of unusual and original talent, who had a very important effect upon him.[34]

The main difference between the playing of Metcherski and that of the other actors, as Shchepkin later noted in his memoirs, was that the Prince acted with a minimum of gestures and spoke in an ordinary tone of voice. This appeared to Shchepkin at first as a weakness in Metcherski's acting. However, he made special mention of the fact that in a certain scene concerned with money, the Prince appeared to be actually grieved, and for the moment made him forget the other actors.[35]

Shchepkin also noted with admiration the astonishing change which took place on the face of the Prince when he was threatened with the loss of his money—a change which transformed his otherwise noble features to those of a "skinflint." Nevertheless, the absolute simplicity of Metcherski's acting, almost without gesture, and of his speaking, "comme tout le monde," seemed to Shchepkin not befitting an actor.

In giving the reasons for his failure to appreciate Metcherski's acting at first, Shchepkin makes very clear the style of acting popular at the time:

> At the time the playing of the actors was considered excellent when none of them spoke in his natural voice, when they declaimed their lines in a completely artificial manner, when they pronounced each word in a strong voice and when almost every word was accompanied by a gesture. The words "love," "passion," "treason" were uttered as loud as possible, but

the actors' facial expression did not carry out the meaning for they remained set and hardly natural. And when, for example, the actor finished a long monologue at the moment of leaving the stage, he had to go off into the wings with his right arm raised.[36]

Until Shchepkin witnessed this particular performance of Metcherski, his own acting had been in the manner of the day. Realizing that the Prince seemed to live the part he was playing, he tried to play the same part in this new way. To his amazement, he found he was unable to speak a single word in a simple, natural manner. Then he tried imitating Metcherski with no more success. He wanted to "feel the part." Finally, on one beautiful day, Shchepkin responded to his stage partner spontaneously. He himself remarked of the result:

> I realized that I had pronounced some words in a very simple way, so simple in fact that, if this had been in life and not in a play, I should not have said this sentence differently.[37]

In discovering the "natural tone" of voice, he was on the threshold of a new way of acting, and it may be said that the realistic school, which was to come to full flower some years later in the Moscow Art Theatre, was born with Shchepkin. This consisted not merely in discarding the old manner of declamation and substituting natural speech, but in the meticulous work on a role in order to give a characterization a realistic foundation. This was Shchepkin's greatest contribution to the art of the Russian stage. For, as Evreinoff points out, many actors before him had heard the natural speech of Prince Metcherski, and no doubt had passed over it as coming from an amateur. It was Shchepkin's good fortune, however, to have been aesthetically ready to receive this innovation and to permit it to direct his painstaking research into new means of artistic fulfillment.[38]

His talent placed Shchepkin in the first rank of actors in the provincial theatres, and his admirers were moved to try to raise enough money to buy him his freedom. But the price Count Volkenstein had set was 10,000 rubles and the sum collected was only 6,000. A certain Prince Repnine supplied the missing 4,000, but this resulted merely in a change of masters. Nevertheless, the historian Bantych-Kamenski provided Shchepkin with the needed amount to become enfranchised, together with his wife and his children. This took place in 1822 when the actor was thirty-four years old. The following year he was engaged to play at the Imperial Theatre in Moscow, where he continued to act for forty years, until his death in 1863.

In 1824 (according to Fülöp-Miller, 1825) a new theatre, the Maly, opened its doors in Moscow and Shchepkin began his famous association with it. Bakshy pays tribute to his art and his influence upon the Maly in these words:

> It was the special merit of Shchepkin that in addition to his exceptional power of impersonation, which harmoniously united both intelligence and sensibility, he always strove to present not just single characters, mutually detached and independent, but the play as a whole, a unity in which all parts bind and determine each other. This practice of the principle of ensemble together with his bitter opposition to every kind of artificiality and affectation in the manner of acting, set its stamp on the work of the Moscow Imperial Dramatic Theatre, the Small (Maly) Theatre, . . . which during the days of Shchepkin and long after his death, became famous for the artistic thoroughness of its productions and even received the name of "The Home of Shchepkin." [39]

RUSSIAN PLAYWRIGHTS AND THEIR INFLUENCE UPON ACTING

Until nearly the middle of the nineteenth century the plays acted on the Russian stage were mostly foreign, or Russian imitations of French, German, or Italian models. The style of acting was influenced by the classic style of the plays.

GRIBOYEDOV

With Griboyedov's *Woe from Wisdom* appeared the first intimation of a play with a truly Russian background. This was a satire on the society of the time, and the characters were skillfully drawn from people of the day. From Griboyedov's own description of his play, ". . . there are twenty-five fools to one reasonable man, and that man, of course, stands in conflict with the society surrounding him."

The play was banned for many years both for production on the stage and publication. It was produced for the first time in full in 1869, forty years after its author's death, and has become "an integral part of the cultural heritage" of the country. The critic P. N. Sakulin remarks of the play, "On the stage we see live, real people with lines from everyday life and extraordinarily colorful speech. . . . Much of it, in the form of pithy proverbs, has become part of popular speech and is immortalized." [40]

Of the handwritten copies which were circulated, A. A. Bestuzhev declared:

A great many characters portrayed boldly and graphically, a vivid picture
of Moscow customs, real emotions, intellect and wit in discourse, hitherto
unknown fluency, and the conversational quality of the Russian language
in the verses . . . all these lure, attract and stagger one. A man with a heart
will not read it without laughing, nor without being moved to tears . . .[41]

PUSHKIN

Pushkin has been called "the founder of the Russian literary language and the father of the new Russian literature." He sought to
reform Russian playwriting, urging that Shakespeare be taken as a
model. In constructing his greatest work, *Boris Godunov,* Pushkin
imitated Shakespeare "in his free and broad delineation of the characters." Pushkin admired Shakespeare because of the lifelike characters which he created. "Verisimilitude of feelings" combined with
"verisimilitude of characters" was the ideal he set for Russian playwriting. "Truth of passions, genuineness of feelings in given circumstances—that is what our reason requires from the playwright,"
Pushkin wrote. Stanislavsky often referred to this statement as a basic
requirement for an actor. Pushkin, too, applied this to the actor as well
as to the playwright. Indeed, he was not in sympathy with the French
classic school of acting, nor did he admire either Karatygin or
Mochalov. On the other hand, he was a friend of Shchepkin and
urged that great actor to write his memoirs.[42]

GOGOL

A truly Russian literature begun by Griboyedov and Pushkin and
continued by Gogol and Ostrovsky gave rise to a realistic school of
acting since the lifelike characters drawn by the playwrights demanded
realistic portrayal on a stage. Nicolai Gogol did much to free the
Russian theatre from the mediocrity into which it had fallen. In addition to his plea for restoration of the great works of Shakespeare,
Molière, Schiller, and Beaumarchais, he urged the creation of Russian
plays "reflecting the life of Russian society and the character of Russian men." [43]

He was greatly concerned with stage practice and was the first in
Russia to speak about the ensemble, which he declared ought to be
both realistic and artistic and which should be directed by none but
the best actor in the play. This same desire to have the entire production create a single artistic impression and to have the performances
of the individual actors subordinated to an overall impression or

organic whole also possessed the actor Shchepkin.[44] The actor and the playwright became lifelong friends, and Gogol seems to have played as important a part as Prince Metcherski in inspiring Shchepkin to a new approach to acting. For just at the time when the actor was experimenting with new ways of making the characters he was playing into living people, the playwright presented him with living people to impersonate.

Gogol also had talent for acting. Ironically enough, he was denied admission to the Imperial Theatre because of the very simplicity of his playing. His ideas concerning both acting and directing were very sound, and similar to those of Shchepkin. In fact, so well did the two friends complement each other that, according to Evreinoff, historians of the theatre argue still as to "whether it was the actor who applied to the stage the theory established by the playwright, or the writer, who with his pen, gave written form to the ideas of his friend, the actor." A comparison of their advice on how to win the audience's applause illustrates this point clearly. Gogol wrote: "The less the actor thinks about making the audience laugh, the more he will succeed in doing it. Laughter will spring from the seriousness with which each person in the play performs his task." [45] Shchepkin, on the other hand, admonished: "Only for God's sake do not seek to make the public laugh since both the droll and the earnest, after all, are derived from the correct view of the thing. . . ." [46]

Gogol also emphasized the need for the ensemble, praising the effect of "a perfectly coordinated harmony of all mutually interrelated parts" which, he felt, was realized in the performance of an orchestra but lacking in stage productions of the period. Shchepkin for his part, was known to refrain from an effective piece of business in his own role in order to promote the general harmonious effect of the performance as a whole.

Shchepkin and Gogol were also in complete accord on how a part should be played, and the influence of their ideas upon Stanislavsky is apparent. For instance, Gogol required the actor to identify with the character "so that the thought and aspirations of the impersonated character be appropriated by the actor himself and that these stay in his mind during the entire performance of the play." He also demanded "truth and naturalness both in speech and in bodily movement." [47] Similarly, Shchepkin wrote in a letter to another actor, Shumsky, "Get, so to speak, into the skin of the person in the play; study his social environment, his educational background, any peculiar ideas he may have, and do not overlook even his past." [48] On another occasion he gave the following counsel:

> Remember, my dear friend, that the stage is averse to carrion: give it a live man, and one not merely physically alive—one who lives with his intellect and his heart . . . . When reading a part, by all means try to compel yourself to think and feel in the manner in which he whom you have to represent thinks and feels. Try, so to speak, to chew and swallow the whole part so that it may become part of your flesh and blood. [49]

Evreinoff suggests that the influence of these two men led artists in the theatre to break away from the sterile imitation of Western theatre. Gogol's *The Inspector General,* or *Revizor,* is regarded by many as "the greatest play in the Russian language extant." [50] Shchepkin was pre-eminently successful in the part of the mayor. Moreover, his influence was so enduring at the Maly Theatre that the actor Davydov, who lived until 1925, "is said to have been a faithful copy of him in this part even in small details." [51]

OSTROVSKY

After Shchepkin's death, the playwright Alexander Ostrovsky continued his tradition at the Maly Theatre. He had a marked influence upon the actors who performed his plays there and was especially responsible for the fine ensemble. Ostrovsky did most to establish not only a national literature but a national theatre as well. His characters were drawn directly from the people; they spoke like people in the audience; they behaved toward one another as people do in life. Moreover, Ostrovsky loved the people and he knew the simplest among them from listening to them "when he was hunting, fishing, visiting country taverns," and "he drew his words and expressions from his talks with them."

Speaking of the reasons for Ostrovsky's greatness Macleod says:

> Now there was a bond of reality in speech between people in the audience and those on the stage. Actors were speaking like other people. Other people could therefore accept them as similar to themselves.
> Then, because he knew and could understand individual characters, their wants and problems, he drew these in the round . . . . people in the audience . . . could feel sympathy or antipathy toward them, as they did in real life. [52]

The playing of Ostrovsky demanded even deeper realism than Gogol. His characters were drawn largely from the middle class, which had begun to assume more importance in 1861 when Alexander II freed the serfs. Because they caused the audience to think, many of his plays were banned by the censor.

The actor who best fitted the playwright's requirements was Prov Sadovsky. He founded his realism on that of Shchepkin, and he and his family continued to perform Ostrovsky at the Maly Theatre, not without criticism from the older generation. It was said of them that "they 'lived' on the stage, even when drinking tea or vodka (and you could tell which it was from the way they appeared to drink it)." This realistic tradition was handed down from father to son in the Sadovsky family as far as the third generation and was still represented at the Maly by the grandson's nephew as late as 1928.[53]

Ostrovsky wrote a play a year from the time he was in his thirties till he died at the age of sixty-three. He was responsible also for the formation of the Society of Russian Dramatic Writers and Opera Composers, and was at the head of the "Artistic Circle" in Moscow. This group, in 1869, asserted "the right of the bourgeoisie to have its own theatre." [54] Their hope was thus to be able to perform many good plays which the tsar's censor had banned.

FREE THEATRES

Numerous private theatres began to open on the outskirts of St. Petersburg, beyond the limits of control of the Imperial Theatre and in Moscow, in various residences of wealthy amateurs. Ostrovsky even performed in his own plays in one of these. The audiences were at first composed of the specially invited.

In 1881, however, a courageous young woman of wealth, who took the name of Anna Brenko, opened the first private theatre in Russia for the general public. She formed her own company of actors, "the flower of non-imperial talent," calling it the Pushkin Theatre.[55] There were several facets of this undertaking which seemed to foreshadow the Moscow Art Theatre. For one thing, the company lived "as a commonwealth, all together." The emphasis was on the ensemble rather than the individual performances. Finally, more time was given the actors for the study of their parts, by comparison with existing standards. In this connection Macleod says:

> Rehearsals usually began a whole fortnight before opening night! First, the author, or Burlak, would read the play to the assembled company. Then there would be a reading round a table, but "in full voice." The second rehearsal was on the stage with the actors reading from the book. Exits, entrances and corrections were noted, and the company went away to

study with the whole plan of the play in their minds. At the third rehearsal they were expected to do without the book; and then followed the "dress rehearsal" which was, however, far from being what we know by that term.[56]

This theatre, however, was short-lived, for with the assassination of Alexander II in March of 1881 all places of amusement were shut down for two months' mourning. However, Anna Brenko continued working for the theatre all her life. To her goes the honor for having opened the "first free acting school for working class amateurs" and for producing on a Moscow stage in 1905, Ostrovsky's most popular play, *The Storm*, in which all parts except her own were played by factory workers.[57]

The abolition of the imperial monopoly in 1882 encouraged private enterprise. In addition to Anna Brenko, one of the first to organize a private theatre was F. A. Korsch, who developed a competent company headed for a time by Davydov. At first this theatre provided the Maly with competition, but very soon Korsch became so sure of his success that he began to pay less attention to purely artistic matters than to the commercial side of the enterprise.[58] One of the first "modern producers" was Lentovsky, who actually paid attention to the stage crowd. He also employed artists to design his sets and costumes. Sometimes his productions surpassed those of the imperial theatres.[59]

DECLINE IN PRODUCTION STANDARDS

However, in the theatres which were springing up in the provinces —and even in the imperial theatres in the last decades of the nineteenth century—the standard of production began to deteriorate. Even before Ostrovsky's death in 1886 the Maly began to lose its fine reputation. The ensemble disappeared and the directors were more concerned with box office returns than with the quality of the plays and players.[60] Davydov, who was for a time in the provinces, complained of the low standard of rehearsal, the number usually being two, with "three as a maximum." He deplored also the "stage diction" assumed by less talented actors, and he tells of one actor's indignant reply to his suggestion that he (Ivan Kozelsky) "stop singing his lines and give Russian speech a Russian inflection according to its meaning," whereupon the actor demanded, "Do you wish me to speak on the stage like a peasant from Pskov?" Moreover he asserted "that he wasn't speaking Russian anyway, he was speaking poetry." [61]

Type casting lasted till 1882, and Macleod pictures conditions at the Maly as crude, with two rehearsals considered sufficient for a comedy and no idea of ensemble, "only a certain give and take between the principals." So it becomes apparent that, by the end of the nineteenth century, Shchepkin's ideas had lost their effectiveness. A flood of inferior problem plays had contributed to making production a matter of "mechanical routine." [62]

Although Ostrovsky had made many suggestions for the reform of the Maly Theatre, they were never given serious consideration by those in charge. They were not even made public until after the death of Stanislavsky. Since the Imperial Theatre was actually run by bureaucrats and lacked artistic direction it could not be successful in actor training. Ostrovsky's demands for stage discipline show a close resemblance to the purposes of Stanislavsky and Danchenko.

Vladimir Ivanovich Nemirovich-Danchenko, who was presently to become the cofounder of the Moscow Art Theatre, ascribes Ostrovsky's failure to influence the young actors to the fact that they were already "slaves of stereotypes" when they arrived at the theatre. "The famous Russian art, proclaimed by Gogol and Shchepkin," declares Danchenko, "had more and more become overgrown with conservatism and sentimentalism, and had become stationary." [63]

Nevertheless, there were some highly gifted actors both in St. Petersburg and Moscow. The Moscow company was generally considered superior to the one in St. Petersburg. It was made so by the presence of such artists as Prov M. Sadovsky, who was to Ostrovsky what Shchepkin had been to Gogol earlier; S. V. Shumsky, a pupil of Shchepkin; and the tragic actress, Fedotova,[64] who was to influence Stanislavsky. According to Varneke, Pissemsky, the author of *Bitter Fate,* having traveled all over Europe and seen many good actresses, found in no other actress such depths of feeling as in Fedotova. She, too, had been a pupil of the Dramatic School, where she had come under the influence of Samarin and Shchepkin. Fedotova shared the honors with another tragedienne, Yermolova, who became the greatest actress on the Russian stage, according to the critics. Stanislavsky referred to her as "the heroic symphony of the Russian theatre." She was completely dedicated to the theatre, and "better than anyone else personified a harmonious synthesis of realism and romanticism." Never depending upon blind inspiration, she preserved Shchepkin's tradition in every detail.[65]

LENSKY

One of the leading actors at the Maly Theatre, and a painter and sculptor as well, Alexander Lensky contributed perhaps the most to the art of the theatre of his time. He was also a teacher at the Moscow

Theatre School and director of the Maly Theatre until 1909. He was the first "to break applause during a scene and to refuse end of act curtain calls." [66]

In his *Notes of an Actor* he exposed some of the affected ideas on acting then in vogue, particularly Diderot's theory regarding the absence of feeling (see pp. 130–133). He maintained, on the contrary, that only extreme sensibility and complete self-mastery can make a great actor.[67] At the Conference of Theatre Workers held in March, 1897, Lensky spoke on "The Causes of the Decline of the Theatre." [68] The question of actor training occasioned a spirited discussion. Many leading actors objected to any training for an actor. They even protested against an actor's having to be subject to the demands of the producer or director. They were led by the actress Strepetova, who, according to Magarshack, shouted at the conference, "Down with dramatic schools! Down with training! Back to Mochalov!" Lensky, on the other hand, emphasized the necessity for the actor to study his art the same as the artist in any other field, and he branded as ridiculous "acting by intuition." [69] He stressed the need for the producer who was artistically competent and advocated the establishment of "permanent companies" and the lowering of the price of admission.[70]

In the light of these events, the creation of a theatre dedicated to the ideas of Shchepkin and Gogol and grounded in the belief of training for the actor was inevitable. It was indeed fortunate that when this need arose events should have already prepared the man capable of creating such a theatre and of developing a method of acting that would shed its influence far beyond its homeland.

❊

Notes

1. René Fülöp-Miller and Joseph Gregor, *The Russian Theatre,* translated by Paul England (Philadelphia: J. B. Lippincott Company, 1930), preface, p. 21.
2. Alexander Bakshy, *The Path of the Modern Russian Stage* (Boston: John W. Luce and Company, 1918), pp. 6–8.
3. Nicolas Evreinoff, *Histoire du Théâtre Russe* (Paris: Edition Du Chêne, 1947), p. 102
4. Bakshy, p. 8.
5. B. V. Varneke, *History of the Russian Theatre, Seventeenth Through Nineteenth Century,* original translation by Boris Brasol (New York: The Macmillan Company, 1951), pp. 30–31.
6. Bakshy, pp. 9–10.
7. Varneke, pp. 68–70; Bakshy, p. 11.
8. Fülöp-Miller, p. 30.
9. Bakshy, p. 11; Varneke, p. 72.
10. Varneke, p. 115.
11. Fülöp-Miller, p. 37.
12. Fülöp-Miller, pp. 31–32.
13. Evreinoff, pp. 207–208.
14. Evreinoff, pp. 210–11.
15. Fülöp-Miller, p. 34.
16. Evreinoff, p. 217.
17. Fülöp-Miller, p. 35.
18. Evreinoff, pp. 211–14.
19. Varneke, p. 151.
20. Evreinoff, p. 223.
21. Evreinoff, p. 231.
22. Joseph Macleod, *Actors Cross the Volga* (London: George Allen & Unwin Limited, 1946), p. 36.
23. Evreinoff, p. 230.
24. Macleod, p. 29.

25. Macleod, p. 30.
26. Evreinoff, p. 228.
27. Evreinoff, pp. 226–28.
28. Evreinoff, p. 227.
29. Macleod, p. 17.
30. Macleod, p. 22.
31. Evreinoff, p. 293.
32. Varneke, pp. 260–63.
33. Fülöp-Miller, p. 35.
34. Evreinoff, p. 235.
35. Evreinoff, p. 235–36.
36. Evreinoff, p. 236.
37. Evreinoff, p. 237.
38. Evreinoff, pp. 237–38.
39. Bakshy, p. 20.
40. Varneke, p. 205.
41. Varneke, p. 204.
42. Varneke, pp. 211–17.
43. Varneke, pp. 300–301.
44. Evreinoff, p. 265.
45. Evreinoff, p. 264.
46. Varneke, p. 287.
47. Varneke, pp. 288–89, 301.
48. Varneke, p. 286.
49. Varneke, p. 293.
50. Bakshy, p. 18.
51. Macleod, p. 26.

52. Macleod, p. 59.
53. Macleod, p. 61.
54. Macleod, p. 62.
55. Macleod, p. 63.
56. Macleod, p. 64.
57. Macleod, p. 66.
58. Varneke, p. 392.
59. Macleod, p. 69.
60. David Magarshack, *Stanislavsky, A Life* (New York: The Chanticleer Press, 1951), pp. 142–43.
61. Macleod, p. 45.
62. Bakshy, p. 21.
63. Vladimir Nemirovich-Danchenko, *My Life in the Russian Theatre*, translated by John Cournos (Boston: Little, Brown and Company, 1936), p. 31.
64. Varneke, p. 358.
65. Varneke, p. 378–80.
66. Macleod, p. 67.
67. Evreinoff, p. 298.
68. Macleod, p. 94.
69. Evreinoff, p. 299.
70. Magarshack, p. 148.

two

Apprentice

The founding of the Moscow Art Theatre by Constantin Sergeyevich Alexeiev, more commonly known as Stanislavsky, and Vladimir Ivanovich Nemirovich-Danchenko was more than a happy accident, as an examination of the backgrounds of its founders will reveal. Less is known about Danchenko than about Stanislavsky, possibly because Danchenko, as a playwright, wrote less about himself and his methods of work, and possibly because, as an actor, Stanislavsky was the more romantic personality of the two.

Born on January 18, 1863, Stanislavsky was the son of a wealthy Moscow business man whose great-grandfather had been a serf. His father owned a factory for making gold and silver thread, where Constantin Sergeyevich spent many years working. However, he always found time for acting and the production of plays.

It was precisely because of his interest in bettering his own acting that Stanislavsky sought almost from the beginning to discover means of improving acting as an art. From his very early days, according to his own testimony in *My Life in Art,* he strove to secure the belief of the audience in the reality of his offerings. In recounting his childhood experience with his brothers and sisters in producing a circus act at home, Stanislavsky complained of his eldest brother's behavior on the day of performance. Vladimir Alexeiev, the only one who could provide the music, apparently did not take his part seriously and sometimes behaved very badly, even going so far as to lie down on the floor before the whole audience in the parlor and refuse to go on playing. He could be placated by the gift of a bar of chocolate, but Stanislavsky declared:

> The performance would be spoiled by his foolish act; all its reality would be lost, and that was the most important thing for us. It was necessary to believe that all this was serious, that it was real. Otherwise it was not interesting.[1]

The atmosphere in the Alexeiev household surely helped to foster in the children of the family an interest in the theatre. For one thing, they were taken at an early age to the theatre, the ballet, the circus, and even to the opera. Sometimes the children of the servants were also taken along, as well as nurse, governesses, and maids. Commenting upon the effect of all this, Stanislavsky wrote:

> The smell of gas, which was used to illuminate theatres at that time, always had a magical influence on me. This smell, connected with my ideas of the theatre and the delight received in it, made me dizzy and called forth strong emotions.

Stanislavsky's parents encouraged his interest. They had organized the first home performance and had taken part in it, when Stanislavsky was seven.[2] Later they and their relatives and neighbors were a willing and often enthusiastic audience at "Constanzo Alexeiev's Circus," and at the marionette theatre which followed. This project filled the days of the young members of the Alexeiev family in their free time and often during their study hours.

In *My Life in Art,* Stanislavsky relates how they overcame their "only obstacle, study and tutors and governesses."

> In the drawer of the table there always lay hidden some piece of theatrical work, the figure of a marionette which was to be painted and dressed, a piece of scenery, a bush, a tree or the plans and sketches for a new production. On the desk lay our books, but in the desk there was always scenery . . . . In the margins of my books and copybooks there were always sketches of scenery. And no one could ever guess whether it was scenery or a geometric drawing.[3]

The admission charge was ten kopecks. Once when a particularly large audience appeared, the young producers decided to move to a larger room in order to realize more profits. The artistic result was less satisfactory than in the smaller room. "We decided that if we were to occupy ourselves with art," Stanislavsky comments, "no thought of money must enter our minds." At this moment, Stanislavsky learned a basic artistic truth.

Further incentive to theatrical production was provided by the elder Alexeiev when an old wing of their country house near Moscow fell into a state of disrepair. This had been the place where the children could romp and play and sing as noisily as they wished without disturbing anyone. Stanislavsky declared:

> Not only they, but the neighbors begged our father not to destroy our club. At last it was decided to put up a new building with a large hall which when necessary could be transformed into an auditorium. Not only the hall with its balcony that served instead of boxes, but even the back part of the building was wonderfully arranged and gave space for dressing rooms, scenery and property. The result was a little theatre.[4]

THE ALEXEIEV CIRCLE

To celebrate the opening of this little theatre four one-act plays were presented by Stanislavsky and his brothers under the direction of their young tutor. The performance was given to celebrate Stanislavsky's mother's birthday, on September 5, 1877. It was important for three reasons. For one thing, it marked the first appearance of Constantin Sergeyevich as an actor when he was not yet fifteen years old. It also was the start of the regular dramatic productions by the members of his family, including his father, which were soon to be organized into the "Alexeiev Circle" under Stanislavsky's own direction. Finally, it was immediately after his performance in the two farces *A Cup of Tea* and *The Old Mathematician* that he made the first critical comments on his acting, thereby beginning his "Artistic Notes." Regarding his acting in the play, *The Old Mathematician,* he wrote, "I played coldly and languidly, without a spark of talent, though I was not worse than the others." With reference to his successes in the first play, as measured by the audience's laughter, he commented: "It was Muzil (a comedian admired by Stanislavsky) who made their laughter, for I had copied even his voice." Magarshack maintains that "it was this habit of unsparing self-criticism which gradually led him to examine analytically the laws of acting and eventually to evolve his famous 'system.'"[5]

Stanislavsky describes the anticipation of this first performance in *My Life in Art*. Since he and his brothers were already studying at the gymnasium in Moscow, they had to go to Moscow to their classes on the day of the performance and return home just before dinner. Stanislavsky was carrying a large box containing wigs, hair, glue, make-up. "The specific odor of the make-up which is so well known to all artists," he writes, "floated into my nose from every crack in the box and made me drunk."

His role in *A Cup of Tea* was one often played by Muzil at the Maly Theatre. In his performance Constantin Sergeyevich tried to copy this actor faithfully, including his hoarse voice and peculiar facial expressions. He felt quite confident, moreover, since he knew his favorite comedian's performance so well. He describes his feelings of excitement at the time:

> What excited me was not my lines, not the meaning of what transpired, for the one-acter was devoid of all meaning, what thrilled me was artistic action, the playing before spectators . . . . I was excited by the madness of the tempo and the rhythm within me which made me hold my breath at times. Words and gestures flew out with the rapidity of lightning. I choked, I lost my breath and could not speak, and my nervousness and lack of restraint were mistaken by me for true inspiration.[6]

In the second role of his debut, that of the old man in *The Old Mathematician,* Stanislavsky felt less confident since he had no model for the part. "At that time," he remarks, "I was still unable to find my examples in life and re-create them on the stage." What he did in this role was to copy different actors in different sections of the part. "Each separate copied section was possible in itself," Stanislavsky declares, "but all the sections taken together were impossible. The part resembled a blanket sewn together of rags, shreds and remnants."

At the time of the performance the young Stanislavsky felt that his better portrayal had been in *A Cup of Tea.* Yet he was criticized for speaking too low and indistinctly and for moving his hands in the air too rapidly. This fact brought him to realize the vast difference between the actor's own impressions while on the stage and the impression created in the auditorium by his acting.

Soon afterward Stanislavsky was invited to play, in a private home, the part of a drunken servant who became more intoxicated with each succeeding entrance. The result was the same. Although he felt himself an excellent copy of a drunkard, the audience criticized him. In a second private performance outside of his home he again played one of the best parts of a favorite actor, and again he felt he was inspired, but "the more it excited me," he declares, "the more the audience criticized my rapid patter, my incoherent diction, my hoarse voice, my murmuring speech, my rapid gestures, my strained and exaggerated efforts." In his third performance he was reproached for lacking "a feeling of true measure." This criticism stimulated him to search for a sense of proportion in all his subsequent work.

In the summertime, when no performance was possible, the younger members of the household began to rehearse French vaudeville skits, which merely resulted in the acquisition of outer technical craftsmanship. In the summer of 1883, when Stanislavsky was twenty, the group decided to write an operetta in which each member was to invent a role that suited him. As might be expected, the play was not a success. It was important, however, for a special circumstance. Stanislavsky's oldest sister, Zinna, suddenly had to step into the leading role, which their cousin had unexpectedly vacated. Stanislavsky writes of how he tortured her in rehearsals. He admits that he had little faith in her, since up to that time she had played only the smallest parts and then only on rare occasions. His joy when her talent revealed itself foreshadowed his future attitude toward his art:

> She could not make her own the strongest and most important moment of the role, without which all that followed would be incomprehensible. I decided not to go any further until she had reached success in the part. With tears of despair in her eyes, my sister played the most important scene, so that we all became seriously affected . . . . The timidity that had chained her was broken by her in her despair and the strong temperament of all artists found its way to the surface. With the same passion with which I had persecuted her, I now glorified her. Without letting her stop to dry her tears, I begged her to continue.[7]

The result of this discovery was the search for a drama that suited Zinna. It was decided to produce *The Practical Man* by Potekhin. While working on this play Stanislavsky devised the scheme of *living the circumstances*. All through the summer rehearsals continued, and it was agreed, Stanislavsky writes, "that on a given day we would live no longer as ourselves but as the people whom we were to play, and under the circumstances of the play in question." As practice made it easier for them to act and speak to one another the way they had decided the characters would act and speak and think under the "given circumstances" of the play, Stanislavsky concludes, "Apparently we were entering into our roles." This was the first play in which he received praise from those who saw it. Although his playing was still a copy of the well-known actor Sadovsky of the Imperial Theatre, what he had taken from him had become his own.

Not only did Stanislavsky's father provide a theatre in his country house at Lyubimovka, but in their Moscow home he converted two rooms connected by an arch into an auditorium and stage. During the week the larger room, which became the auditorium, served as a dining room. To open this little family theatre Stanislavsky rehearsed a new operetta called *Javotta,* which he had brought from Vienna. According to Magarshack, the performance took place in the autumn of 1883.

For the leading part, a young professional who was about to graduate from the Moscow Conservatory was invited to join the home players. The beauty of his voice made up for his ugly appearance and lack of acting talent. Stanislavsky's constant rehearsals gave the chorus a degree of smoothness in spite of his two conflicting methods, which he designated as "to memorize the text so that the words repeated themselves mechanically," and "to live not in our own selves but in our roles as we did in *The Practical Man.*" Discussing this paradox, Stanislavsky says:

> Of course this did not lead us anywhere, for the methods of experience in life continually created a need for impromptu work and the methods of memorizing words completely excluded the possibility of impromptus.[8]

Stanislavsky was keenly disappointed over the preference of the audience for the imported baritone in spite of his bad acting. Magarshack declares "this lack of appreciation of his acting . . . drove him to enter a Moscow School of Acting for a short time." [9] In *My Life in Art* Stanislavsky states that he remained in the Dramatic School of the Imperial Theatre no more than three weeks. Nevertheless, in spite of his short stay and his sporadic attendance necessitated by his work at his father's factory, he was able to discover the weakness in the methods employed. Commenting on the chief fault, that the students were expected to copy their teacher, he writes:

> But they would have done well what was required of them if they had been allowed to do it in their own way. Perhaps it would have been incorrect, but anyway it would have been sincere, truthful and natural, and one could believe them . . . . Remember what Shchepkin writes in his letter: "It is not important that you play well, or ill; it is important that you play truthfully." [10]

He attended largely because of the presence on the board of a very great actress and friend of his family, Glikeria Fedotova, and he left at about the same time that she did. One more comment of his regarding the school bears repeating:

> We were told very picturesquely and with much skill what the play and the parts were supposed to be, that is, of the final results of creative work, but how we were to do it, what road or method to use in order to arrive at the wished-for results—nothing was said about that. We were taught collectively or individually to play a given role, but we were not taught our craft . . . . I was frightened by the thought that like the rest of the pupils, I would be deprived of my own individuality, bad as it was. And I dreamed of one thing only—to be myself, to be that which I can and must be naturally, something that neither the professors nor I could teach me, but nature and time alone.[11]

In spite of the failure of *Javotta,* the Alexeiev Circle continued to be occupied with operettas, and in the summer of 1884, Stanislavsky attempted a truly enormous production after the manner of Lentovsky, the proprietor and manager of the well-known "Hermitage." This, Stanislavsky tells us, was a great park containing ponds for water festivals and water ballets, an operetta theatre which seated several thousand, and an open-air amphitheatre.

Stanislavsky undertook to put on a production of an operetta called *Mascotta* for one performance at the family theatre in the country, providing entertainment for the guests in the garden at the same time. The family circle was augmented by a chorus made up of friends and as many of the servants as could sing. Sometimes the friends came to rehearsal in the early morning and would leave in the small hours of the next morning, or else at six in the morning they would go to Moscow and return for rehearsals in the evening. Since none of the singers could read music, the task of Stanislavsky's older brother was a colossal one. As stage director, Stanislavsky faced no simpler one, for each singer had to be trained individually and there was additional work in decorating the garden.

The picture which Stanislavsky draws of serious work combined with gaiety, laughter, and often lack of sleep suggests a very deep love for the theatre. Yet in evaluating this performance, Stanislavsky is very severe in his criticism of himself in the part of the shepherd, Pipo:

All that is bad in confectionery barber-shop beauty was taken for my make-up—curled mustaches, curled hair, tightly clad legs. And all this for a simple shepherd who always lived near to nature. How can I place my comparatively decent taste in other things alongside of the absence of all taste in my own make-up? . . . there were the same operatic gestures, but all that was good and that we had recently made our own was absent.[12]

Because of his great desire to make acting his profession, he decided to forego the pleasure of going to his family country place the following summer. Accordingly, he stayed alone in the house in Moscow with its marble halls and staircases which lent unusual resonance to his voice exercises. He followed a regular schedule of practice, sometimes till three or four in the morning, continuing this all summer and autumn after working all day in the office. Although he later condemned the method of working before a mirror, he admits that this helped him to realize his faults of gesture and body movement. Another achievement of this summer's work was the improvement of his diction.

This was the year in which the Saxe-Meiningen Players made their first visit to Moscow. However, it was their second visit five years later that made such a profound impression upon Stanislavsky.

Three more operettas were to occupy Stanislavsky as director of the Alexeiev Circle before he turned to serious drama—and that only after a try at opera had convinced him of his unfitness for a musical career. One of the operettas, *Lili,* was inspired by the French actress Anna Judic, then the rage of Paris. According to Stanislavsky his sisters had seen *Lili* performed in Paris and on their return to Moscow recounted the contents of the operetta so vividly that he and his brother were able to write out all the parts.

Lili was perhaps the most successful production presented by the Alexeiev Circle. The *Russian Courier* praised the production for "its good taste," and particularly mentioned Zinna in the leading role and Constantin Alexeiev as the soldier Antoine Planchard, declaring him particularly good in the part of an old man in the third act.[13]

The dialogue had been written in short sentences to simulate French, and the performers were successful in speaking the Russian lines with a French accent and intonation. Stanislavsky declares, "Some of us, especially my older sister, reached perfection but because of the incoherency of our diction at that time . . . it was impossible to tell whether she spoke in French or Russian." The performance was received with applause and was played many more times before enthusiastic audiences. With this production, Stanislavsky admits a degree of achievement when he says:

> Perhaps I did not play the type created by the author, but there is no doubt that I succeeded in creating a true image of a Frenchman translated into the terms of the Russian language. And this was real success in a way, for if I did imitate, it was not the stage I imitated but life. Feeling the national characteristics of the part, I found it easy to justify the tempo and the rhythm of my movements and my speech. This was no longer tempo for the sake of tempo, rhythm for the sake of rhythm, but this was an inner rhythm, although one of general character, typical of all Frenchmen and not of the individual type I played.[14]

Incidentally, *Lili* was presented again two years later, in 1888, and was the last play given by the Alexeiev Circle.

The following winter the Alexeiev Circle devoted itself to a production of *The Mikado,* going to great lengths to secure the proper Japanese atmosphere. They went so far as to invite a troupe of Japanese acrobats who were performing at the circus to live at their home to teach them the Japanese manner of walking, bowing, dancing, and especially how to handle a fan. The extent to which they were willing to go in their devotion to their ideal is evidenced by Stanislavsky's report:

> The women walked all day with legs tied together as far as the knee, the fan became a necessary object of everyday life . . . .
>
> We had Japanese dancing classes and the women learned all the enchanting habits of the geishas. We knew . . . how to fall to the floor doubling up like gymnasts, how to run with mincing steps . . . . We learned to juggle with the fan, throw it under a shoulder or leg, and . . . made our own all the Japanese poses with the fan . . . of which a tremendous amount was distributed in the songs and in the text exactly like notes in music.[15]

The Mikado was a great success. Four performances were given, on April 18, 22, and 25, and on May 2, 1887. It may be assumed that about four months' active work went into the preparation of this production. This is rather amazing when it is remembered that all concerned had other duties to perform beyond rehearsing for the operetta.

Stanislavsky himself was aware of the value of the production to the group, in the agility and ease of body movement which resulted from the juggling, acrobatics, and dancing required. One drawback was Stanislavsky's own inner conflict between the two parts of his activity: as stage director, he sought to discover "a new tone and style of production," whereas, as an actor, he held fast to the operatic stereotype.

The period in Stanislavsky's life which was devoted to rehearsing the Alexeiev Circle appears to have been marked by one major fault which he later overcame and by two characteristics which grew even stronger as his career developed. The fault was the imitation of well-known actors. The two characteristics of promise were, first, a boundless capacity for hard work, and then a tireless search for realistic details in bringing to life the actual milieu of a performance.

The next phase of his career was short-lived. His love of opera had fostered a desire to be an opera singer, and for a short time Stanislavsky studied with Fyodor Kommisarzhevsky, father of Vera Kommisarzhevskaya and Theodore Kommisarzhevsky, both later known in America. However, Stanislavsky realized his inadequacy as a singer at the dress rehearsal of opera scenes which were to have been presented in the "dining-room theatre." He continued to visit Kommisarzhevsky nearly every day just the same, and to discuss art and music with him and his friends. This brief period was not without its effect upon the young Stanislavsky. His slight acquaintance with the necessity for acting to the rhythm of the music impressed him with the importance of rhythm and the difference between outer and inner rhythms. He came to realize the value of mime and "mimodrama," where the content of a scene is expressed by the body alone. He succeeded in convincing Kommisarzhevsky of the importance to singers of complete body control. Thereupon the two experimented with a group of actors and singers in the evenings. With the help of an accomplished pianist who could improvise in changing rhythms the group was required to walk, sit, and move about according to the rhythms of the music being played.

Stanislavsky states simply: "The Conservatory refused to let Kommisarzhevsky start the proposed class." If it had been otherwise, who can say how this might have affected the founding of the Moscow Art Theatre?

Stanislavsky sensed the fault of rhythmic monotony in his own past performances. This he called "dead water," "camel rhythm," and "ox-like rhythm." At the time, however, he was unable to communicate to his satisfaction what he had discovered. However, he put this experience to good use some twenty-five years later in his opera studio. Indeed, he made use of it long before that in his work with actors from the Moscow Art Theatre and its First Studio. Writing of her experience with Stanislavsky in the Moscow Art Theatre, Vera Soloviova makes reference to this:

> Constantin Sergeyevich differentiated between the inner rhythm and the tempo. He explained that inner rhythm is born in your heart, you will move according to your emotions. Tempo is given like tempo de valse or tempo polka . . . . We learned not to dance but to carry music within us —or rather, the music carried us.[16]

In other words, rhythm is used to indicate the pattern of movement while tempo is the external control of that pattern. We speak of the *rhythm* of the ocean tides. The *tempo,* however, will vary depending upon whether the sea is calm or activated by a storm. In like manner, a character may be said to have a certain rhythm, but the tempo of his movements may be changed according to the situation or the mood of the scene.

At this time an event occurred which had an effect upon Stanislavsky's long search for the tools of his career. A group of very talented actors from the Imperial Little Theatre came to play for charity with the Alexeiev Circle in a performance of *The Lucky Man.* Coincidentally, the play was written by Nemirovich-Danchenko, "who was at that time," Stanislavsky declares, "the most popular and talented playwright in Russia." Their famous meeting, however, was almost ten years away. Two of the artists with whom Stanislavsky appeared in this performance were the well-known Glikeria Fedotova, a long-time friend of the Alexeiev family, and Olga Sadovskaya. In working with these professional actors, Stanislavsky made a number of important discoveries. For one thing, although they had played the piece many times before at the Little Theatre, these great artists arrived sometimes a full hour before the appointed time for rehearsal. They were on stage at the specified time, while the amateurs, except Stanislavsky, were often late. Furthermore, the professional actors did not spare themselves, but rehearsed "in full tone," while most of the amateurs spoke in a whisper and had to refer to the book because they did not know their lines. Moreover, Stanislavsky felt inadequate beside these talented professionals. He remarks on the fact that his nervousness prevented him from hearing his cues. His energy was uneven, and he was sometimes loud enough and at other times inaudible. On the other hand, Stanislavsky noted that the artists from the Little Theatre "seemed always to be full of something. Something seemed to hold them at the same temperature of heightened energy and prevented them from sinking . . . ."

Stanislavsky sought the reason for his lack of success from Fedotova, his old friend and former teacher. "You don't know, my friend, from which end to begin. And you don't want to learn," replied the famous old actress. "There is no training, no restraint, no discipline, and an artist cannot live without that." Fedotova not only gave the eager young amateur advice, she offered him a way to carry out her suggestions:

> Play a little oftener with us, and we will teach you, my friend. We are not always like today. We can be severe when the need for it comes. Oh, my friend, we can scold . . . . The artists of today sit with folded hands and wait for inspiration from Apollo. In vain, my friend, he has enough of his own affairs to attend to.[17]

It was Fedotova who made Stanislavsky aware of the importance of looking into the eyes of one's partner to attempt to divine his thoughts and to reply to what he saw revealed in them.[18] This was undoubtedly the basis for Stanislavsky's exercises in *communion* with which students of his System are all familiar.[19]

Stanislavsky had several other experiences in these early days which revealed artistic truths to him. As the Alexeiev Circle was nearing its end, he began to play with other groups. One of these, the Mamontov Circle, was headed by the very wealthy philanthropist and patron of the arts, Savva Mamontov. Working with this group, in which the most talented scenic artists were encouraged and no amount of money or effort was spared, Stanislavsky was nevertheless dismayed at the lack of either talent or technique on the part of the actors. For against a truly splendid scenic background which rivaled the best theatres in Moscow "played completely untaught amateurs, who had not only been unable to rehearse their parts well, but who could not even remember them." It was through these performances, where the entire production was literally thrown together in two weeks' time, that he came to understand the important part played by the actor:

> It was at these performances that I learned this truth, and saw with my own eyes the meaning of completeness and long rehearsals in theatre affairs. I became convinced that in chaos there can be no art. Art is order, grace. What do I care how long they work on the production, a day, or a year? What is important to me is that the collective creation of all the

artists of the stage be whole and complete and that all those who helped to make the performance might serve for the sake of the same creative goal and bring their creations to one common denominator.[20]

By this time Stanislavsky was convinced that he wanted to work in serious drama and no hardships or disappointments could turn him from the course he had chosen. To this end, he accepted every invitation to play whenever and wherever an opportunity presented itself, whether in reputable dramatic circles or in very nearly disreputable amateur halls. Most unpleasant to him was the fact that most of the amateurs used the rehearsals as a means of flirting, and the interest of the audience was less in the performance than in the dances which followed. It was because of the unsavory atmosphere at some of the vaudeville performances with which he became associated that Constantin Sergeyevich Alexeiev, at that time a young man of affairs in Moscow and a director of the Russian Musical Society, decided it would be wiser to conceal his identity from his public. He therefore assumed the name of Stanislavsky, which had belonged to a young amateur whom he had once known and who had stopped playing. He thought that such a Polish-sounding name would be a complete disguise.

There was one performance, however, when his pseudonym proved ineffectual. His part was that of a lover in a questionable French farce; the scene was an actress' dressing room. As he came on stage with a huge bouquet in his hands, he found himself looking into the astonished faces of his parents, his tutor, and the governesses of his sisters, all seated in the center box. The effect must have been like an electric shock. Stanislavsky speaks of it as having the result of changing his playing of the sophisticated, blasé young man of the world so that the character became a "modest well-reared boy—a change which caused the failure of the whole play."

The governesses lamented Constantin Sergeyevich's downfall in French, in German, and in Russian, but his father's comment was: "If you want to play on the side, found a decent dramatic circle and a decent repertoire, but for God's sake, don't appear in such trash as the play last night."

THE SOCIETY OF ART AND LITERATURE

Stanislavsky was shortly to follow his father's advice. He had, in fact, discussed with Kommisarzhevsky the possibility of forming a society that would include amateurs of all the arts and furnish them a

club in which to exercise their talents. At about the same time
Stanislavsky came under the influence of a well-known actor and
director, Alexandre Fedotov, the former husband of his old friend and
teacher, the actress, Fedotova. Fedotov represented the "Society of
Writers and Actors"; Kommisarzhevsky, music and opera; and Count
Salogub, the graphic artists. Stanislavsky joined with these three to
form the Society of Art and Literature during the winter of 1888.
He contributed a large sum of money, nearly 30,000 rubles, a bonus
he had received from his father's business, to obtain and renovate
the premises desired for the society's headquarters.

After a gala opening concert in which actors appeared "in the
role of operatic artists and dancers and the artists of the ballet . . . in
the role of dramatic artists," the theatre of the society presented two
plays directed by Fedotov. They were Molière's *Georges Dandin*, in
which Stanislavsky played the comic role of Sotanville, and Pushkin's
Miser Knight. Salogub designed the scenery and costumes for the
latter piece; Stanislavsky played the tragic part of a miserly old
baron who spends his nights in the cellar of his castle exulting in his
gold pieces purchased at the expense of his honor and decency and
morality, until he is finally crazed by the realization that his death
will leave his treasure to his profligate son.

In preparing this part Stanislavsky was torn between his old
tendency to play the operatic stereotype of an old man and the conception of the role which was in the minds of Fedotov and Salogub. He
was rudely awakened to the artificiality of his conception when he
was confronted with Count Salogub's sketches for the costumes he was
planning for the baron. Stanislavsky describes them in detail:

> Imagine an ancient old man with noble, aristocratic features, in dirty and
> torn leather headpiece that looked like a woman's bonnet, with a long un-
> cut imperial . . . . Long slippers that made the feet look thin and narrow,
> a severe, well-worn, half-buttoned shirt stuck into old breeches . . . . A
> well-defined, aged stoop. The whole figure—tall, thin—bent like a question
> mark. He stooped above a chest and through his thin, bony fingers gold
> pieces flowed into the receptacle below.[21]

Although the first discovery of this conflict brought misery to
Stanislavsky and he begged to be relieved of the part, Fedotov talked
at great length with him and instructed him in acting the part of
the old knight; Salogub showed him paintings of such a character by
the old masters, and finally new ideas began to take root and he

gave up his slavish imitation of the operatic baritone. Stanislavsky characterizes this experience as "an operation that was an amputation, a search and a shaking out of all the theatricality" that he had gathered through his amateur years.

Next Stanislavsky began to work on the outer physical characterization of an old man—his walk, his manner of sitting down and getting up. Through all his efforts he was under the constant criticism and supervision of Fedotov. Finally, on his vacation, he went to Vichy, and worried over the part throughout the summer. He even went so far as to get himself locked in a cellar of an old castle a few miles from Vichy in an effort to simulate the milieu of the play. However, all he gained from this was a severe cold.

In his search for outward means to express the inner life of the character he came to a conclusion which undoubtedly motivated his continual search for means to help the actor:

> The stage directors explained only the results that they wanted. They were interested only in the results. They criticized, telling you what was bad, but they would not tell you how to get at what was desired.[22]

In his work on the comic part of Sotanville in the Molière play, Stanislavsky learned a great deal about false playing. "At the first rehearsal," he tells us, "I was already copying all of the Molière hokum that I had seen, and feeling myself thoroughly at home."

In condemning his own past erroneous ideas of acting, he condemned all the traditional acting of the classics that made all Molière's heroes, for instance, like one another. Stanislavsky was speaking from experience when he asked:

> And how are classical Gothic dramas played? . . . Any high-school boy will show you how high feelings are interpreted in the theatre, how verses are declaimed and chanted with pathos, how costumes are worn, how the actors stride triumphantly over the stage and assume various poses. The gist of the matter seems to lie not in the author and his style, but in Spanish boots, in tights, in swords, in the verses, in the voice badly and falsely placed, in the bearing of the actor, in his animal temperament, in beautiful limbs, in curled hair, in penciled eyebrows.[23]

Fortunately, in this part too he had the advantage of Fedotov's discerning criticism. The director used to demonstrate how a role should be played and his lifelike acting led Stanislavsky to the discovery that the real humor in a scene depends upon the seriousness with which it is performed. As Jilinsky used to say in his classes, "You must play the most ridiculous circumstance with the same degree of concentration that you give to a serious moment." [24] This ability to believe in the seriousness of the circumstances no matter how ridiculous they are was the secret of Fedotov's success in playing and directing Molière. So great was his admiration for his director and teacher, however, that Stanislavsky soon found himself unconsciously copying his master. Nevertheless, he realized that this was an improvement since "a living image is better than a dead tradition."

OUT OF THE QUICKSANDS

Stanislavsky suddenly discovered the key to belief in the comic character of Sotanville. Because one detail in his make-up imparted a lifelike and comic expression to his face he was able to believe in the circumstances of the play. Because of this circumstance, Stanislavsky maintains, "All that was dim became clear, all that was groundless suddenly had ground under its feet, all that I did not believe suddenly found my trust."

After the performance of Sotanville, Stanislavsky declared, "I did not find a new road, but I came to understand my former mistakes, and that is very much." One of his errors, he points out, had been his mistaking "stage emotion, which is only one kind of hysteria, for true inspiration."

At this time in his life another event occurred which also contributed to his artistic success. This was the fact that he fell in love with and chose to marry a young woman who also had been willing to make sacrifices for art's sake. Marie Perevoschikova was a young teacher in a girls' high school in Moscow. According to Magarshack, she assumed the name of Lilina so that her superior should not know of her part in "private theatricals." When her secret was discovered, she was dismissed. Stanislavsky then invited her to join his newly-formed Society of Art and Literature. When they played together in Schiller's *Kabale und Liebe,* the audience realized the young people were in love, although they had not realized it themselves. They were married on July 5, 1889, and "their whole subsequent life was a shining example of real comradeship in art." Lilina became Stanislavsky's partner in every sense of the word, taking part in his stage productions, sharing all his vicissitudes in the theatre, raising two children, and remaining steadfast and loving to the very end of his life. The critic Efros describes her at the time of her joining the

Society of Art and Literature as "enchantingly naive, enchantingly simple, and as enchantingly talented with large bright eyes and beautiful hair." [25] In time she was to become one of the leading actresses of the Moscow Art Theatre.

Gradually Stanislavsky recognized the signposts of the new road. Once on that road, he was to spend the rest of his life trying to mark it clearly for other artistic wayfarers. With each new role, he learned something more about his craft. In *The Usurpers of the Law* by Pissemsky, he was again cast in the role of an old man, as General Imshin. Here, once more, he approached the character from the outside. From his observation of an old man he discovered that space appears between the gums when the false teeth are removed. By moving his lower jaw forward he was able to give this effect. Then by trying to overcome the resultant lisp, he was obliged to speak more slowly than was his custom. The slow rhythm which was occasioned by the effort brought to his mind a very old man, and he was able to divine the inner emotion of the role. Stanislavsky explains this early method which he used:

> I tried first of all to understand and study the physiological cause of the physical process, that is, why the rhythm of action and speech is so slow with old men, why they rise so carefully, why they straighten so slowly, walk so slowly, etc. . . . Before I would rise I looked for something to rest my hands on, and rose with the help of my hands . . . . Conscious relation to action that was typical to old age guided me and as a result I tuned my own feelings to the physiological phenomena of senility. This created a kind of method from the outer to the inner, from the body to the soul, based upon an unbreakable bond between physical and psychical nature.[26]

Referring to this method, Stanislavsky declares, "The technical methods of playing pushed me on to the truth, and the feeling of truth is the best awakener of emotion and the sense of living over a thing, imagination and creativeness."

Strangely enough, in attempting to give critical advice on the performance of another play in which he did not take part Stanislavsky hit upon one of the most valid points in his new approach. His advice was: "Life is never like bad plays on the stage where some people are all black and others are all white. So, when you play a hypochondriac," he continued, "seek where he is happy, virile and full of hope . . . . When you play a good man look for the places where he is evil, and in an evil man look for the places where he is good."

This discovery led Stanislavsky to the realization of his own short-comings in playing the part of General Imshin. "I played a beast," he declared, "but . . . the author himself had taken care of it; what was left to me was to look and see where he was good, suffering, re-morseful, loving, tender and sacrificing and this was new baggage in my actor's train." Finally, in summarizing he said: "When you play an old man, look to see where he is young. When you play a young man, look to see where he is old, etc." Nikolai A. Gorchakov regards this discovery as "the source of the ethical greatness of the Moscow Art Theatre." He says of it, moreover:

> . . . the formula contained the embryo for a completely new method of working with the actor on his roles . . . . Stanislavsky's formula . . . showed the actor the way to psychological independence and to the inner-most secrets of the role he was doing . . . . From this profundity came the "subtext," the "kernel of the role," and the special searches for the internal characteristics that have made the Stanislavsky System famous.[27]

Another conclusion reached by Stanislavsky at this time was that an actor must not copy another actor's portrayal of a role; he must create his own image of the character he is playing. Yet he did not know how to discover the image except through the emotion or through such externals as "pose, costumes, make-up, manner and gesture."[28]

In another role, that of the dishonest stockbroker Obnovlensky in Fedotov's play, *The Ruble,* he came upon the characterization by means of what he describes as a "gift of Apollo." "Like the role of Sotanville," Stanislavsky declares, "after long tortures this role became successful because of an accidental touch in my make-up." It came about because the wigmaker made the mistake of gluing one half of his mustache lower than the other, thus giving to his face "an expression of slyness."

Stanislavsky's biggest role during the Society's second season was that of Peter in Ostrovsky's *Don't Live to Please Yourself but to Please the Lord.* In this part he began to understand inner psycho-logical climaxes in building the role. Nevertheless, Stanislavsky accuses himself of letting the "stencil of the Russian paladin" take possession of him. His description of this stereotype is a valuable comment upon the bad forms of acting that existed and to which even he could succumb:

> Of all existing stencils, the worst is that of the Russian paladin, of the Russian knight, the son of a boyarin or the village strong man with their

width and breadth of soul and character. For these there exists a specific manner of walking, wide gestures that are established once for all, traditional posing, with hands on the hips, a mighty heaving of the head to free it from the falling waves of their hair, a special manner of holding the hat, which is mercilessly crumpled for the mechanical strengthening of passion, brave vocal attempts at the high notes of the register, and a chanting diction in the lyric places of the part. These bad faults have entered so much into the ears, eyes, body and muscles of Russian actors that there is no possibility of getting rid of them.[29]

Stanislavsky felt that the role of Peter was too difficult for his stage of development. He believed that to be the reason for his resorting to the stencil of the Russian paladin and he pointed out the harm that is wrought upon a young actor who undertakes a role which is too difficult for him. Chief among the dangers that he enumerated is resorting to stencils or stereotypes and "staginess," all of which bottle up true emotion within the actor. Stanislavsky points out what takes place under these circumstances:

Nothing is left but to squeeze emotion out of yourself by means of force. There is no greater harm than the harm in the mechanical forcing of the emotions from outside, without the creation of an inner spiritual stimulation. Under this method emotion remains in a drowsy state and the actor begins to strain himself physically. The muscles of the actor are willing tools that are worse than the worst enemies. Every young actor who forces his will to undertake parts too difficult for him only develops his stage muscles, and nothing else.[30]

The next significant influence on Stanislavsky's acting career was occasioned by the second visit of the Duke of Meiningen's company under Director Kronek during the Lenten season in 1890. They made a very definite impression upon the young Stanislavsky. In his own words: "Their performances showed Moscow for the first time productions that were historically true, with well-directed mob scenes, fine outer form and amazing discipline." He later discarded the strict discipline which he had copied from Kronek as he came to realize that such despotism was wrong. He remained indebted to Kronek, however, for his excellent use of the ensemble and for bringing out the inner meaning or "essence of the production."

The faults of the Meiningen Players were clear to Stanislavsky. Chief among these was the fact that less attention was paid to the acting than to the production as a whole. All the energy was centered on the stage direction, on the *mise en scène*, the overall effect, and so much was done to build the right atmosphere that the inferior quality of the acting went unnoticed by a large part of the audience. "The talents of the stage director hid the faults of the actress."

Although Stanislavsky later gave up the traditions of the Meiningen Players, in the early days of the Moscow Art Theatre he was as despotic as Kronek had been. Like Kronek he sat in the producer's chair holding a watch, and when it was time for the rehearsal to begin, he too rang a bell.

One measure of Stanislavsky's greatness, however, was his ability to change when he discovered better methods. Innovations which he introduced were numerous rehearsals—a practice which he had already begun in the days of the Alexeiev Circle and for which he became famous in the days of the Moscow Art Theatre—and the end of the actor's dependence upon the prompter.[31]

At that time circumstances combined to place Stanislavsky in the director's chair. For one thing, the financial status of the Society of Art and Literature declined, and there was not sufficient money to continue the director's salary. In consequence Fedotov left the Society and Stanislavsky assumed his duties. Furthermore they were forced to rent their expensive quarters to the Hunting Club and were invited by its members to give weekly performances for their "family evenings." This custom of presenting a new play every week which is accepted out of necessity in the American summer theatre was the "custom in all other theatres in Moscow." However, those actors were professionals and therefore did not find it so difficult as did the amateurs of the Society.

The well-known actress Fedotova came to their assistance, and with the additional help of experienced actors whom Stanislavsky called in to supplement her work, the Society was able to meet the difficult schedule at the Hunting Club. Fedotova became the head of the dramatic department. Stanislavsky explains the difference between her approach and that of her husband, their former director: "While Fedotov was an artist of *mise en scène* and of the whole production in general . . . Fedotova re-created emotion . . . ." The new directors from the Imperial Theatre, on the other hand, were more external in their approach. The last method inevitably led to the use of stencils because of the hurry necessitated by the weekly performances. On the other hand, certain benefits resulted, such as the gaining of confidence on the stage, the strengthening of the actors' voices, and finally, the attainment of a level of acting which "distinguished them from amateurs." While recognizing the contribution of the new directors in helping to make the difficult program possible, Stanislavsky, nevertheless, realized the dangers of what he characterized as the "factory of stencils." He calls the weekly performances "our sad trade" and declares, "They did not create taste in me nor did they move me forward as an actor."

Another significant event which took place at this time was the coming of Vera Kommisarzhevskaya to live with her father. In a moment of crisis Stanislavsky asked her to step into the part of an actress of the Society who had taken sick. Thus the actress who was later to become famous in Moscow and New York made her debut with Stanislavsky in a one-act play, *Burning Letters*. In the middle of the season the premises of the Hunting Club burned down. As a result the Society had to play under its own auspices.

ON FIRM GROUND

Stanislavsky's first experience in directing serious drama was the production of *The Fruits of Enlightenment*, by Leo Tolstoy, on February 8, 1891.[32] This was a difficult play to produce because of the large cast and what Stanislavsky called "the complexity of the *mise en scène*." He declares, "One needs great experience to make each of the quickly changing groupings interesting and typical." In this production there appeared foreshadowings of the Stanislavsky who six years later was to found the Moscow Art Theatre. For in his approach to the play he tried above everything to be sincere, to find the truth, and to avoid "theatrical and commercial falsehood." "More than all," he asserts, "I wanted living, truthful, real life, not commonplace life, but artistic life."

Furthermore, in producing this play Stanislavsky introduced the rigid discipline for which he was to become famous. There were fines for "lateness at rehearsals, a badly learned part, discussions during work, absence from the rehearsal hall without permission." But Stanislavsky imposed the first fine on himself. His fairness in this, together with his devotion to the work and his great capacity for working, won him the respect and devotion of his co-workers. The seriousness of his approach may be understood from the fact that "garishness of attire, especially as far as the women were concerned, was banned from rehearsals . . . . The tremendous hats of the actresses were not allowed at all. All women were to come without hats."

Perhaps most surprising, but also most revealing of Stanislavsky's serious attitude toward the theatre, is his provision forbidding flirting. While encouraging "serious love," he maintains, "One does not need the atmosphere of flirtation which drags you downward." [33]

The Fruits of Enlightenment was very successful financially, running for several months. In it were many actors who were to become well known in the Moscow Art Theatre. Of the critics' approval, that of two was especially significant. One critic was Nemirovich-Danchenko, whom Stanislavsky was not to meet until six years later. He declared: "No one has ever seen such an exemplary performance on an amateur stage . . . . Tolstoy's comedy was played with a better ensemble and more intelligently than any play is ever played even in the best private theatres in Moscow." Danchenko also had high praise for Stanislavsky's portrayal of Zvezdintsev.

The other critic seemed to utter a prophecy when he wrote that the group "might form a theatre that would raise the mental and moral level of Russian society, that is to say, pursue the real aims of dramatic art." [34] It is indicative of Stanislavsky's innate personal modesty that he omits these critical comments from *My Life in Art*.

At the beginning of the following season the Hunting Club rented new quarters and the Society again was forced to give a performance each week after inadequate rehearsal time. However, Stanislavsky explains:

> . . . so far as our souls were concerned, we prepared one play a year under my directorship and without any hurry. These productions that displayed our artistic work and not our mere craftsmanship we housed in another place and the money we made through them we used for new productions and artistic researches. [35]

ON THE NEW ROAD

The next "yearly artistic production" was Stanislavsky's own dramatization of a story by Dostoyevsky, *The Village of Stepanchikovo*. Stanislavsky achieved a great artistic success in the character of Colonel Rostanov, who is in love with his children's governess. This part was played by Lilina. For the first time, Stanislavsky was completely happy in his part. According to N. A. Gorchakov, he wrote concerning this part, "I became the uncle, while in other roles I had—to a greater or lesser extent—'teased' (that is, copied, mimicked) my own or some-body else's mannerisms." [36] This is what Stanislavsky meant by "organically living the role that has been created within you." Elaborating on this idea, he says:

> In the repertoire of an actor, among the large number of parts played by him, there are some that seem to have been creating themselves in his inner consciousness for a long time. One only has to touch the role and it comes to life without any of the tortures of creation, without any quest or technical work.[37]

Thus for the first time Stanislavsky realized the goal which he set as the ultimate, that is, to *become* the character by completely identifying with the role. "Within the limits of the play," he explains, "I live the life of Rostanov, I think his thoughts, I cease to be myself. I become another man, a man like Rostanov. Do you understand this phrase that is magic for the actor, *to become another?*" In referring to Gogol's allusion to this phenomenon, "Anybody can imitate an image, but only a true talent can become an image," he says:

> If that was true, then I had talent, for in this role (although it was almost the only one) I had become Rostanov, while in my other roles I merely copied and imitated the necessary images and sometimes my own image.[38]

The work was not a financial success because, as Stanislavsky explains, "only a few individuals valued Dostoyevsky on the stage and our work in putting him there." Nevertheless he experienced great artistic satisfaction and the production was highly praised by the writer and critic Grigorovich who was a friend of both Dostoyevsky and Turgenev.

The success which he had achieved with this characterization led Stanislavsky to question the source of that success. That question was the crystallization of the motive for the search that directed his entire artistic life. He wrote:

> I lived through a happy moment in my artistic life. I had received a true gift from Apollo. Were there no technical means for a conscious entry into the paradise of art? When technique reaches the possibility of realizing this hope, our stage craftsmanship will become a true art. But where and how is one to seek those roads into the secret sources of inspiration? This is the question that must serve as the fundamental life problem of every true actor.[38]

Another role in which Stanislavsky was able to play the "image" itself without thinking of it was one in an inconsequential comedy entitled *The Tutor* by Dyachenko. The part was written in French and Russian, and Stanislavsky relates how he was able to speak Russian with a French accent. His French pronunciation was very good because of his frequent visits to the Comédie Française when in Paris. Moreover, he had had experience in the old days of the Alexeiev Circle in the playing of French operettas in the style of Judic. For all these reasons, Stanislavsky entered into the part joyously and played it with the greatest of ease. His own comment was: "I loved the part, the performances gave me pleasure; I had again, for the time being, left the quicksands and was on the true road."

The next special production, *Uriel Acosta*, showed Stanislavsky that certain of his earlier faults still remained. For one thing, he reverted once more to the operatic stereotype in love scenes. Another fault for which he blamed himself was what he called being "out of tune with the text." "The dropping of words from the text," which by the way he attributed to his poor memory, "the unclear interpretation of thought, the crumpling of sentences and words, the quietness of voice and unclear pronunciation," declares Stanislavsky, "interfered not only with my acting, but with the public hearing and understanding me."

In this production Stanislavsky showed the influence of the Meiningen Players. Although he himself in retrospect believed that too much emphasis had been placed upon the external production, nevertheless he also admitted that the performance was unusual for the time in the authenticity of the costuming and in the excellence of the ensemble in the mob scenes. This production brought credit to the Society. It also made a fast friend for Stanislavsky and his art of Alexey Alexandrovich Stakhovich, adjutant of the Grand Duke, and the entire court of the Grand Duke Sergey Alexandrovich. By his own admission this production was also responsible for Stakhovich's becoming "an admirer and a friend" of the Society, and later a friend of the Art Theatre, then one of its directors, and at last, an actor.

According to Stanislavsky, costumes that were historically true to the period and carefully rehearsed mob scenes were a rarity at that time in Moscow. He further declared that the only two styles with which the costumers were familiar were those of *Faust* and those of *Les Huguenots*.

In the triple role of actor, director, and producer Stanislavsky began to realize he needed a partner, particularly to take care of administrative matters. With help he would be able to found a theatre which would reach a larger audience than that of the Society of Art and Literature but which should at the same time continue the high artistic standard already established.[39] He was searching also for competent actors who might form the core of the new group. It was this search that led him to attempt several productions with professional actors and managers.

The first such experience was a production of Gogol's *Inspector General* in a summer theatre outside Moscow. He found the actors letter-perfect in what might be termed a very "slick" performance, with all the usual "stencils" in use. While the actors expressed their willingness to work out the production in accordance with Stanislavsky's understanding of the Gogol masterpiece, when he changed the placement of furniture and exits, they had been so bound by the familiar pattern that they were helpless to create a new *mise en scène*. Moreover, Stanislavsky failed to win their confidence because of the despotic methods he used with them. He succeeded only in confusing them, since there was not enough time to practice the new way of playing. Consequently, the performance was a failure.[40]

That Stanislavsky had profited from his mistake is evident from his second experience with professionals. This time Stanislavsky undertook to produce Hauptmann's beautiful fantasy, *Hannele,* for none other than Lentovsky, the once famous impresario of the "Hermitage Gardens," [41] whose methods he had tried to copy in his home theatre. The play was to be presented in the enormous Solodovnikov Theatre. Stanislavsky expected to learn the method of producing in the professional theatre. However, he was so shocked by Lentovsky's approach to the actors who came to audition, as well as by the disorder and filthy condition of the vacant store where they were called to rehearse, that he found himself delivering a lecture to the old producer. He pointed out what the manager's relation to his actors should be and outlined the minimum requirements for a place of rehearsal in such matters as cleanliness and the simplest physical comforts for all involved. Lentovsky, much to his surprise, responded to the suggestions and the rehearsals proceeded. Stanislavsky made a point of memorizing the full names of all the actors, a greater task in Russian than in English because both the first name and the patronymic are always employed in such semiformal relationships. He attributed his success with the actors in this production to the simple fact that he treated them like anyone else; he declares this was an innovation in the theatre.[42]

The first performance of *Hannele* was on April 2, 1896; it was a great success. Lentovsky presented Stanislavsky with a copy of Gogol's *Inspector General* "with marginal notes in the playwright's own hand, which Gogol had presented to Mikhail Shchepkin, the great actor presenting it, in his turn, to his pupil, Lentovsky." Lentovsky had inscribed it "To a worthier artist. M. Lentovsky." [43]

Stanislavsky succeeded in his production of *Hannele* with professional actors in spite of what was, to them, his sometimes strange method of work. For one thing, he insisted that they must know their parts perfectly by the fifth rehearsal without using their scripts.[44] In working on the play he utilized an accidental light that threw the shadows of the actors grotesquely on the walls and ceiling. He worked to attain the supernatural atmosphere also by his manipulation of the actors' voices, prolonging certain consonants, particularly the sibilants, so that the effect was most unusual. Describing Stanislavsky's effective staging of *Hannele,* Gorchakov says:

> At first the shadows began to run; then everything became intermingled as if one were giddy; after that, everything congealed in an agonizing pause. When Hannele's coffin was carried out, a whispering began that grew into a hurricane and blended with the nightmare of whirling shadows. Stanislavsky created these purely realistic surrealistic devices in 1895! [45]

It seems almost inconceivable that only two weeks after the opening of *Hannele* Stanislavsky's production of *Othello* should have appeared.[46] It was not a success, primarily because the three principals were not adequate for their roles. Lilina could not play Desdemona because of illness, and Stanislavsky, in the Saxe-Meiningen tradition, accepted a completely inexperienced young actress because of her beauty. He was not more fortunate in the actor who played Iago. He undertook to play Othello himself. When a very young man he had been overpowered by Salvini's portrayal of the role and had longed to emulate the great actor's performance. Moreover, when he and his wife visited Venice, the desire to play the part took possession of him again. After meeting with an Arab later in a Paris restaurant, he practiced before a mirror with towels and sheets, transforming himself into a "graceful Moor" in his movements. When it came time for actual rehearsals of the play, he was forced to conduct them in his own flat during his wife's illness. Resorting again to the tactics of

Director Kronek he tried in vain to hide the bad acting behind the production effect of beautiful costumes, making capital of sound effects such as the splash of the oars as the gondola approached, the sound of the chain that fastened it, and the striking of the tower clock.[47] The chief fault, however, and one which he could not disguise, was his own inadequacy in the part. For although he had made the outward movements of the Arab his own to such an extent that he moved in this manner in everyday life, the greater part of the role was far too difficult for him. He was unable to master the gradual development of the jealousy engendered by Iago and to build it truthfully from the very first moment of its inception up to its final climax of "beastlike madness." Nor was he able to handle the difficult transition when the discovery of Desdemona's blamelessness must cast him into the utter despair of remorse. Wrongfully, Stanislavsky depended wholly upon intuition, with the result which he describes so well:

> Of course I was able to reach nothing more than insane strain, spiritual and physical impotence and the squeezing of tragic emotion out of myself. In my strengthless struggle I even lost the little I had gained in other rôles —which I had seemed to possess since the time of *Bitter Fate*. There was no restraint, no control of the temperament, no placing of color; there was only the strain of muscles, the violation of voice and of the entire organism, and spiritual buffers that suddenly grew to all sides of me in self-defense from the problems which I had put before myself and which were too much for me.[48]

Worst of all, the straining showed in his voice and he became hoarse; sometimes he even required the care of a doctor. In addition, his heart became affected by the effort and he also suffered asthmatic attacks. When this happened, his friends tried to persuade him to abandon the production, but he insisted upon going on, partly because of financial necessity and partly, as he admits, because of his personal vanity.

As usual, Stanislavsky learned from his mistakes. The failure of *Othello* brought home to him again the folly of playing a role prematurely. Moreover, the famous Italian actor Rossi came to a performance and asked Stanislavsky to visit him. At that time, he gave his honest evaluation of the performance. Contrary to the Meiningen point of view, he disapproved of the use of colorful scenery and elaborate costumes which diverted the audience's attention, declaring they were devices for the untalented which Stanislavsky did not require. On the other hand, Rossi made Stanislavsky realize his need, in fact his obligation, to do further work on himself.

For his next production for the Society of Art and Literature he chose the well-known melodrama, *The Bells, or The Polish Jew,* by Emile Erckmann and Alexandre Chatrian. The play tells the story of an Alsatian burgomaster, Mathias, who is haunted by the vision of a rich Polish Jew whom he has murdered. Sir Henry Irving made the part of Mathias famous on the English and American stages. The sound of sleigh bells is the prelude to the entrance of the Polish Jew in the first act. Thereafter, he disappears and it is given out that he has been murdered. Mathias' guilt is made clear to the audience by the persistent sound of the sleigh bells which haunts the burgomaster. Even during the wedding scene where the burgomaster's daughter is being married, the sound of the orchestra is finally drowned out by the sound of the sleigh bells "as they overwhelm the guilty Mathias." N. A. Gorchakov says of this production:

> Stanislavsky transferred his directional discovery—the sound-phantom— into the protagonist. The intrusive sound, like Fate, metes out punishment and lacerates the burgermeister. The entire production was subordinated to the music, which was dominated by the sound-phantom.[49]

The final act shows the burgomaster's attic bedroom, which in his feverish nightmare becomes transformed into a court of judgment. Here Stanislavsky displayed his ingenuity as a stage director. It was because the possibilities of the production fired his imagination that he had chosen the play in the first place. He made expert use of the juxtaposition of sound, as of the joyous sounds in the room where people are singing and talking against the wind and the distant but evernearing notes of the sleigh bells outside, as Stanislavsky himself described it "like the chief *leit-motif* of a symphony." [50] In the nightmare scene in the final act Stanislavsky had an excellent opportunity to show his actual producing genius when he transformed the attic chamber into a courtroom and had the actors find their places practically in the dark.[51]

Stanislavsky's own critical evaluation of the production was that he had achieved greater success in his staging than in his acting the part of Mathias, although he says of his performance of this role: "At present, looking backwards, I think that I did not play the part badly. There were the characteristics of an old man, an important, solid citizen, and there was restraint." [52] The production received high praise from a fellow artist. The German actor, Ludwig Barnay, who was well known for his portrayal of Mathias, wrote to Stanislavsky on December 4, 1896, after he had seen a performance:

> Your skill in the sphere of play-production is so great that it puts you among artists of the first rank. Your production of *The Bells* filled me with delight. The acting of yourself and your colleagues in the leading parts of the play, the crowd scenes in the second act, and the feeling of truth that pervaded everything on the stage were so convincing that, taken together, they resulted in a first-rate performance.[53]

There was one point, however, on which the actors in this production drew adverse criticism, the lack of clarity in their phrasing and diction. Stanislavsky's defense in this connection was that they were trying to avoid the insincerity and unnatural manner of speaking then in use by most actors, who either sang or declaimed their lines, taking pleasure in the sound of their own voices. He protested:

> . . . Let some one teach us to speak simply, musically, nobly, beautifully, but without vocal acrobatics, actors' pathos and all the odds and ends of scenic diction. We want the same thing in movement and action. Let them be humble and not completely expressive and scenic in the theatrical sense of the word, but then they are not false, and they are humanly simple. We hate the theatrical in the theatre, we love the scenic on the stage. That is a tremendous difference.[54]

During the following season, 1897, Stanislavsky produced two of Shakespeare's comedies, *Much Ado About Nothing* and *Twelfth Night*. In the first he played Benedick and in the second, Malvolio. The first play gave expression to his preoccupation with medieval life, which resulted from a visit he and his wife had made to Turin, Italy. Here they had come upon a reconstructed medieval town complete with its castle, moat, drawbridge, narrow streets, and cathedral. He had wanted to live in this castle in order to get the feeling of life at that period, but he could not gain permission. This desire reminds one of his earlier experience in Vichy when he had had himself locked up in the cellar of the old castle there.

On his return to Moscow, he cast about for a play that would fit into the scheme of production which he had envisaged. It was this that caused him to schedule *Much Ado About Nothing*. The disparity between Stanislavsky, with his huge frame, and the character of Benedick was a factor, no doubt, in the lack of success of the production. He used realism to the extreme in the effort to make the life of the Middle Ages as natural and familiar to actors and spectators as the life of their own time. He had so immersed himself in the details of the period that he felt as much at home in the stage castle as he did in his flat at the Red Gates. Later he criticized this strict adherence to external realism and used it principally to awaken the actor's subconscious.

One benefit which Stanislavsky gained from the production of *Much Ado About Nothing* was the result of his work on the role of Benedick. Although he still thought the way to discovering the emotion lay in a study of the outer characteristics of the role, his search for a true characterization of the part prevented him from playing the theatrical clichés of such a role. At the same time he admitted that this method was only one way to find the core of the character, and especially useful when the role was not a particularly subtle one or when the characterization came of itself, as it had in some of the lighter parts he had played. As a result of his search for characterization he began to build his characters from his observations of live people around him instead of from studying and reading about fictional characters. Here, at last, he was following the precepts of Shchepkin, who had exhorted his pupils to search for their examples in real life.

The part of Malvolio, which he played in the Society's next production in the fall of 1897, was probably better suited to him. Here the want of a talented stage designer was a great hindrance to the success of the performance. After his success with *Hannele* at the Solodovnikov Theatre, where because of its size his genius had had a chance to exercise itself freely in the staging, he came to feel the need of a really talented scene designer. For his next and last production for the Society of Art and Literature, therefore, he engaged a young man, Victor Simov, who had worked for the Mamontov Circle.[55] The play, Hauptmann's fantasy, *The Sunken Bell,* won great success in the Hunting Club and was carried over into the repertoire of the Moscow Art Theatre. Its first performance took place on January 27, 1898, almost midway between the conception of the idea of the Moscow Art Theatre and its opening performance.

Simov's transformation of the tiny stage of the Hunting Club into the bottom of a chasm in the depth of the woods, with rocks and caves and the suggestion of mountains in the rear, was accomplished by a number of different platforms. Here the wood sprites, the fairy

Rautendelein, the Nickelman, and elves darted about or leaped from rock to rock. For the stage floor was no longer flat, and Stanislavsky and Simov made it almost impossible for the actors to walk in the traditional manner. Stanislavsky worked on this with Simov and declared that the necessity to creep about or leap and climb fostered in the actors a new approach to their parts and awoke their imaginations. In this production he recognized the advantage of "sculptural things," that is, three-dimensional objects, over the traditional painted canvas usually used as a backdrop. "These palpable objects seen by us on the stage," declares Stanislavsky, "are much more necessary and important for us actors than the colorful canvases that we do not see." With this production he admitted to having taken "a great step forward as a stage director," [56] though he was still dissatisfied with himself as an actor.

It is worth noting that at a point following his productions for the Solodovnikov Theatre, when his wife was too preoccupied with the children to be able to take an active part in his theatre life, Stanislavsky actually entertained the idea of giving up the stage. It appears, too, that Lilina was not completely happy because he was forced to spend so much time away from her. Moreover, he was often plagued by doubts as to his career as an actor and he continually felt the need of a codirector and partner who could make up for his lack of a wide literary background.

The opinions of two famous actors of the Maly Theatre were perhaps responsible for keeping his course steady. Nadezhda Medvedeva was the actress whose advice he sought. In a letter to his wife concerning this interview, Stanislavsky makes what proved to be a prophetic comment:

> . . . she kept for some reason talking about my *duty* to do something for the theatre and saying that *my name ought to pass into history.* She has been talking about it for a long time at the Maly Theatre, especially after *Hannele. Lensky thinks so too.*[57]

Magarshack points to certain facts which probably led Stanislavsky to put some faith in Medvedeva's statement. He was, by nature, superstitious. His birth had occurred just one hundred years after that of Volkov, who is usually regarded as the founder of the Russian popular theatre. Furthermore, he was born in the year that Mikhail Shchepkin died. Stanislavsky was a devoted follower of Shchepkin and read everything he had written concerning the art of the theatre.

VLADIMIR NEMIROVICH-DANCHENKO

At this time there were two dramatic schools in Moscow. The one, the Imperial School, belonged to the Maly Theatre and had as its director the well-known actor Lensky. The other was the Philharmonic. It was here that Vladimir Nemirovich-Danchenko began to teach in 1891. Danchenko had already achieved some fame as a dramatist and had received the Griboyedov prize for his play *The New Undertaking*, "for the best play of the season." [58]

From the beginning of his work at the Philharmonic School, Danchenko showed very advanced ideas in play production. He had already evolved some of the techniques which in a few years were to characterize the methods of the Moscow Art Theatre. In the published instructions for the direction of his play *Something New* he declares, "Any setting, gesture, or movement by an actor must depend directly on his internal, subjective life on the stage. The actor's crossing on the stage from right to left and vice versa must flow from the conduct of the character correctly conceived."

Danchenko also was responsible for the "pre-rehearsal phase of working on a play," that is, the discussion and analysis of the play and the characters that took place with the actors seated around a table. He encouraged his students to "reflect, meditate, and dream about the roles and then tell in their own words the lives of the characters not only during the time of the play but beforehand and afterwards." [59] Stanislavsky was working toward the same goal when in the Alexeiev Circle he insisted that on a given day the cast of *The Practical Man* should live according to the given circumstances (see page 31).

Danchenko devoted himself to his teaching and raised the standards of the Philharmonic School. He even succeeded in winning the same consideration as the Imperial School of the Maly Theatre; he shared with Lensky the use of the Maly Theatre during Lent for student performances.[60] It was here that he produced Ibsen's *A Doll's House* with his pupils in 1896.[61] Danchenko calls this the "first real Ibsen production in Moscow." As a result of this he became convinced that the only way to revive the theatre was through the youth of the school.

His next play, *Gold,* was awarded the prize of the Odessa University and was given performances in St. Petersburg and Moscow. However, the initial performances had to be postponed for two months because of the death of Tsar Alexander III. Danchenko utilized the period of mourning for dress rehearsals, which hitherto were unheard of except for "plays of an elaborately decorative character." Danchenko declares, "In contemporary plays the authors saw the actors in their make-up and costumes only at the actual performance, perhaps five minutes before their entrance on the scene, when it was already too late to alter anything." [62]

Danchenko was a great admirer of Chekhov, and the future bond between Chekhov and the Moscow Art Theatre was due to Danchenko's efforts. According to Professor S. D. Balukhaty, Chekhov began to write plays as a protest against the dramatic productions then in style. Balukhaty says: "Chekhov created an original psychological, naturalistic drama, very different from the type of drama which in those days was so firmly established on the Russian stage." [63]

When the original performance of *The Sea Gull* occurred in St. Petersburg on November 11, 1896, it was a dismal failure in spite of the fact that Nina was played by Kommisarzhevskaya,[64] and the best actors of the Alexandrinsky Theatre made up the rest of the company. Danchenko understood the reason for this. He realized that Chekhov's new forms—"pearls of poetry," as he called them—required new techniques in production, new insights into the characters and the means of expressing them. Chekhov's own suggestions later to the Moscow Art Theatre would not have been sufficient. "It must all be done very simply," he said, "just as in life. It must be done as if they spoke about it every day." It took the combined artistry and understanding of Stanislavsky and Danchenko, two years later, to discover "how . . . to utter these simplest phrases simply and yet retain the sense of the theatre and avoid desperate tedium." [65] The best actors of the company at the Alexandrinsky Theatre in St. Petersburg in 1896, however, were not prepared for it. But when in the same year Danchenko again received the Griboyedov Prize for his play, *The Worth of Life,* he protested that it should have gone to *The Sea Gull.*

Although he was a very successful playwright and sometimes even called the successor of Ostrovsky, he devoted himself more and more to his teaching at the Philharmonic and dreamed night and day of a theatre of his own where plays of literary worth could be produced. As a possible partner in his undertaking he thought of Stanislavsky, whose production of *The Fruits of Enlightenment* six years earlier had deeply impressed him. In his critical comments of the performance he had written: "Why, if you did not know that they were amateur actors you would never have believed it!" He declared, furthermore, that the ensemble was better and the comedy more intelligently played "than any play is ever played even in the best private theatre in Moscow." He also had praised Stanislavsky as an actor.[66] Danchenko went to Moscow on June 21, 1897, to learn how the manager of the Maly Theatre had reacted to the list of reforms which he had previously recommended. At the same time he took steps to meet with Stanislavsky.[67]

It is apparent that these two men, Stanislavsky and Nemirovich-Danchenko, were preparing unconsciously for what Gorchakov calls "the revolution of the scenic arts that was to begin in 1897." [68] Stanislavsky seems by temperament and experience to have been fore-ordained for the task that lay before him. He had already developed such techniques for the actor as belief in the given circumstances and communion with one's partner, and had learned to seek his examples in life. Furthermore, he had demonstrated great ingenuity and imagination as a director.

Danchenko gave up a literary career to devote himself to the teaching of acting in the Philharmonic School. How close he was to Stanislavsky in his thinking about the theatre may be seen by examining his recommendations to the Maly Theatre for the improvement of production. These included dress rehearsals; new stage settings, costumes, and furnishings for each production; and "staging plays with some idea of their periods and coloring (rather than using the so-called rich, poor, and Gothic set-up)." [69] Above all else these two men were motivated by a supreme love of their art and a desire to create a theatre in the image of their ideal.

❀

Notes

1. In this chapter, much of my information and all of my quotations from Stanislavsky are taken from his *My Life in Art*, translated by J. J. Robbins (New York: Theatre Arts Books, 1948). Unless otherwise indicated, Stanislavsky references in this chapter refer to this book.
2. David Magarshack, *Stanislavsky, A Life* (New York: The Chanticleer Press, 1951), p. 11.
3. Stanislavski, pp. 50–51.
4. Stanislavski, p. 58.
5. Magarshack, p. 21.
6. Stanislavski, pp. 60–61.
7. Stanislavski, pp. 72–73.
8. Stanislavski, p. 117.
9. Magarshack, p. 35.
10. Stanislavski, p. 88.
11. Stanislavski, p. 90.

12. Stanislavski, p. 121.
13. Magarshack, pp. 45–46.
14. Stanislavski, p. 125.
15. Stanislavski, pp. 126–27.
16. Vera Soloviova, "Memories of the Moscow Art Theatre" (unpublished manuscript), p. 12.
17. Stanislavski, p. 137.
18. Magarshack, p. 52.
19. Stanislavski, *An Actor Prepares*, translated by Elizabeth Reynolds Hapgood (New York: Theatre Arts Books, 1936), pp. 201–209.
20. Stanislavski (*My Life in Art*), p. 143.
21. Stanislavski, pp. 154–55.
22. Stanislavski, p. 159.
23. Stanislavski, p. 162.
24. Andrius Jilinsky, the husband of Vera Soloviova and former member of the First Studio,

died in New York City in 1948.

25. Magarshack, p. 54.

26. Stanislavski, p. 182.

27. Nikolai A. Gorchakov, *The Theatre in Soviet Russia,* translated by Edgar Lehrman (New York: Columbia University Press, 1957), p. 23.

28. Stanislavski, pp. 184–85.

29. Stanislavski, pp. 192–93.

30. Stanislavski, p. 195.

31. Magarshack, p. 74–76.

32. Magarshack, p. 78.

33. Stanislavski, pp. 207–209.

34. Magarshack, p. 79.

35. Stanislavski, p. 211.

36. N. A. Gorchakov, p. 24.

37. Stanislavski, p. 213.

38. Stanislavski, p. 214.

39. Magarshack, p. 114.

40. Stanislavski, pp. 246–47.

41. Magarshack, p. 95.

42. Stanislavski, pp. 248–50.

43. Magarshack, p, 105.

44. Stanislavski, pp. 251–54.

45. N. A. Gorchakov, p. 26.

46. Magarshack, p. 102.

47. Stanislavski, pp. 277–79.

48. Stanislavski, p. 282.

49. N. A. Gorchakov, p. 25.

50. Stanislavski, p. 241.

51. Magarshack, p. 118.

52. Stanislavski, p. 244.

53. Magarshack, p. 122.

54. Stanislavski, p. 245.

55. Magarshack, pp. 126–27.

56. Stanislavski, pp. 262–63.

57. Magarshack, p. 115.

58. Vladimir Nemirovich-Danchenko, *My Life in the Russian Theatre,* translated by John Cournos (Boston: Little, Brown and Company, 1936), pp. 40–42.

59. N. A. Gorchakov, pp. 28–29.

60. Danchenko, p. 46.

61. Magarshack, p. 150.

62. Danchenko, pp. 47–48.

63. *The Sea Gull Produced by Stanislavski,* edited with an introduction by Professor Balukhaty, translated by David Magarshack (New York: Theatre Arts Books, 1952), pp. 9–10.

64. Balukhaty, p. 14.

65. Danchenko, p. 63.

66. Magarshack, pp. 79–80.

67. Danchenko, p. 75.

68. N. A. Gorchakov, p. 29.

69. N. A. Gorchakov, pp. 25–26.

✤

three

Master Builder

The meeting that took place between Constantin Stanislavsky and Vladimir Nemirovich-Danchenko on June 22, 1897, is well known to most students of the theatre. The far-reaching effects of that meeting, however, could not have been even remotely guessed by the two participants.

THE FOUNDING OF THE MOSCOW ART THEATRE

In their reports of the meeting, Danchenko, Stanislavsky, and Magarshack offer slightly different versions. Magarshack declares that Danchenko left his visiting card at the Alexeiev residence on June 21 with a message asking whether Stanislavsky could meet him the next day at the Slavansky Bazaar. He maintains that they met at two o'clock in the afternoon and talked until eight the following morning. According to Magarshack they had never met before.[1] Stanislavsky himself, however, says they had often met but had not "discovered" each other before. He says that Danchenko invited him to the Slavansky Bazaar to discuss a matter of mutual interest, but that they talked from ten in the morning until three the following morning, for "fifteen hours and perhaps longer."[2]

Danchenko states that Stanislavsky replied to his invitation with the following telegram: "Will be very glad to await you June 21 at two o'clock at Slavansky Bazaar."[3] Professor S. D. Balukhaty, historian of the Moscow Art Theatre, in his introduction to Stanislavsky's production notes on *The Sea Gull,* states that the meeting took place on June 22.[4] This is undoubtedly true, as Magarshack also pointed out that Danchenko had asked Stanislavsky to meet him the day following his arrival in Moscow on June 21.[5]

It was the custom for certain actors and other personages, such as Chaliapin, to sit and converse with visitors in one of the famous restaurants of Moscow. Of these the Slavansky Bazaar was one of the most sedate. Danchenko maintains that they had lunch, coffee, and dinner there, and when the air grew too thick with smoke, Constantin Sergeyevich suggested that they retire to his home just outside of Moscow. Danchenko declares: "We began our historic conversation at two o'clock in the afternoon, and finished it at his villa at eight o'clock the next morning." He makes clear that their conversation continued all the way from the Slavansky Bazaar to Lyubimovka. Once there, Stanislavsky began to note down all that they agreed upon and their talk continued until eight o'clock the following morning.[6]

According to Danchenko much of their conversation at first consisted of criticism of the old theatre and their ideas and plans for correcting its faults. The most remarkable thing was that they did not once disagree. They defined, agreed upon, and affirmed new laws for the theatre, and only after a formulation of these laws did their own respective roles emerge from it all.

Danchenko also asserts that he and Stanislavsky "established all the basic principles of this organization." One of these essentials was a matter of emphasis between matters of the stage and those of the office. The old theatre was enmeshed in all the paraphernalia of officialdom and bureaucracy, and its artistic side was subservient to this to such an extent that "the official form became more important than the art content." Stanislavsky and Danchenko resolved to change all this and see to it that the management should bow to the artistic demands of the play, the author, and the actors. Another point decided upon was that each play should have the set, furniture, properties, and even costumes which were appropriate to it. This was an innovation since previously furniture and scenery had been used interchangeably in successive plays. Moreover, the wardrobe of the actor had long been his personal affair and dependent upon his taste rather than on the demands of the play or the wishes of the director. Still another innovation was the abolition of the orchestra in the intermissions, as it was destructive of the continuity of the play's mood.

One of the chief nuisances in the old theatre sprang from the noisy and often late entrance of many in the audience, as well as from their lack of attention during a performance. The founders of the new organization were determined to correct this. They therefore decided to dim the lights before the start of the performance to discourage conversation and to hurry the audience to their seats. They also agreed to keep the lights in the corridor dim during the performance. Ten years later they were able to forbid entrance while the play was going on. Stanislavsky and Danchenko were determined that the actor should be received with the respect and regard to which he was entitled. The members of the audience were to be made to feel happy and grateful for the privilege of entering the theatre. They would be treated as "charming guests," but they would be made "to submit to rules essential for the artistic unity of our spectacle." [7]

The company of the new theatre was to be recruited from the ranks of Danchenko's pupils in the Philharmonic School and from Stanislavsky's actors of the Society of Art and Literature, with the addition of certain professional actors "from Moscow, St. Petersburg, and the provinces." They went over the lists of names very carefully, choosing those who were talented and who would fit into the new group as they envisioned it.

Since Stanislavsky and Danchenko had each been the absolute head of his company, there might have been some difficulty deciding who would be in supreme command of the new theatre. Stanislavsky, however, found the solution to this problem. Believing Danchenko to be far better grounded in the literature of the stage than he was, as well as more experienced in all literary matters by reason of his writing career, he suggested the following division of authority: In all matters pertaining to the literary content, Danchenko was to have the final word or veto, but in all matters concerned with the artistic form of production, Stanislavsky's word was to be the final one.[8] Danchenko admits that Stanislavsky had had more production experience than he. Indeed, Stanislavsky was already well known for the new methods of staging revealed in *Uriel Acosta* and *The Sunken Bell*. The clearest explanation of this divided authority is given by Danchenko:

The entire artistic realm was to be divided into two parts—the literary and the productional. Both of us were to take possession of a whole production, helping each other and criticizing each other. . . . In any event, in the artistic region we would have equal rights. But should there be a difference of opinion and a decision have to be made, he would have the right to veto what he thought objectionable in the productional part, and I would have the same right in the literary part. It came to this: he had the last word in the region of *form,* and I in the region of *content.*[9]

Danchenko was also to assume the greater responsibility for administrative matters, while Stanislavsky was to work mainly with the actors.

Several other matters upon which the two founders agreed in their extraordinary conversation were a more literary style for their printed programs; a curtain which was to be drawn rather than raised; the end of backstage visitors as well as of actors' benefits; and finally, the highest standards of production even at the opening performance.

They also discussed the repertory for the first season, the finances, and what was, according to Danchenko, "the most important and most interesting—the order of rehearsals and the preparation for a production." Both Stanislavsky and Danchenko condemned the old manner of rehearsals, where the actors begin to "walk through" the play, their parts in their hands, from the very first rehearsal, without any previous discussion of the play. In describing the staging and customary furniture "established once and for all for each and every play," Stanislavsky declares:

One scene of the play would take place near the sofa, the next near the table with the two chairs, the third in the middle of the stage near the prompter's box; then again near the sofa, the table and the prompter's box. A painted red cloth with golden and tremendous tassels, also painted, was supposed to represent rich velvet material and real golden tassels. This had a bent corner beyond which one could see a landscape with mountains, valleys, rivers, seas, cities, villages, forests, parks, fountains and all the other attributes of poesy, prettiness and luxury.[10]

Stanislavsky also condemns the customary canvas scenery, which included "canvas doors with the cloth shivering when they were closed or opened and opening and closing of themselves in most cases," and the practice of the stars' bowing to the audience upon entering. It was Stanislavsky's idea to use great painters to design the scenery. Simov, who had been so successful in creating the background for his performance of *The Sunken Bell*, was retained, and other even more famous artists were soon to be added to the company. In the picture which he gives of Simov, Stanislavsky makes clear the real relation of the scenic artist to the play:

. . . he was interested not only in painting in the theatre, but in the play itself, its interpretation, and its qualities from the actors' and stage director's viewpoints. This helped him to enter into the very soul of the theatre. He also understood the dire necessity of helping the inexperienced actors by means of the production.[11]

Danchenko criticizes the old methods of the regisseur, who at the first rehearsal tells one actor to "go to the table at the right" and another, "to the left and sit in the armchair," while a third is directed to "retire to the rear window." There is no apparent justification for any of the movements and no time for the regisseur to explain his reasons for demanding them. Moreover, as the rehearsals proceed, these directions are very apt to be changed by the regisseur, possibly because "he has found it inconvenient for the actress to go to the window on the right while she finds it equally inconvenient to sit in the armchair on the left not for psychological reasons," Danchenko points out, "but simply because it did not correspond to the old acquired habits of the actress."

Furthermore, according to Danchenko, the entire play, whether four or five acts, was always rehearsed each time, and there was never enough time left to do more than rush over the final act. More and more, as the play approached production, the actors took over and began to advise each other, changing the *mise en scène* to suit themselves.[12]

In a letter to Chekhov urging him to release *The Sea Gull* to the new theatre for production, Danchenko characterized himself as a "*littérateur* with taste, capable of understanding the beauty of your [Chekhov's] production, who is at the same time a skillful *régisseur*." [13] This was not unseemly arrogance in view of the fact that for seven years prior to the founding of the Moscow Art Theatre Danchenko had been teaching at the Philharmonic School and had turned out a sizable number of capable actors, among whom were three future members of the Moscow Art Theatre, Moskvin, Meyerhold, and the great Olga Knipper. Moreover, his method leaned toward that finally arrived at by Stanislavsky. In describing the "processes" which he sought Danchenko asserts:

. . . the instruction went far beyond the bounds of first experiments in stage technique. Psychological movements, everyday features, moral questions, emotional mergings with the author, aspiration toward frankness and simplicity, the quest of vivid expression and diction, mimicry, plastics, self-assurance . . . .[14]

Stanislavsky had not yet discovered the way to inner truth. Also, as he himself points out, the actors in the new group were for the most part students or amateurs, and their lack of experience had to be covered "by the luxuriousness of costumes, decorations, scenery, properties and a production that might dazzle the spectator." [15]

The same method of preparing a play for production was followed by both men. The play was discussed carefully before the beginning of rehearsals. Then one scene was taken at a time, and sometimes repeated for hours and even days in order to reach the correct interpretation of its meaning.[16]

Following their historic eighteen-hour conversation, Stanislavsky and Danchenko arranged to visit each other's performances in the coming season in order to evaluate the personnel for their new theatre. They also came to know each other better and discussed each other's performances frankly.[17]

The chief problems that filled their days throughout the next year were the search for a suitable theatre and, most important, the raising of funds. Stanislavsky himself contributed 10,000 rubles, approximately $5,000 in those days. His wife, Lilina, offered to act for the new theatre without salary for an unspecified time.[18] The rich Moscow merchant, Morozov, became a shareholder in the new company; he contributed 10,000 rubles. He was later to build a new theatre and buy out all the other shareholders except Stanislavsky and Danchenko.[19]

The budget for the first year of the new theatre was only 28,000 rubles or $14,000. Salaries, therefore, had to be apportioned accordingly. Moskvin came to them for 100 rubles a month, and Olga Knipper played leading parts at the start for only 75 rubles a month. The members of the group, however, were all motivated by a common devotion to the ideal theatre.

Having made arrangements for a theatre and decided upon a repertoire, Stanislavsky and Danchenko began rehearsals of their opening play, *Tsar Fyodor*, on June 14, 1898.[20] They worked in a sort of barn or shed in Pushkino, about 23 miles from Moscow. In his speech to the actors before this first rehearsal, Stanislavsky sounded a very lofty note:

> For me this theatre is a long-hoped for, long-promised child. It is not for the sake of material gain that we have waited so long for it. No, it is the answer to our prayer for something to bring light and beauty into our humdrum lives . . . . If we do not come to this enterprise with clean hands we shall defile it, disgrace ourselves and be scattered to the ends of Russia . . . . Do not forget either that our goal is to bring enlightenment into the lives of the poor, to give them some aesthetic enjoyment amid the gloom in which they have been living. We are attempting to create the first thoughtful, high-minded, popular theatre—and to this great goal we are dedicating our lives.
>
> Be careful not to crush this beautiful flower, else it will wilt and its petals fall . . . .
>
> For the sake of such a purpose let us leave trivial matters at home, let us gather here in a common effort . . . . Let us be guided by the motto of "common work, friendly work" . . . .[21]

The summer in Pushkino was a period of great activity. Stanislavsky kept "a chronicle" in which he put down the order of each day, what plays were to be rehearsed (often there were rehearsals of two different plays in the same day) and everything that occurred. Rehearsals began at eleven every morning and lasted until five in the afternoon. After the actors had dined and had bathed in the river, the second rehearsal took place from seven to eleven at night. In addition to the company rehearsals, Stanislavsky or Danchenko often worked alone with an actor.[22]

Danchenko, who had been finishing his work on a novel, did not come to Pushkino until July 25, more than a month after rehearsals had begun. Stanislavsky, on the other hand, worked on rehearsals of *Tsar Fyodor* and other plays in the repertory until August 12.[23] At that time the general rehearsals were taken over by Stanislavsky's assistant, Sanin; Stanislavsky retired to his brother's estate until September 20 to rest and to prepare the staging of *The Sea Gull*. At the same time Danchenko was to begin discussions of *The Sea Gull* with the actors.[24]

Later Stanislavsky took Sanin; Lilina; the stage designer, Simov; the costumer; and one or two other actors on an expedition to several ancient Russian cities to search for material and atmosphere for the costumes and scenery for *Tsar Fyodor*. In Rostov they were permitted to spend a night in the palace of Ivan the Terrible. Thus they were able to steep themselves in the atmosphere, and Simov made many sketches of the palace as well as of the museum treasures. In Nizhny-Novgorod, which for centuries had been famous for its fair, they were able to purchase many of the costumes and properties used in *Tsar Fyodor*. Stanislavsky had come to realize the need for "color spots" in a production, rather than the creation of the entire production in its original luxurious form. He had found these color spots on his journey.

When Stanislavsky came to the Hermitage Theatre in the fall to continue the rehearsals, he was greatly disappointed at its state of disrepair. It had previously been used as a sort of variety house, with acrobats, clowns, and even trained animals as part of the entertainment, and it had been left in a shocking state. Accordingly the whole company set about cleaning and redecorating. Stanislavsky writes: "We were forced to invent new methods of turning a stable into a temple, and of creating an interior that would be bearable for cultured people." [25]

The rehearsals proceeded in the face of staggering difficulties. For one thing, the heating system had to be repaired, and this at a time when the weather was far below freezing. At the same time it became necessary to agree upon a name for the new theatre. Stanislavsky says that Nemirovich-Danchenko suggested the Moscow Art and Popular Theatre as a name, saying they must decide without further delay. Danchenko, on the other hand, states that for the first year it was called the Art-Accessible Theatre because they were dedicating "morning holiday performances" to workers at very moderate prices. He explains, "We wanted our theatre to be generally accessible, we wanted the main part of our audience to consist of the intelligentsia in moderate circumstances, and of the student bodies." [26]

Danchenko says that the attitude of the press toward the new undertaking was "either frankly hostile or definitely mocking." The papers were either silent or printed items such as this: "Is it not true, that all this is a whim of grown but naive human beings, the wealthy merchant-amateur Alexeiev and the delirious litterateur Vladimir Nemirovich?" [27] Danchenko and Stanislavsky ignored such attacks and redoubled their efforts toward a unified production.

Stanislavsky had another obstacle to overcome. He had still to convince the newcomers, mostly professional actors from the provinces, of the rightness of his methods. Sometimes they insisted that "the stage demanded visualized action, a loud voice, a rapid tempo, and full-toned acting." By this was meant, not "the fullness of inner emotion and living over the part," Stanislavsky comments, "but the fullness of shouting, exaggerated gesture and action, and a primitively vulgar delineation of the role, fed by animal temperament." When these quarrels arose, Stanislavsky either called upon those members of the company who had been with him in the Society of Art and Literature to demonstrate his methods or went upon the stage himself and acted out the part as the recalcitrant actor had said it couldn't be done.[28]

Although Stanislavsky was far from his ultimate goal at this point, no one understood this better than he. The difference between the other theatres and the new Moscow Art and Popular Theatre lay principally in the fact that, according to Stanislavsky, all the other theatres practiced conventionalized theatrical truth, and they wanted another, "a real artistic, scenic truth."

In reply to the charge that the new theatre was seeking for naturalism in its production, Stanislavsky declared:

> We never leaned toward such a principle. Always, then as well as now [1924], we sought for inner truth, for the truth of feeling and experience, but as spiritual technique was only in its embryo stage among the actors of our company, we, because of necessity and helplessness, and against our desires, fell now and then into an outward and coarse naturalism.

Stanislavsky gives a very clear statement of what it was that the new theatre was revolting against:

> We protested against the customary manner of acting, against declamation, against overacting, against the bad manner of production, against the habitual scenery, against the star system which spoiled the ensemble, against the light and farcical repertoire which was being cultivated on the Russian stage at that time.[29]

The opening performance took place on October 14, 1898, with the presentation of *Tsar Fyodor*. The audience was astonished at the realistic setting, especially in the garden scene, where the decorations were placed along the footlights, creating the "fourth wall." A few grumblers muttered, "An imitation of the Meiningen players . . ." and "Archaeological details. What a rummaging in the museums." However, the play was well received by the critics. The first hurdle had been successfully cleared.[30]

Nevertheless, after *Tsar Fyodor* dark days followed. *The Merchant of Venice*, the revival of *The Sunken Bell* and *Men above the Law*, *Antigone*, and *Greta's Happiness* (a modern play put into the repertoire by Danchenko over Stanislavsky's objection) were all failures.[31]

The finances of the new theatre were in a precarious state. The money which had been contributed by the stockholders was all used up. When they decided to revive *Hannele*, which had been so successful when done by the Society of Art and Literature, they ran into religious objections from the Metropolitan of Moscow before the first performance. Finally even the performances for workingmen had to be canceled because they had not been submitted to the proper censor. This was the situation until the opening of *The Sea Gull* on December 17, 1898.[32] It was largely because of Danchenko's constant importuning that Chekhov had given the new theatre permission to produce this play.

GREATER REALISM IN ACTING THROUGH CHEKHOV

This first production of a Chekhov play marked the beginning of greater realism in the acting of the Moscow Art Theatre. Whereas in *Tsar Fyodor* every effort had been made to depict the external details as realistically as possible, during the rehearsals of *The Sea Gull* it became increasingly evident that the actors needed an extra dimension in portraying these characters. Chekhov had drawn them with so much understanding and had given so much meaning to the simplest words they spoke that the actor was forced to seek the inner life of each one and attempt to express this on the stage. This created a quality of inner realism which the actors had not hitherto possessed.

Even before the opening of *Tsar Fyodor* Stanislavsky had prepared the staging of *The Sea Gull* down to the finest details of movement, grouping, and characterization, even to the tone of voice of an actor at a given moment (see page 69). In retrospect, Stanislavsky admitted to "despotic" methods at this period and even condemned the director (himself), who, "hiding in his study . . . made a detailed *mise en scène* that agreed with his emotions, his inner sight and hearing" but paid no attention to "the inner emotions of the actor." [33]

It is hardly necessary to point out the importance of this "score," as Stanislavsky called it, for *The Sea Gull*. The original contains the text of Chekhov's play on one side, and on the other, Stanislavsky's notes concerning such things as the motives of the characters, the subtext of the lines, and the complete plot of the action, lighting, and sound. We are indebted to David Magarshack for his translation of the entire score and the text, together with the introduction by Professor Balukhaty.

The Moscow Art Theatre made Chekhov popular. Without that organization he might never have achieved his present fame. The production of *The Sea Gull* marks the spiritual birth of the Moscow Art Theatre, and a new phase of its acting was achieved through continuing work on the subsequent Chekhov plays.

The wonder is that this could come about in spite of the fact that Stanislavsky and many of the others had found the play "strange and monotonous after its first reading." He frankly admits, "During the course of many evenings Vladimir Ivanovich hammered all the beauties of Chekhov's work into my head." He characterizes Danchenko's ability to talk one into liking a play as a fault, since often much of what he had related was found to be his own rather than the author's creation.[34]

It is surprising to see how close the ideas of Danchenko and Stanislavsky were in their approach to Chekhov. The key to this approach, Danchenko declared, was enunciated by Chekhov in a remark which he made during the rehearsals for *The Sea Gull* at the Alexandrinsky Theatre in St. Petersburg: "They act too much. It would be better if they acted a little more as in life." Danchenko declares that this expresses the significant difference between "the actor of the old theatre" and the actors of the Moscow Art Theatre. His elaboration of this point illuminates that difference:

> The actor of the old theatre acts either *emotion:* love, jealousy, hatred, joy, etc.; or *words,* underlining them, stressing each significant one; or a *situation,* laughable or dramatic; or a *mood,* or *physical self-consciousness.* In a word, inevitably during every instant of his presence on the stage he is *acting* something, representing something. Our demands on the actor *are* that he should not act anything; decidedly not a *thing;* neither feelings, nor moods, nor situations, nor words, nor style, nor images. All this should come of itself from the individuality of the actor, individuality liberated from stereotype forms, prompted by his entire "nervous organization . . . ."[35]

Danchenko defines the actor's individuality as "the immense region of his imagination, his heredity, all that manifests itself beyond his consciousness in a moment of aberration." He maintains that it is the purpose of rehearsal to "awaken" this individuality, and finally, "in

such a degree . . . to incarnate oneself into a role that the words of
the author become for the actor his own words."

From Balukhaty comes this reference to Stanislavsky's prescription
for acting Chekhov:

> Stanislavsky asserted that there could be no greater mistake than to at-
> tempt to "act" in a Chekhov play; what the actor, according to Stanislavsky,
> had to do was "to *be*," that is to say, to live, to exist, by "getting under
> the skin" of the Chekhov character by "penetrating into the most secret
> places of his heart." [36]

Stanislavsky admits that the actors' "spiritual technique was only
in its embryo stage" at this time and therefore, while they sought "a
real artistic, scenic truth," that is to say "the truth of feeling and
experience," they still were forced to proceed "from the outward to
the inward." [37] Accordingly, Stanislavsky prepared his detailed *mise en
scènes*, using scenic movement "as an expression of the active emotional life of the characters," emphasizing the natural concrete realism
of the scene, conceived against the social background of the life of
the characters in the play." He even went so far as to endow every
person "according to his character or his emotional state of mind,
with his own way of walking, his own rhythm as it happens in everyday life." He took great care that the "behavior" and "action" of
each character or group "should conform in the spectator's mind to
his perception of life as it really is, to its general content and
form." [38]

This undoubtedly made it easier for the audience to become identified with the characters and accounted for the praise of the critics,
one of whom remarked that the performance was "not simply an
interpretation of the play, but an embodiment of it."

With Simov, the stage designer, Stanislavsky worked out new ways
of giving the impression of the "fourth wall" by placing a bench across
the footlights and seating a part of the "stage audience" with its
back to the real audience for the opening scene. There were innovations, too, in the treatment of interior scenes, with the suggestion of
adjoining rooms lending greater reality to the setting.[39]

The use of lighting and sound effects was revolutionary. Special
attention was paid to lighting at the beginning of an act. Every effort
was made to have the lighting correspond to the time of the stage
action. For example, at the opening of *The Sea Gull* the stage was in
darkness except for the light of a lantern hung on a post because the

curtain for Trepleff's play hid the moon.[40] Danchenko admits, however, that in the beginning they went to extremes in their efforts to achieve realistic lighting. "There were times, indeed," he asserts, "when the stage was so dark as to render invisible not only the actors' faces, but even their figures." [41] This is particularly interesting when one recalls that on his visit to America Stanislavsky criticized the stage lighting employed by Arthur Hopkins in *The Hairy Ape*. His ideas had changed considerably, since he is said to have objected to "the too frequent use of dark stage effects" in America:

> I cannot see how a producer can darken his stage time and time again, obscuring his leading character, deliberately robbing the latter of one of his most effective means of expression, namely, his eyes and facial expression . . . . But why should producers conceal from the public men with faces as fine and expressive as Barrymore and Warfield? [42]

Whatever the early faults, and both Stanislavsky and Danchenko are frank to admit them, the score for *The Sea Gull* shows the beginnings of the method of the Moscow Art Theatre that was one day to develop into the Stanislavsky System.

According to Balukhaty, the main concern of both producers was "to make the performance one indivisible whole from the artistic point of view." The result was the wonderfully created ensemble and the "carefully coordinated connexion between all the elements of the performance so as to achieve one single interpretation of the ruling idea of the play." [43] Stanislavsky set out to "fire the spectator's imagination with the material of the play, to evoke in him a rich association of ideas, to awaken his slumbering feelings and moods."

To accomplish his purpose Stanislavsky made extensive use of sound effects. There were several categories and they served different purposes. There were sounds of nature, such as thunder, wind, rain, and the familiar cricket. Then there were the ordinary sounds of daily life, such as bird songs and the barking of a dog or the sound of "harness bells," the clatter of dishes, the ringing of a doorbell. Sounds were introduced as "indications of the actual real life which takes place on stage," or for the "intensification of some definite mood," or as "an indication of the emotional state of mind of a character." Again sound was used to show contrast or heighten a significant moment, as the sound of laughter in the dining room after Nina's final exit, when Konstantin stands motionless before he goes out to shoot himself.[44]

Another innovation introduced by Stanislavsky in his score for *The*

Sea Gull and retained by the Moscow Art Theatre was what Danchenko refers to as "appropriate objects and characteristic minutiae for the persons of the play." Danchenko stresses the value of Stanislavsky's use of stage properties in attracting the audience and in "assisting in endowing the scene with a mood of reality." In his opinion, however, their greatest value lay in their usefulness to the actor, who in the old theatre found himself "outside time and space." [45] In this connection Balukhaty says:

> And the new theatre learnt how to re-create the external truth of life and at the same time provide a proper understanding of the inner life of the characters by disclosing their innermost feelings and their closest inter-relationships with each other.[46]

Stanislavsky admired Chekhov's ability "to create inward and outward artistic truth" and his understanding of "how to make the best possible use of inanimate objects on the stage, and how to instill life into them." Here Magarshack and Balukhaty quote an identical passage of Stanislavsky, except for the last three lines, which appear only in Magarshack:

> Twilight, sunset, sunrise, a storm, rain, the songs of awakening birds, the trampling of horses over a bridge, the rattle of a carriage as it drives off, the striking of a clock, the chirping of a cricket . . . are necessary to Chekhov not for the sake of their external effects but for the revelation of the life of the human spirit. For it is impossible to separate us and everything that takes place in us from the world of inanimate things, light and sound among which we live and on which human psychology depends so much.[47]

In *My Life in Art* Stanislavsky writes in less detail than Magarshack and Balukhaty about the "technique and methods for the artistic interpretation of Chekhov" which he originated in the Moscow Art Theatre. He praises the playwright for having "discovered" to them "the life of things and sounds," saying, "The properties that surrounded us on the stage took on an inner relationship with the soul of the actor." [48] Stanislavsky had not yet discovered the way to creative playing at all times and under all circumstances. At this period, he admits, "Our creativeness was based on accident." Explaining this in greater detail, he asserts:

> Passing from the outward to the inward we were often successful in piercing some of the mysteries, and then we would strike on the inner line of the development of the role. There would be a spark and then the flame of real feeling and a miracle.[49]

This is what Stanislavsky refers to as "the line of the intuition of feelings." It is a sense of the reality of the character which comes to the actor intuitively and in part because Chekhov's characters are so like living people whom the actor has known. Stanislavsky refers to it also as "the eternal in art . . . the eternal which Chekhov has given to the theatre of the world and to the art of the theatre." He declares, furthermore:

> Chekhov gave that inner truth to the art of the stage which served as the foundation for what was later called the Stanislavsky System, which must be approached through Chekhov, or which serves as a bridge to the approach of Chekhov. Playing Chekhov, one is not forced to search for the feeling of truth, which is such a necessary element of the creative mood.[50]

It was at such times that Stanislavsky found the ability to live his part; in his own words, "the words and actions of the part were transformed into the actor's own words and actions." This he characterized as "a creative miracle—the most important and necessary sacrament of the soul for the sake of which it is worth making every possible sacrifice in our art." [51]

"What is so wonderful about Chekhov's plays," Stanislavsky says, "is not what is transmitted by the words, but what is hidden under them, in the pauses, in the glance of the actors, in the emanation of their innermost feelings." [52] This discovery and playing of the "subtext" also became an important part of the Stanislavsky System.

The reception given the production of *The Sea Gull* at its opening performance on December 17, 1898, at the Moscow Art and Academic Theatre in Karetny Row was different from that at the Alexandrinsky Theatre in St. Petersburg exactly two years and one month before. Of the numerous accounts of the second opening night, Danchenko writes most eloquently of the deep silence in the audience and on the stage at the end of the first act. The curtain closed after Masha, "played beautifully by Lilina," has opened her heart to the doctor and spoken of her hopeless love for Konstantin. The actors, believing the first act had been an utter failure, were almost hysterical; Knipper, according to Stanislavsky, fainted. Then, "as if a dam had burst or a bomb exploded—all at once there was a deafening crash of applause from all: from friends and from enemies." The curtain opened showing the stupefied actors. According to Danchenko, the curtain was drawn no less than six times.[53]

Stanislavsky describes the scene backstage with "congratulations and embraces like those of Easter night and ovations to Lilina, who played Masha and who had broken the ice with her last words which tore themselves from her heart . . . ." [54]

In the words of one critic reported by Balukhaty, "Most of the spectators walked about the corridors and foyers in the intervals looking curiously as though they were celebrating their own birthdays."

On the whole the press was appreciative, praising the producer's subtle understanding of the play's spirit and atmosphere, the "harmonious ensemble." They conceded that the Art Theatre had "won a great victory." Although *The Sea Gull* was on the whole less successful than the other Chekhov plays and remained in the repertory only until December, 1905, the work on this first Chekhov production had opened a new chapter in the acting of the Moscow Art Theatre.[55] Furthermore, four years later, Franz Schechtel, the architect who designed the stage and auditorium for the theatre's new home, placed his design of a "flying sea gull" on the moss green draw curtains, and

this has remained the emblem of the Moscow Art Theatre [56] ever since.

In reply to questions as to how his characters should be played, Chekhov gave only the barest hints. Yet Stanislavsky came to realize the full import of the author's laconic remarks and to discover the kernel of the character from them. In *The Sea Gull,* for example, Stanislavsky began to play Trigorin in truly elegant attire, in spotless white clothes including vest and hat. Chekhov's comment to him after seeing the special performance which was arranged for him was simply, "Wonderful. Listen, it was wonderful! Only you need torn shoes and checked trousers."

It took Stanislavsky a year in this case to realize Chekhov's full meaning. While he was playing the part, he came to understand that Chekhov had meant to imply not only Trigorin's lack of taste but also his lack of talent as a writer. Only the young girls like Nina who cast themselves at his feet never notice till too late that they have created his genius out of their infatuation.

In order that Chekhov might see the theatre's production of *Uncle Vanya* the whole company, including wives and children and all the stage assistants, undertook a journey to the Crimea where the playwright was living because of his illness. Again the laconic words, two in fact, illuminated the final scene in the play for Stanislavsky. Referring to Astrov's final departure, Chekhov said, "He whistles. Listen, he whistles. Uncle Vanya is crying, but Astrov whistles." When Stanislavsky put the author's direction into practice, another facet in Dr. Astrov's character became clear. Although he has lost his faith in people, he is happy in his devotion to nature, and as he drives away from the place where he has found temporary happiness, he whistles.[57]

The third season of the Moscow Art Theatre, 1900–1901, saw three productions by Stanislavsky: Ostrovsky's *The Snow Maiden,* Chekhov's *The Three Sisters,* and Ibsen's *An Enemy of the People.* The production of the first play was noteworthy for Stanislavsky's use of realistic detail in conjunction with his ingenious treatment of the fantastic. For example, when Jack Frost appeared, he brought with him a grizzly bear. At the same time the trees and bushes which had been visible on the mountain side in the background suddenly came to life before the eyes of the audience and turned into fantastic wood demons in the snow. A realistic touch was achieved by having the villagers sink into a snowdrift which was actually a trough filled with salt placed along the front of the stage parallel with the footlights.

OUT OF THE SUBCONSCIOUS

It was during the rehearsals of *The Snow Maiden* and of *The Three Sisters* that something occurred which was not fully understood by Stanislavsky until several years later. Both happenings illustrate the power of the memory in awakening the subconscious. On the first occasion the rehearsal had been proceeding normally until the actress Olga Sadovskaya complained that she was distracted by two baskets, suspended from the ceiling, which cradled two old men, icon painters, lying on their backs painting the ceiling of the king's palace. When the cradles were lowered for the men to rest, Stanislavsky noticed that his imagination lagged; when, however, the baskets were raised to the ceiling again, his imagination was stimulated anew. The reason for this was not apparent until years later when Stanislavsky visited Kiev's St. Vladimir Cathedral. As he listened to the distant singing of a prayer, alone in the cathedral, there came to his mind the recollection of an earlier visit he had made while the cathedral was being built. At that time, too, he had been alone, but the stillness had been broken by "the singing of the icon painters who were suspended in cradles beneath the dome and were painting it slowly as though they were anointing it with oil." [58] The sight of the icon painters at the rehearsal had unconsciously recalled the atmosphere of the cathedral in Kiev, which was exactly what Stanislavsky required in rehearsal.

A similar occurrence took place during the rehearsals of *The Three Sisters*. In spite of Stanislavsky's carefully prepared *mise en scène* the play was showing no progress and the rehearsal had come to a standstill, when suddenly Stanislavsky was moved to a realization of what the mood of the play should be. For while everyone was sitting about the stage disconsolately, someone began to scratch on a wooden bench and the sound was like that of a mouse. Whether the sound in the darkness was in some way connected with a previous experience when he had been in a similar state of mind, Stanislavsky was unable to remember. However, in his words, "a spiritual spring was touched," [59] at that moment. He declared, "For some reason it made me think of a family hearth; I felt a warm glow all over me; I sensed truth and life, and my intuition began to work." He suddenly understood the Chekhov characters and he realized why the author had felt the play was a gay comedy. For the characters were not "wallowing in their depression, but were longing for gaiety and laughter." So,

for the second time, Stanislavsky's intuition had come, not by accident as was usually the case, but out of his subconscious.

The Three Sisters required three years' work to reach a satisfactory
production. Thereafter it became more and more successful, as did
Stanislavsky's portrayal of Vershinin's part, although he himself was
never completely satisfied with it. Nevertheless Olga Knipper, the
Masha of the play, has written an account of his portrayal, which
characterizes it as having "great nobility, restraint and purity." "I
cannot recall the scene of my parting from this Vershinin without
tears," she declares.[60]

It was in the part of Dr. Stockman in Ibsen's *An Enemy of the
People,* however, that Stanislavsky achieved complete fusion with the
part. "In my actor's perceptions I felt myself more at home on the
stage in the role of Stockman than in any other role in my repertoire,"
Stanislavsky writes. "In it I instinctively followed the line of the
intuition of feelings." (See page 77.) In playing the part, Stanislavsky
put all thoughts of politics out of his mind and concentrated upon
Stockman's love for truth. In consequence, the political implications
were all the stronger for the audience.

It is in this play that Stanislavsky may be said to have discovered
inner technique. That is, he allowed his inner image of the character
of Stockman to create the external characteristics of the man, as "the
short-sighted eyes which spoke so eloquently of his inner blindness
to human faults, the childlike and youthful manner of movement, the
friendly relations with his children and family. . . ." [61] In explaining
how the outer image "flowed naturally from the inner image, and
the soul and body of Stockman-Stanislavsky became one organically,"
he says:

> I only had to think of the thoughts and cares of Stockman and the signs
> of short sight would come of themselves, together with the forward stoop
> of the body, the quick step, the eyes that looked trustfully into the soul of
> the man or object on the stage with me, the index and the middle fingers
> of the hand stretched forward of themselves . . . as if to push my own
> thoughts, feelings and words into the soul of my listener. All these habits
> came of themselves, unconsciously, and quite apart from myself. From where
> did they come? [62] (See illustration facing page 88.)

Stanislavsky was to find the answer to this question several years
later, and the discovery was another link in the chain of events which
led to his finding at last the way to awaken the subconscious, to induce

the creative state. He found that the particular gestures and movements, which he thought at the time had come to him out of the air, had arisen unconsciously out of his memory. "Little by little," he writes, "I found accidentally the sources of many of the elements of the inner and outer images." For example, he recognized his stretching of the index and middle fingers when he met "a learned man" in Berlin whom he used to meet in a sanitarium in Vienna. His manner of stamping his foot in the part he realized he had taken from a well-known music critic. At this time he made a further discovery. "I had only to assume the manners and habits of Stockman, on the stage or off," he writes, "and in my soul there were born the feelings and perceptions that had given them birth." In explanation of this phenomenon he says:

> In this manner, intuition not only created the image, but its passions also. They became my own organically, or, to be more true, my own passions became Stockman's. And during this process I felt the greatest joy an artist can feel, the right to speak on the stage the thoughts of another, to perform another's actions, as if they were my own.[63]

His fellow actors were astounded at "this fusion of Stanislavsky and Stockman." According to the testimony of one of them, "Those who happened to be near him on the stage were absolutely convinced that they were in the presence of a new person." Leonidov, who became a prominent member of the Moscow Art Theatre, explained the fusion by the similarity in the characters of Stanislavsky and Stockman. Ibsen's character fought for the truth and Stanislavsky "fought against everything that he thought false in the theatre," Leonidov declared, adding, "It was indeed impossible to separate Stanislavsky from Stockman."

The actress Nina Litovtseva, wife of Kachalov and later one of the producers of the theatre, speaks of the power of the last scene, when the boys in the roles of Stockman's sons were moved to tears by Stanislavsky's playing. "That was one of the most remarkable crowd scenes I ever saw," she declares. In this scene Magarshack points out, "Stanislavsky used scarcely any gestures at all." It is significant that in the role of Stockman, where Stanislavsky reached such complete fusion with the character by means of the "intuition of feeling," he no longer depended upon the externals upon which he had hitherto lavished so much care.[64]

To what extent the acting of the Moscow Art Theatre was superior to that of other Russian theatres of the time may be judged by the ovation the company received on its first visit to St. Petersburg at the close of the 1900–1901 season in the spring. During a festive dinner, one of the speakers declared that Stanislavsky and Danchenko had killed the ancient theatrical routine and put truth in its place. Another referred to the former way of speaking, gesturing, and walking, and closed his speech with the statement that this company had, instead of actors and actresses, "men and women who deeply believe." [65]

In March, 1901, the Moscow Art Theatre opened a dramatic school. Those accepted were required to play in crowd scenes and as walk-ons in order for Stanislavsky and Danchenko to judge their suitability for a stage career. They were required also to attend all rehearsals of the company. The following spring they were given an examination, and if successful were admitted to the school. [66]

In 1902 an event of great importance took place. At a moment when the finances of the Moscow Art Theatre were in a critical state, Morozov, the wealthy merchant who had been the friend and benefactor of the theatre from its beginning, came to their rescue. He bought up the shares of all the stockholders except Stanislavsky and Danchenko, and advanced nearly 50,000 rubles for the building of a new theatre. Actually he reconditioned the existing theatre in Kamergersky Lane and this became the permanent home of the Moscow Art Theatre.

Stanislavsky points out the unusual feature of Morozov's approach to the task of rebuilding the auditorium and stage. Contrary to the usual practice, only about a quarter of the total was spent on the auditorium, the foyer, and other rooms intended for the use of the audience; the greater part was spent on the stage and the actors' dressing rooms. The stage itself, as well as the floor below it, revolved, and there was a trap which could be raised or lowered to form a mountain, a chasm or a river as the play required. [67]

According to Magarshack, the new theatre in Kamergersky Lane was opened on November 19, 1902, with Tolstoy's *The Power of Darkness*. Stanislavsky, on the other hand, writes of a decision to open the new theatre with a play by Gorky entitled *Small People;* this Gorky completed before *The Lower Depths,* which was originally expected to be the opening play. In the list of Moscow Art Theatre productions the first play to be given in the Kamergersky Theatre is *Small People;* the date here is October 25. In the same list the opening date for Tolstoy's *The Power of Darkness* is November 5. [68]

For Tolstoy's play Stanislavsky, Simov, his stage designer, and several others visited the actual village where the action of the play supposedly took place. There they spent two weeks studying all the phases of village life. They went so far as to bring back an old man and an old woman to supervise the presentation of village customs. The result was the reproduction on stage of a Russian village which was true to the smallest detail. However, it was not until the old peasant woman replaced the actress playing Matryona at one rehearsal that "the spiritual darkness and power" of the village was displayed. It was impossible to retain her in the part because she not only departed from Tolstoy's text but used oaths that would never have passed the censors. Nevertheless she demonstrated to Stanislavsky the difference between unjustified naturalism, where the properties and sounds existed for themselves, and true naturalism which is justified by the actor's inner experience.[69]

In preparing to present Gorky's *The Lower Depths*, Stanislavsky followed his old method of depending upon the atmosphere of the play to give him the feeling or emotion, and then extracting the image from the feeling. This time Stanislavsky and others in the company visited the Khitrov Market. This was a part of the city peopled entirely by derelicts, robbers, and other criminals. Some who had known better times occasionally were engaged to copy parts for actors. After spending some time there in company with the prototypes of Gorky's play, Stanislavsky was able to understand and feel the play's inner meaning, which he believed to be "freedom at any cost." His imagination and creativeness were awakened more readily than they could have been by lengthy discussions of the play. Nevertheless, he was not completely satisfied with his playing of the part of Satin. Although he attempted to find the creative mood through the feelings, he did not relive the part intuitively and sometimes he played the result, the idea which Gorky expressed in the character of Satin.[70]

THE SEARCH FOR NEW FORMS

Not until Stanislavsky was working on three plays by Maeterlinck, *The Blind, Interior,* and *The Unbidden Guest,* did he begin to search for new forms of expression. Realizing that impressionist painting and music were more successful in expressing the fantastic and imaginative yearnings of the mind and heart than the voice of the actor, he studied the works of modern painters and sculptors and composers.

Meeting with Meyerhold, who had left the Moscow Art Theatre several years before to establish a theatre in the provinces, Stanislavsky discovered that he also was seeking a more modern expression, and, in fact, that he believed he had already discovered a new method for contemporary theatre. Accordingly, Stanislavsky established the Studio on Povarskaya Street to help Meyerhold realize the dreams which he himself shared, namely, "to introduce impressionism in the theatre and find a beautiful and conventionalized scenic form for its expression."

When, after a summer and autumn spent in rehearsals, the Studio at last displayed the results of its labors in a presentation of Maeterlinck's *The Death of Tintagiles* and Hauptmann's *Schluck und Jau,* Meyerhold's talent was apparent in the imaginative groupings and in the ingenious *mise en scène.* However, the inexperience and inadequacy of the young actors was also apparent. Stanislavsky came to realize that the vast gap between the director's dreams and ideas and their realization could only be bridged by actors trained in a completely new technique. To achieve such a production would require much more time and money than was practicable, especially since the 1905 Revolution had broken out at that time. Therefore Stanislavsky was obliged to liquidate the Studio after reimbursing the actors at his own expense.[71]

Apparently the experience with the Studio on Povarskaya Street and with Meyerhold's methods brought Stanislavsky to the realization of the greater importance of the actor in a production. He also repudiated dependence upon the scene designer and all the externals and production tricks which he had learned from the Meiningen Players. His great concern was with the discovery of the laws of acting, which he was sure existed.[72]

In spite of Stanislavsky's dissatisfaction, the acting of the Moscow Art Theatre must have been of a very high standard, for when the entire company went on its first European tour, the critics gave its performances the highest praise. In describing a performance of *Tsar Fyodor,* which the Kaiser attended, one of his staff wrote:

> The acting reaches such artistic heights that one forgets one is in a theatre, one lives over the soul-shaking historic events. All that is theatrical is absent . . . . Although one does not understand a single word, the performance is so engrossing that one completely forgets the words and lives over the tragedy together with the actors.[73]

Danchenko gives a more detailed account of the critical acclaim. According to him the Berlin critic, Alfred Kerr, praised them for achieving "the spirit of clarity . . . of simplicity, of an inwardly fortified repose, which the excellent art of Reinhardt has not yet reached." [74]

In Dresden the reviewers reached a lyric height. They referred to "this evening of artistic, sacred rapture and never-to-be-forgotten impressions of an art which presents equally the highest inner and the highest outer truth." In Vienna the critic Ludwig Bauer declared, "Perfection on the stage has been actually realized," and the *Neue Freie Presse* compared the ensemble to "a brilliantly rehearsed and conducted orchestra." [75]

SELF-EXAMINATION AND OBSERVATION

In spite of the success of the tour, Stanislavsky was still dissatisfied with himself as an actor and intent on finding the cause of what seemed to him his lack of creativeness. In the summer of 1906 he went to Finland for his vacation. Sitting on a cliff overlooking the sea each morning, he began to recall the events of his artistic career. Why was it that great actors like Salvini, Duse, and Yermolova seemed able to make their parts better with each succeeding performance, while the more he played a role, the less satisfied he became? He went over his role of Doctor Stockman and recalled the living memories which had awakened his feelings and perceptions of the character. Suddenly the live feelings of Stockman returned to him and he recognized the difference between his first creativeness in the part and the loss of this in subsequent performances, when he had been accustomed to play "the physical signs of absent emotion."

In other words, he had formed the habit of playing the outer characteristics without experiencing the emotions that led to them. He attributed this to "muscular memory," which is especially conspicuous in actors. He carefully examined his other roles and tried to discover the source of their creativeness. In the process he reached the conclusion that a spiritual as well as physical make-up was necessary for each performance.[76]

When he returned to Moscow for the 1906–1907 season, Stanislavsky's mind was still occupied with the search for the means of creativity. While he was playing a familiar role he unexpectedly came to a full realization of "the creative mood." It became clear to him, also, that one of the things that constituted a genius was the presence of this creative mood, which came without effort and was most conducive to inspiration. The less talented the actor, the less often this condition visited him. Stanislavsky's chief concern became "how to create a favorable condition for the appearance of inspiration by means of the will, that condition in the presence of which inspiration was most likely to descend into the actor's soul." He began to realize that the less talented actor might, by means of systematic exercises, learn to reach this creative mood which comes of itself to the genius. He observed his own reactions on and off stage, as well as the reactions of his fellow actors, when rehearsing new parts with them. In fact, he was accused of turning the rehearsals into a laboratory and the actors into guinea pigs. Still he continued his observations, particularly of great actors, native and foreign. In all of these he noted a common characteristic—the responsiveness and lack of tension in their bodies. As this freedom from strain gradually became habitual with him, and as a result he began to feel much more comfortable on stage, Stanislavsky made a second discovery. The exercises which directed his attention upon what was taking place within him also served to keep his attention from straying beyond the footlights. Moreover, he was not only more comfortable at these times, but it was then that the creative mood was "most pleasant" and he even forgot that he was on the stage. While watching a performance of a visiting star, he noticed this same freedom from strain as well as the focusing of attention upon the stage alone. From this discovery he was able to formulate several generalizations. For one thing, the actor's concentration on the life on the stage produces concentration on the part of those in the audience and awakens their imaginations and emotions. He found, also, that the actor's concentration affects all of his senses; it "embraces his mind, his will, his emotions, his body, his memory and his imagination." Finally, Stanislavsky came to the conclusion that the first requisite for creativeness is "the complete concentration of the entire nature of the actor."

Stanislavsky was building the foundation of his System, not on theory but from self-examination and his observation of great actors. Three basic elements were the relaxation of the muscles and the concentration of attention, and then "the feeling of truth." This last he defined as "scenic truth," which is different from truth in life. He emphasized the importance of the actor's believing in what happens on the stage and in what he is doing, although all the while he is perfectly conscious that he is surrounded by canvas flats instead of the walls of a room, and by stage properties which are sometimes far from the truth. Yet the actor must react to the unreal life on the stage as if it were real. It is this magic *if* which converts stage life into scenic truth, which gives rise to truthful emotions, to truthful relations of the actor to the events taking place on the stage and to "the properties, the scenery, the other actors, . . . to their thoughts and emotions." The feeling of truth also contributes to an understanding of the inner justification of stage movement and postures. For example, Stanislavsky realized that if he merely assumed a pose of stretching, the result was not the same as if he stretched himself for the purpose of reaching something. In the latter case he could believe in what he was doing and the audience would in turn believe him. This is what he meant by subjecting an exercise to his feeling of truth.[77]

Still experimenting in February, 1907, Stanislavsky produced Knut Hamsun's symbolic play, *The Drama of Life*. Here he gave all his attention, both in directing and in acting, to the "inner character" of the play and its roles. Moreover, to emphasize the inner techniques, all movement by the actors was eradicated except in the ensemble. The liberal part of the audience praised the impressionistic effects which Stanislavsky achieved with his new production methods, as, for example, the effect of a group of workmen of gigantic size in poses that resembled a Meunier sculpture. He was not satisfied, however, in the achievements of the actors, and realized more than ever their need for systematic training. As a result, he began to pay more and more attention to the discovery of the natural laws which he was convinced "exist for the purpose of awakening another and higher superconscious region of creativeness," and which he asserted could only be approached by "the conscious technique of the actor." *The Drama of Life* was significant also for another reason. It was in this play that Leopold Sulerzhitsky worked for the first time as Stanislavsky's assistant, becoming his closest friend and greatest ally in the working out of his System.

Stanislavsky was still searching for the appropriate means of expressing abstract conceptions when accidentally he came upon a simple principle which opened up many new production possibilities. One day, when he had invited those interested in finding new methods of production to meet with him at his home, he suddenly wanted a piece of black velvet that apparently had disappeared before their eyes. After an extended search the velvet was found draped over the

1. Stanislavsky as Dr. Stockman in Ibsen's Enemy of the People *(1900).*
Bronze statuette by S. Sudbinin.

2. *Stanislavsky as Vershinin in Tchekhov's* Three Sisters. *His last appearance on the stage was in this part in 1928.*

3. *The Moscow Art Theatre, auditorium looking toward the stage with sea gull on the curtain.*

4. The Moscow Art Theatre from the street.

back of a chair. Not only had it become invisible but it had given the chair the effect of a small table, and all because it had been standing in front of a wall on which another piece of black velvet was hanging. With this rediscovery of the old principle that black obscures objects to the sight when placed against a black background, Stanislavsky was able to produce all sorts of unusual effects, even changing the shapes of actors' bodies and causing them to disappear and appear again as from nowhere. He used these effects to advantage in his production of *The Life of Man,* by Andreyev; Stanislavsky was eager to produce it because of its abstract nature. Here the black velvet was used as a background and walls; furniture, doors, and windows were outlined in rope of various colors, depending upon the mood of the scene. The effect produced by the scenery alone was unreal, ghostly. Even more startling was the effect of the actors, who appeared unexpectedly and disappeared mysteriously into the cavernous background. Yet in spite of the success of the production and the fact that the theatre was hailed for having discovered "new paths in art," Stanislavsky was not satisfied, and he felt that the actors had only repeated what they had accomplished much earlier in *The Polish Jew* and *Hannele.* Moreover, they had not succeeded in bringing to life on the stage the true soul of Andreyev's play, but had depended upon external means and tricks of production for the performance of mysticism and the abstract.[78]

In his next production, *The Blue Bird,* Stanislavsky was successful in bringing to life the beauty and symbolism of Maeterlinck's poetic fairy tale. The black velvet was used to advantage, as well as blue crepe de chine, which obscured the bodies of the "unborn souls" and allowed only their faces to show.[79] In the summer of 1908, Stanislavsky visited Maeterlinck to obtain the author's approval of certain changes in the play which he felt would enhance its production.[80] The beauty and spirituality of Stanislavsky's conception of this play are vividly reflected in his speech delivered to the players at the first rehearsal of *The Blue Bird* in 1908. Pointing out the importance of their justifying the author's confidence in them and the need for penetrating as deeply as possible into the author's mysticism, Stanislavsky explained the main idea of the author, saying:

Man is surrounded by the mysterious, the awful, the beautiful, the unintelligible . . . . We are drawn toward the mysterious, we have forebodings, but we do not comprehend . . . . The most important things are hidden from man. Thus he lives absorbed in material blessings, getting farther and farther from spiritual, contemplative life . . . . Sometimes we attain real happiness, out in the open fields in the sunshine but this happiness, like the blue bird, becomes black as soon as we enter the shadow of the ill smelling town. Children are nearer to nature . . . . That is why Maeterlinck, in *The Blue Bird,* has surrounded himself with children to undertake the journey through mysterious worlds . . . . Let us, too, attempt to turn back to youth.

The production of *The Blue Bird* must be made with the purity of fantasy of a ten-year-old child. It must be naive, simple, light, full of the joy of life, cheerful and imaginative like the sleep of a child . . . .[81]

Stanislavsky wanted the production to "thrill the grandchildren and arouse serious thoughts and deep feelings in their grandparents." In addition to discussing his ideas on the costuming and music to be used for *The Blue Bird,* he admonished the actors to prepare themselves "independently." He said:

I speak of your personal life, observation which will broaden your imagination and sensitiveness. Make friends of children. Enter into their world. Watch nature and her manifestations surrounding us. Make friends of dogs and cats and look into their eyes to see their souls. You will be doing the same as Maeterlinck did before writing the play, and you will come closer to the author.[82]

The Blue Bird remained in the repertory of the Moscow Art Theatre for a great many years and was usually given on Saturdays for children.[83] Writing of the production which he saw in 1924, Oliver Sayler declared, "*The Blue Bird,* as Stanislavsky has visualized it, is the supreme height of imaginative beauty in the modern theatre." [84]

Stanislavsky's approach to Turgenev's *A Month in the Country* was completely different. Here he felt the importance of directing the audience's entire attention to the inner workings of the characters. In order to avoid anything of a distracting nature, therefore, he returned to the methods he had employed in *The Drama of Life,* eliminating movement and gestures as much as possible. He insisted, for example, that at times the characters should sit on a bench or a divan throughout a whole section of a scene "so as to display the inner essence and the word picture of the spiritual lacework of Turgenev." [85] Stanislavsky placed great emphasis upon the need for actors to communicate their thoughts and emotions to one another. To carry out his ideas, he departed radically from Moscow Art

Theatre tradition and held his rehearsals in private on the small rehearsal stage. Here he prepared the production according to his System. Moreover, he now worked out one of the most important parts of that System, namely, that each role is made up of many "problems and pieces" and that the actor must understand these problems or tasks and know what he wants to do in order to work them out as well as how to arouse his creative imagination to accomplish this. Olga Knipper, for one, found it difficult to make herself one with the character of Natalya Petrovna and at one time left the rehearsal in despair. It was not an easy task, as Stanislavsky himself admitted, "to turn the whole cast at one stroke to what we have been trying to achieve gradually and systematically." [86] The experiment, however, earned the respect of the actors for the System.

Another result of Stanislavsky's preparation of *A Month in the Country* was that he began to pay close attention to the best means of analyzing a role and to take careful note of his own inner reactions and perceptions as he prepared to play the part of Rakitin. He also began to appreciate more fully something which he had previously only surmised, that the actor must learn not only to work on himself but on his role as well; and this opened up a whole new field for study.[87]

ADOPTION OF THE STANISLAVSKY SYSTEM

With the production in 1911 of Tolstoy's *The Living Corpse* (sometimes called *Redemption*), the Moscow Art Theatre formally adopted Stanislavsky's System. Much to Stanislavsky's surprise, Danchenko in an address to the entire company insisted that the actors should study the "new methods of work" and that the theatre should accept them. The actors, however, did not immediately conform without protest. Possibly the cause was Stanislavsky's own inability to put his ideas into sufficiently simple words, as he himself admits.[88] He realized his need for further experiment, and it was for this reason that a year later he founded the First Studio.[89]

The year 1911 is famous in the history of the Moscow Art Theatre also for the production of *Hamlet* under Gordon Craig. In 1908 Stanislavsky had invited the English scenic artist to produce *Hamlet* at the Moscow Art Theatre and had placed the entire theatre at his disposal, even going so far as to make himself Craig's closest assistant.[90]

Stanislavsky's temerity in doing this, as well as the difficulty of bringing Craig's ideas to fulfillment, can be glimpsed from a remark of Huntley Carter, the English critic, who said: "The extreme difficulty of the undertaking will be fully understood by those who know the indefinite character of Mr. Craig's ideas as expressed, say, in his designs for costumes. Such designs are the despair of the well-meaning wardrobe mistress." [91]

A problem arose, however, from the impossibility of converting Craig's scenic designs for the great screens that were to form the background into practical stage units. Moreover, on opening night shortly before curtain time a near catastrophe occurred when the screens began to fall. The performance was saved by the quick work of the stage hands, but it was necessary to give up Craig's plan to shift the scenes in full view of the audience.[92]

Gorchakov considers "Craig's contribution to the Moscow Art Theatre—and through it to the Russian theatre— . . . the abstract primitivism of three dimensional shapes on the stage." Through different combinations of "the huge but narrow screens," the various scenes of the play were suggested. Gorchakov declares that "Craig asserted the need for blending the music, the lighting, and the movement of the architectural forms into a single musical quality. The synthesis of music, lighting, and architecture was also new for the Russian theatre." [93]

For the next several years Stanislavsky devoted himself to research in his System, working with Sulerzhitsky in the First Studio. In 1914, in preparation for his part of Salieri in the Moscow Art Theatre's production of Pushkin's tragedy, *Mozart and Salieri,* he spent a great deal of time with the great Russian basso, Fyodor Chaliapin. At this time he discovered another important element in his System, the *through-action* of the part. Stanislavsky considered this a necessary stimulus for freeing the actor's subconscious and for enabling it to assist in the creation of the role and "directing it towards the ruling idea of the play."

THE REVOLUTION

With the outbreak of the Revolution in 1917 Stanislavsky occupied himself more and more with work in the Studios. He supervised the First Studio's production of *Hamlet* in 1918. This was his most successful presentation of a Shakespeare play. In the same year he opened his Opera Studio.[94] During the first five years after the Revolution the Soviet control of the theatres was less strict than later. Moreover, it was the desire of the government to preserve examples of the "old culture." [95] This may explain why the Moscow Art Theatre was able to present *The Cherry Orchard* almost on the eve of the Third Revolution. An audience of a thousand of the common people applauded it and went away in silence. During this period the audience was composed for the most part of factory workers and peasants, often uneducated and quite ignorant of the Moscow Art Theatre and its ways. To Stanislavsky fell the task of teaching them decorous behavior in a theatre, such as "how to sit quietly, how not to talk, how to come into the theatre at the proper time, not to smoke, not to eat nuts in public, not to bring food into the theatre and eat it there, to dress in their best so as to fit more into the atmosphere of beauty that was worshipped in the theatre." Several times Stanislavsky was forced to speak to the audience from the stage. The success of these efforts to educate the theatre audience amazed even Stanislavsky. Moreover, it justified his belief that the theatre was not the place for propaganda and that even the "simple spectator longs for the life beautiful." [96]

MEYERHOLD

Strangely enough, the one who protested most strongly against the new government's policy of protection of the old culture and its tolerance of the repertory of the Moscow Art Theatre during the first years following the Revolution was Vsevolod Meyerhold.[97] As one of Danchenko's most brilliant pupils at the Philharmonic, in company with Moskvin and Olga Knipper, he had been brought to the Moscow Art Theatre at its founding. There, during the first four years, he had played Shuisky in *Tsar Fyodor,* Konstantin in *The Sea Gull,* Malvolio in *Twelfth Night,* Ivan the Terrible in *The Death of Ivan the Terrible,* and Tusenbach in *The Three Sisters.* He had gone with the company to the Crimea to visit Chekhov, whom he greatly admired.[98] However, in 1905, when the studio in Povarskaya Street ended in failure, Meyerhold broke completely with the Moscow Art Theatre and openly rejected their realistic method.

One of the chief causes for the disagreement between Stanislavsky and Meyerhold was the latter's insistence upon the domination of the director and the transformation of the actors into puppets responsive in their speech and movement to the director's will. Although both men wanted the audience to be drawn into cooperative activity with the actors, Stanislavsky was eager that they should forget the artificiality of the emotional experience and even the fact that they were in a theatre, while Meyerhold did everything to make both actors and audience aware of the theatricality of the situation.

Meyerhold's theatre was the Symbolical Theatre. He believed it would lead to a revival of the theatre of antiquity, which was to him the theatre in its highest form. To this end he revived the style of the Italian theatre of improvisation, the *commedia dell'arte,* as well as other methods of stylization, and above all, the grotesque.[99]

With the coming of the October Revolution, Meyerhold created the "October in the Theatre" movement; the purpose of this was to make the theatre serve the political aims of the Bolshevik government. He organized "theatrical shock troops" for propagandizing the public, which was to a large extent illiterate. The new ideas were dramatized especially at railroad stations. In recognition of these services, Meyerhold was honored with the title of "People's Artist" and he was placed in charge of the Theatre Section of the new Commissariat of Education.[100]

In his bitter rejection of Stanislavsky's System of psychological realism Meyerhold went to extremes to discredit the acting of the Moscow Art Theatre. He believed that movement was superior to speech. For this he turned to biomechanics, which used the body in a series of plastic movements and gestures to make clear his (the director's) scheme of the play. This method of precise gesture was borrowed from the Chinese and Japanese theatres.[101] Meyerhold adapted his system of gymnastic exercises to the Bolshevik idea that the purpose of art is propaganda. Since people could be united only through their similarities, and since the inner life of man is made up of individual differences, the externals were the only concern of the propaganda theatre. Meyerhold sought to have the actor represent the character through perfect control of the physical movements of the body. Further outward features of individuality disappeared when he devised a simple blue working coverall for both actors and actresses instead of the various costumes previously worn by the characters.

Another facet of Meyerhold's experiments was known as "constructivism." The conventional stage settings were discarded because of their association with the "false bourgeois atmosphere of individualism," and in their place were constructions of steel or wood. Platforms on different levels, scaffolds, ramps, elevators, cranes, moving staircases, and revolving wheels provided a suitable background and environment for Meyerhold's "motor-symbolism." He often achieved very startling effects. In *The Magnificent Cuckold,* for instance, a large wheel represented the actors' changing emotions, revolving at maximum speed when the outraged husband was supposedly fuming with jealousy.[102] Norris Houghton, who attended Meyerhold's rehearsals of this play in Moscow, describes the lover entering down a slide and knocking down his sweetheart, who stood at the foot of it. This was meant to symbolize the spirit of their meeting.

Meyerhold's style covered many widely different phases. While his first period was devoted to movement, his second period was static and preoccupied with a succession of poses on the part of his actors. He was undoubtedly a very gifted director, but he was not consistent. For all Meyerhold's open denunciation of the Stanislavsky System, Houghton discovered to his amazement that Meyerhold's apprentices were required to study it.[103]

Above all, Meyerhold's theatre was a theatre of satire. He took great liberties in presenting the classics and gradually became bold in satirizing even the Soviet bureaucracy. As a result, he was denounced by the government he had once so strongly supported. His greatest success from the point of view of the staging was his production of *The Inspector General,* although he was sharply criticized for the liberties he took with Gogol's comedy. He will probably be best remembered for his brilliant staging of the bribery scene, with its semicircular background of seventeen folding doors, from each of which a "rat-faced" official appeared with a fistful of banknotes clutched in his outstretched hand.[104] Meyerhold's use of symbolism came to a climax at the close of this play, when the actors "froze in rigid distorted poses" and after a few seconds of darkness were replaced by "mannequins in the same ridiculous poses." Gorchakov declares: "With this closing chord, Meyerhold for the first time revealed his secret to the audience . . . . Even in the 'proletarian dictatorship' the world struck him as merely an exhibit, a collection of benumbed puppets who were the playthings and victims of fate." [105]

Meyerhold's productions of Pushkin's *The Queen of Spades* and *La Dame aux Camélias* were both given in defiance of the Party's directive that all plays should present "socialist realism." According to Orlovsky, it was *The Queen of Spades* which brought about the closing of the Meyerhold Theatre. Orlovsky declared: "In this production he made a complete departure from 'Meyerholdism' and created an excellent and talented production full of deep, tragic meaning." [106] Gorchakov, on the other hand, maintains that *La Dame aux Camélias,* "one of Meyerhold's most outstanding works, turned out to be his final one." He declares: "It was the swan song both for Meyerhold and for his wife (Zinaida Raikh, who played Marguerite Gautier)." Here, at last, was no experimentation for the sake of effect, no "directorial tricks." It represented "a return to Ithaca—the Odyssey of the Russian Theatre," for in it Meyerhold very nearly "returned to the Moscow Art Theatre style that he had left in his youth." Meyerhold came back to impressionism with the use of a white wall, a curving staircase of white marble, gleaming candles, golden candelabra, and costumes and furniture of the period. The acting, too, was realistic. Marguerite died in an armchair, her back to the audience. Gorchakov believed that Meyerhold's final presentation "implied an enormous protest against the wretched naturalistic debasement of the theatre by the Bolsheviks . . . against the dismal truth of life in the staging of Soviet plays." The Soviet critics denounced him for not having shown the "social and tragic clash of the characters in its social content" and for daring to give "a lyrical treatment, a muted tone" to the "elegiac and esthetic drama of moods." [107]

However, although *La Dame aux Camélias* was presented in 1934 and the Party critics hurled abuses at Meyerhold from all sides, it was not until January 3, 1938 that his theatre was closed by government decree. Even those who had not agreed with his revolutionary methods sympathized with him, but only one man was courageous enough to offer him asylum. Gorchakov says of this: "There was only one great figure who called upon the disgraced genius, even though that figure had always personally found Meyerhold's work infinitely distasteful. The individual in question invited Meyerhold to work in his studios. His name was Constantin Stanislavsky." [108]

A year later and ten months after Stanislavsky's death, Meyerhold delivered a courageous speech before the First All-Union Congress of Directors in Moscow. While admitting many mistakes, he asserted the right to experiment. Finally he denounced the Soviet theory of Soviet realism or antiformalism and declared that what was taking place at the time in the best theatres of Moscow as an achievement of the Soviet theatre was "frightful and pitiful." Declaring that "the theatre is art! And without art, there is no theatre!" he accused the government of stifling creativeness and he asserted:

Where once there were the best theaters of the world, now—by your leave—everything is gloomily well-regulated, averagely arithmetical, stupe-

fying, and murderous in its lack of talent. Is that your aim? If it is—Oh!—
you have done something monstrous! . . . In hunting formalism, you
have eliminated art! [109]

Meyerhold was arrested by the NKVD the day following his speech.
Shortly after his arrest his wife was found brutally murdered in her
apartment. Meyerhold reportedly did not die until after World War
II.[110]

NEW PRODUCTION TECHNIQUES

Gorchakov calls attention to the fact that Stanislavsky's imaginative
staging of *The Mikado* antedated "Meyerhold's first experimentation
with stylization" by twenty years, and Tairov's innovations "in
rhythm and in associating the gestures of the actors with music" by
thirty years. Stanislavsky describes the scene with the fans which he
introduced in the production:

> The poses with the fan depended on the arrangement of the groups, or
> rather on a kaleidoscope of continually changing and moving groups.
> While some swept their fans upward, others lowered and opened theirs
> near their very feet; others did the same to the right, still others to the left,
> and so on.
> When this kaleidoscope came into action in the crowd scenes, and fans
> of every size, color, and description swept through the air, the soul was in
> ecstasy from the theatrical effect. Many platforms were prepared so that
> from the fore-stage where the actors lay on the floor to the background
> where they stood some feet above the ground, the entire arc of the stage
> could be filled with fans.[111]

Stanislavsky explains his distribution of the "Japanese poses with
the fan" among the songs and words spoken by the actors. He declares:
"In this manner, every passage, bar of music, and strong note had its
definite gesture, movement and action with the fan."

Stanislavsky had used symbolism successfully both in his production
of *The Blue Bird* and in a more abstract style in *The Life of Man*.
With the production of *Cain* in 1921, Stanislavsky advanced further
in his experiments with rhythm and the use of sculptural decor. In
the scene in hell he peopled the stage with gigantic figures executed
by the sculptor, N. A. Andreyev. The principles of sculpture dictated
the groupings of the characters also. The gateway to Paradise was
suggested by "gigantic columns" and the lighting was particularly
effective against the sculptured forms.[112]

The audience of peasants and workers displayed their appreciation at the dress rehearsal; when the performance was over they left the theatre in silence, "as if they were leaving a temple of worship after prayer." [113] Nevertheless the play was withdrawn from the repertory after about eight performances, probably because of Soviet censure. Gorchakov sees in this production the Moscow Art Theatre's protest against the civil war which the Bolsheviks had fomented throughout the country. It was so interpreted by a Soviet critic.[114] A more realistic reason for the choice is advanced by Magarshack, who believes the small cast appealed to Stanislavsky because of the catastrophe which had befallen the company the preceding year. At the close of the regular season, a group of the actors including Knipper and Kachalov had gone south on a guest tour to Kharkov, and their return had been cut off by the sudden advance of the White Army of General Denikin.[115] This group in exile was known as the "Prague Group of the Moscow Art Theatre." So for several years the fine ensemble that had taken so many years to build was destroyed. The two groups were reunited, fortunately, when Stanislavsky took the company abroad in 1922.[116]

One of the best examples of the difference between Meyerhold and Stanislavsky is in their use of the grotesque. Gozzi, the author of *Turandot,* referred to the grotesque as "a manner of exaggerated parody." Meyerhold declared that the grotesque "is ignorant of details and acts merely from its own originality, appropriating everything that corresponds to its *joie de vivre* and to its capricious and scoffing attitude toward life." The definition might be said to characterize Meyerhold's own attitude toward life. Stanislavsky, on the other hand, told the actors who were rehearsing Gogol's play, *Dead Souls*: "The grotesque is perhaps the highest form of art, but to bring it off successfully one must first of all cultivate the soil and the roots from which this quite remarkable living plant springs." [117] Earlier, in *My Life in Art,* he had said that the symbolic and the grotesque are alike in that the source of each is "not in the mind, but in the inner soul." By this it is apparent that he meant the grotesque must be justified by the inner life of the character and of the play. "It is necessary to play a role hundreds of times," he said, "to crystallize its essence, to perfect the crystal, and in showing it, to interpret the quintessence of its contents. The symbol and the grotesque synthesize feelings and life." [118]

On his return from America in 1924, Stanislavsky was appalled at the innovations in production that were taking place under the Soviet "reformers." The new directors were attempting to compensate for the lack of content in the new Soviet writers by resorting to external techniques that were highly theatrical and were often an end in themselves. Many of the new theatre's techniques were borrowed from the circus, the motion pictures, or the music hall.[119] Stanislavsky and his colleagues in the Moscow Art Theatre were still primarily concerned with making the life of the human spirit come alive on the stage. For new means to accomplish this Stanislavsky sought unceasingly. He insisted, moreover, that the life of the spirit "will not be reached by . . . acrobatics, constructivism, blatant luxury, rich productions . . . simplicity (even to the complete removal of the scenery), false noses, . . . or by any of the other external devices and exaggerated effects . . . usually justified by the stylish word 'grotesque.' " [120]

Stanislavsky, however, showed himself a master of brilliant theatrical technique when it was called for. In 1926 he produced a play by Ostrovsky, *Goryacheye Serdtze,* translated as *The Burning Heart* or *The Ardent Heart* or *The Warm Heart* in observance of the hundredth anniversary of the playwright's birth. In this play Stanislavsky left the manner of playing which he had discovered through Chekhov's plays and adopted what Orlovsky called "artistic maximalism"; he had used this term to explain Vakhtangov's technique, defining it as "realism, scenic truth, and at the same time, theatrical brilliance all to the maximal limit." Writing of Stanislavsky's production of *The Ardent Heart,* Orlovsky says: "Characterizations of the cast were sharpened almost to the point of the grotesque . . . . Here, however, there was this difference: under the comic treatment lay real human feelings and sincere experience." [121]

In the cast of this Ostrovsky play were many of the young actors from the new Dramatic Studio which he had formed upon his return from America. It constituted a triumph for Stanislavsky and the Moscow Art Theatre in terms of their most important contribution to the new theatre, their training of new actors. Furthermore, it demonstrated one of the most valuable facets of Stanislavsky's genius, "the constant growth of his artistic sensibilities," [122] his ability to adapt to changing circumstances, to give up even what once seemed sacred. This flexibility, this adaptability was perhaps the secret of Stanislavsky's youthfulness. At sixty-three he could bring the wisdom and knowledge of his great experience to vitalize the production methods so popular with younger Soviet directors and in doing so surpass their achievements. He accomplished this, moreover, without mutilating the original text of the author as Meyerhold and many other Soviet directors, not excepting Nemirovich-Danchenko, were prone to do. The best evaluation of Stanislavsky's new technique comes from Gorchakov, who says:

> Stanislavsky transmuted the comic chimeras of the satire into reality, and he changed the ideal into the material. He showed "comedy from within," and the grotesque element came from the depths of the spirit. All this was the victory of the Moscow Art Theatre and the Stanislavsky System over all the methods of the reformers, who always approached satire and fantasy from without, from the form, from movement, or from propagandistic notions.[123]

The first four years following his return from his American tours marked a period of rich activity for Stanislavsky. In addition to *The Ardent Heart* he produced Beaumarchais' satire *The Marriage of Figaro,* an adaptation of the French melodrama *The Two Orphans,* which he called *The Sisters Gerard,* and four Soviet plays, as well as several operas; and in his studio he worked for a long time rehearsing a dramatization of Dickens' story *The Battle of Life.*[124] Fortunately Nikolai M. Gorchakov (not to be confused with the historian, Nikolai A.), who had directed this last play at the Vakhtangov Theatre and who had come to the Moscow Art Theatre from the Third Studio in 1924, kept stenographic notes of Stanislavsky's rehearsals of the Dickens' adaptation as well as of several other plays. These he later published in *Stanislavsky Directs.* The report of rehearsals of *The Battle of Life* illustrates how Stanislavsky applied his System and contains his own explanation of its basic principles.

Stanislavsky himself defines his System or method as "the way to the actor's correct state of being on the stage," which is "the normal state of a human being in life." For an actor to achieve this, Stanislavsky says:

> He must be physically free, must control his muscles, and must have limitless attention. He must be able to hear and see on the stage the same as he does in life. He must be able to communicate with his partner and to accept the given circumstances of the play completely.[125]

The next principle calls for the performance of the correct "inner psychological and outer physical actions" in the "progressive unfolding of the play" as demanded by the "theme of the play, its idea, its characters, and the given circumstances." Stanislavsky suggests the use of what he calls the "magic if," that is, the actor must ask himself what he would do if all that happens to the character happened to him. This will lead him to discover the correct *actions* for the character, or as Stanislavsky says, help the actor "to begin to do on the stage." Finding all the reasons and justifications for the character will make the actor's actions and the character's actions "fuse automatically."

Playing the correct actions will cause the correct feelings to arise, provided the actor has analyzed the play and the character correctly.

At this time Stanislavsky and Danchenko adopted a plan for rehearsals which gave much of the work to their assistants. Stanislavsky, for example, would hold the preliminary rehearsals of a play at his home in Leontyev Lane. After these had covered the groundwork, the assistant director was permitted to continue, all the while keeping in close touch with Stanislavsky, who in the meantime supervised the work on the design for the sets, the costumes, and the lighting. Then, when the play was considered thoroughly prepared, Stanislavsky came to the rehearsal and there began a period of careful grooming, and if all was satisfactory, dress rehearsals and even the opening performance were scheduled.[126] However, if he was not satisfied with the results, Stanislavsky would sometimes take the entire production into his own hands, and, as happened in the case of the production of *Dead Souls* in 1931, the opening might be postponed for a year or more.[127]

The success of Stanislavsky's training of both actors and directors was displayed in the Moscow Art Theatre's production of Bulgakov's *The Days of the Turbins* in 1926. All the actors, as well as the director, I. Sudakov, were young people who had been trained by Stanislavsky. Writing of this production, Gorchakov declared:

> These actors turned a "stage fact" into real life . . . . The Moscow Art Theatre showed with unprecedented power the warmth, the sincerity, and the living breath of everything that was happening . . . . With the production of *Days of the Turbins* the Moscow Art Theatre presented the Soviet theatre with new and expert actors completely trained by the Stanislavsky System.[128]

The production of *The Days of the Turbins* was significant for another reason as well. Ten years after the Revolution, when most of the plays presented were devoted to the glorification of the Soviet way of life, the Moscow Art Theatre presented a play by the only

Soviet playwright ever to portray White Guardsmen, the enemies of the Revolution, in a human way. The play showed the effect of the Revolution upon the Turbin family, who were White Russians. Many of those in the audience had relatives who had been in the White Army, who had perhaps lost their lives in the civil war. Sometimes the women fainted or became hysterical and had to be carried out of the theatre.[129] The play scored a tremendous success, and on opening night the militia had to be summoned to restore order. Stanislavsky's emphasis upon "simplicity in art and scenic truth" moved the audience more than the "revolutionary forms of 'biomechanics' or 'constructivism.' " [130]

The Soviet press, however, were critical both of the playwright Bulgakov and of the Moscow Art Theatre. At one point during rehearsals of *The Days of the Turbins* there had even been an attempt to ban its presentation, and subsequently a controversy arose over the question of restoring it to the repertory of the Moscow Art Theatre. Each time Stalin expressed himself in favor of the play which showed the enemy to be both powerful and intelligent. In the first instance Stanislavsky himself had complained to Stalin of the proposed ban. Gorchakov interprets this gesture on the part of Stalin as an overture "to win over the most important of the Russian theatres, with their world-wide reputation." [131] Gorchakov maintains, however, that the following year, as part of the celebration of the tenth anniversary of the Revolution, Stanislavsky produced the play *Armored Train 14–69* by the Soviet playwright Vsevolod Ivanov, and in directing it he appears to have contradicted the fundamental principles of his System. For one thing he took a "Bolshevik attitude toward the White movement," which constituted a complete reversal of *The Days of the Turbins,* which was still in the repertory of the Moscow Art Theatre. In *Armored Train* for example, he told the actors playing the White Guardsmen: "You are not 'crusaders,' but traitors betraying your country . . . . You artists must make your hearts burn with indignation at them. For this you must find a merciless and realistic attitude to your roles—especially if that work is to open the audiences' eyes to the ulcers of the past." [132]

Gorchakov interprets this apparent reversal on Stanislavsky's part as merely the use of the actor's technique of "getting used to a character," in this case "his new role as a director of Soviet plays." The production was distinguished nonetheless for the absence of stereotypes. Even the "revolutionary mass" was presented as "an

assemblage of brilliant individuals." Kachalov's performance of the
partisan leader was a living portrait of the finest qualities of the
Russian muzhik, instead of the usual stereotype. The author himself
paid tribute to the Moscow Art Theatre's perceptive approach to a
play, as well as to their ability to make the characters, including all
the members of a crowd, come alive. *Armored Train 14–69* was, however, the only propaganda play which Stanislavsky directed.[133]

Huntley Carter, who visited Moscow at that time, drew a comparison
between the theatres of Meyerhold and Stanislavsky. One theatre had
a smooth road at the beginning because it made itself the servant of
the Revolution. The other met with unfair criticism and bitter objections from the Communists, merely because of the fact that it had
its origin in the former life which many of them wanted to destroy.
Carter praised Stanislavsky and the Moscow Art Theatre for remaining true to their artistic principles even while they sought to understand the demands of the new way of life. Stanislavsky's magnanimity
is illustrated by the fact that he visited the Meyerhold theatre to see
the productions of his former pupil, while not always sympathetic to
their style and methods. At a performance of *Mandate* by the Soviet
playwright Erdmann, Carter sat next to Stanislavsky, who remarked to
him: "It is very good. But you see Meyerhold is becoming more
academic. He has got back to the flat stage and screens, and he is
still very fond of the carefully arranged ensemble." [134]

Another production of Stanislavsky's in 1927 was of greater importance than that of the Soviet play *Armored Train 14–69*. It was
Beaumarchais' *The Marriage of Figaro*. Stanislavsky preserved the
continuity of the sparkling comedy by using the revolving stage and
changing the scenery in full view of the audience.[135] The production
was noteworthy, also, for his individualization of each member of the
crowd. However, the significance of this production lay in Stanislavsky's use of new inner technique and the discovery of new laws
governing the actor's psychological technique. He demanded that
the actors make a thorough study of themselves in the given circumstances of the play, and especially of their physical actions or movements. Since almost every movement in life is fostered by thought and
inner action, movement on stage or physical action gave the actor the
key to what the character was thinking and what actions he wished
to perform. The work with the actors on *The Marriage of Figaro*
was the source of Stanislavsky's last step in his System, which he was
to call the "method of physical actions." Speaking of the value of

this new technique, Gorchakov says: "Concrete movements, concrete objectives on the part of the actor, tear him away from himself and bring him to a different reality. This is the reality of the character's spirit, along with his psychology. And it is not limited to psychology alone; the character of a person *is* his system of movements." [136]

During all four years following his American tour, Stanislavsky continued to act in his former parts. Huntley Carter saw him in *The Lower Depths* in 1927 and praised his performance.[137] In 1928, he started to write his second book, in which he wished to make his System available in practical form to actors. On October 27 of this same year the Moscow Art Theatre celebrated its thirtieth anniversary with a gala production which included several acts from the plays in its repertory. Stanislavsky delivered a speech which was an affirmation of his artistic principles and a plea for the preservation of the traditions of the Russian theatre, as well as a defense of the plays in their repertory. He also explained the Moscow Art Theatre's inability to change its "face," as it were, to satisfy the Revolutionary elements before a corresponding inward change had taken place. In addition, he played his old part of Vershinin in the first act of *The Three Sisters*. This was his last appearance as an actor, and the part was one of his greatest. Near the end of the act he experienced severe pains in the chest, but he forced himself to go on to the end so as not to spoil the celebration. However, the doctor called to his dressing room diagnosed the attack as angina pectoris. Although his illness made a semi-invalid of him, Stanislavsky did some of his most important work during his last ten years. He was forced to spend the next three months in bed and could not leave the house until four months later, when he went first to the Black Forest and then to a seaside town near Nice to recuperate. He remained away from Russia for a year and a half. During that time he wrote the *mise en scène* for the production of *Othello,* which he had been working on with Leonidov in the title role. Actually Stanislavsky had condemned his former method of the director's working out all the actions beforehand, but in this case there was no choice.[138]

At the beginning of Stanislavsky's recuperation in Germany, in December, 1929, a very fortuitous event occurred. The American dramatic critic Norman Hapgood, and his wife, Elizabeth Reynolds Hapgood, who had come to know Stanislavsky well during the American visits of the Moscow Art Theatre, were in the Black Forest at that time. Learning that Stanislavsky was at Badenweiler, they went to visit him and urged him to complete the book on his System, upon which he was at work. Mrs. Hapgood, an accomplished linguist, had learned Russian at the Sorbonne. Stanislavsky was touched when she offered to translate his book into English and to secure an American publisher. Mr. and Mrs. Hapgood urged Stanislavsky to obtain permission to remain in Europe long enough to complete the book. Furthermore, they volunteered to raise sufficient money to guarantee his stay for the necessary period. Stanislavsky moved to Nice at the beginning of 1930 to be near the Hapgoods, and Mrs. Hapgood made the first translation of the now well-known *An Actor Prepares* at that time; it was published in 1936 by Theatre Arts Books.[139] Unfortunately, Stanislavsky saw only the page proofs of the Russian edition before his death two years later.[140]

Upon his return to Moscow in the fall of 1930, Stanislavsky began the supervision of Gogol's *Dead Souls*. He was not satisfied with the work of his assistant producer and took over the staging himself (see page 101). At the same time he occupied himself with working in his dramatic and operatic studios and continued to prepare the next book on his System. In 1933 he began what was his last play with his students, Ostrovsky's *Artists and Their Admirers*. He worked for three years on this in the studio in his home in Leontyev Lane, and the young actors kept careful notes of all he said. In the cast were the youngest of his students, a number from the middle group, and from the original members of the Moscow Art Theatre only Kachalov.[141] He spent all of his time on practical and theoretical lessons rather than on the production. According to Orlovsky, he seemed to feel the need to hurry to hand down his knowledge and observations to these young people, who went home after the lessons and wrote down what Stanislavsky had taught them. His System had not yet been passed by the censor for publication, and these rehearsals, more useful for these young actors than several years of acting experience, made it possible for them to apply the Stanislavsky System in their future productions and to teach it later on. In 1934 he founded a new Studio with his sister Zinna as his assistant, and he continued his work with his students until a few months before his death on August 7, 1938.[142]

The last two productions which Stanislavsky directed for the Moscow Art Theatre were Bulgakov's *Molière* and Molière's *Tartuffe*. The first was presented in 1936 after two years of rehearsal. Nikolai M. Gorchakov was the assistant director. The play was not successful and Stanislavsky and Danchenko withdrew it after about eight performances.[143] In spite of the fact that it did not please the Soviet critics the production was important because during its rehearsals Stanislavsky introduced new methods for working out the "trunkline" or controlling action which united all the characters with their separate problems into one dramatic whole. Here, too, Stanislavsky made further developments in his "method of physical actions." Gorchakov declares:

> The actors were no longer absorbed in delving within their own experiences but were entirely submerged in the concrete actions and deeds that flowed logically out of one another. He revealed a new method for working over the inner current of visions that accompany the actor's thoughts in playing a role.[144]

Stanislavsky did not live to finish his work on *Tartuffe,* but his students carried the production to its completion. Gorchakov maintains that he began rehearsals of this play in the spring of 1938,[145] only a few months before his death. This is evidently in error, since when Mrs. Hapgood visited Stanislavsky in May, 1937, she saw him rehearsing *Tartuffe.*[146] It is a strange coincidence that this play was on a tentative list which Stanislavsky had suggested when he and Danchenko were trying to form the repertory of their new theatre. Danchenko, however, had dismissed it as a "mere artistic trifle," along with *Twelfth Night* and *Much Ado About Nothing.*[147] Stanislavsky began his work on *Tartuffe* with a small selected group of actors from the Moscow Art Theatre. Their work represents Stanislavsky's final experiments in discovering new means for developing the actor's internal technique. He emphasized the need for even successful actors to return to the laboratory, as it were, and declared that this was the best way to make sure that their acting had vitality and youthfulness and was free from stereotypes or bad habits. The finer the actor, the more often he would "return to school." Stanislavsky applied all the elements of his system to these rehearsals, including his latest chapter, his "method of physical actions"; this he considered the key to the whole System. By this means he believed the actor could achieve "metamorphosis" or identification with the role. For he maintained that only by completely believing in the circumstances given by the playwright could the actor achieve reality in his performance and in his relation to the other characters. The simple physical tasks which the actor is called upon to carry out constitute the basis for his belief in the circumstances of the play. Moreover, the physical actions are the result and often the source of inner, psychological actions.

Stanislavsky was eager to bequeath his System to the actors who worked with him. For this reason his primary concern in the rehearsals of *Tartuffe* was to give the actors practice in applying the method of physical actions. He used improvisations to a great extent, giving the actors tasks to fulfill similar to those demanded by the text of Molière's play. By this means the actor was led to believe in the inner justification of the simplest "physical actions" and finally to fusion with the role.[148] According to Toporkov, who was a member of the group from the Moscow Art Theatre rehearsing *Tartuffe,* Stanislavsky explained the basis for his new technique in this way:

> Emotions must not be recalled and fixed. One can only recall the line of physical actions . . . . In rehearsing the scene, begin from the simplest physical actions; make them extremely truthful; search for the truth in every trifle. You will then acquire faith in yourself and in your actions . . . . We know how to do the simplest physical actions, but these physical actions (depending on the supposed circumstances) go over into the psychophysical.[149]

Both Stanislavsky and Danchenko had the same goal in mind for the actual performance; both men condemned the acting of the old school which depended upon declamation or sterile overacting; but it was Stanislavsky who was able to discover the means of creating a living character out of a role. He evolved his techniques through self-analysis and observation of great actors like Salvini, Rossi, and Duse.

Stanislavsky's studies and experiments were concerned with finding ways for the actor to bring about the creative state when inspiration has a free path, to call forth live emotions or feelings at the moment of performance, to understand the role completely, and finally, to reincarnate it. He never wearied of his experiments or of his teaching. He established the First Studio in 1912, and in 1934, only four years before his death, he started a new studio. His main objective and that of the theatre of which he was so great a part was to portray the life of the human spirit, and he never relinquished his efforts to make that portrayal alive and truthful.

N. M. Gorchakov bears witness to the amazing vitality of Stanislavsky's teaching:

He was continually moving ahead. His directorial approach was never dogmatic. . . .

Stanislavsky was constantly discovering new and better methods and exercises for this training.[150]

In the beginning, when the Moscow Art Theatre presented the plays of Chekhov, Stanislavsky found the right technique for their performance. Commencing with the atmosphere, the environment, he worked to make the everyday objects which surrounded the actors reflect the external truth of everyday life and disclose the inner life of the characters as well. Later, he was able to reverse this approach and start with an intuitive idea of the character, and after a complete understanding of his inner life, his motives, and the "trunkline" of his psychological actions, to discover the externals of the character. This led him to see the bond between the inner psychological actions and the external physical actions, and finally to evolve his method of physical actions.

The productions which Stanislavsky directed show the touch of the master's hand. Realism, symbolism, and the abstract were all forms with which he was successful. Finally, toward the end of his life, when the Revolution spurned the psychological realism which the Moscow Art Theatre had made famous, Stanislavsky showed his skill in the use of bright theatricality and even of the grotesque.

Stanislavsky dedicated himself to working with each young generation of actors and directors. Until the end of his life he sought to improve and simplify the techniques he had discovered and he never hesitated to discard the old in favor of the new, provided that the "new" offered a better means of attaining scenic truth.

Notes

1. David Magarshack, *Stanislavsky, A Life* (New York: The Chanticleer Press, 1951), pp. 136–52.
2. Constantin Stanislavski, *My Life in Art,* translated by J. J. Robbins (New York: Theatre Arts Books, 1948), pp. 293, 299.
3. Vladimir Nemirovich-Danchenko, *My Life in the Russian Theatre,* translated from the Russian by John Cournos (Boston: Little, Brown and Company, 1936), p. 75.
4. *The Sea Gull Produced by Stanislavski,* edited with an introduction by Prof. S. D. Balukhaty, translated by David Magarshack (New York: Theatre Arts Books, 1952), p. 40.
5. Magarshack, p. 136.
6. Danchenko, pp. 76, 83–86.
7. Danchenko, pp. 83–93.
8. Stanislavski (*My Life in Art*), pp. 294–95.
9. Danchenko, p. 107.
10. Stanislavski, p. 319.
11. Stanislavski, pp. 308–309.
12. Danchenko, pp. 96–98.
13. Danchenko, p. 140.
14. Danchenko, p. 46.
15. Stanislavski, p. 308.
16. Danchenko, p. 95.
17. Stanislavski, p. 294.
18. Danchenko, pp. 113–16.
19. Stanislavski, pp. 387–88.
20. Danchenko, pp. 136–37, 144.
21. *Stanislavski's Legacy,* translated by Elizabeth Reynolds Hapgood (New York: Theatre Arts Books, 1958), p. 3.
22. Stanislavski, p. 301.
23. Magarshack, p. 161.
24. Danchenko, p. 148.
25. Stanislavski, p. 324.
26. Danchenko, p. 117.

27. Danchenko, p. 167.
28. Stanislavski, pp. 305–306.
29. Stanislavski, pp. 330–31.
30. Danchenko, p. 171.
31. Magarshack, pp. 158, 161.
32. Danchenko, pp. 172–73, 175–77, 180–81.
33. Stanislavski, p. 322.
34. Stanislavski, p. 321.
35. Danchenko, p. 159.
36. Balukhaty, p. 123.
37. Stanislavski, pp. 330, 333.
38. Balukhaty, pp. 108–10.
39. Balukhaty, pp. 78, 107, 126.
40. Danchenko, p. 184.
41. Danchenko, p. 164.
42. Robert Albert Johnston, "The Moscow Art Theatre in America" (unpublished doctoral dissertation, Northwestern University, 1951), p. 87.
43. Balukhaty, p. 122.
44. Balukhaty, pp. 110–12.
45. Danchenko, p. 161.
46. Balukhaty, p. 122.
47. Magarshack, p. 184.
48. Stanislavski, p. 350.
49. Stanislavski, p. 333.
50. Stanislavski, p. 351.
52. Balukhaty, p. 130.
53. Danchenko, pp. 186–87.
54. Stanislavski, p. 356.
55. Balukhaty, pp. 73–74, 76–77, 82.
56. Magarshack, p. 231.
57. Stanislavski, pp. 358, 366.
58. Magarshack, pp. 208–10.
59. Stanislavski, p. 373.
60. Magarshack, pp. 221–23.
61. Stanislavski, p. 404.
62. Stanislavski, p. 405.
63. Stanislavski, pp. 405–406.
64. Magarshack, pp. 212–15.
65. Stanislavski, pp. 377–78.
66. Magarshack, pp. 226–27.
67. Stanislavski, pp. 387–89.
68. Stanislavski, pp. 391, 577.
69. Stanislavski, pp. 401–403.
70. Stanislavski, pp. 397–98.
71. Stanislavski, pp. 426–38.
72. Magarshack, p. 274.
73. Stanislavski, p. 447.
74. Danchenko, p. 284.
75. Danchenko, pp. 300, 309, 310.
76. Stanislavski, pp. 458–61.
77. Stanislavski, pp. 462–67.
78. Stanislavski, pp. 474–97.
79. Vera Soloviova, "Memories of the Moscow Art Theatre" (unpublished manuscript), p. 13.
80. Stanislavski, pp. 498–503.
81. *Acting, A Handbook of the Stanislavsky Method,* compiled by Toby Cole (New York: Crown Publishers, 1955), pp. 218–19.
82. Cole, pp. 220–21.
83. From a personal conversation with Vera Soloviova.
84. Oliver M. Sayler, *Inside the Moscow Art Theatre* (New York: Brentano 1925), p. 46.
85. Sayler, p. 543.
86. Magarshack, pp. 305–307.
87. K. S. Stanislavski, *Die Arbeit des Schauspielers an der Rolle,* zusammengestellt von

J. N. Semjanowskaja; redigiert, kommentiert und eingeleitet von G. W. Kristi (Berlin: Henschelverlag, 1955), p. 8.

88. Stanislavski, p. 526.

89. P. Markov, *Moskovsky Khudozhestvenny Teatr, Vtoroi* (*Moscow Art Theatre, Second,* Moscow, 1925), p. 1.

90. Magarshack, p. 294.

91. Huntley Carter, *The New Spirit in Drama and Art* (New York: Mitchell Kennerley, 1931), p. 202.

92. Stanislavski, pp. 520–22.

93. Nikolai A. Gorchakov, *The Theatre in Soviet Russia,* translated by Edgar Lehrman (New York: Columbia University Press, 1957), p. 47.

94. Magarshack, pp. 342–50.

95. Nikolai A. Gorchakov, *The Theatre in Soviet Russia,* p. 113.

96. Stanislavski, pp. 550, 553–56.

97. Nikolai A. Gorchakov, *The Theatre in Soviet Russia,* p. 113.

98. Stanislavski, p. 367.

99. Nikolai A. Gorchakov, *The Theatre in Soviet Russia,* pp. 54, 61, 67–69.

100. Norris Houghton, *Moscow Rehearsals* (New York: Harcourt, Brace and Company, 1936), p. 89; René Fülöp-Miller and Joseph Gregor, *The Russian Theatre,* translated by Paul England (Philadelphia: J. B. Lippincott Company, 1930), p. 61.

101. Nikolai A. Gorchakov, *The Theatre in Soviet Russia,* pp. 203–204.

102. Fülöp-Miller, pp. 67–68.

103. Houghton, pp. 20–21, 39–40.

104. Fülöp-Miller, pp. 69–70, 124.

105. Nikolai A. Gorchakov, *The Theatre in Soviet Russia,* p. 214.

106. Serge Orlovsky, "Moscow Theatres 1917–1940," in Martha Bradshaw, ed., *Soviet Theatres 1917–1941* (New York: Research Program on the U.S.S.R., Ann Arbor, Mich.: Edwards Brothers, Inc., 1954), p. 95.

107. Nikolai A. Gorchakov, *The Theatre in Soviet Russia,* pp. 344–45.

108. Nikolai A. Gorchakov, *The Theatre in Soviet Russia,* p. 362.

109. Nikolai A. Gorchakov, *The Theatre in Soviet Russia,* p. 362.

110. Orlovsky, pp. 95–97.

111. Stanislavski, p. 127.

112. Nikolai A. Gorchakov, *The Theatre in Soviet Russia,* p. 141.

113. Stanislavski, p. 556.

114. Nikolai A. Gorchakov, *The Theatre in Soviet Russia,* pp. 140, 421.

115. Magarshack, p. 353; Stanislavski, p. 557.
116. Nikolai A. Gorchakov, *The Theatre in Soviet Russia*, p. 235.
117. Magarshack, p. 381.
118. Stanislavski, p. 344.
119. Nikolai A. Gorchakov, *The Theatre in Soviet Russia*, pp. 236–37.
120. Nikolai A. Gorchakov, *The Theatre in Soviet Russia*, p. 432, citing Stanislavski, *Moia Zhizn' v Iskusstve (My Life in Art)*, p. 695.
121. Orlovsky, pp. 53–54.
122. Magarshack. p. 370.
123. Nikolai A. Gorchakov, *The Theatre in Soviet Russia*, p. 238.
124. Magarshack, p. 369.
125. Nikolai M. Gorchakov, *Stanislavsky Directs*, translated by Miriam Goldina (New York: Funk and Wagnalls Company, 1954), pp. 119–21.
126. Magarshack, pp. 370–71.
127. Magarshack, pp. 581–82.
128. Nikolai A. Gorchakov, *The Theatre in Soviet Russia*, pp. 238–39.
129. Nikolai A. Gorchakov, *The Theatre in Soviet Russia*, pp. 186–87.
130. Orlovsky, pp. 55–56.
131. Nikolai A. Gorchakov, *The Theatre in Soviet Russia*, p. 187.
132. Nikolai A. Gorchakov, *The Theatre in Soviet Russia*, pp. 243–44.
133. Nikolai A. Gorchakov, *The Theatre in Soviet Russia*, p. 336.
134. Huntley Carter, "The New Age of the Moscow Art Theatre—Ten Years under Soviet Power," *Fortnightly Review*, Vol. CXXIII, New Series (January–June, 1928), pp. 58–71.
135. Magarshack, p. 370.
136. Nikolai A. Gorchakov, *The Theatre in Soviet Russia*, pp. 239–41.
137. Carter, p. 70.
138. Magarshack, pp. 376, 379.
139. From conversations with Mrs. Hapgood after the celebration of the sixtieth anniversary of the Moscow Art Theatre, October, 1958, and on February 22, 1960.
140. Magarshack, p. 400.
141. Orlovsky, p. 72.
142. Magarshack, pp. 387, 398–400.
143. Nikolai M. Gorchakov, *Stanislavsky Directs*, pp. 353, 390.
144. Nikolai A. Gorchakov, *The Theatre in Soviet Russia*, p. 329.
145. Nikolai A. Gorchakov, *The Theatre in Soviet Russia*, p. 346.
146. From a conversation with Mrs. Hapgood on February 26, 1960.
147. Magarshack, p. 159.

148. Nikolai A. Gorchakov, *The Theatre in Soviet Russia*, pp. 346–49.

149. Vassily Toporkov, *Stanislavskii Na Repetitsii*, pp.

149–50, as cited by N. A. Gorchakov, *The Theatre in Soviet Russia*, p. 450.

150. Nikolai M. Gorchakov, *Stanislavsky Directs*, pp. 393, 395.

four

The Studios of the Moscow
Art Theatre

When in February, 1909, Stanislavsky offered to teach the art of living a role to any of the actors who wished to learn, he met with very little enthusiasm.[1] With the help of Sulerzhitsky, he then began to teach some of the young actors and actresses who were either supernumeraries or pupils in the Moscow Art Theatre school. Still unsatisfied with the result, he decided that Sulerzhitsky should teach the System in a private dramatic school which one of the actors in the company ran. After several years, a group of Sulerzhitsky's pupils was accepted in the Moscow Art Theatre.[2]

Writing of the audition of Sulerzhitsky's pupils, Vera Soloviova, one of the younger actresses of the Moscow Art Theatre at that time, remarks:

> I remember well the appearance of a group of students from the Adasheff School where Sulerzhitsky was teaching. In the group were Eugene Vakhtangov, Lida Daykun and Maria Ouspenskaya. . . . All three were accepted. It was the year of the production of *The Living Corpse* [1911]. All of us youngsters had to play gypsies in the scene where Theodore Protasov comes to the gypsies. . . . We, the people who had been at the Moscow Art Theatre already about two years, felt as if we were veterans and looked with disdain on the newcomers. Besides, these people who came from the school showed much more interest in Stanislavsky's exercises and were more serious and systematic than we who were already Stanislavsky's guinea pigs.[3]

Most of the young actors, however, soon began to appreciate the value of Stanislavsky's theories and approached him to give more time to teaching them.

THE FIRST STUDIO

Accordingly, in the fall of 1912, Stanislavsky hired quarters formerly occupied by a motion picture theatre in the same building once used by the Society of Art and Literature. "Here," says Stanislavsky, "we gathered all who wanted to study the so-called Stanislavsky System, for this was the main purpose of the founding of the Studio." Thus the First Studio, as it came to be called, was born. "Its aim," in Stanislavsky's own words, "was to give practical and conscious methods for the awakening of superconscious creativeness." [4]

Stanislavsky was not able to give as much time as he wished to the work of the Studio. For this reason Sulerzhitsky was placed at its head and he conducted Stanislavsky's exercises "for the creation of the creative feeling, for the analysis of the role, and for the construction of the willed orchestration of the role on the bases of consistency and the logic of emotion." [5]

Stanislavsky's former autocratic attitude as producer apparently disappeared with the formation of the Studio. He offered its members an opportunity to "appear in a scene from a play, to submit scale-models of sets, to demonstrate the result of his researches in stage technique or to offer some literary material for the stage." [6] Richard Boleslavsky asked whether the group of young actors and actresses could work on a play. Stanislavsky consented, and they chose a rather melodramatic work by the Dutch playwright, Heijermans, dealing with the sinking of a merchant vessel, the "Good Hope," because of the greed and parsimony of the shipowners. The play is known by various titles: *The Wreck of Hope, The Loss of Hope* and *The Good Hope*. The young Richard Boleslavsky was the director, and the leading role, that of "Jo," the girl whose lover is drowned, Stanislavsky gave to Vera Soloviova. [7]

All this while the members of the Studio continued to work in the Moscow Art Theatre and their schedule was so heavy that at one point it seemed impossible for the Studio work to continue, to say nothing of preparing a play in addition to the one being readied on the parent stage. Nevertheless, Stanislavsky insisted that the performance of *The Good Hope* must take place, even in the face of the impossible. Accordingly, the Studio rehearsals occurred at night after the day's work at the Moscow Art Theatre, and often continued till the next morning. Final rehearsals were taken over by Sulerzhitsky and then by Stanislavsky. The dress rehearsal took place before the older actors of the theatre, Danchenko, Benois, the scenic artist, and other invited guests. Stanislavsky was delighted with the result, and in *My Life in Art* he says: "The rehearsal was exceptionally successful and clearly displayed in all who took part in it a certain special and until that time unknown simplicity and depth in the interpretation of the life of the human spirit."

Public performances started on January 15, 1913. The money from the tickets sold went for the Studio, but the actors continued to work without pay. The newspapers gave high praise to the Studio production. The older actors realized the possibility of competition for the first time. Speaking of the effect of the newspaper criticism upon this group—the older generation, who up to this point had not willingly accepted his System—Stanislavsky declares: "They began to pay a great deal of attention to what I said about the new methods of acting. My popularity began to awaken again, especially among the young people." [8]

The second production of the First Studio was Hauptmann's naturalistic play, *The Festival of Peace*. It was directed by Eugene Vakhtangov, who is generally considered to have been one of Stanislavsky's most gifted pupils. However, Vakhtangov's direction so emphasized the dark side of life, without showing any of the brighter aspects, that Stanislavsky became very angry and accused Vakhtangov of ignoring one of the main points of his teaching, that in showing the darker side of anything one must try to find its few brighter aspects. Indeed, if it had not been for the intervention of some of the older actors of the Moscow Art Theatre, including Kachalov, *The Festival of Peace* would not have been permitted a performance for the public. The play was a success, however, and Gorky was especially pleased with it. Unlike Stanislavsky, he approved of propaganda on the stage. [9]

One of the techniques used by Stanislavsky to develop the elements of his System was the improvisation of dramatic situations. It is interesting to note that Gorky first suggested the idea of a theatre of improvisation when Stanislavsky visited him in Capri in February, 1911, some time before the formal opening of the First Studio. Although the possibility appealed strongly to Stanislavsky, it was not actually carried out by the Moscow Art Theatre. Gorky outlined such a plan in a letter which he wrote to Stanislavsky on October 12, 1912, pointing out the advantages of this method of developing characters and plot spontaneously.[10] The technique was adopted by the First Studio and in a letter to Gorky, Sulerzhitsky remarked on the success of the Studio in improvisations.[11]

In addition to the practical working out of the System, Stanislavsky and Sulerzhitsky hoped to accomplish something else with the First Studio. "Sulerzhitsky and I dreamed of creating a spiritual order of actors," Stanislavsky declares in *My Life in Art.* "Its members were to be men and women of broad and uplifted views, of wide horizons and ideas, who knew the soul of man and aimed at noble artistic ideals . . . ." They would have liked to do away with the charge of admission and make their theatre free to all comers, even as a temple is free. Moreover, they envisioned a theatre on a large estate at some distance from the city, where the spectators could come and be refreshed before the performance. Most of all, however, the actors were to take part in communal living, working together on the farmland in the spring, the summer, and the fall, and devoting themselves to the work of the Studio performances in the winter. Because of Sulerzhitsky's experience with the Dukhobors in Canada, he was to be in charge of this farming experiment also. He was a Tolstoyan and had an affinity for nature.

Most of this dream, of course, was impossible of realization. However, Stanislavsky bought some land on the Black Sea near the town of Eupatoria, and for several summers some members of the First Studio actually lived there, planting, building, cooking, each one carrying out his communal duty under Sulerzhitsky's direction. Speaking of the experiment, Stanislavsky says:

> The fame of the primeval group spread through all of the Crimea, and attracted excursions of the curious, who came to see the wild actors of the Studio of the Moscow Art Theatre. The entire enterprise aimed at the bringing together of the actors in good and interesting conditions of life, amidst healthy physical work, after the close and nervous atmosphere of the stage that always spoils peaceful relations. This summer life in the lap of nature was not in vain. It really brought the actors of the Studio very close to each other.[12]

Through the gentle influence of Sulerzhitsky the members of the Studio found a responsive chord in the writings of Charles Dickens. When it was decided to dramatize one of his works, *The*

Cricket on the Hearth was chosen, and it became, in 1914, the third production of the First Studio. It was dramatized and directed by a young member of the Studio, Boris Sushkevich. Stanislavsky and Sulerzhitsky worked on the last rehearsals. Stanislavsky says: "Sulerzhitsky put all his heart into this work. He spent many high feelings, spiritual strength, warm beliefs, and beautiful dreams on the actors of the Studio, until they were literally infected with his ardor, which made the production unusually spiritual and touching." [13] Michael Chekhov, nephew of the dramatist, played the part of Caleb Plummer, the toymaker; Vera Soloviova, the role of his blind daughter, Bertha, who was in love with their demanding landlord, Mr. Tackleton, played by the brilliant Eugene Vakhtangov.[14]

The critic, Solus, had this to say:

> Of the performers, let us put in the first place the blind girl, Bertha. Her expressive face was at times filled with great tragedy, and never ceased to answer the demands of the artistic measure.
>
> The part was played by the young actress, Vera Soloviova, a great and true talent illuminated by her charm and youth.

"It was in this production, perhaps," Stanislavsky declares, "that there sounded for the first time those deep and heartfelt notes of superconscious feeling in the measure and the form in which I dreamed of them at that time." Stanislavsky ascribed this in part to the intimacy of the performance in the small theatre of the Studio, where the stage was on a level with the audience and the spectator felt close to the actors. Moreover, he believed that this same effect was not likely to occur in the customary large theatre "where the actors were forced to raise and strain their voices and to stress their acting theatrically." [15] Gorchakov compares the effect of *The Cricket on the Hearth* upon the First Studio to that of *The Sea Gull* upon the Moscow Art Theatre. He says:

> Mildness, genuineness, and intimate humaneness such as the Russian theater had never seen before streamed forth from the stage to the small auditorium. The heart and soul of the presentation was Sulerzhitsky. He blended the Tolstoyan idea with great love for life and the world. The devotion with which Sulerzhitsky preached the ideas of lofty dedication and service to art is not to be found in any of the other great personalities associated with the Russian theater.[16]

Two other productions of the First Studio demand special mention. In 1916, *Twelfth Night* was produced under the direct supervision of Stanislavsky. Of this production Oliver Sayler commented:

> *Twelfth Night* at the Studio fulfills its Elizabethan character not only by the simplicity of its staging, but also by a rare combination of taste and refinement with gusto and hearty rowdyism . . . . Under Stanislavsky, the two moods, equally typical of Tudor demeanor, receive their just emphasis in a deft blending which reconstitutes the age of Shakespeare's England.[17]

In 1921, Strindberg's *Eric IV* was staged by Eugene Vakhtangov with Michael Chekhov in the title role. In this production there appeared the first change from the Stanislavsky tradition of psychological realism. Vakhtangov wrote of it:

> This is an experiment of the Studio in its search for theatrical forms. Up until now the Studio, true to Stanislavski's teaching, has doggedly aimed at obtaining mastery of inner experience; now the Studio is entering a period of search for new forms. This is the first experiment. Experiment, to which our own times have directed the Studio. The Revolution demands that we take the petite bourgeoisie off the stage. The Revolution demands of us significance and vividness.[18]

Gorchakov's description of the settings reveals the imagination of Vakhtangov in making the background mirror the inner meaning of the play:

> The twisted columns of the palace, the spots of gold, the rust-spotted bronzes, gave an impression of Erik's decline and impending death. There were huge columns of straight lines, broken off here and there; these were fragments not of a palace, but of a prison—a prison for Erik.[19]

Vakhtangov's production of *Eric IV* gave a clue to the direction which the work of the First Studio was to take during the next several years under the leadership of Michael Chekhov.

By 1924 the First Studio had grown up and established itself, with governmental as well as parental permission, as the Moscow Art Theatre Second. Its first production, *Hamlet,* was directed by Michael Chekhov, who also played the title role, with A. I. Cheban as the King and Vera Soloviova as the Queen. Their performances displayed such brilliant command of their roles that actors from other theatres came many times to see them.[20] Their use of exaggerated stage make-up to suggest masks, the juxtaposition of opposing forces in sharp outline heightened by the careful editing of soliloquies, and the transference of the setting to the Middle Ages revealed the brilliant theatricality usually associated with Meyerhold.

Of Soloviova's performance as the Queen, the critic P. Markov wrote in *Pravda* in 1926, "It is possible that only Soloviova (the Queen) possessed the high style of tragedy of modern expressionism which reached severe precision and simplicity."

Among other productions of the Moscow Art Theatre Second were Euripides' *Orestes*, *Balladina* by Slovatsky, and *Uncle Tom's Cabin*. In the last two, Soloviova played the leading roles. In the second, as in *The Lower Depths* in America, she played first the younger sister and later the older sister—in this case, the part of Balladina herself. In the last she played Eliza. It is interesting to note that except for the parts of Bertha in *The Cricket on the Hearth* and Sonya in *Uncle Vanya*, which were really ingenue parts, Soloviova always played strong, tragic roles. Writing of her in his book, *Moscow Art Theatre Second*, the critic P. Markov says:

> Her path lay from psychologically sharp drama to tragedy. You can see this if you follow the parts she played—she played a person who has in her the possibility of full feelings which are suppressed. That was her "Jo" in *Good Hope* and *Daughter of Jorio* [D'Annunzio] . . . . In *Daughter of Jorio* it sounded as if the actress tore off the controlled form . . . and threw into the audience the scream of real pain, words, feelings . . . From Soloviova we are entitled to expect the incarnation of tragedy on the stage.[21]

Although Stanislavsky was saddened when the First Studio went its own way instead of staying within the fold of the Moscow Art Theatre, there was no real break between the two groups. The large playhouse on Theatre Square bore a close resemblance in its interior to the Kamergersky Theatre. The ushers of the two theatres dressed identically and the sea gull remained the insignia of both. Indeed there was a close interrelationship, as seen in the fact that many of the actors of the Moscow Art Theatre Second not only remained as members of the original company but even joined it at times to play certain roles. Furthermore, the Moscow Art Theatre itself sometimes performed on the stage of the Moscow Art Theatre Second.[22]

Writing of his second visit to the Moscow Art Theatre in 1924, Sayler compares the role of Michael Chekhov in the Moscow Art

5. *Caleb Plummer's Toy Shop in Act II of* The Cricket on the Hearth *at the First Studio of the Moscow Art Theatre. Vera Soloviova as Bertha, Michael Chekov as Plummer, and Eugene Vakhtangov as Tackleton.*

6. *Stanislavsky at work on his System in 1938 shortly before his death.*

Theatre Second with that of the two founders of the Moscow Art
Theatre. He declares:

> . . . like them, he has round him a faithful band of co-workers, trained to
> play together by years of intimate association. Including Tchehoff [Chek-
> hov] himself, I count an even dozen artists in the theatre's first line today
> who were the backbone of the First Studio ensemble back in the winter of
> 1917–1918: Ivan Bersenieff, Boris Sushkievitch, Valentine Smuishlyaieff,
> Alex Tcheban, V. Gotovtseff, A. Geyrot, and Mlles. Vera Soloviova, Sophia
> Giatsintova, Maria Durasova, S. Birman, and Nadiezhda Bromley.[23]

According to Soloviova, the only member of the First Studio now
teaching in America, when Michael Chekhov left Russia in 1928,
the productions of the Moscow Art Theatre Second returned to
psychological realism. Nevertheless, the acting was much richer in
interpretation and much more colorful because of the years of experimentation under Vakhtangov and Chekhov. Moreover, Vakhtangov always had insisted upon Stanislavsky's artistic truth as the
foundation for his work.[24] His influence was evident in the combination of realism with theatricality in the brilliant tones that characterized the production of *The Flea,* the dramatization of a story by
Leskov, which was produced by the Moscow Art Theatre Second in
1924–1925 under A. Diky's direction and of which Orlovsky remarks:
"As a theatrical achievement, the production of *The Flea* can only be
compared to Vakhtangov's production of *Princess Turandot.*[25]

Chekhov put great reliance on the mood or atmosphere as a spur to
inspiration. He drew attention to the contrast that often existed
between the atmosphere that surrounded the actor on stage and his
own inner mood, as, for instance, when the scene is one of great gaiety
and festivity but the actor comes to it with an inner grief. Chekhov
depended not so much upon reality as upon potentiality for arousing
inspiration. Gorchakov maintains that he believed the actor should
be able to summon up an image of the role as a whole from the
creativeness of his imagination.[26]

One of the techniques which Chekhov suggested to accomplish this
was the "psychological gesture," [27] that is to say a physical characterization of the role. Chekhov also used the psychological gesture to
approach the "different attitudes" of the character toward other
people in the play.[28]

Soloviova gives this explanation of the difference between Stanislavsky and Chekhov:

Sometimes we thought that all we got from Stanislavsky was not enough. Michael Chekhov and Vakhtangov, who were the most devoted and favorite actors of Stanislavsky, started experiments in abstract forms. Once Stanislavsky and Chekhov talked for five hours, not being able to agree about affective memory. The thing was that Chekhov never had to worry about emotions. He only needed to imagine a character he was to play to see him. He used to say he could find in himself, without any trouble, all the feelings of the character. Not everybody had that ability. This was the only point of disagreement between them.[29]

Another favorite of Moscow audiences was Dickens' *The Cricket on the Hearth,* which remained in the repertory of the Moscow Art Theatre Second until 1931. That production's tenth anniversary in 1924 also marked the five hundred and sixty-first performance of this play, which had started the First Studio on its road to fame. Four of the original players were in the "tenth jubilee" production—Maria Durasova as Mary Peerybingle, Nadiezhda Bromley as Mistress Fielding, Vera Soloviova as Bertha, and Boris Sushkevich as Caleb Plummer, the part which in the original production had been played by Michael Chekhov.[30] After playing in the anniversary performance of *The Cricket on the Hearth,* Soloviova went to Lithuania to join her husband, Andrius Jilinsky, who had been made Director of the Lithuanian State Theatre. Two years later, however, she was recalled to Moscow for the twentieth anniversary of *The Good Hope.* She had played the part of Jo nearly five hundred times.

In spite of the audiences' appreciation of *The Flea* and *The Cricket on the Hearth,* however, the Department of Agitation and Propaganda leveled the criticism of "aestheticism" and "eclecticism" against the Moscow Art Theatre Second, accusing it of "going back to Leskov and Dickens" when a "new Soviet revolutionary repertory" was in order.[31] As the group continued its creative experiments and neglected the directive demanding that all plays exemplify "socialist realism," which amounted to the extolling of the Soviet way of life and condemning any other, it incurred the displeasure of the Party Central Committee. As the First Studio, the group had been nurtured on the Tolstoyan philosophy of Sulerzhitsky and then on Vakhtangov's idealistic expressionism; upon reaching its maturity and becoming the Moscow Art Theatre Second, it had been influenced by Michael Chekhov and his devotion to the anthroposophy of Rudolph Steiner. All of these philosophies were completely alien to Soviet materialism.[32] At first it was proposed to move the entire theatre to Kiev.

However, at a banquet one evening the artistic director, Bersenev, made the fatal mistake of discussing with the English ambassador the treatment which the theatre had been receiving. This proved its undoing; finally, the end of 1936 saw the dissolution of the Moscow Art Theatre Second. Its members were scattered among other theatres in Moscow and its outlying districts.[33]

THE SECOND STUDIO

In 1916, a group of Stanislavsky's students formed the Second Studio, amounting to a third generation of actors. Stanislavsky himself explains the need for the different studios as arising from the fact that the different generations that grew up after the Revolution were each exposed to different environments and so found it difficult to understand one another well and could not fuse with one another.[34] Unlike its predecessor, the Second Studio remained principally a school.

However, upon the return of the Moscow Art Theatre from abroad in August 1924, its company was so depleted by the number of actors who had chosen to remain in America that Danchenko and Stanislavsky decided to take the entire Second Studio into the Moscow Art Theatre. Actually this was not done; instead the Second and part of the Third Studio were consolidated into a new Dramatic Studio and School of the Moscow Art Theatre. The purpose of this was to train young actors and directors as a supplementary group which could be drawn upon to add to the thinning ranks of the Moscow Art Theatre, occasioned by the retirement of its older members. The full course of the school was three years, and Stanislavsky worked closely with its students, at the same time occupying himself with an outline of his System for publication.[35] How successful he was in creating fine actors from these young people was demonstrated two years later in 1926, when the Moscow Art Theatre presented *Days of the Turbins* with a cast composed entirely of the young generation.[36]

THE THIRD STUDIO

It is paradoxical that the man who accomplished most in the discovery of new forms was also closest to Stanislavsky's teachings. Eugene Vakhtangov left the First Studio and established a dramatic school of his own shortly after his production of *The Festival of Peace*, to which Stanislavsky had objected so violently. In 1920, however, he returned to Stanislavsky and to the First Studio, and his school became the Third Studio of the Moscow Art Theatre. His death in 1922, four months before the Moscow Art Theatre's departure for its American tour, was a source of great grief to Stanislavsky.[37]

Although Vakhtangov's artistic life with the Moscow Art Theatre and its First and Third Studios covered the short span of less than ten years, his influence has continued and his name is remembered with honor. He accepted the ideals of the Bolshevik Revolution and was in the forefront of the search for new theatrical forms. In the realization of his artistic aims, he succeeded in synthesizing the teachings of Stanislavsky and the new ideas introduced by Meyerhold. He played the part of Tackleton in the First Studio's production of *The Cricket on the Hearth*. His production of *Eric IV* was one of the earliest departures from the traditional style of Stanislavsky toward that of brilliant theatricality.[38]

When Stanislavsky established a studio for the Habima Players from Palestine, he placed it under the direction of Vakhtangov. His production of *The Dybbuk* with that group won recognition. According to Huntley Carter, Vakhtangov was strongly influenced by Tibetan philosophy and interested in Yoga, and he employed it in teaching acting.[39] This was also true of Stanislavsky and Chekhov.

In his studio, Vakhtangov was as highly respected by his students as Stanislavsky was in the Moscow Art Theatre. Like Stanislavsky too, Vakhtangov had an enormous capacity for work, as well as the ability to see an actor's mistake almost immediately. These two facts may have accounted for the perfection of his work.

The two productions which Vakhtangov completed with his Third Studio were Maeterlinck's *The Miracle of St. Anthony* and Gozzi's *Princess Turandot*. The first revealed his genius so vividly that it was called "The Miracle of Eugene Vakhtangov." No detail was too small for his attention, and every gesture, every detail of make-up and costuming, as well as every part, whether that of a principal or a walk-on, was in harmony with the basic idea of the production. Serge Orlovsky declares: "The spectator was so filled with belief in the holiness of St. Anthony that there were people who swore they saw brightness coming from the head of the actor, Zavadsky, who played St. Anthony, and they could not be convinced that no shining took place." [40]

Vakhtangov worked on *Turandot* during his fatal illness. At the dress rehearsal, Stanislavsky was so delighted with what had been achieved that at its close he hurried to congratulate his pupil, who at that time was too ill to be present. Vakhtangov never saw the public performance of his work. He died of cancer on May 29, 1922. Shortly afterward the Third Studio became the "Vakhtangov Theatre." [41] According to Orlovsky, in *Turandot* and *The Miracle of St. Anthony* Vakhtangov had succeeded in giving "a dazzling theatrical presentation, full of the living feelings and passions of man." Vakhtangov's fame spread beyond Russia when, in 1926, his theatre took the two productions, *The Miracle of St. Anthony* and *Turandot,* to Berlin, Paris, and Stockholm; in all three cities they were widely acclaimed.

What Vakhtangov was able to achieve has been defined by his pupil Zakhava as "a synthesis of the two basic concepts of theatrical art" as epitomized by Stanislavsky and Meyerhold respectively, "content and form, truth of feeling and theatricality." "These Vakhtangov wanted to unite in his theatre," Zakhava declared. His intention was "that this theatre should express the organic unity of the 'eternal' basis of the art with theatrical form, directed by a sense of the contemporary." [42] Vakhtangov believed in "theatrical realism." Gorchakov asserts: "Vakhtangov's work . . . seemed to reconcile two mutually exclusive principles—Meyerhold's grotesquerie and Stanislavsky's truth-to-life. The synthesis produced an irony that belonged to Vakhtangov and his theatre alone." [43] Gassner maintains that next to Stanislavsky his influence has been the most fruitful.[44]

Fortunately Vakhtangov's deep understanding of Stanislavsky can be seen from the notes from his diary which were arranged by Zakhava, the director of the Vakhtangov Theatre, and originally made available for translation by the Group Theatre. They first appeared in *New Theatre Magazine* in 1947, and were reprinted in the book compiled by Toby Cole entitled *Acting, A Handbook of the Stanislavski Method.*[45]

The method of Vakhtangov was used by Chekhov in his productions with the Moscow Art Theatre Second, with this difference, that Chekhov sometimes constructed his bright theatrical forms without the foundation of truthful human feelings.

THE FOURTH STUDIO

The Fourth Studio of the Moscow Art Theatre was founded in 1921 and was under the direction of Burdzhalov, one of the Art Company's original members and a member of Stanislavsky's Society of Art and Literature before the Moscow Art Theatre was founded.[46] This Studio did not seek new forms nor did it develop as Vakhtangov's Studio had.

It was content with presenting translations of the classics, for which it became known in Moscow. After Burdzhalov's death in 1924, it existed for a short time as a regional theatre and later became the Realistic Theatre under the direction of N. P. Okhlopkov.[47]

THE OPERA STUDIO

In 1918 the Bolshoi Opera Theatre of Moscow sought the help of the Moscow Art Theatre in improving the dramatic calibre of its performances. Accordingly, Stanislavsky agreed to organize a studio where the established singers might come for advice on acting in opera and the younger ones could put themselves under his systematized training.[48]

The stenographic notes taken by a member of this Studio of the lectures given here by Stanislavsky between 1918 and 1922 have been translated by David Magarshack. They are entitled "The System and Methods of Creative Art" and have been published in England with an essay by Magarshack on the Stanislavsky System in a book called *Stanislavsky on the Art of the Stage*.[49]

After his heart attack in 1928, on the occasion of the thirtieth anniversary of the Moscow Art Theatre,[50] Stanislavsky continued to work with his Opera Studio but did so in his own home on Leontyev Lane, which also housed his Opera Theatre. It was here that Joshua Logan came to observe rehearsals in 1931.[51] Here, also, Norris Houghton visited Stanislavsky and was permitted to watch his rehearsals of *Carmen* four years later.[52]

In 1934 Stanislavsky decided to form a new Dramatic and Operatic Studio to experiment further in his latest theories of arousing creativity and preparing a role. Because of his ill health, however, he did not actually begin his work in this Studio until the winter of 1935. It appears that Houghton actually saw this group, with which Stanislavsky continued to work except for intervals when his illness forced him to remain in bed, until two months before his death on August 7, 1938.

Stanislavsky founded the Studios for the express purpose of experimenting with his System and of teaching it to young people who would carry on his work. In spite of his frequent heart attacks he continued his activities in the Studio whenever he was strong enough. In September, 1937, after spending seven months in a sanitarium outside of Moscow, he was able to resume his work for two months.

His dedication to art is evident in everything he did and is particularly illuminated by his words to his students at this time:

> Very soon I shall no longer be with you, but if I am one of the links, however small, in the chain which is handed down by great men from century to century, I have the right to tell you, don't lose any time and learn from me while it is not yet too late.[53]

One of Stanislavsky's dearest wishes was for the continuity of his teachings. Fortunately, before he died, he was permitted some consciousness of the possibility of its realization. He knew that through the efforts of Mrs. Hapgood the first book on his System had been published in America in 1936.

Because of his correspondence with Mrs. Hapgood and her visit to him in 1937, Stanislavsky knew also that his second book would be published in America as soon as he finished it. Although he worked on the manuscript until shortly before his death the following year, the material which now forms *Building a Character* did not reach Mrs. Hapgood until some time after the close of World War II. It was published by Theatre Arts Books in 1949.[54]

Stanislavsky founded the First Studio as a laboratory for the System or method which he was devising. The older generation of Moscow Art Theatre actors, and even Nemirovich-Danchenko, had been at first unwilling to participate in his experiments. The younger generation offered more fertile soil.

There were two other reasons for Stanislavsky's founding the succeeding Studios. The first was his desire to train young actors and directors according to his System in order to supply a reservoir of talent for the Moscow Art Theatre. His second purpose was to offer established actors the opportunity of experimentation and exploration to revitalize their performance and insure their continuing interest in perfecting their technique. The Studios were, in effect, a lifeline for his System guaranteeing the continuity of the principles to which he had devoted the greater part of his life. It was, in fact, Stanislavsky's pupils from the First Studio who carried his System to America.

Notes

1. David Magarshack, *Stanislavsky, A Life* (New York: The Chanticleer Press, 1951), pp. 310–11.
2. Constantin Stanislavski, *My Life in Art* (New York: Theatre Arts Books, 1948), p. 525.
3. Vera Soloviova, "Memories of the Moscow Art Theatre" (unpublished manuscript), pp. 54–60.
4. Stanislavski, p. 531.
5. Stanislavski, pp. 531–32.
6. Magarshack, p. 333.
7. Soloviova, p. 22.
8. Stanislavski, pp. 532–33.
9. Stanislavski, pp. 334–35.
10. Maxim Gorky, *Reminiscences* (New York: Dover Publications, 1946), pp. 188–202.
11. Magarshack, pp. 320–333.
12. Stanislavski, p. 539.
13. Stanislavski, p. 539.
14. Soloviova, pp. 23–24.
15. Stanislavski, pp. 539–40.
16. Nikolai A. Gorchakov, *The Theatre in Soviet Russia*, translated by Edgar Lehrman (New York: Columbia University Press, 1957), p. 245.
17. Oliver M. Sayler, *The Russian Theatre* (New York: Brentano, 1922), p. 88.
18. Serge Orlovsky, "Moscow Theatres, 1917–1941, The First, Second and Third Studios of the Moscow Art Theatre," in Martha Bradshaw, ed., *Soviet Theatres* (New York: Research Program on the U.S.S.R., 1954), p. 14.
19. N. A. Gorchakov, *The Theatre in Soviet Russia*, p. 436.
20. Orlovsky, p. 39.
21. P. Markov, *Moskovsky Khudozhestvenny Teatre, Vtoroi*

(*Moscow Art Theatre, Second,* Moscow, 1925), pp. 169–70.
22. Oliver M. Sayler, *Inside the Moscow Art Theatre* (New York: Brentano, 1925), pp. 166–69.
23. Sayler, *Inside the Moscow Art Theatre*, p. 166.
24. Soloviova, pp. 42, 44.
25. Orlovsky, pp. 39–40.
26. N. A. Gorchakov, *The Theatre in Soviet Russia*, pp. 247–49.
27. Michael Chekhov, *To the Actor* (New York: Harper and Brothers, 1953), pp. 63–84.
28. Chekhov, pp. 150–151.
29. Soloviova, p. 55.
30. Sayler, p. 162.
31. Orlovsky, p. 40.
32. N. A. Gorchakov, *The Theatre in Soviet Russia*, p. 249.
33. Orlovsky, pp. 94–95.
34. Stanislavski, p. 534.
35. Sayler, pp. 175, 178–79.
36. Orlovsky, pp. 55–56.
37. Magarshack, p. 356.
38. Orlovsky, pp. 42–43.
39. Huntley Carter, *The New Spirit in the Russian Theatre* (London: Brentano's Ltd., 1929), pp. 182–83.
40. Orlovsky, pp. 14–15.
41. Orlovsky, pp. 14–15.
42. Orlovsky, pp. 42–43.
43. N. A. Gorchakov, p. 251.
44. John Gassner, *Masters of the Drama* (New York: Dover Publications, 1940), p. 540.
45. *Acting, A Handbook of the Stanislavski Method,* compiled by Toby Cole (New York: Crown Publishers, 1955), pp. 116–124.
46. Sayler, p. 210.
47. Orlovsky, pp. 17–18.
48. Stanislavski, *My Life in Art,* p. 558.
49. Stanislavsky, *Stanislavsky on the Art of the Stage,* translated, with an introductory essay on Stanislavsky's System by David Magarshack (London: Faber and Faber Limited, n.d.), p. 78.
50. Magarshack, pp. 376–78.
51. Constantin Stanislavski, *Building a Character,* translated by Elizabeth R. Hapgood, introduction by Joshua Logan (New York: Theatre Arts Books, 1949), pp. xiii–xv.
52. Norris Houghton, *Moscow Rehearsals* (New York: Harcourt, Brace and Company, 1936), pp. 82–84.
53. Margarshack, p. 395.
54. Stanislavski, *Building a Character,* p. viii.

five

Sources of Early American
Acting Techniques

Theories of acting current in America from 1890 to 1918 were European in origin. Around them centered two major controversies, namely whether or not acting can be taught and whether or not the actor should feel the emotions of the character he is portraying.

DIDEROT'S PARADOX

The point of view has usually been founded upon one or the other of two famous essays on acting, Diderot's "Paradox of Acting" [1] or Talma's "Reflections on Acting." [2] The first of these was written toward the end of the eighteenth century, but it was not published until 1830, forty-six years after Diderot's death. The paradox arises out of Diderot's conviction that the actor himself should not feel the emotion which he enkindles in the audience. He explains that the actor "feels neither trouble, nor sorrow, nor depression, nor weariness of soul. All these emotions he has given to you. The actor is tired, you are unhappy, he has had exertion without feeling, you feeling without exertion." In fact, Diderot declared, ". . . in complete absence of sensibility is the possibility of a sublime actor." [3]

Although the strongest impression of Diderot's essay was made by the seeming contradiction between the emotion portrayed by the actor and his emotionless inner state while on the stage, Diderot actually made a number of other points with which almost every student of acting must agree. Above all, he made a strong plea for discipline and conscious control as opposed to inspiration. He continually stressed the need for the actor to copy nature.

It is not so much the actor's feeling the emotion as his being overcome by it, and so carried from his true course, that Diderot deplored:

> The man of sensibility is too much at the mercy of his diaphragm to be a great king, a great politician, a great magistrate, a just man, or a close observer, and, consequently, an admirable imitator of Nature.[4]

Diderot's definition of sensibility is actually the crux of the whole discussion and is worthy of scrutiny by his followers as well as his opponents:

> Sensibility, according to the only acceptation yet given of the term, is, as it seems to me, that disposition which accompanies organic weakness, which follows on easy affection of the diaphragm, on vivacity of imagination, on delicacy of nerves, which inclines one to being compassionate, to being horrified, to admiration, to fear, to being upset, to tears, to faintings, to rescues, to flights, to exclamations, to loss of self-control, to being contemptuous, disdainful, to having no clear notion of what is true, good, and fine, to being unjust, to going mad.[5]

This strongly suggests that Diderot equated *sensibility* with an excessive display of emotion or lack of self-control. Otherwise he could not have written:

> Great poets, great actors, and, I may add, all great copyists of Nature, in whatever art, beings gifted with fine imagination, with broad judgment, with exquisite tact, with a sure touch of taste, are the least sensitive of all creatures.[6]

Diderot seems to imply, moreover, that an actor may experience emotion in the search for the character he is to portray. In describing preparation made by Clairon, reigning French actress from 1743 to 1788, he says:

> I have no doubt that Clairon goes through just the same struggles . . . in her first attempts at a part; but once the struggle is over, once she has reached the height she has given to her spectre, she has herself well in hand, she repeats her efforts without emotion.[7]

Finally, Diderot demonstrates that his concern is less with whether or not the actor feels the emotion of his part than that he control himself when he says: "And after all, what does it matter to us whether they feel or do not feel, so long as we know nothing about it."

This is certainly one of the sources of the so-called "external" school of acting.

TALMA'S SENSIBILITY AND INTELLIGENCE

Adherents of the other side of the question often take for their source the great French tragedian and favorite of Napoleon, Talma, and his famous essay, "Reflections on Acting." Written as a preface for the autobiography of Lekain, in a series of dramatic memoirs, it was published in 1825, only one year before Talma's death.

"Reflections on Acting" made its first appearance in English in 1877 when Sir Henry Irving had it translated and printed in a British monthly, *The Theatre*. In 1883, Irving had it reprinted in pamphlet form with a preface which he wrote for it. He considered Talma's essay the answer to the need for a "permanent embodiment of the actor's art." [8]

Talma's chief contention that "sensibility and intelligence . . . are the principal faculties necessary to an actor," seems at first glance to be the direct opposite of Diderot's thesis that the great actor is free from sensibility. However, Diderot says "the actor must have *penetration* and no sensibility." Upon examination it seems that Talma's definition of sensibility includes penetration:

> To my mind, sensibility is not only that faculty which an actor possesses of being moved himself, and of affecting his being so far as to imprint on his features, and especially on his voice, that expression and those accents of sorrow which awake all the sympathies of the art and extort tears from the auditors. I include in it the effect which it produces, the *imagination* of which it is the source, not that imagination which consists in having reminiscences, so that the object seems actually present (this, properly speaking, is only memory), but that imagination which, creative, active, and powerful, consists in collecting in one single fictitious object the qualities of several real objects, which associates the actor with the inspiration of the poet, transports him back to the past, and enables him to look on at the lives of historical personages or the impassioned figures created by genius—which reveals to him, as though by magic, their physiognomy, their heroic stature, their language, their habits, all the shades of their character . . . .[9]

The fundamental difference between the beliefs of Diderot and Talma can be understood in the light of Talma's expansion of sensibility to include "that faculty of exaltation which agitates an actor, takes possession of his senses, shakes even his very soul, and enables him to *enter into* the most tragic situations and the most terrible of the passions *as if they were his own*." (Italics supplied.)

The difference between Diderot and Talma is precisely in this idea of the actor's identification with the character he is portraying. Diderot rejects identification while Talma maintains:

> Everyone possesses it [sensibility] in a greater or less degree. But in the man whom nature has destined to paint the passions in their greatest excesses, to give them all their violence, and show them in all their delirium, one may perceive that it must have a much greater energy; and as our emotions are intimately connected with our nerves, the nervous system of an actor must be so mobile and plastic as to be moved by the inspiration of the poet as easily as the *Aeolian harp sounds with the least breath of air that touches it*.[10]

In contrast to this Diderot asserted: "A great actor is neither a pianoforte, nor a harp, nor a spinnet [sic], nor a violin, nor a violoncello; he has no key peculiar to him; he takes the key and the tone fit for his part of the score, and he can take up any . . . ."[11]

Talma believed that the actor could not succeed in deeply impressing his audience and moving the coldest of them without "an excess of sensibility." However, he dismissed inspiration like Diderot, though for slightly different reasons:

> The poet or painter can wait for the moment of inspiration to write or to paint. In the actor, on the contrary, it must be commanded at any moment. That it may be sudden, lively, and prompt, he must possess an excess of sensibility. Nay, more, his intelligence must be always on the watch and acting in concert with his sensibility, and regulate its movement and effects, for he cannot, like the painter and the poet, efface what he does.[12]

Talma reported that Lekain broke with the traditional cadenced declamation or "sing-song psalmody" which had characterized the French theatre up to his time and dared to speak for the first time on the French stage in the "true accents of nature." Moreover, he insists that "actors ought at all times to take nature for a model, to make it the constant object of their studies"; and he deplored the fact that in spite of the advice "offered by Molière in his *Impromptu de Versailles*" and by Shakespeare in Hamlet's advice to the players, "the false system of pompous declamation has been established in almost all theatres of Europe and proclaimed as the sole type of theatrical imitation." [13]

That Diderot and Talma both considered Lekain an excellent actor bears witness to the fact that they had the same goal but believed in different means of attaining it. Diderot described Lekain as "a cold man, who is without feeling, but who imitates it excellently." However, he based his conclusion upon the fact that Lekain reputedly was able to see a diamond earring on the floor and push it toward the wings with his foot in the midst of the tragic scene he was playing at the time. His reasoning was to be brilliantly refuted a hundred years later by George Henry Lewes, the English critic.

Talma, on the other hand, felt that Lekain's efforts "to impart a sort of reality to the fiction of the stage" could only be realized by an actor who had "received from nature an extreme sensibility and a profound intelligence," and he considered that "Lekain possessed these qualifications in an eminent degree."

In discussing the qualities of Lekain, Talma showed how fine acting could compensate for physical appearance. He said:

> Nature had refused to Lekain some of the advantages which the stage demands. His features had nothing noble in them; his physiognomy was common, his figure short. But his exquisite sensibility, the movement of an ardent and impassioned soul, the faculty he possessed of plunging entirely into the situation of the personage he represented, the intelligence, so delicately fine, which enabled him to perceive and produce all the shades of the character he had to paint—these embellished his irregular features and gave him an inexpressible charm.[14]

That Talma was not only a great actor but a great student of acting technique is ably demonstrated by the course of study which he suggested for "the actor who possessed this double gift," sensibility and intelligence:

> In the first place, by repeated exercises he enters deeply into the emotions, and his speech acquires the accent proper to the situation, of the personage he has to represent. This done, he goes to the theatre not only to give theatrical effect to his studies, but also to yield himself to the spontaneous flashes of his sensibility and all the emotions which it involuntarily produces in him. What does he do then? In order that his inspirations may not be lost, his memory, in the silence of repose, recalls the accent of his voice, the expression of his features, his action—in a word, the spontaneous workings of his mind, which he had suffered to have free

course, and, in effect, everything which in the moments of his exaltation
contributed to the effect he had produced. His intelligence then passes
all these means in review, connecting them and fixing them in his memory,
to re-employ them at pleasure in succeeding representations.[15]

The significant feature of Talma's advice is its emphasis on the
recall of "the *spontaneous* workings of his mind . . . *everything* which
in the *moments of exaltation contributed to the effect* he had produced," rather than of the effect itself. It is true that he did suggest
that the actor should recall "the accent of his voice, the expression of
his features." Nevertheless, all that follows proves beyond a doubt
that Talma's concern was with the cause rather than the effect, with
the inner emotional state that brought about the outer visible result.
In this respect he bears a close resemblance to Stanislavsky, as indeed
he does in his concern for the points which follow.

Speaking of Lekain's ability to regulate movement, he said:

> He regarded this as a very essential part of his art. For action is language
> in another form. If it is violent or hurried, the carriage ceases to be noble.
> Thus, while other actors were theatrical kings only, in him the dignity
> did not appear to be the result of effort, but the simple effect of habit.
> He did not raise his shoulders or swell his voice to give an order.[16]

His concern with truthful acting caused him to give very thorough
directions for such seemingly technical matters as the speaking of
lines and pausing. He said of Lekain, "his pauses were always full of
deep significance." The reasons advanced by Talma for using certain
techniques were always based upon actual circumstances:

> There are, in fact, certain circumstances in which it is necessary to solicit
> oneself before we confide to the tongue the emotions of the soul or the
> calculations of the mind. The actor, therefore, must have the art of thinking
> before he speaks, and by introducing pauses he appears to meditate upon
> what he is about to say. . . . His attitudes and features must indicate
> that during these moments of silence his soul is deeply engaged; without
> this his pauses will seem rather to be the result of defective memory than
> a secret of his art.[17]

He discussed also two other common occurrences affecting the
mode of utterance. In one, deep emotion is manifested in the face
before the words are spoken. Talma said that in some situations "a
person strongly moved feels too acutely to wait the slow combination
of words" and therefore "the sentiment that overpowers him escapes

in mute action before the voice is able to give it utterance." His direction in that case is very clear: "The gesture, the attitude, and the look ought, then, to precede the words, as the flash of the lightning precedes the thunder." At all times his technique arises out of the motivations rather than the result.

In the other situation, that of "the person transported by the violence of feeling," Talma said:

> The words come to his lips as rapidly as the thoughts to his mind; they are born with them and succeed one another without interruption. The mind of the actor, then, ought to be hurried and rapid; he must even conceal from the audience the effort he makes to prolong his breath.[18]

Talma warned that the "slightest pause would destroy the illusion because the mind would seem to participate in this pause," adding that "passion does not follow the rules of grammar."

There are two other points which Talma stressed that approach very closely Stanislavsky's beliefs. The first is that the actor can make use of his own emotional experiences in portraying different characters upon the stage. In Talma's words, "He meditates on these, and clothes the fictitious passions with these real forms." The second is that the actor can find in his own emotional reactions, at least the seeds for other impulses that at first seem foreign to his nature. "Thus the sentiment of a lofty emulation enables us to divine what envy may feel; the just resentment of wrongs shows us in miniature the excess of hatred and revenge." [19]

Regardless of all the other points covered by Diderot and Talma, succeeding generations of actors have espoused the cause of one or the other in their acceptance or rejection of a single proposition, that an actor should identify himself with the character he is playing.

DISCIPLE OF DIDEROT

Constant Coquelin, the French comedian for whom Rostand wrote *Cyrano de Bergerac,* took note of this fact in his essay entitled "Art and the Actor":

> The theatrical world is divided into two opposing camps in regard to the question whether the actor should partake of the passions of his part— weep himself in order to draw tears—or whether he should remain master of himself throughout the most impassioned and violent action on the part of the character which he represents; in a word, remain unmoved himself,

the more surely to move others, which forms the famous paradox of Diderot.

Coquelin declares himself to be in agreement with Diderot. His position, however, is not altogether persuasive:

> Well, I hold this paradox to be literal truth; and I am convinced that one can only be a great actor on condition of complete self-mastery and ability to express feelings which are not experienced, which may never be experienced, which from the very nature of things can never be experienced.

However, somewhat later, Coquelin appears to accept the other point of view when he says:

> The actor makes up his personage. He borrows from his author . . . he draws . . . on his own experience and imagination . . . . He sees it [his part], grasps it—it does not belong to him, but *he inhabits its body, is fairly it!* [20]

In another place, he gave expression to somewhat the same idea when he declared, "It is with this individual *self* that he makes you by turns shiver, weep or smile."

Coquelin agreed with Talma when he suggested that "just as their sorrows often serve great poets as the inspiration of their best verses, so ours may serve us in the creation of great parts." Notwithstanding this, he insists ". . . the actor needs not to be actually moved." Coquelin's account of what Brander Matthews called his method of "getting inside the skin of a character" bears a strong resemblance to Michael Chekhov's use of creative imagination in creating a character.[21] According to Matthews, Coquelin told an interviewer:

> When I have to create a part, I begin by reading the play with the greatest attention five or six times. First, I consider what position my character should occupy, on what plane in the picture I must put him. Then I study his psychology, knowing what he thinks, what he is morally. I deduce what he ought to be physically, what will be his carriage, his manner of speaking, his gesture. These characteristics once decided, I learn the part without thinking about it further; then, when I know it, I take up my man again and, closing my eyes, I say to him, "Recite this for me." Then I see him delivering the speech, the sentence I asked him for; he lives, he speaks, he gesticulates before me; and then I have only to imitate him.[22]

Coquelin aroused the opposition of Sir Henry Irving and of Dion Boucicault by a later paper entitled "Actors and Acting," which appeared in *Harper's Monthly* for May, 1887. Irving's reply, "Mr. Coquelin on Actors and Acting," in June of the same year, in the magazine *Nineteenth Century,* was followed, two months later, by Dion Boucicault's comment, "Coquelin—Irving," in *North American Review.* Coquelin answered both in *Harper's Weekly* for November 12, 1887, in two separate articles.[23]

Coquelin again asserted his belief that the actor "should never feel the shadow of the sentiments to which he is giving expression at the very instant that he is representing them with the utmost power and truth." Yet in the very next paragraph, he said: "Study your part, *make yourself one with your character,* but in doing this never set aside your own individuality." [24] (Italics supplied.)

In his reply, Irving concerned himself for the most part with refuting Coquelin's stand that "an actor should never exhibit real emotion," declaring: "Eloquence is all the more moving when it is animated and directed by a fine and subtle sympathy which affects the speaker though it does not master him." [25]

Boucicault also took the occasion to refute Coquelin's main position regarding emotion and the actor. Coquelin cited Hamlet's advice to the players, "in the torrent and tempest of his passions to beget a temperance that will give it smoothness," to prove his position. "But it may be said this is meaningly," wrote Boucicault, "an advice to repress rant." Boucicault expressed his opinion that the "perfectly trained artist" can "give rein to his passional spasm while retaining his seat and control of Pegasus."

Furthermore he implied that Coquelin's "method of building up a character" was applicable only to comedy. He praised it, calling it "an admirable lesson to comedians" which "should be preserved by an imperishable record in the archives of our art," but went on to add: "But as comedy is largely a physiological study, tragedy is largely pathologic. Doubtless there are many great tragic figures in the drama that should be treated from the outside, as are the great comic figures; but this part of them is comedy. . . ." [26]

Boucicault registered an objection to what he called "the application of Zolaism to our art," and, as an example, he compared a performance of Bernhardt's with one by Rachel from *Adrienne Lecouvreur.* Bernhardt had emphasized the physical suffering of the girl dying of poison and showed her "in convulsions, writhing between her two lovers." Boucicault said, "The spectators watch the throes of death as if they were present at a terrible operation."

Rachel, on the other hand, brought out the agony of her soul at parting from her young lover. "There was no vulgar display of physical suffering excepting in her repression of it." In this Boucicault touches upon a point made repeatedly by Stanislavsky, namely, that the stage is not the place to show clinical aspects of sickness.[27]

THE NATURAL SCHOOL OF ACTING

Nearly all actors, whether they adhered to the emotional or the antiemotional point of view, have professed "nature" as their guide, although their methods have had very little else in common. This was true as far back as the eighteenth century, when the controversy existed between "art" and "nature." Marie Françoise Dumesnil, Clairon's rival at the Comédie Française, exclaimed, "Yes, 'nature.' How many use this word without knowing its meaning." Dumesnil expressed the essence of her philosophy of acting when she wrote: "To imbue oneself with great emotions, to feel them immediately and at will, to forget oneself in a twinkling of an eye in order to put oneself in the place of the character one wishes to represent—that is exclusively a gift of nature and beyond all the efforts of art." [28] Half a century earlier, Michel Baron, who had been called "the most celebrated of Molière's disciples and France's first great tragic artist," also earned for himself the epithet of the "most natural player of his time." It was said that before going on stage Baron would speak aloud or whisper to whatever actor might be about to enter with him, in order to *be* the character.[29]

Examples could be multiplied indefinitely. However, it is apparent that this use of "natural" acting means the actor's identification with the character he is portraying.

BOUCICAULT

One of the earliest exponents of this theory in America was the playwright Dion Boucicault, who protested so strongly against Coquelin's antiemotional attitude. Five years before the publication of his answer to Coquelin, during one of his visits to England, Dion Boucicault addressed an audience of actors and actresses at the Lyceum Theatre, London. The theatre was lent for the occasion by Sir Henry Irving. The address, entitled "The Art of Acting," was first printed from a stenographic report in the *Era* for July 29, 1882.[30] Boucicault began his address by refuting the idea which had been previously advanced in the press that acting could not be taught, and he pointed to Paris, where acting was taught. He also mentioned Sardou, Alexandre Dumas, and others who were "in the habit of teaching the actors how the characters they have drawn should be played," and referred to the fact that "all active managers such as Mr. Irving, Mr. Wilson Barrett, Mr. Bancroft, Mr. Hare, Mr. Kendall all teach the younger actors and actresses how to play their parts . . . because there is no school . . . to teach them acting."

Boucicault then defined what he meant by acting. From his definition, it is evident that he believed in the actor's identification with the character:

> Acting is not mere speech! It is not taking the dialogue of the author and giving it artistically, but sometimes not articulately. Acting is to perform, to be the part; to be it in your arms, your legs; to be what you are acting; to be it all over, that is acting.[31]

Like Stanislavsky, Boucicault divided his subject into two parts, the actor's work on himself and that on the character.

The first part of the address covered such matters as voice, gesture, and walking. On all of these Boucicault gave valuable advice, always with wit. He said that using a loud voice was not necessarily the way to be heard, and he emphasized the importance of speaking distinctly, of giving every vowel and consonant its full value, in order to make sure of being heard in a large auditorium. He pointed out that the consonants give strength to speech, and the vowels, expressiveness and beauty. The next thing for the young actor to learn, according to Boucicault, is "to measure his breath." "The first fault of a young public speaker is that he begins with a rush, and then falls in the distance." He called special attention to *l, m, n,* and *r,* the "four liquids in the alphabet . . . out of which you cannot possibly compose an unmusical word." His criticism displayed a fine understanding of phonetic values, particularly in his discussion of the mispronunciation of vowels.

He was frank in voicing his objection to the dropping of the final *r* by the English, and mentioned also the mistake of some who substituted a *w*. He drew attention also to the "fault of young actors and actresses" of condensing their words, giving as examples, "syllble" for "syllable," and "apptite" for "appetite."

Boucicault referred to the changing fashions in voice for the playing of tragedy, and called attention to the popular notion that the tragedian never used his natural voice on the stage. He characterized the use of the treble voice of the previous century by "the great French tragedians before Talma and the great English tragedians before Kean" as "the tea pot style"; next came "the period when the tragedian played his part on the double bass." Even in his day the medium voice used was not the actor's natural voice, according to Boucicault, who declared that he had "fought out this very question with the great tragedians in France," who seemed to be "afraid of destroying the delicate illusion of the audience." [32]

With regard to gesture, Boucicault emphasized the point that there can be no hard and fast rule about anything in the theatre, since the finest effects are often achieved by great actors' "inverting the well known rules." Nevertheless, he offered a rule generally followed in the use of gesture, namely, that "all gesture should precede slightly the words that it is to impress or illustrate," since "the gesture indicates slightly to the mind what is going to be given in words, and the words complete that idea and satisfy the mind of the audience." Boucicault deplored the fact that such simple matters, instead of being known to every actor, are "transmitted, gipsy-like, in our vagrant life from one generation to another."

Next Boucicault discussed "the lost art of walking," and recommended examination of the "Greek friezes where the lines of persons are represented in the true attitude of a person walking."

Another point upon which Boucicault commented was the conventional means of "taking an exit" where the actor would commence a speech on one side of the stage, then cross, saving the last few words "to take him off." He spoke of the common occurrence of an actor's asking him to write a few words to take him off.

The remaining part of his lecture Boucicault devoted to the study of character. Here he stressed the importance of listening:

> Now, the finer part of the acting is to obtain an effect, not altogether by what is given you to speak, but by listening to what another person speaks, and by its effect upon you, by continuing your character while the other man is speaking.[33]

In fact he went so far as to suggest that if an actor concentrates his attention upon listening, he will be relieved of "that vanity sickness that we call stage fright." There is a close resemblance to Stanislavsky's "circle of attention" [34] in Boucicault's explanation:

If the man fixes his mind upon some other object, if the mind is over *there*, not *here* on himself, ease will naturally follow, because he is naturally there as a listener. That is his first lesson; when he has accomplished this he must come to the study of character.[35]

Boucicault admonished his audience that they should study character "from the inside," not "from the outside." Furthermore, they should be less concerned with whether a part would fit them than whether they could fit into the part. However, he advised young people about to go on the stage to try to select the kind of character that was more suited to their natural endowments, pointing out that an actor who could play Hamlet well might be altogether unsuited to the requirements of Othello. The lecture ended on a plea for instruction for young actors. Eight years after this address, for several months before his death in 1890, Boucicault taught at the school for acting established by A. M. Palmer at his Madison Square Theatre in New York City.[36]

IRVING

Sir Henry Irving was in agreement with Boucicault on three fundamental points regarding acting. He also was an advocate of the natural school of acting; he believed that acting could and should be taught; and he was of the opinion that the actor should identify himself with his role. In an address which he gave at Oxford in 1886, he praised Burbage, Betterton, Garrick, and Kean as the "four greatest champions in their respective times on the stage of nature in contradiction to artificiality." He referred to the praise of Burbage [37] given by Richard Flecknoe, the seventeenth century critic, for "so wholly transforming himself into his part, and putting off himself with his clothes, as he never (not so much as in the 'tiring house) assumed himself again until the play was done"; and even when he was not speaking, "with his looks and gesture maintaining it [his part] still to the heights." [38]

Five years later, at the opening of the Philosophical Institution at Edinburgh, Irving made another address. At that time he defined the actor's business as "primarily to reproduce the ideas of the author's brain, to give them form and substance and color and life, so that those, who beheld the action of a play may, so far as can be effected, be lured into the fleeting belief that they behold reality." At the same time, Irving gave Macready's definition of action: "To fathom the depths of character, to trace its latent motives, to feel its finest quiverings of emotion, is to *comprehend the thoughts that are hidden under words* and thus possess one's self of the actual mind of the individual man." [39] (Italics supplied.) "To comprehend the thoughts that are hidden under words," or, as we are more accustomed to say, "to read between the lines," Stanislavsky called playing the "subtext." [40]

In his explanation of the force of the actor's intention, Irving anticipated Stanislavsky's principle of the interaction of the mind, the will, and the feelings.[41] Irving declared:

> It is in the representation of passion that the intention of the actor appears in the greatest force. He wishes to do a particular thing, and so far the wish is father to the thought that the brain begins to work in the required direction, and the emotional faculties and the whole nervous and muscular system follow suit.[42]

In regard to actor training, Irving maintained:

> The actor must at the start be well endowed with some special powers, and by training, reading and culture of many kinds, be equipped for the work before him. . . . No genius can find its fullest expression without some understanding of the principles and method of a craft.[43]

Irving took exception to Diderot's theory that "an actor never feels the part he is acting":

> It is of course true that the pain he suffers is not real pain but I leave it to any one who has ever felt his own heart touched by the woes of another to say if he can imagine a case where the man who follows in minutest detail the history of an emotion, from its inception onward, is the only one who cannot be stirred by it—more especially when his own individuality must perforce be merged in that of the archetypal sufferer.[44]

On the other hand, Irving's approval of Talma's point of view was expressed in the introduction which he wrote for "Reflections on Acting." Here he deplored the "want of a permanent embodiment of the principles" of acting, "a *vade mecum* of the actor's calling, written by one of themselves, and by an artist universally recognized as a competent expositor." He considered Talma's essay the answer to this need.

"Talma knew," said Irving, "that it was possible for an actor to feel to the full a simulated passion, and yet whilst being swept by it to retain his consciousness of his surroundings and his purpose." [45] Here, again, Irving's thinking brings to mind Stanislavsky, who used to illustrate this same phenomenon with Salvini's remarks: "An actor lives, weeps, and laughs on the stage, and all the while he is watching his own tears and smiles. It is this double function, this balance between life and acting that makes his art." [46]

Irving phrased an idea which may be a key to the mystery when he said, "The essence of acting is its apparent spontaneity." [47] Many great actors of all times have suggested ways of achieving this goal.

LEWES

As early as 1875, George Henry Lewes, the English writer and critic, in a volume entitled *On Actors and the Art of Acting*,[48] brought together many of his earlier critical pieces. The book is still one of the most searching and intelligent pieces of dramatic criticism of the actual performances of leading actors of his time, including Kean, Macready, Rachel, Ristori, and Salvini. It contains as well, some of the most discerning comments on "the art of acting."

Like Irving, Lewes was on the side of those who believed that acting could be taught. In a letter to Trollope he called attention to the "chaotic state of opinion on the subject of acting in many minds of rare intelligence." "Another general misconception," Lewes continued, "is that there is no special physique nor any special training necessary to make an actor."

On some very important points of technique, Lewes anticipated Stanislavsky by nearly twenty-five years. For instance, what Stanislavsky called "emotion memory" or "affective memory," is suggested in the following:

> It is from the memory of past feelings that he draws the beautiful image with which he delights us. He is tremulous again under the remembered agitation, but it is a pleasant tremor, and in no way disturbs the clearness of his intellect. He is a spectator of his own tumult; and though moved by it, yet so master it as to select from it only those elements which suit his purpose. We are all spectators of ourselves; but it is the peculiarity of the artistic nature to indulge in such introspection even in moments of all but the most disturbing passion and to draw thence materials for art.[49]

The similarity between this passage and the following by Stanislavsky is easily apparent:

> Another reason why you should cherish those repeated emotions is, that an artist does not build his role out of the first thing at hand. He chooses carefully from among his memories and culls out of his living experiences the ones that are most enticing. He weaves the soul of the person he is to

portray out of emotions that are dearer to him than his everyday sensations.[50]

Also in his comment on the "deficiency of pathos" in Salvini's acting of *Othello* Lewes came very close to Stanislavsky in the statement, "Tragic pathos to be grand should be *impersonal*." He explained it in these words:

> Instead of our being made to feel that the sufferer is giving himself up to self-pity, we should be made to see in his anguish the expression of a general sorrow. The tragic passion identifies its suffering with the suffering of mankind. The hero is presented less as moaning over his lot, exclaiming: "I am so miserable!" than as moaning over his and the common lot, exclaiming: "O, this misery!" . . . the more he pities himself the less you pity him. Grief, however intense, however wild its expression, when borne with a sense of its being part of our general heritage, excites the deepest sympathy; we feel most keenly *for* the sufferer in feeling *with* him.[51]

That Lewes believed the actor should feel the emotions of the character he is portraying is apparent from his discussion of "the greatest actor, the creative artist":

> When an actor feels a vivid sympathy with the passion or humor he is representing, he *personates,* i.e., speaks through the *persona* or character; and for the moment *is* what he represents. He can do this only in proportion to the vividness of his sympathy, and the plasticity of his organization, which enables him to give expression to what he feels.[52]

Following this picture of what an actor should strive to be, Lewes offered a definition of the unacceptable performer:

> The conventional artist is one who either, because he does not feel the vivid sympathy, or cannot express what he feels, or has not sufficient energy or self-reliance to trust frankly to his own expressions, cannot *be* the part, but tries to *act* it, and is thus necessarily driven to adopt those conventional means of expression with which the traditions of the stage abound. Instead of allowing a strong feeling to express itself through its natural signs, he seizes upon the conventional signs, either because in truth there is no strong feeling moving him, or because he is not artist enough to give it genuine expression; his lips will curl, his brow wrinkle, his eyes be thrown up, his forehead be slapped, or he will grimace, rant, and "take the stage," in the style which has become traditional, but which was perhaps never seen off the stage; and thus he runs through the gamut of sounds and signs which

bear as remote an affinity to any real expressions as the pantomimic conventions of ballet-dancers.[53]

Lewes referred to remarks of Talma several times. While he made no reference to Diderot, he presented a more striking paradox, in his words, "the antimony, as Kant would call it—the contradiction which perplexes judgment":

> If the actor lose all power over his art under the disturbing influence of emotion, he also loses all power over his art in proportion to his deadness to emotion. If he really feel, he cannot act; but he cannot act unless he feel.

Lewes expanded the paradoxical question and at the same time clarified his position with regard to it:

> The condition being that a man must feel emotion if he is to express it, for if he does not feel it he will not know how to express it, how can this be reconciled with the impossibility of his affecting us aesthetically while he is disturbed by emotion? In other words: *how far* does he really feel the passion he expresses? It is a question of degree. As in all art, feeling lies at the root, but the foliage and flowers, though deriving their sap from the emotion, derive their form and structure from the intellect.[54]

Lewes considered Shakespeare's "brief but pregnant advice to the players" in *Hamlet* proof that he "had mastered the principles of the art of acting." In Hamlet's admonition, "In the very torrent, tempest, and, as I may say, whirlwind of passion, you must acquire and beget a temperance that may give it smoothness," is to be found, according to Lewes, "the cardinal principle in all art, the subordination of impulse to law, the regulation of all effects with a view to beauty." In a paraphrase of this passage Lewes actually gave an amplification of Talma's requisite for the actor of sensibility and intelligence:

> He must be at once passionate and temperate: trembling with emotion, yet with a mind in vigilant supremacy controlling expression, *directing* every intonation, look and gesture. The rarity of fine acting depends on the difficulty there is in being at one and the same moment so deeply moved that the emotion shall spontaneously express itself in symbols universally intelligible, and yet so calm as to be perfect master of effects, capable of modulating voice and moderating gesture when they tend to excess or ugliness.[55]

Stanislavsky expressed the same idea in these words:

Never lose yourself on the stage. Always act in your own person. You can never get away from yourself. The moment you lose yourself on the stage marks the beginning of exaggerated false acting.[56]

As great an actress as Mrs. Fiske so genuinely approved of Lewes' work that she declared to Alexander Woollcott:

Here we have the soundest and most discerning treatise on the subject I have ever read, the only good one in any language. Every actor would agree with it, but few could have made so searching an analysis, and fewer still could have expressed it in such telling, clarifying phrases . . . . We'll have to rename it "The Science of Acting" and use it as a textbook for the National Conservatory when the theater's ship comes in.[57]

THE PARADOX OF DUAL CONSCIOUSNESS

This faculty of "dual control" as it were, which Shakespeare, Talma, Lewes, Irving, and Stanislavsky, as well as a great many other authorities on the subject, have declared necessary for effective performance, has been well named by William Archer, the eminent Scots critic and translator of Ibsen's works. He called it "the divided mental activity." As early as 1888, Archer's critical writings on the "artistic value of real emotion," taken from the records and testimony of actual performers and entitled "Masks or Faces," was first given to the public. It is still a valuable contribution to critical thought on acting, as is evidenced by the fact that it was reprinted in 1957. In it Archer first examined in detail Diderot's "Paradox," and then he turned to an investigation of what he considered the "real paradox of acting." This he called "the paradox of dual consciousness." [58] As far as Diderot's paradox was concerned, Archer declared that Diderot's theory was not well established, since he had rarely gone to the theatre during the years before he formulated his doctrine.

Archer declared the controversy to be "entirely modern," adding that "the emotional theory held the field unquestioned" in ancient times as in the time of Shakespeare, who, he maintained, "has said what might well have been the last words upon it." Since the dispute arose at the end of the eighteenth century, Archer concluded that Diderot's theory, if correct, was a comment upon the acting of French tragedy at the time. Moreover, Diderot had given credit to Remond Sainte-Albine and the Italian actor, Ricaboni, for starting the controversy. Sainte-Albine was the author of a work called *Le Comédien*, which dealt with the qualities necessary for an actor and was extravagantly emotional in its point of view. Archer pointed out that Diderot's "anti-emotional extravagances" were merely a protest against the "emotional extravagances" of Sainte-Albine and Sticotti. The latter was the Italian actor who in 1769 readapted into French the anonymous English adaptation of Sainte-Albine's work. Finally, Archer condemned Diderot's different interpretations of sensibility and suggested that by using sensibility to mean hysteria, Diderot with his own hand had removed the paradox.

Archer next turned to his investigation of the "paradox of duel consciousness." In order to discover what part the emotions play in an actor's portrayal of a role and how far an actor identified with the character he was representing, Archer inquired of leading English and American actors and actresses concerning their state of mind during emotional scenes, their ability to control tears while acting, and the realistic effects upon the audience of real and simulated feeling.

Archer offered proof of real emotion accompanied by real tears in the acting of such famous persons as David Garrick, Mrs. Siddons, her niece, Fanny Kemble, Adelaide Neilson, Charlotte Cushman, and Tommaso Salvini.[59] He quoted Clara Morris as saying:

> You must feel, or all the pretty and pathetic language in the world won't make other people feel . . . . I do everything to get my feelings thoroughly aroused. Then I only have to look out for the other danger and keep from being overcome myself. All the tremolo and false sobs in the world will never take the place of real emotion.[60]

Archer gave his own observation of Ellen Terry's performance:

> No one who was near the stage on the first night of *The Amber Heart* can doubt the reality of Miss Ellen Terry's tears. In the second act they literally streamed down her cheeks, while her whole frame was shaken with weeping. Her emotion was not, of course, uncontrollable, but for the moment it was uncontrolled; and I may add that the effect upon the audience was instant and intense.[61]

Archer's evidence, for the most part, points to agreement in theory and practice of actors before his time as well as of those who were his contemporaries not alone in England, but in France and America as well. Generally they expressed themselves in favor of real emotion, but most of them emphasized the need for the actor's remaining in control of that emotion. Archer quoted two widely separated sources with remarkably similar points of view in the American actress, Clara Morris, and the eminent French actor, M. Albert Lambert *père*. Clara Morris spoke out strongly against the danger of "losing oneself in a part," declaring:

> As to really losing oneself in a part, that will not do: it is worse to be too sympathetic than to have too much art. I must cry in my emotional *roles* and feel enough to cry, but I must not allow myself to become so affected as to mumble my words, to redden my nose, or to become hysterical.[62]

The expression of Lambert *père* is important for several reasons. For one thing, it suggests the uses of "emotion (affective) memory" advanced by Stanislavsky.[63] Furthermore, the first statement is almost identical to that used by Joseph Jefferson to sum up his philosophy of acting.[64] Lambert *père*, however, was more concise in his definition of terms:

> For a general law of my own acting I hold to this: A warm heart, a cool head. By "heart" I mean the mental powers that can sustain emotion at a high pitch of intensity, that by a mere exertion of the will can summon tears, struggles for breath, torments, all the nuances of anguish, whether by *recalling like situations observed or experienced in real life* or by *deliberately identifying oneself with the character played*. By "a cool head" I mean a superintending faculty that never nods—a kind of instinct of artistic self-preservation that contrives to channel even the most impassioned outburst into conformity with the principles of an art learned and reflected upon.[65] (Italics supplied.)

PERSONAL EMOTION

The next part of Archer's inquiry was concerned with discovering whether an actor experienced emotions similar to those of the character he was playing and whether his personal sorrow affected his acting.

Archer received abundant proof that in playing scenes where the emotion called for was that of grief or sorrow, actors either consciously recalled a similar moment from their own lives, or the scene, sometimes even the words that the actor was required to speak, revived the memory of an actual sorrow and so gave reality to the emotion he was playing. Archer mentioned eight prominent actors, all of whom had assured him that their own sorrows had affected their acting "for good."

Among the instances taken from history is the anecdote of the

Greek actor Polus, who, "clad in the mourning habit of Electra, took from the tomb the bones and urn of his son," and substituted this for the urn supposedly containing the ashes of Orestes. "This anecdote," Archer maintained, "shows that a protagonist whom the Athenians reckoned great believed in the good effect of real emotion on the stage." Archer also called attention to Quintilian's views regarding emotion:

> The great secret . . . for moving the passions is to be moved ourselves; for the imitation of grief, anger, indignation, will often be ridiculous, if our words and countenance alone conform to the emotion, not our heart. . . . Wherefore, when we wish to attain verisimilitude in emotion, let us put ourselves in the place of those who really suffer; and let our speech proceed from the very state of mind which we wish to induce in the judge. Will he grieve who hears me declaim unmoved? . . . Will he weep who sees me dry eyed, . . . But how shall we be affected, our emotions not being at our command? This, too, I shall try to explain. What the Greeks call φαντασίας, we call *visiones;* whereby the images of things absent are so represented to the mind, that we seem to see them with our eyes, and to have them present before us. Whoever shall have conceived these thoroughly, will have complete power over his emotions.[66]

The secret of control over the emotions, then, according to Quintilian, lies in the ability of vivid recall of *"the images of things absent."* Stanislavsky expressed an almost identical idea in speaking of emotion memory:

> Can you picture to yourself what our emotion memory is really like? Imagine a number of houses, with many rooms in each house, in each room innumerable cupboards, shelves, boxes, and somewhere, in one of them, a tiny bead. . . . That is what it is like in the archives of your memory. It has all those divisions and sub-divisions. Some are more accessible than others. The problem is to recapture the emotion that once flashed by like a meteor. . . . If you learn how to be receptive to these recurring memories, then the new ones as they form will be more capable of stirring your feelings repeatedly.[67]

For more up-to-date evidence Archer turned to the diaries of Macready, in which the actor attested to the effect of the death of his daughter upon his acting in the part of Virginius. When at one point in the second act his thoughts had turned to this child, he had been nearly overcome by his emotion. Referring to a later performance of the same role, which was in his opinion one of his most brilliant, he admitted the powerful effect upon his acting of the thoughts of another child he had lost. Salvini reported a similar experience when his own little daughter was at home dying and tears choked his voice and his "sobs went . . . to the heart of the audience." The great Italian actress, Ristori, similarly attested to the effect of her own experience upon her emotion in the scene she was playing:

> I have occasionally been so overcome by the analogy between a fictitious situation and an event in my own life, that I have had to put forth all my strength in order to retain my self-control, and have not always entirely succeeded! The effects obtained under such mental conditions are naturally stronger because they are true.[68]

Archer declared however, that most of his informants agreed that a too recent sorrow was harmful. He gave as an example of this point, an occurrence at the Lyceum Theatre "during the historic run of *Hamlet*" in the 1874–1875 season. Mr. H. L. Bateman, its manager, died during a performance in which his daughter, Miss Isabel Bateman, the Ophelia to Irving's Hamlet, had to go on playing after a short intermission. Miss Bateman's own estimate of the result is valuable:

> The effect of the real experience . . . was anything but beneficial to my performance. In my effort for self-control I believe I never acted so badly; it remains in my memory as a terrible nightmare, and I have had a horror of the part ever since. . . . On the other hand, . . . my acting has been greatly influenced for good by real but more remote sorrows.[69]

Miss Bateman's comment on her experience as "a terrible nightmare" which "stayed in her memory" is evidence, if any were needed, of the claims for "emotion memory." Furthermore, Stanislavsky seemed to imply the use of "more remote" emotional experience when he said: "Time is a splendid filter for our remembered feelings —besides it is a great artist. It not only purifies, it also transmutes even painfully realistic memories into poetry." He elaborates this idea when he says:

> Theoretically you might suppose that the ideal type of emotion memory would be one that could retain and reproduce impressions in all the exact details of their first occurrence, that they would be revived just as they really were experienced. Yet if that were the case what would become of our nervous systems? How would they stand the repetition of horrors

with all the original painfully realistic details? Human nature could not stand it.[70]

In summarizing the findings of his investigation into the use of real emotions on the stage Archer maintained:

> I have shown that the actor does, in some cases indubitably feel with his character, the imagined emotion happening to coincide with a real emotion in his real life. It is pretty clear, too, I think, from the answers I have quoted, that the effect upon the actor of this mingling of real with imagined emotion differs in degree rather than in kind from the effect of the imagined emotion. . . .[71]

Stanislavsky expressed a similar idea when he said: "Our emotion memories are not exact copies of reality—occasionally some are more vivid but usually they are less so, than the original." [72]

Archer was a believer in what he termed "the Life School," that is to say he advocated the actor's observing both his own emotions and those of people around him, and using his observations in portraying character. He cited instances from the experiences of Talma, Rachel, Macready, M. Albert Lambert *père,* Salvini, Ellen Terry, Isabel Bateman, and others to prove that "the actor's habit of mind prompts him, as he goes through life, to seize upon and treasure up details which may be of use in his art," adding, however, that "this seems often to occur without any distinct act of will."

According to Archer, Macready made notes in his diary of a visit to Bedlam "when preparing to play Lear," and Ellen Terry prepared for her first performance as Ophelia by "a long visit to Banstead Asylum." The testimony quoted by Archer revealed agreement on two points, namely, the practical value for the actor of both personally experienced emotions and emotions observed in others, as demonstrated by the following:

> "A thousand times," writes Salvini, "I have availed myself of emotions experienced in real life, adapting them to other personages and situations."
>
> "There have been events," writes Mrs. Bancroft, "which have so impressed me that when opportunity offered, I have reproduced them."
>
> "As a casual onlooker," writes Miss Isabel Bateman, "I have noted effects of real emotion, and stored them up for possible use." [73]

The following is Stanislavsky's comment:

We use not only our own past emotions as creative material but we use feelings that we have had in sympathizing with the emotions of others. It is easy to state *a priori* that it is utterly impossible that we should have sufficient emotional material of our own to supply the needs of all the parts we shall be called upon to play in a whole lifetime on the stage.[74]

Archer concluded this part of his inquiry with this statement: "There can be no doubt that emotional experience, and the study of emotion in others, are of the greatest value to actors." He even went so far as to declare, "Even those of my informants who deny this are probably more dependent than they think on the unconscious action of their memory in registering real-life effects. This point is well illustrated by John Drew's response to Archer:

I have consciously noted facts in real life for future use, but have never yet had opportunity to put them into practice. I have been able, however, to trace effects made to certain incidents automatically registered in my memory, though at the time of using them I fancied them imaginary or invented.[75]

In discussing the difference between the feelings or emotions of a participant in an incident and those of an onlooker, Stanislavsky emphasized a number of points. First he drew attention to the importance of emotion memory for "inner creativeness":

Our whole creative experiences are vivid and full in direct proportion to the power, keenness and exactness of our memory. If it is weak the feelings it arouses are pale, intangible and transparent. They are of no value on the stage because they will not carry across the footlights. . . .[76]

and

Sometimes impressions once received continue to live in us, grow and become deeper. They even stimulate new processes and either fill out unfinished details or else suggest altogether new ones.

With regard to the effect of an event upon an onlooker, he said:

There is, of course, no reason why the onlooker should not experience very strong emotions. He may even feel the incident more keenly than the participating parties. . . . Their feelings are different.

Stanislavsky also suggested the possibility of a third source of emotion memory:

> There is another possibility—a person might not participate in an incident either as a principal or an onlooker. He might only hear or read about it. Even that would not prevent his receiving deep and powerful impressions. It would all depend on the strength of the imagination of the person who wrote the description or told about it, and also on that of the person reading or hearing the story.[77]

Miss Janet Achurch, another of Archer's informants, gave evidence of using all sources of emotional stimulation when she wrote: "It is impossible for me to help it. Everything that comes, or ever has come into my own life, or under my observation, I find myself utilising. . . ." Her next comment is the crux of Archer's dissent from Diderot. She continued, "and in scenes of real personal suffering I have had an *under-consciousness* of taking mental notes all the time." [78]

As pointed out earlier, Diderot made much of the fact that the great French actor Lekain, at the height of a deeply emotional scene in which he had just emerged from his father's tomb "with blood-stained hands" after the murder of his mother, was able to take note of a diamond earring, which had "fallen from an actress' ear," and push it "toward the wing with his foot." Diderot declared that this incident proved Lekain to be "a cold man, who is without feeling, but who imitates it excellently." [79] Archer, on the other hand, maintained that this incident merely afforded an example "of the manifold activity of consciousness at any given moment." He called this faculty "divided mental activity" and cited authorities for the phenomenon from the experiences of men and women both on and off the stage. "Why should stage emotions be supposed to absorb all a man's faculties," he asked, "when the most poignant emotion in real life does nothing of the sort? On the contrary, it will often sharpen our senses in every direction, producing not anaesthesia, but hyperaesthesia." [80]

In a chapter entitled "The Brownies of the Brain," Archer elaborates on his concept of "divided mental activity" and gives several examples of its actual effect. He writes:

> The real paradox of acting, it seems to me, resolves itself into the paradox of dual consciousness. If it were true that the actor could not experience

an emotion without absolutely yielding up his whole soul to it, then Diderot's doctrine, though still a little overstated, would be right in the main. But the mind is not so constituted. . . .

There are many "brownies," as Mr. Stevenson puts it, in the actor's brain, and one of them may be agonising with Othello, while another is criticising his every tone and gesture, a third restraining him from strangling Iago in good earnest, and a fourth wondering whether the play will be over in time to let him catch his last train.[81]

Archer offered many illustrations of "the two or more strata of consciousness, or lines of thought, . . . in the mind while acting." He considered Fanny Kemble's analysis of her own state of mind on stage the "classic" example:

The curious part of acting to me, is the sort of double process which the mind carries on at once, the combined operation of one's faculties, so to speak, in diametrically opposite directions; for instance, in the very last scene of Mrs. Beverley, while I was half dead with crying in the midst of the *real* grief, created by an entirely *unreal* cause, I perceived that my tears were falling like rain all over my silk dress, and spoiling it; and I calculated and measured most accurately the space that my father would require to fall in, and moved myself and my train accordingly in the midst of the anguish I was to feign, and absolutely did endure. It is this watchful faculty (perfectly prosaic and commonplace in nature), which never deserts me while I am uttering all that exquisite passionate poetry in Juliet's balcony scene, while I feel as if my soul was on my lips, and my color comes and goes with the intensity of the sentiment I am expressing: which prevents me from falling over my train, from setting fire to myself with the lamps placed close to me, from leaning upon my canvas balcony when I seem to throw myself all but over it.[82]

Clara Morris, in a later century, not only attested to the same "divided mental activity" but even suggested the subconscious process which fed her imagination while on the stage:

There are, when I am on the stage, three separate currents of thought in my mind; one in which I am keenly alive to Clara Morris, to all details of the play, to the other actors and how they act, and to the audience; another about the play and the character I represent; and, finally, the thought that really gives me stimulus for acting. For instance, when I repeat such and such a line it fits like words to music to this underthought, which may be of some dead friend, of a story of Bret Harte's, of a poem, or maybe even some pathetic scrap from a newspaper.[83]

Archer noted: "Miss Morris is here speaking of parts which from frequent repetition have lost their effect upon her." However, Clara Morris' use of an image drawn either from personal experience or from observation as a source of emotional stimulation is quite in harmony with the suggestions of actors or critics already noted, from Quintilian to Stanislavsky.

Thus far the methods of acting technique examined have suggested a division of actors into two groups, which, to borrow from Boucicault, can be named as those who work "from the inside" and those who work "from the outside." (See page 142.) The first are usually grouped under the "natural" school and the second are often referred to as "external." However, toward the end of the nineteenth century another method appeared which affected American acting until 1925 [84] and which apparently was responsible for developing a technique even more external than that advocated by Coquelin and his followers. The system was called Eurhythmics.

Introduced to America by Steele MacKaye, the brilliant producer and playwright who established the first acting school in America, the Delsarte System was extremely popular as a method of teaching speech and acting during the last thirty years of the nineteenth century.[85] Delsarte was a French teacher of music and singing and an opera coach, who apparently also coached some actors and clergymen. His "science," as he claimed it to be, was "pseudophilosophy" founded upon Catholic doctrine, by which all things show a "trinitary organization." The essences of being, according to Delsarte, were life, mind, and soul, their agents being vocal sound or tone, words, and movement, respectively.

Under the influence of MacKaye, the emphasis was placed upon gesture (the expression of the soul) and pantomime. The Delsarte System became a system of aesthetic or "harmonic" gymnastics; many of the exercises were apparently invented by MacKaye. The other two founders of what has been referred to as the "new elocution" were Professor Lewis B. Monroe and the Reverend William R. Alger. Monroe was one of the organizers of Boston University's School of Oratory, and Alger, a Unitarian minister in Boston, studied with MacKaye and then with Delsarte's son in Paris. MacKaye lectured widely on the Delsarte System. However, a series of twelve lectures which he gave in 1878 probably had the greatest effect in establishing "Delsartism" as a method of instruction in many leading theatrical schools in America. Three students of the Boston School of Oratory and auditors at the lectures were Charles Wesley Emerson, the founder of the Emerson College of Oratory in 1880; Silas S. Curry, who subsequently established the School of Expression of Boston; and Franklin Sargeant,[86] MacKaye's assistant in his Lyceum Theatre School in New York City in 1884 and later head of the Lyceum School of Acting, the Empire Theatre Dramatic School (1897), and the American Academy of Dramatic Arts.[87] Another student of Monroe's, later a popular platform reader, was Leland Powers, who in 1904 founded the Leland Powers School of the Spoken Word.[88]

Emerson, Curry, and Powers were all influenced by Delsarte's system, and while rejecting some of its phases, seemed to accept the division of expression into spiritual, mental, and physical aspects. Of the three, Curry departed furthest from the method of Delsarte. After studying it for many years, he attempted to evaluate it. He ascribed its popularity to the excellence of MacKaye's lectures on the subject,[89] but he took exception to the claim that "if the body is right, the voice will be right." He also criticized Delsarte for putting too much emphasis upon pantomime, thereby sacrificing "unity of expression." Curry gave credit to Delsarte for pointing out the influence of the body upon the voice and the importance of "preliminary training or attuning of the whole body," which had been neglected previously.[90] However, he rejected the idea that "everything is, in its elements, a trinity":

> Thus, the Delsarte system is built upon a series of trinities, beginning with the Universe as composed of God, consciousness, cosmos; God as love, wisdom and power; Man as soul, mind and life; and the organism or physiognomic man, as torso, head and limbs, each in correspondence as to significance, the first term of each group being spiritual, the second rational, and the third passional or vital. . . . Then there are three kinds of motions: about a center, toward a center and from a center; also, with corresponding significance, which can be applied to all the agents of the body and to their actions. This, in a word, is the Delsarte system, artificial and untrue, bringing narrowness, one-sided views of nature and perversion, to any one who gets within its constricting grasp.[91]

Curry declared that MacKaye was the only teacher of the Delsarte System who could make the "purposes of the exercises" clear. He complained of the fact, moreover, that "some who put themselves forth as great expounders of Delsarte . . . have obtained a little smattering from copying the note books of Mr. MacKaye's pupils' pupils." [92]

In spite of the fact that the emphasis in body training has changed, the evidence indicates that Steele MacKaye himself, in his interpretation of Delsarte, made a considerable contribution to acting technique. As late as 1925, when his son was gathering material for the father's biography, the actress Mary Shaw wrote him:

> During my first years on the stage, I heard your father give a series of talks on "Art of Expression by Gesture and Attitude." What he told and demonstrated in those talks has been the influence that illuminated all my strivings to interpret roles in the theatre. Years of effort and some achievement have proved to me how eternally true his "Basic Laws" of expression are. All the deepest joy that has come to me from great sculpture, painting, and acting has been the recognition in them of the truths his genius made so clear. . . .[93]

Mary Shaw was an actress of some prominence from 1900 until 1922.[94]

Although the picturization of various body positions used to illustrate the Delsarte principles must seem extremely artificial to students of a later generation, in fairness to the system it is well to bear in mind MacKaye's comment upon Delsarte:

> It was always his aim to get at fundamentals out of which positions will form spontaneously and *one of the worst violations of nature is to externally fix a position for each emotion.*[95]

In her study of the teaching methods of Curry and Stanislavsky, Coger gives a vivid description of Curry's beliefs and practices. Curry was the first teacher to advocate specific training for the mind. His belief in the effect of the mind upon the voice is well illustrated from the following excerpt taken from *The Province of Expression*.

> As we look upon a man stirred by great ideas which are so vivid as to stimulate and coordinate the experience of the soul, the eyes twinkle and flash, the face glows, the very textures of the muscles of the man are modulated so that the voice vibrates with emotion in ways that physiology and the science of sound have never been able to fathom. The whole man is expanded and exalted; and from the crown of his head to the soles of his feet every part of the body is speaking.[96]

Curry stressed the need for training in concentration and observation for developing the imagination. In *Imagination and the Dramatic Instinct* he maintained that the development of the imagination calls for "simple concentration, reposeful observation and the free and easy giving of ourselves to the objects around us." His explanation of feeling as resulting from "a vivid realization of relations or associations," and his example of a mother holding a little coat which recalls her little boy and the joys and hopes of other days is, of course, close to Stanislavsky's use of "emotion memory." In company with Talma, Lewes, Archer, and many others, Curry subscribed to the idea of the "dual nature" of the performer, insisting that he should feel genuine emotion while speaking, but that he must have conscious control of the situation at the same time. Curry asserted that body training was necessary for voice development but that both should be subservient to right thinking and feeling.[97] He, therefore, added emphasis upon the mental and emotional elements.

"All work for expression must be from within, outwards," Curry insisted. "While it seeks knowledge of every phase of expression, yet, in its practical application it must proceed from the mind to the body."

Another method which Curry condemned as mechanical was that based upon the scientific knowledge of voice which Dr. James Rush expounded in his *Philosophy of the Human Voice* in 1828.[98] There is no doubt that Rush made a significant contribution to the study of speech education in his treatment of the phonetic values of syllables, as well as in his study of pitch, stress, quality, and inflection. Rush has been credited with being the first investigator to see that mind is inseparable from the physical phenomena of self-expression. His system, originally a scientific method of voice training, was especially valuable in correcting defects of voice. However, in the hands of Rush's followers, beginning with the actor, James Murdoch,[99] it became a highly artificial method for expressing the outward attributes of emotion by the arbitrary control of stress, force, and voice quality. Curry commented upon an actual lesson given by a follower of Rush:

> "*Sorrow*: to be rendered by low pitch, long quantity, aspirate quality and slow time. *Joy*: rendered by high pitch, short quantity, pure tone and quick time," etc., etc. Any one in his senses who will observe nature, can see that sorrow is given in all pitches, and that joy is not confined to a high pitch.[100]

Paradoxically, most existing systems claimed nature as their model, and there was something of value in almost every one. That some of them reached a perverted form which at times approached the ridiculous was, for the most part, the fault of the overzealous efforts of their practitioners.

Notes

1. Denis Diderot, "The Paradox of Acting," in Denis Diderot, *The Paradox of Acting* and William Archer, *Masks or Faces* (New York: Hill and Wang, 1957).
2. Talma, "Reflections on Acting" in Brander Matthews, ed., *Papers on Acting* (New York: Hill and Wang, 1958).
3. Diderot, pp. 19–20.
4. Diderot, p. 56.
5. Diderot, p. 43.
6. Diderot, pp. 17–18.
7. Diderot, p. 16.
8. Henry Irving, Introduction to "Reflections on Acting," in *Papers on Acting*, p. 42.
9. Talma, pp. 48–49.
10. Talma, p. 49.
11. Diderot, p. 46.
12. Talma, p. 50.
13. Talma, pp. 45–47.
14. Talma, p.53.
15. Talma, pp. 50–51.
16. Talma, p. 55.
17. Talma, pp. 55–56.
18. Talma, p. 56.
19. Talma, pp. 57–58.
20. Constant Coquelin, "Art and the Actor," in *Papers on Acting*, pp. 26–27.
21. Michael Chekhov, *To the Actor* (New York: Harper and Brothers, 1953), pp. 21–34.
22. Coquelin, "Notes on Talma," in *Papers on Acting*, p. 274.
23. Brander Matthews, Introduction to "Actors and Acting, A Discussion by Constant Coquelin, Sir Henry Irving, and Dion Boucicault," in *Papers on Acting*, p. 162.

24. Coquelin, p. 173.
25. Irving, "Actors and Acting," in *Papers on Acting,* p. 181.
26. Boucicault in *Papers on Acting,* pp. 184–85.
27. Conversation with Vera Soloviova; Stanislavski, *An Actor Prepares,* translated by Elizabeth Reynolds Hapgood (New York: Theatre Arts Books, 1936), pp. 150–51.
28. "A Reply to 'Reflections on Dramatic Art' of Clairon," Toby Cole and Helen Krich Chiney, eds., *Actors on Acting* (New York: Crown Publishers, 1949), pp. 174–75.
29. Michel Baron, in *Actors on Acting,* pp. 158–59.
30. Matthews, "Notes on Dion Boucicault," in *Papers on Acting,* p. 280.
31. Boucicault, in *Papers on Acting,* pp. 146–47.
32. Boucicault, in *Papers on Acting,* p. 149.
33. Boucicault, in *Papers on Acting,* p. 155.
34. Stanislavski, *An Actor Prepares,* pp. 70–71.
35. Boucicault, in *Papers on Acting,* p. 155.
36. Matthews, "Notes on Dion Boucicault," in *Papers on Acting,* p. 280.
37. Henry Irving "Four Great Actors," *The Drama* (New York: Tait, Sons and Company, 1892), pp. 116–17.
38. Richard Flecknoe, "Discourse of the English Stage," in J. E. Spingarn, ed. *Critical Essays of the Seventeenth Century* (England: Oxford, Clarendon Press, 1908), p. 95.
39. Irving, "The Art of Acting," *The Drama,* pp. 178–79.
40. Nikolai M. Gorchakov, *Stanislavski Directs,* translation by Miriam Goldina (New York: Funk and Wagnalls Company, 1954), p. 402.
41. Stanislavski, *An Actor Prepares,* p. 233.
42. Irving, "The Art of Acting," *The Drama,* p. 193.
43. Irving, "The Art of Acting," *The Drama,* p. 187.
44. Irving, "The Art of Acting," *The Drama,* p. 194.
45. Irving, "The Art of Acting," *The Drama,* p. 194.
46. Stanislavski, *An Actor Prepares,* p. 252.
47. Irving, Introduction to Talma, in *Papers on Acting,* pp. 42–43.
48. George Henry Lewes, *On Actors and the Art of Acting* (New York: Grove Press n.d.).
49. Lewes, p. 94.
50. Stanislavski, *An Actor Prepares,* p. 166.
51. Lewes, p. 228.
52. Lewes, p. 146.
53. Lewes, pp. 146–47.
54. Lewes, pp. 93–94.
55. Lewes, p. 88.

56. Stanislavski, *An Actor Prepares*, p. 167.
57. Alexander Woollcott, *Mrs. Fiske, Her Views on Actors, Acting, and the Problems of Production* (New York: The Century Company, 1917), p. 104.
58. William Archer, *Masks or Faces*, in Denis Diderot, *The Paradox of Acting*, and William Archer, *Masks or Faces* (New York: Hill and Wang, Inc., 1957), p. 184.
59. Archer, *Masks or Faces*, pp. 107–12.
60. Archer, *Masks or Faces*, p. 120.
61. Archer, *Masks or Faces*, p. 122.
62. Archer, *Masks or Faces*, p. 126.
63. Stanislavski, *An Actor Prepares*, pp. 178–79.
64. Joseph Jefferson, *Rip Van Winkle, The Autobiography of Joseph Jefferson* (New York: Appleton-Century-Crofts, Inc., n.d.), p. 337.
65. Archer, *Masks or Faces*, p. 129.
66. Archer, *Masks or Faces*, p. 106.
67. Stanislavski, *An Actor Prepares*, p. 164.
68. Archer, *Masks or Faces*, p. 136.
69. Archer, *Masks or Faces*, p. 137.
70. Stanislavski, *An Actor Prepares*, p. 177.
71. Archer, *Masks or Faces*, p. 141.
72. Stanislavski, *An Actor Prepares*, p. 177.
73. Archer, *Masks or Faces*, p. 149.
74. Stanislavski, *An Actor Prepares*, p. 179.
75. Archer, *Masks or Faces*, p. 149.
76. Stanislavski, *An Actor Prepares*, pp. 175–76.
77. Stanislavski, *An Actor Prepares*, pp. 177–78.
78. Archer, *Masks or Faces*, p. 149.
79. Diderot, p. 38.
80. Archer, *Masks or Faces*, pp. 96–97.
81. Archer, *Masks or Faces*, p. 184.
82. Archer, *Masks or Faces*, p. 184.
83. Archer, *Masks or Faces*, p. 185.
84. Fred Blanchard, "Professional Theatre Schools," in Karl R. Wallace, ed., *History of Speech Education in America* (New York: Appleton-Century-Crofts, Inc., 1954), pp. 635–37.
85. Claude L. Shaver, "Steele MacKaye and the Delsartian Tradition," in *History of Speech Education in America*, pp. 202–203.

86. Shaver, pp. 204, 213.
87. Percy MacKaye, *Epoch* (New York: Boni and Liveright, 1927), Appendix, lii–liii.
88. Edyth Renshaw, "Five Private Schools of Speech," in *History of Speech Education in America,* pp. 306–307.
89. S. S. Curry, *The Province of Expression* (Boston: School of Expression, 1891), p. 336.
90. Curry, pp. 357–58.
91. Curry, pp. 359–60.
92. MacKaye, *Epoch,* Appendix, li–lii.
93. MacKaye, *Epoch,* p. 63.
94. Glenn Hughes, *A History of the American Theatre* (New York: Samuel French, 1951),
pp. 326, 339, 346, 360, 385.
95. MacKaye, *Epoch,* Appendix, li–lii.
96. Leslie Irene Coger, "A Comparison for the Oral Interpreter of the Teaching Methods of Curry and Stanislavsky" (unpublished doctoral dissertation, Northwestern University, 1953), p. 86.
97. Coger, pp. 99, 100, 112, 126, 134.
98. Curry, p. 312.
99. Lester L. Hale, "Dr. James Rush," in *History of Speech Education in America,* pp. 228–32, 235, 163.
100. Curry, p. 313.

six

Theories and Methods of Acting
in America from 1900 to 1925

At the beginning of the twentieth century, the training of actors in America entered a new phase. Opportunities for apprenticeship in the old stock companies were rare, and well-known actors were less and less inclined to private teaching. Schools of acting then became popular.[1]

POPULAR METHODS

The methods taught belied their claim of being "natural," as evidenced by a comment by Franklyn Fyles, a New York drama critic and one-time play collaborator with David Belasco. Attempting to give a picture of everyday dramatic school training, Fyles wrote:

> A class in dramatic expression . . . may consist of a roomful of young men and women striking extravagant poses in unison. . . . Or they may be prostrating themselves on the floor to lie there sprawling like swimmers and crying like lunatics. They are practising a system of stage culture. A row of pupils . . . make faces of love, hate, and other intense feelings, accompanied by highly emotional exclamations. . . . Pictures of visages in all manner of grimace, from pleasure to anguish are imitated in the practice of expression.[2]

Textbooks used during the early years of the century, and sometimes even much later, reveal an emphasis upon the *conscious control of the outward appearance of emotion.* The methods showed to a great extent the effect of either Steele MacKaye's formulation of Delsarte or Dr. Rush's Voice Culture, first popularized by the actor James Murdoch.[3]

An actor who helped to make Rush's method popular was F. F. Mackay. His book, entitled *The Art of Acting* and subtitled *The Analysis of Expression and its Application to Dramatic Literature,* which was republished in 1913, contained a commendatory letter, dated May 1, 1892, from no less a person that Edwin Booth.[4] Mackay lived a long life, from 1830 to 1923.[5] His death occurred in the year in which the Moscow Art Theatre paid its first visit to the United States. Mackay went beyond the attempt to express emotion by controlling the quality and inflection of the voice. He sought to regulate the movements of the body and even of the eyes!

> The ecstasy of all those emotions that come from impressions which produce exhilarating sensations, elevating the mind and lifting it above the plane of work-a-day life, as joy, hope, adoration and other benevolent emotions, turn the eyes upward with a look of supplication that seems to say, "Help me, all you powers above," to realize this seeming good.
>
> In anger and jealousy, the eye is constantly in motion, looking out on all sides as if on guard against an attack. In hatred, which is settled anger, the eyes have a fixed and sullen look, as if fully prepared for revenge, and only waiting the opportunity for executing their plot.[6]

A revision of the original text brought out by his son, Charles Mackay, as late as 1934, differed very little from the original except in its title, *Elementary Principles of Acting, A Textbook Aid for Teachers and Students Based on the Art of Acting by F. F. Mackay.* This edition contained an endorsement by Walter Hampden, who declared: "It carried me back many years to the time when I read with so much profit to myself your father's book, so highly recommended by Edwin Booth." [7] The book contains F. F. Mackay's definitions of the science and the technique of acting:

> The student needs to know human emotions and the various outward forms by which they are usually manifested. This knowledge so systematized and arranged as to be easily remembered and referred to, is the science underlying the art of acting. The premeditated use of those forms of voice, pose and gesture by which emotions are generally expressed in nature constitutes the technique of acting.[8]

Here, also, are listed the "Seven Modes of Utterance," which are "Effusive, Explosive, Expulsive, Sighing, Sobbing, Panting, and Gasping," and the types of stress which may be "Thorough Stress, Radical Stress, Median Stress, Final or Vanishing Stress and the Stress of Tremor." "Stress of Tremor" is explained in detail:

> Stress of tremor, the language of weakness results from the inability of the muscular power to resist, without vibration, the power of a mental impression . . .
> It is, therefore, the exponent of all emotion in the rage or ecstasy of impassioned force.[9]

The following note regarding the practice of certain selections from Shakespeare appears to place the emphasis upon the effect rather than the cause: "If the student wishes to practice on the Macbeth speeches mentioned above, he should try to attain a tremor of the whole body."

Estelle H. Davis,[10] a student of Mackay's and during the 1920s and 1930s a teacher of speech at Barnard College and Columbia University, and director of the University's Laboratory Players, presented Mackay's doctrine faithfully:

> Certain emotions tend to cause one to try to make contact with others —giving, sharing, sacrificing for. In these the body should *move out* from its center.
> In envy, greed, fear, the person curls in upon himself, shrinking from contact.
> In short, those stock positions were to be used as an artist uses a manikin or as a sort of "short hand" version of the bare bones of a pose. Then, from his imagination and also from his observation of himself and those around him, the actor was to fill in the real character.[11]

The problem for the student actor was compounded by the use of the same vocabulary in both approaches. For example, "Idealism, Imagination, Sincerity, and the greatest of these is Sincerity." [12] It seems fair therefore, to assume that the ideal or image of good acting held by those who recommended opposite approaches was to a large extent, the same. On the other hand, most of the available writing on the subject stressed the objective or goal, while very little was put down regarding the actual means of attaining it.

THE THEORIES OF FOUR PROMINENT ACTORS

Joseph Jefferson, Richard Mansfield, Louis Calvert, and William Gillette, four actors prominent in America at the turn of the century and later, have recorded in their memoirs or addresses some very definite precepts and beliefs. Jefferson and Mansfield had this in common, that neither believed that acting could be taught. Calvert and Gillette, on the other hand, have made important contributions to the discussion of acting methods.

JOSEPH JEFFERSON

Jefferson was apparently familiar with previous points of view on the subject. In his autobiography entitled *Rip Van Winkle* he said: "Much has been written upon the question as to whether an actor ought to feel the character he acts or be dead to any sensations in this direction." His conclusion was that the methods actors employ depend upon "their own natures," and he asserted that this fact renders the teaching of the art by any strictly defined lines a difficult matter.[13] His often-quoted prescription for himself, "For myself, I know that I act best when the heart is warm and the head is cool," is an almost exact translation of a statement by the French actor, M. Albert Lambert *père* (see p. 149).

With regard to the study of acting, Jefferson seemed to equate technique with mechanical matters such as voice and gesture:

> Many instructors in dramatic art fall into the error of teaching too much. The pupil should first be allowed to exhibit his quality and so teach the teacher what to teach . . . .
>
> It is necessary to be cautious in studying elocution and gesticulation, lest they become our masters instead of our servants. . . . But, even at the risk of being artificial, it is better to have studied those arbitrary rules than to enter a profession with no knowledge whatever of its mechanism.[14]

While not actually an advocate of the teaching of acting, since he believed acting to be "more a gift than an art," Jefferson advised that "A clear and unmistakable outline of a character should be drawn before an actor undertakes a new part"; and he cautioned against the actor's depending, instead, upon "our ghostly friends Spontaneity and Inspiration to pay him a visit," adding, "should they decline to call, the actor will be in a maze and his audience in a muddle." As Talma and many others before him had done, he pointed out that Hamlet's advice to the players, "these simple instructions of not more than a dozen lines contain the whole art of acting."

Jefferson warned against certain faults in acting. One he called "the unnatural trick of speaking soliloquy and side speeches directly to the audience." Another which he mentioned was an actor's attracting attention to himself and away from the important point on the stage "by the introduction of some unimportant by-play" or movement "done from ignorance" or even at times, to Jefferson's regret, "through jealousy."

In warning against distracting the attention of the audience, he emphasized the "value of repose," admonishing the actor "as soon as he ceases to be the interesting figure" to "observe the action of the other characters," adding, "this is the most natural by-play and the least likely to do harm." Since Jefferson was gifted also as a painter, many of his comparisons were taken from that art. In developing the idea of the need to refrain from unimportant movement on stage and to pay attention to "the action of the other characters," he said:

> It acts like the distance in a picture, which, being subdued, gives strength to the foreground. But the tyro is generally fearful that he will fail to attract attention, whereas obscurity instead of prominence may at times be the most desirable. To do nothing upon the stage seems quite simple, but some people never acquire this negative capacity.[15]

That Jefferson himself "paid attention to the action of the other characters" is evidenced by the tribute of the actor Francis Wilson, who in his biography of Jefferson wrote:

> But the eye was the great feature of his face. There was mildness, sweetness, frankness, fun, jollity and especially was there riveted attention in it when he listened—and no man to my knowledge ever listened better.[16]

Jefferson recounted an anecdote about Macready's having asked the criticism of a fellow player, Mrs. Warner, of his performance of an honest man accused of theft for the first time in his life. Mrs. Warner reportedly declared that whereas in his earlier performances he had spoken with "a depth of feeling and sincerity," Macready had fallen into the habit of giving his responses glibly and like one who has committed a great many thefts in his life. This story had served to remind Jefferson that he had been making a similar mistake, and he sought to overcome it "by listening to each important question as though it had been given for the first time, turning the question over in his mind as if to find the words for the reply; and by making the pauses interesting to the audience by the manner of pantomime." He declared, as Irving had done earlier, "It is the freshness, the spontaneity of acting that charms."[17]

Except for a few illustrations from his own experience, like the one above, however, Jefferson's advice for the most part consisted of general observations such as the proposition that "imagination . . . enters largely into the best form of acting," and the one just quoted regarding spontaneity. In pointing out the difference between the artist and the actor, he made the point which Gillette illustrated so well several years later:

> The artist is continually painting new pictures, but the actor must not only paint over and over again night after night the same emotions, but paint them as if he had never felt them before.[18]

RICHARD MANSFIELD

Although Richard Mansfield did not believe that acting *per se* could be taught, nevertheless, according to Wilstach, "he spent a deal of valuable time teaching people how *not* to act.[19] His efforts covered a wide range, extending from the less experienced actors in his company to his star—in the case of the young Margaret Anglin, whom he engaged to play Roxanne. When Mr. Palmer, the manager of the Madison Square Theatre, suggested that he "be more lenient," Mansfield replied:

> I am only kind. Roxanne is a great part. Only one who has suffered can play such a role. This girl has temperament and the emotions, but she is young and inexperienced. I cannot persuade her spirit. I must rouse it.[20]

In an address at the University of Chicago, Mansfield stressed the necessity for vocal culture, painting, deportment, and languages in training for the stage. He spoke of the "old days" when less was known about voice training, and referred to the fact that Edmund Kean, Kemble, and even Edwin Forrest had no voice left when, at the end of *Richard III,* they cried out, "A horse! A horse! My kingdom for a horse!"

Wilstach declared that Mansfield's own voice "grew in strength, depth, flexibility and endurance the longer he lived." His mother had been an opera singer and he attributed this control to her method. At any rate, "he was able to finish an evening of 'Cyrano,' 'Richard,' 'Peer Gynt,' or any lengthy role stronger vocally than when he began, though he was all but prostrated physically." John Corbin, the drama critic, said, "Mansfield's voice is pure gold."

As early as 1893, in an open letter to the press, Mansfield pleaded that the wealthy men "who lose a million at the turn of a hand, who build palatial clubs, vast hotels, and what not else for the glory of the nation," should build and endow a National Theatre. Seven years later, as the first speaker at a series of lectures on the drama at the University of Chicago, he made a similar plea. At this time, oddly enough, he lamented the lack of training for the actor and even declared, "We need a recognized stage and a recognized school."

However, Mansfield believed the school for the training of actors should be "a hard, hard school . . . of unmerciful criticism." He even went so far as to declare:

> You can teach people how "to act acting," but you can't teach them "to act." Acting is as much an inspiration as the making of great poetry and great pictures. What is commonly called acting, is acting acting. This is what is generally accepted as acting. A man speaks lines, moves his arms, wags his head, and does various other things—he may even shout and rant; some pull down their cuffs and inspect their finger nails; they work hard and perspire, and their skin acts. This is all easily comprehended by the masses and passes for acting, and is applauded; but the man who is actually the embodiment of the character he is creating will often be misunderstood, be disliked, and fail to attract . . .[21]

Wilstach declares: "He continually impressed his players with the necessity of feeling deeply the emotions of a role and reflecting them in their faces." He even invented a pantomime exercise for facial control which he urged his actors to practice. The actor was called upon to express through his eyes and changes in his facial expression the emotions that a child feels as he watches the approach of a storm which holds him indoors, and finally the joy as it recedes. This exercise would seem to demonstrate Mansfield's belief in the creative imagination as the spur to awaken live feelings. He himself declared, "Imagination is necessary to make a poet or an actor."

Describing him as "beau, wit, poet, painter, musician, and master of his own and many kindred arts," Wilstach said of Mansfield's art of make-up:

> He gave a painter's attention to his make-up, which he described as "painting a portrait on the canvas of the face." This portrait he illuminated with all the emotions of the role he was playing. In spite of the elaborate care he gave to the variety and detail of his make-up, he always subordinated it to the expression which he projected from within.[22]

According to Wilstach, "Mansfield understood an audience's respect for sincerity and never found anything too difficult to do or too trifling to slight." He expended great care in studying a character he was to play. "His performance of a role . . . was to him a sacred work, almost sacramental. In his make-up for Ivan the Terrible he discarded at the last moment the full flowing beard he had intended and used instead "a few straggling hairs—as though his beard had been eaten away by moths." After the performance a visitor backstage told him his make-up for the part had been an "amazingly accurate duplicate of the Kremlin portrait . . . said to have been painted in the Tsar's lifetime" and recently seen by the visitor.

Similarly, the "little, swiftly pattering run, almost like a child's," which Mansfield adopted for a moment in the final act, was said by a famous American doctor to have been an actual characteristic of the "nervous and physical decay of which Ivan IV is supposed to have died." Mansfield called these coincidences "Little instinctive returns to the actual in a player's treatment of an historical figure," and found their explanation in Hamlet's words to Horatio, "There are more things in heaven and earth, Horatio, than are dreamt of in your philosophy."

There apparently was a touch of the mystic about him, for he claimed to have dreamed the exact events which transpired in the visit of D'Oyly Carte's secretary with the offer of an engagement.

Even his complete identification with a role was accomplished by a sort of self-hypnosis. On this point Wilstach declared:

> He strove with all the hypnotic force of his imposing intellect to transform himself—*mind, heart,* and *body*—*into the role he was acting.* If one could *be,* it was not difficult to *do. Being and acting fused. He became a character* and *allowed the character to act.*23 (Italics supplied.)

Mansfield's preparations on the day of performance started with a long walk in the afternoon. After this, he partook of a "light repast at five o'clock" in solitary silence, which was unbroken until his arrival at the theatre and in his dressing room, "never less than two and sometimes three hours before his entrance."

Finally Wilstach recounts:

> When the call came for his entrance and he emerged from his dressing room a metamorphosis had taken place. It was not the actor who went

upon the scene, it was the character. By some process, and it has been called self-hypnosis, he became the person he was playing.

He carried the manner to and from and into his dressing room. He acted the role all the evening on and off the scene, and it fell away from him only as he put aside the trappings and emerged from the dressing room his own self bound for home.[24]

So great was his identification with the particular part that his reactions to the environment of the stage and backstage were entirely in the character of the person he was playing.

Mansfield himself made this admission:

Inspiration only comes to those who permit themselves to be inspired. It is a form of hypnotism. Allow yourself to be convinced by the character you are portraying that you are the character. He would be a poor, miserable pretense of an actor who, in the representation of any historical personage were otherwise than firmly convinced, after getting into a man's skin (which means the exhaustive study of all that was ever known about him), that he is living that very man for a few brief hours.[25]

In the extreme care that went into a portrayal of his characters, Mansfield resembled Stanislavsky. However, the method by which the two men arrived at their characterizations was different. Mansfield spoke of projecting himself "by force of his will into another being, into another sphere."

Stanislavsky, too, spoke of the momentary excitement of the sudden and complete fusion of the actor's life with the part he is playing. On the other hand, he never believed that the actor becomes the character. He speaks of "that closeness to your part [which] we call perception of yourself in the part and of the part in you." He made very clear, however, that the emotions which the actor experiences in the part are his own, arising out of a "position analogous to that of the character." [26]

Both Mansfield and Stanislavsky compared the development of a part to the birth of a child. However, the emphasis in each case was different. Mansfield declared:

. . . the toil, the patient study . . . the growing into the soul of the being we delineate, the picture of his outward semblance, his voice, his gait, his speech, all amount to a labor of such stress and strain, of such loving anxiety and care, that can be compared only in my mind to a mother's pains.[27]

Stanislavsky explained the metaphor in this way:

> Our type of creativeness is the conception and birth of a new being—
> the person in the part. It is a natural act similar to the birth of a human
> being.
>
> If you follow each thing that happens in an actor's soul during the
> period in which he is living into his part, you will admit that my compari-
> son is right. Each dramatic and artistic image created on the stage, is
> unique and cannot be repeated, just as in nature. . . . In the creative
> process there is the father, the author of the play; the mother, the actor
> pregnant with the part; and the child, the role to be born.[28]

With Mansfield it was "the toil," "the labor . . . of such stress
and strain," the "loving anxiety and care" that he compared to the
mother's pain at childbirth; with Stanislavsky, it was the very act of
creativity that he equated with the bringing into the world of a new
life. Moreover, in Mansfield's case, it was almost like the transmigra-
tion of his soul into that of the character; with Stanislavsky, it was
the creation of an entirely new entity, that of the actor in the role.

WILLIAM GILLETTE

The career of William Gillette, well known both as playwright and
actor and identified with the character of Sherlock Holmes almost as
closely as Jefferson was with Rip Van Winkle, covered a long period.
Born in 1855, by the time of his death in 1937 he had made himself
known to several generations.[29] In 1910 he put on a revival of his five
best-known plays; in 1917, he was seen in Clare Kummer's comedy, *A
Successful Calamity;* and in 1918, he played in Barrie's *Dear Brutus*
with Helen Hayes as his dream daughter.[30]

In 1913 he addressed a joint meeting of the American Academy of
Arts and Letters and the National Institute of Arts and Letters held in
Chicago. This address was published in the seventh number of the
proceedings of the Academy and Institute under the title of "The
Illusion of the First Time in Acting." [31] It was one of the first fairly
extensive discourses on acting methods in America which actually
gave some practical suggestions to the actor.

First, Gillette lamented the lack of adequate guides for the actor
such as exist for the "followers of other occupations and professions"
that would enable him to apply his efforts "in the most advantageous
direction." This state of rudderless confusion was augmented, Gillette

declared, by the "inane, contradictory, and ridiculous things that are written and printed on the subject."

Gillette declared: "Shakespeare has stated . . . that the true purpose of the Play is to hold the Mirror up to Nature—meaning, of course, human nature." Furthermore, he maintained that no one could "read a Play," that "the play—if it is Drama—does not even exist until it appears in the form of Simulated life." [32]

Gillette's principal concern was to show how the actor breathes life into the characer he has to portray. He accomplished this by the use of satire, referring to the faults in acting as "character assassination." The most obvious of these, "the sing-song or 'reading' intonation, the exaggerated and grotesque use of gesture and facial expression, the stilted and unnatural stride and strut," he passed over quickly, alluding to them ironically as "inherited blessings from the Palmy Days." [33]

The two most common classes of defects, "bubbling over with Dramatic Death and Destruction," Gillette labeled the "Neglect of the Illusion of the First Time" and the "Disillusion of Doing It Correctly." He mentioned a third class, also, which he called the "Illusion of Unconsciousness of What Could Not Be Known." "However," Gillette declared, "all these groups are closely related, and the 'First Time' one is fairly representative." He pointed out that the difficulty arose because the actor is "fully aware—especially after several performances—of what he is going to say," but the character he is portraying "does not know what he is going to say."

Gillette suggested the correct way for an actor to simulate life in his next remarks:

> Now it is a very difficult thing—and even now rather an uncommon thing—for an actor who knows exactly what he is going to say to behave exactly as though he didn't; to let his thoughts (apparently) occur to him as he goes along, even though they are there in his mind already, and (apparently) to search for and find the words by which to express these thoughts, even though these words are at his tongue's end. That's the terrible thing—at his tongue's very end! [34]

Gillette suggested further techniques when he maintained "matters of speech, of pauses, of giving a character who would think time to think; in behavior of eyes, nose, mouth, teeth, ears, hands, feet, etc., while he selects his words to express the thought." [35]

The next passage was close in meaning to Stanislavsky's discussion of the actor's need for "simple actions," ". . . the details that will put life into his part." [36]

This menace from Death from Neglect of the Illusion of the First Time is not confined to matters and methods of speech and mentality but extends to every part of the presentation, from the most climactic and important action or emotion to the most insignificant item of behavior—a glance of the eye at some unexpected occurrence, the careless picking up of some small object which (supposedly) has not been seen or handled before. Take the simple matter of entering a room to which, according to the plot or story, the Character coming in is supposed to be a stranger; unless there is vigilance the actor will waft himself blithely across the threshold, conveying the impression that he has at least been born in the house . . . .[37]

Stanislavsky, too, made a point of the actor's entering a room. The following excerpt from *An Actor Prepares* will illustrate the importance which he attached to it:

"Let us say that one of the persons in the play has to come into a room. Can you walk into a room?" asked Tortsov.

"I can," answered Vanya promptly.

"All right then, walk in. But let me assure you that you cannot do it until you know who you are, where you came from, what room you are entering, who lives in the house, and a mass of other given circumstances that must influence your action. To fill all that in so that you can enter the room as you should, will oblige you to learn something about the life of the play." [38]

Gillette called attention to the importance of having the right "Spirit of the Presentation as a Whole," in addition to the care needed for every single item:

Each successive audience before which it is given must feel . . . that it is witnessing, not one of a thousand weary repetitions, but a Life Episode that is being lived just across the magic barrier of the footlights. That is to say, the Whole must have that indescribable Life-Spirit or Effect which produces the Illusion of Happening for the First Time. Worth his weight in something extremely valuable is the Stage Director who can conjure up this rare and precious spirit! [39]

In speaking of the second group of defects from the "Disillusion of Doing it Correctly," Gillette commented, "speaking, breathing, walking, sitting, rising, standing, gesturing, in short behaving correctly, when the character under representation would not naturally or customarily do so." "Drama can make its appeal only in the form of Simulated Life as it is Lived," declared Gillette, "—not as various authorities on Grammar, Pronunciation, Etiquette, and Elocution happen to announce at that particular time that it ought to be lived." [40]

Actually, Gillette was making a plea for truthfulness in acting, for the use of the actor's own self or personality in the part, when he said "Among those elements of Life and Vitality, but greatly surpassing all others in the importance, is the human characteristic or essential quality . . . Personality." [41]

Both Gillette and Stanislavsky recognized that by nature an actor may be unsuited for a certain part. Stanislavsky warned:

> Here is another menace: some actors do not fully realize the limitations placed on them by nature. They undertake problems beyond their powers to solve. The comedian wants to play tragedy, the old man to be a jeune premier, the simple type longs for heroic parts and the soubrette for the dramatic. This can only result in forcing, impotence, stereotyped, mechanical action. These are also shackles and your only means of getting out of them is to study your art and yourself in relation to it.[42]

Gillette spoke of famous actors who had been unsuccessful when they "undertook parts, as they occasionally did, unsuited to their Personalities." He recalled Salvini's failure as Hamlet and Booth's unfitness for Othello. At the same time he condemned the point of view that is not satisfied with the actor "who represents with marvellous power and truth to life the characters within the limited scope of his Personality," but demands instead that a performer be "able to assume an unlimited number of totally divergent roles." This Gillette dismissed as "a question of pure stage gymnastics." [43]

LOUIS CALVERT

Louis Calvert, like Mansfield, was born in England, but he became an important part of the New York stage in the first decade of this century.[44] Like Gillette, Calvert expressed the wish that the actor might have some guiding principles, as did other artists. He lamented the fact that there was "no body of literature on the actor's art to which the novice might go for guidance." [45]

He especially regretted the absence of any actual records of how the great actors of the past had performed, and deplored the fact that biographies and autobiographies of famous actors emphasized the triumphs which they had accomplished but not the methods that they had employed in achieving them. He declared that Joseph Jefferson, in his long autobiography, had written only a few pages of great value. Furthermore, he pointed to the stage's need for a library and a museum of its own "where the history of the actor's art could be coherently presented and studied."

Although Calvert maintained that there were some simple essentials that every young actor would do well to know at the outset and which he could learn from others, he was quick to insist that he did not want "to be suspected of formulating a technique of acting." Rather he wished to assist the beginner "in finding his own technique."

Nevertheless, Calvert's book, *The Problems of the Actor,* comes closer to offering a technique for the novice than anything available in America before Stanislavsky's *An Actor Prepares,* which was not to appear until some eighteen years later. Moreover, a study of the two reveals singular agreement.

Calvert declared that his effort had been to derive from his own experiences some truths which might be of service to the beginning actor, and to state as concretely as possible some of the simple principles which bitter experience had made him believe were sound. He advised the actor to strive for simplicity and truth. Here, the closeness to Gillette and Stanislavsky is evident. Gillette spoke of Simulated-Life and Stanislavsky, of Faith and a Sense of Truth.

As indispensable qualifications for an actor Calvert listed Enthusiasm, Humanity, Imagination, Voice and Personal Appearance. Humanity, he believed, came from "a consideration and sympathy for men and women." "If we are to reproduce faithfully real people and real emotions as our life work," he wrote, "it is essential that we know people sympathetically, and like them, and feel with them when they laugh or sigh."

Stanislavsky said "a real artist must lead a full, interesting, beautiful, varied, exciting and inspiring life . . . . He should study the life and psychology of the people who surround him, of various other parts of the population, both at home and abroad." [46]

Of imagination, Calvert said, "When acting takes on the imaginative, creative qualities (as all great acting must do) it is art."

The fine ensemble acting of the Duke of Meiningen Company influenced both Stanislavsky on their Russian tour and Calvert on their visit to Drury Lane, London, 1875. He recounts his impression of a performance of *Julius Caesar* in which he was deeply moved by the actor who played the servant to Octavius Caesar. Later he learned that the role had been played by one of the company's best actors. Calvert used this as an illustration of his conclusion: "We should not judge a part by its length but by the possible 'moments' there may be in it. No part is so small but one can learn something from it." Similarly, Stanislavsky said "There are no small parts, only small actors."

Calvert had some very telling things to say about voice training, and he stressed the importance of learning techniques which enable an actor to "seem" to speak naturally. He maintained that the young actors who avoid voice training do so because of "the striving for realism and naturalness which characterizes so much of what we do in the theatre today." However, he believed that the "sonorous tone and studied utterance of actors of the old school" was the result of too little rather than too much of such study, and insisted that elocution—by which he undoubtedly meant voice and diction—was still essential for the actor.

Calvert discussed at some length what he called "getting into one's part." "We should forget our voice, and hands and feet while on the stage," he declared, "and fix the whole attention on living the character we may be playing." To assist the actor in "getting into the character," he advised him to analyze the character in his "mental laboratory" and "dissolve him into his component parts."

First, however, Calvert recommended that the actor read the entire play, or at least hear it read. He called attention to a very real danger in the use of sides: "The script we study should contain the whole of the scenes in which we have a share," otherwise the actor runs the risk of "getting a knowledge of the words before he has any idea . . . of the character of the man he is to portray." Calvert warned against learning the lines of a part before knowing why the character says them; he pointed out the danger for the beginner of having a small part in a road company, saying: "One can learn little about the art of acting by repeating the same few lines three hundred times." Moreover, he added, "He is likely to fall into the habit of parroting his lines and going through the scanty stage business he may have with scarcely a thought of its bearing on the play."

"The man, the character, should come first, then his thoughts, then his words," Calvert said, adding, "We must know, not only those thoughts the character expresses, but also we must know the thoughts he does not express." This ability to think the character's thoughts, Calvert considered essential to present a lifelike characterization. "If the lines we speak are the total of the part," he maintained, "our portrait can only be a silhouette." He suggested that during rehearsal the actor should devise very definite thoughts which he could think as reactions to the partner's speeches.

This is very close to what Stanislavsky referred to as the "inner monologue" which he recommended during performance as well. In *Stanislavsky Directs,* the book which is an almost stenographic report of some of the Russian director's rehearsals, there is a detailed explanation of this line of thought which should spring from the mental reactions of the listening actor to his partner.[47]

Calvert selected the role of Shylock to demonstrate his method. The first step was to acquire a thorough understanding of his character; the next was to "become Shylock." The means suggested was the use of the actor's own remembered experience, what Stanislavsky referred to as "affective memory." In the effort to portray the qualities of an "avaricious, revengeful old usurer," which Calvert had decided upon as the qualities of Shylock, he recalled his reactions in his childhood to a little boy he had disliked:

> I remember the cold blooded way in which I weighed the possibilities of slipping up behind him and kicking him, and making my escape. I daresay any one can recall such moments; and if one fixes his mind on them, he can bring to the surface those old primitive instincts which convention has since tended to soften and iron out. If we concentrate on such moods for a time, it is amazing how clear the motives and the psychology of a Shylock may become.[48]

The third step which he recommended for becoming the character is, in reality, improvisation. Taking the scene between Bassanio and Shylock when the former comes to ask for a loan, Calvert transferred the whole thing to the current period and also changed the dialogue into everyday speech. The purpose of this was "to practice thinking —above all thinking—and walking and gesticulating, smiling, and shrugging as such a man would." "As a result," Calvert declared "his emotions have become clearer in the light of our own emotional experiences."

The chief difference between this and Stanislavsky's use of improvisation lies in the fact that the latter is more active, involving as it does, playing with the partner.

The final step in Calvert's preparation was "to get back into the atmosphere of the play, to associate this new self we have found with the time and place and the people imagined by the dramatist." Calvert discussed the great change in the actor's use of his hands since the days of Kemble and Kean, when "every emotion had a set gesture by which it should be expressed," and "gesturing was a canonized thing; a certain position of the hands indicated pity, another, supplication, another, horror." While not condemning the "old conventions," and making the assumption that conventions then current would "in the future seem quite as quaint and futile," Calvert, nevertheless, concluded: "We have been bringing the stage closer to real life—as we suppose . . . . So it is from real life and real emotions, not from tradition, that an actor must learn his gestures today." Warning against copying a gesture or bit of business which other actors used effectively unless "it seems to fit our part," Calvert advised, "We should never force a gesture on our character, it is better to wait until the character forces a gesture on us." His conclusion was: "It may be said that nowadays, the gestures grow from the character of the person we represent, rather than from the lines he speaks." His final word was, "Thought should always precede our gestures; they should always grow from something inside." For Calvert maintained that "a thorough study of the characteristics of the man the actor is playing will obviate the need for him to think about how to move his hands or his shoulders." This bears a close resemblance to Chekhov's use of leading centers.[49]

Many of the points which Calvert emphasized were close in meaning to points made by Stanislavsky, with this difference: Calvert, like many others before him, set up broad general goals that the actor should strive for without giving any clear, well-defined course of action for attaining them. For instance, Calvert prescribed "a certain mental discipline . . . which will force us to keep our minds unswervingly on the character" and urged the actor to accomplish this by devising "ways which will aid his concentration and make him proof against the distractions that increasing familiarity with the part is pretty apt to bring."

Stanislavsky, on the other hand, devoted an entire chapter of some twenty pages to the "Concentration of Attention," including exercises to improve the power of observation. He directed the actor how to look at an object. "It is essential to reeducate ourselves to look and to see on the stage, to listen and to hear. To be attentive and to appear to be attentive are two different things," he said. "Make the test for yourselves and see which way of looking is real, and which is imitative." Stanislavsky directed the actor to carry his power of observation into his daily life as well as to "concentrate with all his being on whatever attracts his attention, to look at an object, not as any absent-minded passerby, but with penetration." "Otherwise," he warns, "his whole creative method will prove lopsided and bear no relation to life." [50]

Calvert called attention to "the many thoughts behind the spoken words." This Stanislavsky referred to as the subtext.[51] Calvert asserted that the actor should actually feel the emotions he portrays and not merely simulate them: "The actor who really moves audiences to laughter or tears does not trick them; he himself feels keenly the various emotions he seeks to express; his task is to innoculate his hearers with the same emotion."

Calvert disapproved of Coquelin and accused him of "concerning himself merely with the externals and superficialities, the visible attributes of Cyrano, instead of feeling him." On the other hand, he considered Ristori the greatest tragedienne he had ever seen.

Calvert was of the same mind with Talma, Lewes, Salvini, and Stanislavsky when he said, "It seems to me that all passion must be kept under a certain control and within the pale of art." He advised the actor "to give way to uncontrolled passion" while rehearsing in private in order "to develop his powers of expressing it," but added, "While acting, we must always remain master of our resources."

Calvert was something of a paradox, for he seems to have been ahead of his time in many instances and yet not entirely free of the older methods, as shown by the space he devoted to gesture and his inclusion of directions for the eye movements. Although Calvert maintained that the actor must be imbued with the emotion he is expressing and should, to a certain extent, blind himself to everything else, even to the fact that he is playing before an audience, on the other hand he offered a very technical analysis of Constance's speech from *King John*, beginning with the lines, "Arm, arm, you Heavens, against these perjured kings!" Here, he carefully detailed the use of pause, force, tempo, and intensity.

Stanislavsky, too, devoted much time to matters of pause, intonation, and emphasis. The purpose, however, was always to lend importance to the words the actor speaks and help him to "create the life of a human spirit in a role or a play." [52] Speaking of the need for phrasing, he says:

> This division into measures and the reading of a text according to it, oblige us to analyze phrases and get at their essence. If we do not do this we cannot know how to say them. This habit of speaking in measures will make your speech more graceful in form, intelligible and profound in content, because it forces you to keep your mind constantly on the essential meaning of what you are saying when you are on the stage. Until you achieve this there is no use either in your attempting to carry out one of the principal functions of the words, which is to convey the illustrated subject of your monologue, or even in doing the preparatory work of creating this subtext.[53]

In relation to the use of pause and intonation, Stanislavsky remarked:

> . . . a listener is affected not only by the thoughts, impressions, images, connected with the words, but also by the color tones of the words, the intonations, the silences, which round out what the words left unexpressed.
>
> Intonations and pauses in themselves possess the power to produce a powerful emotional effect on the listener.[54]

Stanislavsky continually emphasized the importance of the actor's creating an inner stream of images for the words he speaks. His direction is clear: "To an actor a word is not just a sound, it is the evocation of images. So when you are in verbal intercourse on the stage, speak not so much to the ear as to the eyes." [55]

Calvert's insistence on the actor's "living the character" and his advocacy of improvisation and the actor's use of his own "remembered experience" bear a striking resemblance to the technique of Stanislavsky. Calvert may well have been influenced by another famous English actor and director, Granville-Barker, who had visited Stanislavsky and praised his methods.[56] At any rate, Calvert's book, *The Problems of the Actor,* made a considerable contribution to acting technique in America. The critic of *Drama* magazine asserted that it was the best book that had been written on the subject.[57] If it had received wider recognition, it might have prepared the way for a more sympathetic acceptance of the Stanislavsky System, two decades later.

Notes

1. Fred C. Blanchard, "Professional Theatre Schools in the Early Twentieth Century," in Karl R. Wallace, ed., *History of Speech Education in America* (New York: Appleton-Century-Crofts, Inc., 1954), pp. 618–20.

2. Franklyn Fyles, *The Theatre and Its People* (New York: Doubleday, Page and Company, 1900), pp. 26–27.

3. Blanchard, p. 618.

4. F. F. Mackay, *The Art of Acting* (New York: F. F. Mackay, 1913), Frontispiece.

5. Oral Sumner Coad and Edwin Mims, Jr., *The American Stage: The Pageant of America,* Vol. XIV, ed. Ralph Henry Gabriel (New Haven: Yale University Press, 1929), p. 254.

6. F. F. Mackay, p. 209.

7. Charles Mackay, *Elementary Principles of Acting* (New York: Samuel French, 1934), xii.

8. Charles Mackay, p. 6.

9. Charles Mackay, pp. 144–45.

10. Mrs. Davis was the wife of the actor Samuel Coit, and co-author of E. H. Davis and Edward Mammon, *The Spoken Word in Life and Art* (New York: Prentice-Hall, 1932), and of Letitia Raubicheck, E. H. Davis, and Adele Carrl, *Voice and Speech Problems* (New York: Prentice-Hall, 1931).

11. From a letter of June 16, 1958 from Dr. Letitia Raubicheck to this writer. Dr. Raubicheck, who was director of Speech of New York City

Schools until 1958, studied with Mrs. Davis and collaborated with her in Raubicheck, Davis, and Carrl, *Voice and Speech Problems.*

12. Charles Mackay, p. 2.
13. Joseph Jefferson, *Rip Van Winkle: The Autobiography of Joseph Jefferson* (New York: Appleton-Century-Crofts, Inc., n.d.), p. 336.
14. Jefferson, p. 343.
15. Jefferson, p. 342.
16. Francis Wilson, *Joseph Jefferson, Reminiscences of a Fellow Player* (New York: Charles Scribner's Sons, 1906), p. 5.
17. Wilson, pp. 340–41.
18. Wilson, p. 245.
19. Paul Wilstach, *Richard Mansfield* (New York: Charles Scribner's Sons, 1909), p. 443. The information about Richard Mansfield and the quotations, unless otherwise noted, are from this source.
20. Wilstach, p. 317.
21. Wilstach, pp. 443–44.
22. Wilstach, p. 234.
23. Wilstach, p. 237.
24. Wilstach, p. 426.
25. Wilstach, p. 444.
26. Constantin Stanislavski, *An Actor Prepares* (New York: Theatre Arts Books, Inc., 1936), pp. 288–89.
27. Wilstach, *Richard Mansfield,* p. 443.
28. Stanislavski, *An Actor Prepares,* pp. 294–95.
29. George Freedley and John A. Reeves, *A History of the Theatre* (New York: Crown Publishers, 1941), p. 327.
30. Glenn Hughes, *A History of the American Theatre* (New York: Samuel French, 1951), pp. 359–60.
31. William Gillette, "The Illusion of the First Time in Acting," in Brander Matthews, ed., *Papers on Acting,* Notes (New York: Dramatic Museum of Columbia University, 1915), p. 275.
32. Gillette, pp. 31, 34.
33. Gillette, p. 38.
34. Gillette, pp. 39–40.
35. Gillette, p. 41.
36. Stanislavski, *An Actor Prepares,* pp. 287–89.
37. Gillette, pp. 41–42.
38. Stanislavski, *An Actor Prepares,* p. 287.
39. Gillette, p. 43.
40. Gillette, p. 44.
41. Gillette, p. 45.
42. Stanislavski, *An Actor Prepares,* p. 279.
43. Gillette, pp. 46–48.
44. Hughes, pp. 349–50.
45. Louis Calvert, *Problems of the Actor* (London: Simpkin, Marshall, Hamilton, Kent and Company, Ltd., n.d.). All the quotations from Calvert which follow are from his *Problems of the Actor.*

46. Stanislavski, *An Actor Prepares*, p. 181.
47. Nikolai M. Gorchakov, *Stanislavsky Directs*, translation by Miriam Goldina (New York: Funk and Wagnalls, 1954), p. 377.
48. Calvert, p. 72.
49. Michael Chekhov, *To the Actor* (New York: Harper and Brothers, 1953), pp. 88–91.
50. Stanislavski, *An Actor Prepares*, pp. 73, 86.
51. N. M. Gorchakov, *Stanislavsky Directs*, p. 402.
52. Constantin Stanislavski, *Building a Character*, translated by Elizabeth Reynolds Hapgood (New York: Theatre Arts Books, 1949), p. 159.
53. Stanislavski, *Building a Character*, p. 123.
54. Stanislavski, *Building a Character*, p. 137.
55. Stanislavski, *Building a Character*, p. 113.
56. Jean D'Auvergne, "Moscow Art Theatre," in *Fortnightly Review*, Vol. 101 (May, 1914), p. 793.
57. Vanderveort Sloan, "Problems of the Actor," in *Drama*, Vol. 8 (May, 1918), p. 295, cited by Louis Hetler, "The Influence of the Stanislavsky Theories of Acting on the Teaching of Acting in the United States" (unpublished doctoral dissertation, University of Denver, 1957), p. 48.

❊

seven

Changes in American Stage Practice from 1890 to 1925

In America, from 1890 to 1925, the staging of plays showed far more drastic changes than the methods of acting. This was in part, the result of the disappearance of the old stock companies and the emergence of the commercial producer. Some changes represented improvements over the old ways, but others were, unfortunately, the forerunners of theatre practices still regarded as undesirable since they seem to have placed the theatre in the category of commerce rather than art.

STAGE PRACTICE IN THE OLD STOCK COMPANIES

Although it was under the old stock companies that the American theatre grew to maturity, there were many weaknesses in their common stage practice. Chief among these were insufficient time for proper study, inadequate rehearsal, and very little "stage direction," as directing was then called.

The old stock company somewhat resembled a repertory company in that several different bills were presented in the same week. The actors often had to learn new parts while they were performing in another play, as they do in summer stock today. Otis Skinner, whose early training was gained at the Philadelphia Museum in 1877, gives a vivid description of the result of having too many parts to learn in too short a time:

Many a Saturday night I have gone to my lodgings with three parts to study for Monday matinee and night, and walked the floor till daybreak, my forehead wound in a wet towel to avoid falling asleep, cramming the words into my brain somehow—anyhow.[1]

Because of this practice the actor sometimes did not arrive at the true meaning of the character.[2]

The situation caused by too little time for preparation was made worse by inadequate rehearsals; the chief concern was with lines and "stage business," and once these were set, the play was considered ready for performance. Dress rehearsals were almost nonexistent.[3] John Drew, describing his early experiences under his famous mother's management, mentions a humorous incident which occurred because there had been no dress rehearsal, when the actors could accustom themselves and one another to their costumes. Accordingly, when Drew appeared in the red coat and white wig of a British officer, Ada Rehan, who was never able to control her laughter if anything seemed at all amusing, burst out laughing because, in his white wig, Drew reminded her of a sheep.[4]

Skinner refers to the lack of constructive direction, declaring: "One got a general idea of exits and entrances, of the *mise en scène,* with instructions to give the star the center of the stage and keep out of his way." That actors used "tricks" as short cuts in a long part is not surprising. Skinner describes some of these:

> Parts were scantily studied, inadequately rehearsed and slovenly performed. . . . If we said anything approximating the meaning of our lines, we were doing well. I learned the useful arts of faking and winging. To "wing" a part meant to have the manuscript of it tucked in your sleeve or your pocket, or thrust into the framework of the wing near your exit to be seized and scanned between scenes. Should you see an individual gazing intently into his hat while playing an intense, dramatic scene you knew he had his part concealed there. Writing sketchy cues on your cuff was an old trick.[5]

Skinner even admits that he never studied the part of the Admiral in a play called *Blackeyed Susan.* In a court-martial scene where he was seated at a table, he placed the part in the open book in front of him and read the lines.

Despite their faults, however, the old stock companies produced a great many actors and actresses who achieved fame. It seems fair to assume, therefore, that either there were many gifted performers or the audiences' demands at that time were different from those of today.

There were, of course, many exceptions to this haphazard type of production. In 1870, a New York drama critic wrote:

> When the accursed star system, and the general disorganization of the stage accompanied the other disorganizations of the war, Wallack's *alone* held fast to the good, and even now, at Wallack's alone can one see the whole of a fine play finely played. Good actors gravitate to it, attracted as it were by an innate feeling that there is the management where study and refinement will be turned to account, and there assemble audiences capable of appreciating artistic results of both.[6]

Wallack's fame, however, was soon to be eclipsed by Augustin Daly, who was to be the leading American manager for the next twenty-five years. Admittedly, Daly had received his inspiration from Burton's and Wallack's theatres.

THE EXALTATION OF THE METICULOUS

Much has been written about the Daly Company and about Augustin Daly himself. Judge Joseph Daly has written an extensive biography of his famous brother; various actors, among them John Drew and Otis Skinner, make frequent reference in their memoirs to the time spent under his management. It appears that the Daly Company was unique in a number of ways, particularly in the high standards of production and the rigid discipline enforced. Daly's insistence upon a standard that approached perfection, regardless of the number of rehearsals required, as well as the strict discipline which he imposed upon his actors, suggests Stanislavsky and his relation to the Moscow Art Theatre.

John Drew, who was the leading man of Daly's Company for thirteen years, asserts that first nights were as smooth as later ones. This smoothness of performance and excellence of ensemble won Ellen Terry's commendation.[8] The Daly Company received high praise during a London visit. The *Saturday Review* commented:

> There is not now in London, an English company as well chosen, as well trained, as brilliant in the abilities of its individual members, or as well harmonized as a whole, as the admirable Company which Mr. Daly directs. They suggest the Comédie Française at its very best. Every performance shows that they are controlled by a single mind strong in the knowledge of its own aim and ability.[9]

During the Washington engagement of *Masked Ball* Frederick Febvre, doyen of the Comédie Française, remarked on the ensemble effect in a letter to John Drew: "There is team play and accord in your company, and every one plays for the whole and not for himself." [10]

Drew himself pays Daly a compliment when he writes:

It would be difficult to imagine a company in which there was greater accord than there was at Daly's. Everything was so fine, and the associations were so pleasant. No one took offense if the morning greeting was not as friendly as it should have been for we were, in a sense, like a family. . . . Both in and out of the theatre each had consideration for the others. Our relations were more than cordial; they were affectionate.[11]

George Clarke, who frequently quarreled with Daly, twice so seriously as to cause him to leave the company, nevertheless admitted that he could not keep away in spite of the fact that he could receive more money from other managers. He insisted that he never found the same artistic atmosphere anywhere else.[12]

Mrs. Gilbert, who was one of the "Big Four" of Daly's Company and whom Daly affectionately addressed in her later years as "Grandma," suggested the word "watchfulness" as most descriptive of his influence. In 1901, two years after Daly's death, when she herself was eighty, she wrote in her *Reminiscences*:

He was so watchful, so keen to see any falling off in one's reading of a part—so quick to modify any little mannerism or foolish trick in a beginner's work; to me there doesn't seem anyone left to say, "Don't!" [13]

Coming to Daly's after experiencing for several years the haphazard methods of direction which prevailed in the old stock companies, Otis Skinner describes this "second phase of stage direction" to which he was subjected as "a period of intense instruction—the exaltation of the meticulous, with the actors made into an automaton—parrots of the director." [14]

According to Skinner:

The master director was never more effective than when he was running under forced draft; alert, nervous, inventive, insistent in perfecting the smallest gesture and the subtlest modulation of voice (I have known him, on occasion, to be dissatisfied with the crook of his leading lady's forefinger and to straighten it out, to adjust the pose of her head and turn of her foot) . . . .[15]

Judge Daly re-enforces this impression in commenting upon Clara Morris, whose "triumph had not been effected without extreme preparation. Long rehearsals with her ambitious and painstaking manager had shaped every movement and guided every inflection." [16] As is well known, Daly made Ada Rehan a star. According to Deshler Welch, Daly was completely responsible for her achievement:

> Mr. Daly taught Miss Rehan expression, movement, suppression, advance, yielding, anger, grief, terror, despair, desolation, joy, happiness, merriment . . . elocution and declamation and general stage deportment.[17]

On the other hand, William Winter, while crediting the manager with having "aided in her professional education," nevertheless insists that "in the main her conquest has been due to personal charm, originality of mind, acute and winning sensibility, abundant animal spirits. . . ." [18]

Regardless of which point of view is correct, Skinner makes the comment in connection with his last engagement with Ada Rehan that "acting was no longer a pleasure; it was an obligation; Augustin Daly was dead and without him she was helpless." [19] He adds, however, that she was ill, "often too ill to come to rehearsal."

Admirable as Daly's management was in many ways, it was not without faults. His rigorous discipline earned for him the title of "autocrat" of the stage. He demanded strict obedience to his orders; infractions were punishable by fines. A letter in his own hand dated 1894, five years before his death, and preserved in the Robinson Locke Scrapbook, directs his stage manager "to deduct the full penalty for all grievous stage waits from any one so guilty unless it is explained to your satisfaction and you agree to remit the fine. The penalty is $5 for each offense." [20]

There were fines, too, for being late, for leaving the theatre after once having entered and reported, and for speaking to the manager on business outside of his office.[21]

John Drew mentions as another limitation of the Daly theatre, "desire for novelty which sometimes had led the manager astray." Referring to the Daly production of *A Midsummer Night's Dream,* he says: "Henry Irving and many others called attention to the extraordinary and fussy confusion of the staging."

Another weakness of Daly's brought severe censure from the critic, Norman Hapgood. Hapgood alleged that in the production of *School for Scandal* Daly padded the part of Lady Teazle for Ada Rehan, even going so far as to transfer a speech from Charles Surface to allow her to make the last impression on the audience. Hapgood's comment upon the procedure in scenes where she was a member of a group casts doubt upon the complete success of the ensemble. He complains that she sat at the side while the rest of the group were speaking, and when her turn came, she took the center of the stage and the others "faded off." Hapgood accuses Daly of trying "to make the whole play over into nothing but a background for Lady Teazle," declaring:

> The grossest instances of this tendency were in the scenes between Sir Peter and Lady Teazle. When Miss Rehan spoke, Sir Peter obediently pretended he was dead. When he spoke, Miss Rehan went over to an interpolated musical instrument and pounded for the attention of the audience. . . .[22]

Whatever his faults may have been, Daly's emphasis upon smooth production and his efforts toward perfection were contributions to the improvement of stage practice. Daly believed that an actor should be able to play any part and he insisted upon versatility in the members of his company. According to his brother, his "purpose was to break away from tradition; to free actors from the trammels of 'lines' into which they had settled as in a groove. . . . He astonished his players by throwing them into parts for which they thought they had no fitness." [23]

In 1898, one year before Daly's death, J. Rankin Towse paid him tribute for continuing to have a stock company in spite of the fact that many other managers were abandoning that system:

> Mr. Daly is the last surviving representative of the type of manager who formed, developed, and preserved the best traditions of the stage and justified the claims of the theatre to be numbered among the arts. . . . He has proved almost to demonstration that stock companies are indispensable to a healthful dramatic condition.[24]

Nevertheless, there appears to be some contradiction between Daly's insistence upon a fine ensemble and the fact that toward the end of his career he elevated Ada Rehan from leading lady to star.

THE STAR SYSTEM AND BOX OFFICE APPEAL

The chief objection to the so-called "star system" was, of course, that it centered the attention upon one player, using the rest of the company merely to emphasize the star's importance. The very word "supporting" players, still in use, bears witness to the evils of the system which followed the era of the stock company and which, unfortunately, still exist.

It was Charles Frohman who earned the epithet, "the star-maker"; it was he who had the beautiful Empire Theatre built at Fortieth Street and Broadway in 1893. Although he called his company the Empire Theatre Stock Company, it was not that in the true sense of the word because of the presence of a star in all productions.[25]

His choice of actors, as well as of the plays to be presented, was dictated by their audience appeal, and he made the "box office" rather than "artistic faith" the motivating power behind every production.[26]

Nevertheless, Charles Frohman developed a great many actors and actresses, among them Ethel Barrymore, Henry Miller, Maude Adams, Robert Edeson, May Robson, Arthur Byron, Margaret Anglin, John Drew, William Gillette, Julia Marlowe, Blanche Bates, and William Faversham. Each of these became a star. He placed the importance of the actor above that of the play, and he contended that the American public preferred personalities to plays. He asserted that the doers of great deeds appeal more strongly to the imagination than the deeds.[27]

Frohman's biographer, Isaac F. Marcosson, attributes to him the "genius for singling out gifted young women," declaring: "He conducted their rehearsals with a view of developing all their resources and to show every facet of their temperament." [28] This statement gives us no idea, however, of his actual stage practice.

Charles Frohman began his career managing a road company of *Hazel Kirke,* Steele MacKaye's realistic drama. He got his start as a producer because he was canny enough to see the appeal of Bronson Howard's *Shenandoah.* His success at the beginning of this century was phenomenal. According to Glenn Hughes, "he operated five theatres in New York City, one in London, and he controlled the bookings in several hundred others scattered throughout the United States. . . . Yet this theatrical tycoon, the first of his kind, was reported to be excessively modest, even shy."

For all his emphasis upon the commercial side of the theatre, Charles Frohman apparently maintained a close personal relationship with the stars under his management. When he was about to sail for London on the "Lusitania," Ethel Barrymore made a special trip from Boston to say goodbye to him. Speaking of his tragic death in the sinking of the "Lusitania," she writes of him with warmth and affection:

> . . . We had to accept the terrible fact that Mr. Frohman had gone. For many years, he had been my very best friend. He had taken the place of parents and I had gone to him with not only my theatre troubles, but all my troubles. He had always been understanding and wonderful.
>
> Nothing was ever quite the same after that for me.
>
> I shall always remember him with love. A wonderful, golden man.[29]

Near the close of her *Memories,* Ethel Barrymore mentions him again: "And, incidentally, in all the years I have never ceased to miss Mr. Frohman." Maude Adams' retirement from the stage at an early age, so soon after Frohman's death, has been ascribed to her dependence upon him.

DAVID BELASCO AND THE PERFECTION OF REALISTIC DETAIL

Charles Frohman was largely responsible for David Belasco's coming to New York to be the stage manager of the Madison Square Theatre and later of the Lyceum, both of which were operated by Frohman's brother, Daniel. In the beginning of the twentieth century, Belasco became Charles Frohman's chief rival. Coad and Mims report that after Frohman's death he was the dean of American producers and regarded as the patriarch of the American theatre.

Many actors and actresses publicly acknowledged the value of Belasco's training. Among those were Jane Cowl, Judith Anderson, Mrs. Leslie Carter, Frances Starr, Leonore Ulric, Mary Pickford, David Warfield, Leo Dietrichstein, Lionel Atwill, and Arthur Byron.[30] It was an accepted fact that Belasco made a star out of Mrs. Leslie Carter, who came to him without any training for the stage.

By his own account he subjected Mrs. Carter to a rigorous routine for a period of two years. This consisted of a systematic course in calisthenics and dancing "for the cultivation of grace and repose," long walks daily, and planned vocal instruction. Belasco asserts that her breathing, enunciation, and voice placement corrected and improved as a result of the voice training, and that the physical exercises overcame her fault of "too much facial expression from nervousness."

After months of technical exercises Belasco permitted Mrs. Carter to read aloud to him until "she grew accustomed to hear herself speak." Then came short scenes, including that of the second player's speech in *Hamlet,* to make her speak "trippingly on the tongue." By this time, Belasco declares, "She had acquired sufficient technique to utilize to the best advantage all her natural gifts of imagination and emotion." To teach her to make "sudden transitions of intense emotions," Belasco played a scene from *Oliver Twist* with her in which he himself impersonated Bill Sikes.[31]

Of Belasco's actual stage practice, there are occasional statements only. They offer little concrete example of any method. In an interview with Ada Patterson which appeared in *Theatre* in 1906, he says:

> During six weeks of rehearsal I give my attention to two things in my cast. I suppress that which is undesirable and develop that which is desirable. I do it first by talking to each person about his or her part. I tell the story as my mother used to tell me stories in my boyhood, with the desire to interest and instruct. I gain the person's confidence. I talk until there is a sudden brightening of the eyes and an intake of breath. . . . I know then that he has the idea, and I pass on to the others. . . . There are so many things I do without being able to give the reason for them that I suppose I am, as you say, psychic.[32]

In his autobiography, *The Theatre through Its Stage Door,* Belasco declares:

> At the outset I suggest little to my people, in order to make them suggest more. I appeal to their imagination, emotion, and intelligence and draw from them all I can. When I can get no more from them, I then give them all there is in me. I coax and cajole, or bulldoze and torment, according to the temperament with which I have to deal.[33]

Belasco seems to have paid great attention to what is generally called the "reading of lines," for he maintained:

> I believe in little things. I know their value. The transitions of tone are marvelous factors in gaining effects. In life the transitions often tell the entire story of emotion. The tones follow the gamut of feeling. Therefore I work hard upon the tonal effects in my plays.[34]

By his own admission Belasco sometimes "kept his people on the stage twenty hours at a stretch, making some of them read a single line perhaps fifty times, experimenting with little subtleties of intonation or gesture, and going over bits of business again and again." [35]

This may well be an exaggeration; Belasco was given to overstatement. Both Winter and Timberlake in their biographies of the famous producer take occasion to correct inaccuracies or exaggerations in Belasco's own account of his achievements.

One example of this is Winter's correction of Belasco's claim to having established "a new style of acting and playwriting," even as early as when he was stage manager for Daniel Frohman at the Madison Square Theatre. Winter writes, "Another of Belasco's completely mistaken and indeed comically errant notions is set forth in the following paragraph from his 'story' ":

> Coming to New York as a stranger, I knew I had a task before me *to introduce the new style* of acting which I felt was destined to take the place of the melodramatic method. . . . For a long time I had promised myself to give the public *a new style of acting and playwriting, all my own.* . . . New York audiences had been trained in a school of *exaggerated stage declamation, accompanied by a stage strut, and large classic, sweeping gestures,* so, when *I introduced the quiet acting,* we were laughed to scorn, and the papers criticized our 'milk and water' methods. *It was all new,* and those who saw went away stunned and puzzled. We were considered extremists at the Madison Square Theatre, but we persisted, with the result that *our method* prevails today. The italics are mine.—W.W.) [36]

Winter refutes Belasco's contention with examples of actors whose performance exemplified "quiet acting," including in his list Betterton, Garrick, Macready, Edmund Kean, Jefferson, and Edwin Booth, "an actor who could speak blank verse as if it were the language of nature, and always did so."

The famous old critic also points out that Daly's company had drawn unfavorable comment in 1875 from the San Francisco *Evening Bulletin,* whose critic was "displeased by the delicate, refined, '*quiet*' acting which had charmed New York":

> The Fifth Avenue Theatre Company have a style of their own. It is emasculated of vigor, force in action, and anything like declamation in reading. It is *quiet, elegant, languid;* making its points with a French shrug of the shoulders, little graceful gestures, and rapid play of features. The voice is soft, the tone low, and the manner at once subdued and expressive. It pleases a certain set of fashionables, but to the general public it is acting with the art of acting left out.[37]

Timberlake also takes exception to this particular claim of Belasco, calling it an "absurd statement" which "revealed once again his capacity for exaggeration and self assertion":

Even in Belasco productions the critics were occasionally placed under the painful necessity of calling attention to actors who reeled, staggered, clutched scenery and bawled out their lines in a manner that quite o'erstepped the modesty of nature. Hamlet's advice to the players was written 280 years before Belasco invaded New York, and, despite the latter's acknowledged directorial ability, it is doubtful if he had single handedly improved the basic recipe for the art of acting.[38]

No one has denied that from the very beginning of his career Belasco lavished great attention on details, sparing no effort to make the settings for his plays as realistic as possible. The extreme to which he was willing to go was illustrated in his production of *The Governor's Lady,* where he reproduced in exact detail a well-known restaurant of his day.

An example of Belasco's inventive genius can be seen in the effect he achieved in *The Darling of the Gods.* The inspiration for the "River of Souls" came quite by accident. After an all-night rehearsal Belasco was completely discouraged with the stage effect, which was supposed to give the appearance of a Japanese purgatory where "the bodies of the dead floated between Heaven and Hell," and he gave orders for the set to be struck. When everything had been removed except a gauze curtain lighted from the rear by two calcium lights, the form of a stage carpenter walking behind the scrim cast "eerie shadows on the shifting gauze." This was exactly the effect Belasco had been working for. The scene which he finally achieved gave the effect which today is produced by the Linnebach rear projector. The *New York Sun* commented on the "sheer, unearthly beauty . . . with its plasticity of wave, its haunting lights and the dim wraiths that flit through this Oriental Styx." [39]

Winter's statement of Belasco's contribution is given in his summation of the "Nature of Belasco's Talents and Services":

> . . . his judgment, taste, and expert skill in creating appropriate environment, background, and atmosphere for a play and the actors in it are marvellous. His attention to detail is scrupulous; and his judgment is prompt and usually unerring. No theatrical director within my observation,—which has been vigilant and has extended over many years,—has surpassed him in the exercise of that genius which consists in the resolute, tireless capability of taking infinite pains.[40]

It seems regrettable that the plays he chose were not always worthy of the limitless time, care, and effort which he lavished upon them.

The Merchant of Venice was Belasco's only production of a classic for the professional stage. It was that production, with David Warfield as Shylock, that Stanislavsky saw and praised. Timberlake quips: "He was spared *The Bachelor Father* and *Lily Sue*."

Alexander Woollcott laments that Belasco's poor taste associated him always with second- and third-rate plays. Commenting upon the fact that his generation "witnessed the greatest flowering of dramatic literature since the glory that was Greece," he remarks that Belasco never produced any of the plays of the great contemporary playwrights, although "Ibsen, Tchekhov, Andreyev, Hauptmann, O'Neill, Synge, Galsworthy, Shaw, Barrie, Barker, Dunsany and Brieux were writing them"; instead, he "seems to have spent all his years in the theatre in a kind of puzzled and timorous avoidance of the company of its great men." [41]

Arthur Hornblow's appraisal of Belasco in his own time is more generous:

> The secret of Belasco's success is that he is never in a hurry. Unlike some of his brother managers, who hastily throw their plays on the stage, he takes his time. Each play is carefully prepared and rehearsed—sometimes as long as a year being spent on one production—and as a result he seldom has to record a failure.[42]

> Belasco's contribution to the American drama is that of a producer and stage director rather than of an author. His plays, mostly melodramas, have little permanent value, but as a creator of stage effects, in elaboration of detail, in arrangement of actors and stage pictures, he is recognized to be without a master in the modern theatre.[43]

To Belasco, together with Mrs. Fiske and her husband, manager Harrison Grey Fiske, as well as many other fine actors including Richard Mansfield and Joseph Jefferson, must be given the credit for opposing the theatrical trust known as "The Syndicate." The trust included Klaw and Erlanger, New York booking agents; Nirdlinger and Zimmerman, theatre managers of Philadelphia; and Al Hayman and Charles Frohman, owners of the Empire Theatre in New York City. By applying the methods of "big business" to theatre management, these men seized control of most of the theatres in large cities across the country and attempted to force their terms upon actors and managers in booking their productions. Actually, the power of the Syndicate was broken by the coming of the three Shubert brothers from Syracuse. They "eventually created a nation-wide network of their own theatres, challenging the Syndicate in every center, and opposing Trust with Trust." [44] The result was not one master but two!

Summing up the accomplishments of the first decade of the twentieth century, Glenn Hughes comes to the conclusion that although the theatre "was active, prolific and popular, it was for the most part lacking in artistic distinction" except for revivals or the "work of contemporary foreigners such as Ibsen and Shaw." His reasons are these:

> There were many gifted actors before the public, and there were skillful producers behind the scenes, but the bulk of their efforts was expended on plays of momentary interest. Harrison Grey Fiske, Arnold Daly, Winthrop Ames, and a few others carried "the banner of the ideal," but the great majority were content to wring dollars from the sentimental or the sensational type of entertainment.[45]

IN PURSUIT OF THE IDEAL

Harrison Grey Fiske was the editor of what George Freedley has called "that fine theatrical newspaper, the *New York Dramatic Mirror*." [46] In 1890 he had married Minnie Maddern, who as Mrs. Fiske became one of America's leading actresses. He was her manager, and in 1894 he presented her in *A Doll's House*. In 1901 he leased the Manhattan Theatre for his wife and was thereafter responsible for many other fine productions of Ibsen with Mrs. Fiske in the leading roles. Considerable study made her interpretation of Hedda in *Hedda Gabler* a fine achievement.[47]

Fiske also introduced the Polish actress, Bertha Kalich, to New York audiences. W. B. Leavitt in his *Fifty Years in Theatrical Management* characterizes Fiske as a "prominent producing manager, personally directing the rehearsals and supervising all the details of the production of plays which he presents." [48]

The other "contemporary foreigner" whose works were presented during this period was George Bernard Shaw; and the man most often associated with his plays, both as actor and producer, was Arnold Daly. Originally an office boy of Charles Frohman's, Daly became an actor in 1892, and beginning in 1904, he introduced American audiences to a number of the Irish playwright's works. In 1903 Daly had played Marchbanks in the first professional production of *Candida* in New York; the play was a hit and lasted for 133 performances.[49] The following year he was responsible for Shaw's writing *How He Lied to Her Husband* to "fill out the evening" for *The Man of Destiny*, which Daly was currently playing.[50]

In 1904 Daly revived *The Man of Destiny* for eight performances and in 1905 he opened a two months' repertory season with six plays of Shaw; at this time he introduced *Mrs. Warren's Profession.* For this last, he and his leading lady, Mary Shaw, were arrested and taken to court "for presenting an immoral play"; but in spite of much furor in the press, they were acquitted.[51]

In 1907 Daly revived *Candida;* this he played with Margaret Wycherly. As late as 1915, Arnold Daly was still presenting a repertory company in three Shaw plays.[52]

Winthrop Ames was distinguished as a producer in two connections. In 1909 he was appointed the director of the New Theatre, the magnificent marble structure erected on Central Park West by the directors of the Metropolitan Opera House as a result of much agitation on the part of a group of theatre lovers to get some wealthy men to build and endow a repertory theatre for the presentation of the classics and the best American plays. The New Theatre was the first endowed repertory theatre in America,[53] although ten years earlier the well-known Boston critic, Henry Austin Clapp, had strongly advocated an endowed repertory theatre.

The New Theatre opened on November 6, 1909 with a revival of Shakespeare's *Antony and Cleopatra,* and Sothern and Marlowe as guest stars. There were five productions during the first year, with such actors as Louis Calvert, Grace George, Rose Coghlan, and Matheson Lang in prominent parts.

It was apparent soon after the first performance, however, that the acoustics were faulty and the house so large that the actors were almost inaudible. Moreover, "the public did not show any great enthusiasm for the ambitious venture." Nevertheless, Ames continued his efforts in the interest of art and opened the second season at the New Theatre with a revival of *Twelfth Night,* in which Annie Russell played Viola and Louis Calvert, Sir Toby. The repertory consisted of another Shakespeare revival, *The Winter's Tale; The Witch,* John Masefield's adaptation of *Anne Pedersdotter,* a play by the Norwegian, Hans Wiers-Jenssen; *A Son of the People,* by Sophus Michaelis; Maeterlinck's poetic play, *Sister Beatrice,* which was given with the fourth act of Ibsen's *Brand;* and finally, on October 1, 1910, Maeterlinck's *The Blue Bird.* The New Theatre continued its run of *The Blue Bird* until November 7. Then it was moved to another theatre and the repertory at the New Theatre continued.[54]

Four more productions were added before the close of the year, including another Shakespeare revival, *The Merry Wives of Windsor,* and another Maeterlinck play, *Mary Magdalene.* In January, 1911, Ames presented the American premiere of Josephine Preston Peabody's prize-winning play, *The Piper,* which had been chosen to open the new Shakespeare Memorial Theatre in England.[55] Edith Wynne Matthison played the part of the Piper.

However, in spite of the excellence of the productions and the superiority of the choice of plays, the New Theatre was a financial failure, and after its brave attempt at repertory for two seasons, the theatre was taken over by commercial interests and renamed The Century. In addition to its tremendous size and poor acoustics, two other factors believed to have contributed to its demise were "the mixing of the star and repertory systems (which are antithetical), and the lack of an important body of native plays." [56]

Ames' second significant venture was the opening, in 1912, of the "Little Theatre," which was, in Arthur Hornblow's words:

> . . . a small auditorium with no balcony and very small seating capacity but decorated and upholstered as exquisitely as a royal boudoir, where under the intelligent direction of Mr. Winthrop Ames, are presented from time to time plays of a higher intellectual order than are usually to be seen in Broadway theatres.[57]

Opening with *The Pigeon* by Galsworthy, the next year Ames presented a fantasy by Laurence Housman and Granville-Barker entitled *Prunella.* This was followed by Shaw's comedy, *The Philanderer,* which ran for 103 performances.[58]

Ames continued his interest in European playwrights. His participation, in 1913, in Professor George Pierce Baker's Harvard "47 Workshop" in acting, directing, scenic design, costume design, and lighting, along with such other outstanding men and women of the theatre as Alexander Dean, Theresa Helburn, John Mason Brown, Walter Prichard Eaton, Kenneth Macgowan, Mary Morris, Osgood Perkins, Robert Edmond Jones, Lee Simonson, Donald Oenslager and many others, bears witness to the extent of his dedication to artistic production.[59]

Another producer who attempted to break away from the star system was the actress-manager Grace George. In 1915 she made a gallant effort to establish a stock company at the Playhouse with a group of top-rank actors, which included Louis Calvert, Conway Tearle, Ernest Lawford, and Mary Nash. She succeeded in reviving Langdon

Mitchell's brilliantly amusing comedy, *The New York Idea,* and presented the American premiere of Shaw's *Major Barbara.* She too found, however, that "modern theatrical conditions imposed well nigh insurmountable difficulties in the way of maintaining a permanent stock organization." [60]

Several years earlier, her husband, William A. Brady, had made an abortive attempt to establish a repertory company at the Playhouse, for which effort he earned what may seem like extravagant praise from W. B. Leavitt:

> His work has been of inestimable value, and he is following in the footsteps of his illustrious predecessor, Augustin Daly, in establishing a dramatic repertoire company of the highest class at his new theatre, the "Playhouse," and there is no one better qualified than he is to duplicate Mr. Daly's achievements in this generation. Both were animated by the same ambition to maintain the highest possible dramatic standards. [61]

Leavitt's comment is further witness to one more sincere, if unsuccessful, attempt to reinstate a repertory theatre in New York City.

Arnold Daly, Mary Shaw, Mrs. Fiske, Winthrop Ames, and Grace George were a part of what Dickinson calls The Insurgent Theatre, [62] and while their attempts to reform the commercial theatre came to nothing, the strivings toward a new theatre showed some signs of progress in other quarters. Dickinson is of the opinion that the very failure of Ames' New Theatre served to point out the need for "a change of impulse" in that "the stimulus of investment must give way to the stimulus of creation." He finds a causal relation between the New Theatre's capitulation and the interest in smaller scale production that followed. He points out three great needs that any new theatre must meet: "a better system of expense values; a more dependable and enlightened audience; an impulse coming from the artists rather than from the investors." [63]

THE RISE OF THE LITTLE THEATRE

These needs were met near the end of the first decade of the twentieth century by the little theatres which began to spring up in different sections of the country. Notable among these was that in Ravinia Park in Chicago, under Donald Robertson; Wisconsin's Dramatic Society; the Wisconsin Workshop in Milwaukee; the Chicago Little Theatre of Maurice Browne and his wife, Ellen Von Volkenburg; and the little theatre established by Sam Hume in association with the Arts and Crafts Society of Detroit. There were many and varied avowed purposes of the different little theatres, such as the presentation of plays not likely to be produced by the commercial theatre, the fostering of native playwrights, meeting community needs, improving the taste of the audience, and last but not least, improving the methods of acting and staging. Usually the actors worked for the mere joy of creating, and there was no fee except for the director. In many cases there was no rental charge for the theatre building, which sometimes was located in a college or university.

One of the little theatres connected with a college was that of the School of Drama of the Carnegie Institute of Technology. Here students were prepared for professional careers on the stage, and here, too, in their own little theatre, the School of Drama offered selected groups of citizens of Pittsburgh the opportunity of seeing plays free of charge and well produced by such capable directors as Donald Robertson, B. Iden Payne, and William Poel.

Another group connected with a university was the famous "47 Workshop" established in 1912 by Professor George Pierce Baker at Harvard, with his students and a group of young women from Radcliffe. It was intended as a laboratory in play production and was founded for the purpose of providing the members of Professor Baker's classes in playwriting with the benefits of subjecting their work to a critical audience and of supplying the young playwrights with practical experience in all phases of production.[64] Many of Baker's students became the founders of little theatres in New York City. Notable among these were Eugene O'Neill, Theresa Helburn, and Lee Simonson.

THE NEIGHBORHOOD PLAYHOUSE

Three of the most outstanding little theatres in New York City were The Neighborhood Playhouse, The Provincetown Playhouse, and The Washington Square Players, which later became The Theatre Guild. The first of these, The Neighborhood Playhouse, began as an outgrowth of the Henry Street Settlement, "a flowering of its spirit and work." [65] It was formed to provide an outlet for neighborhood talent and was a reality in fact before it had a theatre building of its own. It owed its existence to the generosity of Alice and Irene Lewisohn,[66] who were soon joined by Agnes Morgan. Several years later Helen Arthur, a young lawyer and a secretary at the Shubert office and former member of Professor Baker's Harvard "47 Workshop," became the group's business manager.[67] Writing of the organization more than forty years later, Alice Lewisohn declares, "The Neighborhood Playhouse grew from the need to integrate the media of production at a time when photographic representation dominated the commercial stage." It acquired its own home at the corner of Grand and Pitt Streets in the lower East Side on February 12, 1915. After presenting its first play, *The Shepherd*, which was concerned with the revolutionary movement in Russia and with Tolstoyan ideas of non-resistance, it turned to two plays by Galsworthy, *The Silver Box* and *The Mob*. Galsworthy was present at the second and praised it highly. He even declared that it was superior to the London production which he had directed.

The Neighborhood Playhouse achieved fame, however, with its production, in the season of 1921–1922, of *The Grand Street Follies*, an original burlesque of well-known theatre personalities, somewhat in the whimsical manner of Balieff's *Chauve Souris*, which had just taken New York by storm. Because of its great success, *The Grand Street Follies* became a yearly institution. In seven years The Neighborhood Playhouse had grown from the children's clubs of the Henry Street Settlement and their festivals into a theatre. Engaging a permanent company in 1924, it continued to encourage folk art and to present more unusual programs than those of the other two little theatres in New York. Among these were the appearance of the distinguished Hindu poet, Rabindrinath Tagore, and the actor, Jacob Ben-Ami. The latter presented a program in Yiddish before he had learned English. In the 1924–1925 season the Neighborhood Playhouse presented Joyce's *Exiles* and the Sanskrit comedy, *The Little Clay Cart*. These were followed by *The Dybbuk*.

Because of their enthusiasm over the productions of the Moscow Art Theatre and the method of Stanislavsky, the managers of The Neighborhood Playhouse made arrangements to have their students study with Richard Boleslavsky, a former member of the Moscow Art Theatre and its First Studio, during the summer and in evening classes in the fall of 1923. This marked the first time the Stanislavsky System was taught in America. Boleslavsky also directed two of the three plays which the Playhouse presented as its opening bill in 1923. An attempt at repertory in 1926 was unsuccessful and Miss Lewisohn asserts that the financial pressures, the handicap of location, the physical dimensions of the building, and the growing intensity of the work made it necessary to close The Neighborhood Playhouse the following year. Its ideals and its method of integrating all the crafts of the theatre were continued, however, when the Neighborhood Playhouse School of the Theatre was created a year later. Since its founding in 1928 it has been one of the staunchest supporters of the Stanislavsky System in New York City.

THE PROVINCETOWN PLAYERS

The second of these little theatres and perhaps the most famous of the three, The Provincetown, was created in the summer of 1915 in "an old fish house on a wharf" in Provincetown, Massachusetts, by a group of writers and artists, among whom were Susan Glaspell and a "shy, dark boy, named Eugene O'Neill." Actually it was not until the end of the second summer that the group formed the idea of continuing their work in New York. It was then that they took the name The Provincetown Players, and at the suggestion of O'Neill, they called their home in Greenwich Village at 139 MacDougal Street, The Playwrights' Theatre. During the first season their announcement carried the following statement:

> The impelling desire of the group was to establish a stage where play-wrights of sincere, poetic, literary and dramatic purpose could see their plays in action and superintend their production without submitting to the commercial manager's interpretation of public taste.[68]

The Provincetown gave O'Neill his opportunity. In helping him to fame, it became famous. The relation between O'Neill and The Provincetown may be compared to that of Chekhov and the Moscow Art Theatre.

O'Neill gave the theatre a claim to fame on another score. James Weldon Johnson has said: "The Provincetown Playhouse was the initial and greatest force in opening up the way for the Negro on the dramatic stage." The Provincetown's service to the Negro consisted in its presentation of the first all-Negro play, O'Neill's *The Dreamy Kid,* and the use of Negro actors in Negro roles in this and other plays, O'Neill's *The Emperor Jones* and *All God's Chillun Got Wings,* and Paul Green's *In Abraham's Bosom.* Charles Gilpin created the title role in *The Emperor Jones,* and the Provincetown tasted success for the first time. In a revival of this play in 1924 Paul Robeson played the leading part. The following year the Province-town presented him in his first performance as a singer. With the success of *The Emperor Jones* the Provincetown lost its amateur standing. O'Neill's play was taken uptown to the Selwyn Theatre for four special matinee performances, which lengthened into five weeks. It was subsequently transferred to the Princess Theatre where it played two hundred performances and then started a road tour that lasted two years. O'Neill's next play, *The Hairy Ape,* on which, in its direction, the Broadway producer-director, Arthur Hopkins collaborated with the Provincetown's James Light, was finally taken over by Mr. Hopkins and moved uptown to the Plymouth on April 17, 1922, a little over a month after its opening at the Provincetown.

In 1923 The Provincetown Players was dissolved because the founders felt that the purpose and atmosphere of the original no longer existed. Accordingly, the name was changed to the Experimental Players, although the playhouse, now at 133 MacDougal Street, still went by the name of The Provincetown Playhouse. Under the reorganization the directors were Eugene O'Neill, Kenneth Macgowan, and Robert Edmond Jones. Under their guidance the Provincetown continued until 1925.

In the old days before 1920, the members of the Provincetown had lived and worked together, and their work became their play. Their oneness of purpose is reminiscent of the Moscow Art Theatre. Speaking of the difference under the new regime, Deutsch remarks:

> For, despite the fact that Jones used to gather the players in the club room and read to them from Stanislavski's "Life in Art," the spontaneous group-life of the days before the arrival of fame and fortune was not there.

For the season of 1924–1925, Macgowan and his codirectors leased the Greenwich Village Theater and succeeded in running the two playhouses with a permanent company in repertory. In the prospectus, the advantage of "the security of permanent employment and . . . of constant work together" was mentioned. A further claim made was that "all will work toward a creative ensemble." This may well have been a result of a visit of the Moscow Art Theatre. In April, 1923, Macgowan had written in *Theatre Arts Magazine* under the title of "And Again Repertory":

> The visit of the Art Theatre is . . . a lesson in the most essential part of the art of the theatre. It shows us sharply individualized characterizations, a virtuosity of impersonation on the part of each player, the highest proficiency and the most sincere and sustained spiritual effort, and the welding together of all the various performers of a play into an ensemble of fluid, varied yet concerted and pointed quality.[69]

Deutsch credits the visits of the Moscow Art Theatre as well as the "recollections of the old Provincetown camaraderie" with the attempt on the part of the members of the Provincetown, including the stage crew, to come together in weekly dinners in what she terms "a mildly self-conscious communal 'life in art.'" In the group activity that existed for a time, at least, all contributed their time and effort to the enterprise, whether in planning promotion or publicity or in seeking out necessary stage properties. Because of their economic security, Deutsch remarks that "the actors had the energy and time to read plays together, direct each other in informal rehearsals, study voice production and Dalcroze . . . ." [70] This may be taken as an indication of what a professional, well-regarded group of American actors were doing in 1924 and 1925 in the way of self-improvement.

That the Provincetown Players were in sympathy with the Moscow Art Theatre seems evident for reasons other than Jones' recourse to *My Life in Art*. For one thing, after the Art Company had returned to Russia, several of its artists who remained behind were connected with the Provincetown as directors or actors. In October, 1924, Stark Young's play, *The Saint,* was directed by Richard Boleslavsky, Robert Edmond Jones, and Stark Young, and the part of Paris Pigeons was played by Maria Ouspenskaya, one of the actresses who had chosen to stay in America; and in November, 1926, the Provincetown presented *Princess Turandot,* adapted from the Russian version which had such an outstanding success as directed by Stanislavsky's gifted pupil, Vakhtangov. The New York production was directed by Leo Bulgakov, another pupil of Stanislavsky, member of his First Studio and of the Moscow Art Theatre. His wife, Barbara Bulgakov, played the title role.

In 1925, however, the MacDougal-Greenwich Village Theatre combination had been dissolved. James Light and Eleanor Fitzgerald had assumed the leadership of the Provincetown, retaining the name, Experimental Theatre, Inc., while Macgowan, Jones, and O'Neill continued to operate the Greenwich. At first subscribers were invited to subscribe to plays offered at either house or to those offered at both houses at reduced prices. The Provincetown announced the return to its original purpose of offering opportunities to new American playwrights and of favoring experimental plays. O'Neill remained on the Board of Directors.

The new playwrights and experimental plays, unfortunately, did not materialize in great enough numbers to secure financial success.

The Provincetown put on Paul Green's *In Abraham's Bosom,* which did not draw audiences until after it was awarded the Pulitzer Prize. It was directed by Jasper Deeter and brought the Negro actor, Frank Wilson, to prominence. Paul Green was the first authentic American folk dramatist, and the Provincetown performed a service for him that was similar to its service to O'Neill. It also produced *Him,* by the poet e. e. cummings, and again drew enthusiastic audiences. However, financial difficulties multiplied until a gift of $15,000 from Otto H. Kahn sparked a drive for more funds, and the group took the bold step of renting the Garrick Theatre uptown. "The Provincetown Playhouse in the Garrick Theatre" promised much.

However, success was out of reach. Their production of Thomas H. Dickinson's play, *Winter Bound,* the story of two girls who sought solitude on a snowbound farm in Connecticut, aroused much stimulating discussion but made no money. Aline MacMahon played the part of Tony, a sculptress. The play was the subject of much controversy in the press, wherein it was compared to *The Captive* and *The Well of Loneliness.* An attempt was made to raise money by a review of scenes from past Provincetown successes. This included a scene from *Desire Under the Elms* with Walter Huston, songs from *Fashion* sung by Mary Morris, as well as singing by Paul Robeson, but Heywood Broun's appeal for funds at the end of the evening was unsuccessful. The Wall Street crash was anything but conducive to theatre fund-raising. The Provincetown was forced to close with the final performance of *Winter Bound* on December 14, 1929. Because of it, however, an unforgettable page in the American Theatre had been written.

THE WASHINGTON SQUARE PLAYERS

The origin of the Washington Square Players was not very different from that of the Provincetown Players. They were at first a group of intelligent, alert, socially-minded residents of the neighborhood who used to meet in Washington Square and talk theatre late into the night. Some of the group had had previous experience with the theatre. All were idealists, eager for experiment.

Their first choice of a location was an old stable at 133 MacDougal Street. This they had to abandon because of many legal complications which finally caused the landlady to change her mind about renting them the quarters. Therefore, finding themselves without a theatre and the season half over, they welcomed the opportunity to rent a tiny theatre aptly called The Bandbox located uptown, on East 57th Street, for Friday and Saturday evenings. It had recently been abandoned by another group, The New York Play Actors, Incorporated, because of lack of public attendance.

The Washington Square Players opened on February 19, 1915, with a bill of one-act plays. The Bandbox had a seating capacity of 300. It was sold out for the first performance, and nearly sold out for the second. Forty-three performances of fourteen one-act plays were presented during their first season. The actors received no pay. In their second season, which opened on October 4, 1915, the program was expanded from two to six performances a week; the admission price was raised from $.50 to $1.00; and some of the actors were paid a salary.

By the third season, in the fall of 1916, they were able to give up the Bandbox theatre and move downtown to the Comedy Theatre, which was situated on Forty-first Street near Broadway. The Players now added workshops and a school. The group had expanded from 12 to 25 the second season, and in the third, to about 100. In addition to 47 one-act plays, they had presented three full-length plays, *Aglavaine and Selysette, The Sea Gull,* and *Ghosts.* The Director was Edward Goodman. The use of one-act plays, Dickinson believes, was a strategy that in part explained the early success of the Washington Square Players.[71]

Walter Prichard Eaton ascribes the founding of the Washington Square Players to two motives, the desire for self-expression and discontent with existing conditions in the commercial theatre. He declares, moreover, that the group was influenced by the success of the Abbey Theatre and the Moscow Art Theatre. In their prospectus the Washington Square Players expressed their belief in the future of the American theatre and they deplored the state of the American drama in a season in which only one play by an American playwright had won the Drama League's endorsement. They declared that a higher standard could be reached only as the outcome of experiment and initiative; they expressed the belief that hard work and perseverance, coupled with ability and the absence of purely commercial considerations, might result in the birth and healthy growth of an artistic theatre in this country.

Although the acting was sometimes uneven, the Washington Square Players presented many plays that the public could not have seen except for them. Among these were Andreyev's *The Life of Man,*

Ibsen's *Ghosts,* Chekhov's *The Sea Gull* and a revival of Shaw's *Mrs. Warren's Profession. The Sea Gull* may have been beyond their powers of interpretation at the time, but it showed "what far-off goals these young people had their gaze upon—an Art Theatre like that in Moscow!" [72]

A list of the early actors includes the names of Katharine Cornell, Rollo Peters, Helen Westley, and Roland Young. Its scene designers were Lee Simonson, Robert Edmond Jones, and Rollo Peters; its directors, Edward Goodman and Philip Moeller. Among the actual founders were the actress Helen Westley, the patent attorney and playwright Lawrence Langner, designer Lee Simonson, directors Philip Moeller and Edward Goodman, and the banker Maurice Wertheim.

The last production of the Washington Square Players was given in the spring of 1918; many of the group's members went into the army.

About a year and a half later, a month after the Armistice, Langner, Moeller, and Westley felt that they should try to reactivate the group and form a new art theatre. After several meetings in which other former members of the Washington Square Players joined, it was decided to form a cooperative professional acting company. Langner and Wertheim each contributed $500 and the name the Theatre Guild was chosen. The Garrick Theatre on West 35th Street was made available to the new group at a low rental through the generosity and goodwill of Otto H. Kahn, who had been a friend of the Washington Square Players. Writing of the Theatre Guild's first ten years, Eaton declares its steady growth and success were due to the passionate devotion to an idea which has been held by many a lone artist of the theatre in times past, and which animated the founders of the Moscow Art Theatre. "And what is that idea?" asks Eaton, and then defines it, declaring:

> Merely that the theatre is bigger than any workers in it, and in its ideal condition will not be employed for either personal or commercial exploitation, but for the creation, as carefully and lovingly as lies within one's power, of the best drama of one's time, drama honestly reflecting the author's vision of life or sense of style and beauty. This idea, if it is sincerely held, carries as corollary the belief that in their hearts many theatregoers must also prefer it to any lower standard. [73]

Thus one of the little theatres grew up, and, for a time at least, successfully met the challenge of the commercial theatre. However, even before the death of its three directors, the Theatre Guild, too,

had succumbed to the pressure of Broadway. In a theatre where production costs are continually rising and where stagehands can command higher salaries than some of its actors, it is inevitable that art
should be sacrificed. How the face of the New York theatre appears
to the outsider is made brilliantly clear by the impressions of a visiting
European director. In the spring of 1960, Willi Schmidt, the director
of the Schiller Theatre in Berlin, came to New York under the
auspices of the Institute for Advanced Studies in the Theatre Arts
to direct a production of Schiller's *Love and Intrigue.* In an article
written for *Equity,* the official organ of Actors Equity Association, he
offered some advice to American actors as a result of his New York
experience:

> . . . I would show this society which tolerates you only to use your
> talent for business (show-business in my ears is an ugly word); I would
> show this society that the dignity of a nation will not be judged by her
> ability to make money, but by her ability to produce art. In your case, I
> would try to show that the theatre is the most stimulating means of
> expression.[74]

The Neighborhood Playhouse, the Provincetown Players, and the
Washington Square Players, which sired the Theatre Guild, were all
admittedly influenced by the Moscow Art Theatre during its visits to
New York in 1923 and 1924. Moreover, Stanislavsky and his company
gave added impetus to a trend that had already begun some years
before. This was the attempt toward more realistic staging and the
creation of a truly lifelike ensemble.

Notes

1. Otis Skinner, *Footlights and Spotlights* (Indianapolis: Bobbs-Merrill Company, 1923), p. 41.
2. Skinner, p. 80.
3. Skinner, pp. 80, 123.
4. John Drew, *My Years on the Stage* (New York: E. P. Dutton and Company, 1921), p. 36.
5. Skinner, pp. 40, 41.
6. Oral Sumner Coad, and Edwin Mims, Jr., *The American Stage: The Pageant of America,* Vol. XIV, ed. Ralph Henry Gabriel (New Haven: Yale University Press, 1929), p. 234.
7. Coad and Mims, p. 236.
8. Marvin Felheim, *The Theatre of Augustin Daly* (Cambridge: Harvard University Press, 1956), p. 28.
9. Drew, p. 124.
10. Drew, p. 174.
11. Drew, p. 95.
12. George Parsons Lathrop, "The Inside Working of the Theatre," *Century Magazine,* LVI (June, 1898), pp. 265–75.
13. A. H. Gilbert (Mrs. G. H.) *The Stage Reminiscences of Mrs. Gilbert* (New York: Charles Scribner's Sons, 1901), pp. 223–24.
14. Skinner, p. 352.
15. Skinner, p. 146.
16. Coad and Mims, p. 240.
17. Deshler Welch, "Some Reminiscences by Deshler Welch," *The Book-Lover's Magazine,* Vol. 111 (April, 1904), p. 496.
18. William Winter, *Ada Rehan: A Study* (New York, 1891), pp. 17–18.
19. Skinner, p. 270.

20. Robinson Locke Collection of Dramatic Scrapbooks: Augustin Daly.
21. Felheim, pp. 32, 33.
22. Felheim, p. 281–82.
23. Coad and Mims, p. 237.
24. J. Rankin Towse, "A Critical Review of Daly's Theatre," *Century Magazine*, LVI, 2, (June, 1898), pp. 261–64.
25. Glenn Hughes, *A History of the American Theatre* (New York: Samuel French, 1951), p. 238.
26. Coad and Mims, p. 279.
27. Hughes, p. 239.
28. Coad and Mims, p. 303.
29. Ethel Barrymore, *Memories* (New York: Harper and Brothers, 1955), p. 205.
30. Craig Timberlake, *The Bishop of Broadway* (New York: Library Publishers, 1954), p. 407.
31. David Belasco, *The Theatre Through Its Stage Door*, ed. Louis V. Defoe (New York and London: Harper Brothers, 1919), pp. 96–98.
32. Ada Patterson, "David Belasco Reviews His Life Work" (Chats with American Dramatists, No. 6), in *Theatre*, VI (September, 1906), p. 248.
33. Belasco, p. 94.
34. Patterson, p. 249.
35. Timberlake, pp. 406–407.
36. Winter, p. 152.
37. Winter, pp. 158–59.
38. Timberlake, p. 110.
39. Timberlake, pp. 224–25, 319.
40. Winter, pp. 159, 160.
41. Timberlake, pp. 379, 380.
42. Arthur Hornblow, *A History of the Theatre in America* (Philadelphia: J. B. Lippincott and Company, 1919), Vol. II, pp. 335–36.
43. Hornblow, p. 340.
44. Hughes, pp. 317–18.
45. Hughes, pp. 353–54.
46. George Freedley and John A. Reeves, *A History of the Theatre* (New York: Crown Publishers, 1941), p. 329.
47. Alexander Woollcott, *Mrs. Fiske, Her Views on Actors, Acting, and the Problems of Production Recorded by Alexander Woollcott* (New York: The Century Company, 1917), pp. 63–67.
48. W. B. Leavitt, *Fifty Years in Theatrical Management* (New York: Broadway Publishing Company, 1912), p. 294.
49. Hughes, pp. 281, 333.
50. Freedley, p. 572.
51. Hughes, pp. 335–39.
52. Hughes, p. 357.
53. Hornblow, p. 323.
54. Hughes, pp. 349–51.
55. Freedley, p. 584.
56. Hughes, p. 349.
57. Hornblow, pp. 335–36.
58. Hughes, pp. 357–58.
59. Hughes, pp. 363–64.
60. Hornblow, p. 335.

61. W. B. Leavitt, p. 294.
62. Thomas H. Dickinson, *The Insurgent Theatre* (New York: B. W. Huebsch, 1917), pp. 20–23.
63. Dickinson, pp. 28, 75.
64. Dickinson, pp. 106–114.
65. Dickinson, p. 162.
66. Hughes, p. 370.
67. Alice Lewisohn Crowley, *The Neighborhood Playhouse, Leaves From a Theatre Scrapbook* (New York: Theatre Arts Books, 1959), p. 31. The following information on the Neighborhood Playhouse is from this very illuminating work.
68. Helen Deutsch and Stella Hanau, *The Provincetown* (New York: Farrar and Rinehart, Inc., 1931), p. 17. The information on the Province-town Playhouse is taken from this work.
69. Kenneth Macgowan, "And Again Repertory," *Theatre Arts Magazine*, VII (April, 1923), p. 90, quoted by Robert Albert Johnston in "The Moscow Art Theatre in America" (unpublished doctoral dissertation, Northwestern University, 1951), p. 271.
70. Deutsch, pp. 130–31.
71. Dickinson, pp. 172–84.
72. Walter Prichard Eaton, *The Theatre Guild, The First Ten Years* (New York: Brentano, 1929), pp. 19–21, 26.
73. Eaton, pp. 4–6.
74. Willi Schmidt, "The American Actor," in *Equity*, Vol. XLV, No. 4 (April, 1960), p. 6.

eight

American Reaction to Stanislavsky
and the Moscow Art Theatre

American reaction to Stanislavsky and the Moscow Art Theatre resulted from what was known about them in the United States before their visits here in 1923 and 1924 and also from the effects of these visits. Therefore this reaction can be divided into two periods, the first from 1906 to 1923, and the second, or immediate, from 1923 to 1925.

FROM 1906 TO 1923

America was introduced to the art of the Russian stage during the first two decades of the twentieth century in two widely different ways. One was through the demonstration of Russian artists of the stage and ballet who performed in America; the other was through the reports of American and English visitors to Moscow of what was taking place in Russia itself. These latter appeared in American and English periodicals, and in some cases in books printed in the United States.

RUSSIAN CULTURAL AMBASSADORS

Two Russian artists who came to this country in March, 1905 were to have a great impact on the American theatre, even before the Moscow Art Theatre reached its artistic maturity. Paul Orlenev brought his company, the St. Petersburg Players, to New York, with Alla Nazimova and himself in leading roles of the repertoire.

In Nazimova, American audiences saw for the first time a pupil of

Stanislavsky and an exponent of the "new acting." Originally a student of Danchenko for three years at the Philharmonic Dramatic School, at nineteen she was one of those chosen for another year's experience with the Moscow Art Theatre. At the end of that year, she chose to play leading roles in the provincial theatre rather than remain with the Moscow Art Theatre in minor roles.[1]

Orlenev's company was praised in New York for two seasons and played a repertoire of Gorky, Dostoyevsky, Strindberg, Alexis Tolstoy, Ibsen, Chekhov, and Hauptmann in Russian. Nevertheless, Orlenev was not successful in his management; and in spite of a sponsoring committee composed of such leaders as Edith Wharton, Richard Watson Gilder, Ethel Barrymore, and Mrs. Harry Payne Whitney, the company was forced to return to Russia before the end of the second season. Nazimova had made such a favorable impression, however, that the Shuberts gave her a five-year contract to remain in America and perform Ibsen in English. She learned the language in six months' time and in November, 1906, she began a series of Ibsen plays with which she was identified in America for more than thirty years. After her first performance the critic of the *New York Times* called her interpretation of Hedda Gabler superior to that of Mrs. Fiske.[2]

Two months later, with her next production, *A Doll's House,* the critics realized that theatrical history was being made. Instead of displaying her own personality in the different roles of Hedda and Nora, Nazimova revealed two completely different personalities in the two characters. There was praise for her acting as well as for the art which could make this possible. The statement which she made in an interview which appeared in the *New York Times* of November 18, 1906, gives evidence of the naturalness of her acting: "Almost every day at rehearsal the actors would mistake some of my lines for directions I was giving them—just because I simply talked my words." [3]

Nazimova's impact on the American theatre was provocative and lasting. Some critics, notably William Winter, stood firm against the onslaught of both Ibsen and realism in acting, and William Gillette defended the "personality" of the actor.[4] Nazimova, however, is credited with having introduced in this country the Russian inspired acting of psychological realism which America was to see in full flower in the Moscow Art Theatre performances of 1923 and 1924.

In 1908 the great Russian basso, Fyodor Chaliapin, came to sing at the Metropolitan Opera House. For some inexplicable reason he was not appreciated in New York at that time. When he returned thirteen years later, however, he met with such success that the police had to control the crowds which fought to hear his *Boris Godunov*. It is significant that in the meantime he had triumphed in London and Paris.

The failure, also in 1908, of another great artist, the actress Vera Kommisarzhevskaya, is equally inexplicable. The only possible reason for her lack of public support is the fact that she came without any publicity and was practically unknown except among the Russian immigrants on the East Side. In her performances of Ibsen's *A Doll's House*, Gorky's *Children of the Sun*, Ostrovsky's *The Girl Without Dowry*, Sudermann's *The Fires of St. John* and *Battle of the Butterflies*, and Molière's *Misanthrope*, she received the praise of the critics; but this could not counteract the public's neglect and she remained only a short while. Sayler is of the opinion that her failure here contributed to her early death two years later.

Further interest in Russian theatre art was awakened in America in 1910 by the visit of Pavlova and Mordkin, who introduced the exquisite loveliness and exotic imagination of the Russian ballet. A year later, when Morris Gest imported the "vanguard" of the Russian ballet, America saw for the first time the magnificent settings and brilliant costumes of the great Russian artist Leon Bakst.[5]

Early in 1916, largely through the efforts of Otto H. Kahn, a millionaire who was a patron of the arts, America saw the Diaghileff Ballet and the paintings of the great Russian artists, Alexander Benois and Alexander Golovin. Benois, Roerich, and Dobujinsky had become associated with the stage design of the Moscow Art Theatre. The following year the Diaghileff Ballet Company appeared again and toured the country. This time they were joined by the great Nijinsky, who had been released from a prison camp in Austria. Among the many Russian artists who came to this country and remained were Fokine, according to Sayler the greatest director of modern Russian ballet, and Mordkin.

In 1920 two other artists came to New York. One was Nicolas Roerich, the famous Russian painter and scenic artist; the other was the actor Jacob Ben-Ami, who began his American career in the Yiddish theatres of Second Avenue and the Bowery [6] and made his English-speaking debut under Arthur Hopkins. As recently as 1959 Ben-Ami appeared in a successful Broadway production, *The Tenth Man*.

REPORTS FROM MOSCOW

The Moscow Art Theatre made its first European tour in 1905. The rhapsodic accounts of their success in Paris and Berlin stimulated journalists, critics and persons interested in the theatre to make the long journey to Russia to see them upon their return from abroad.

As early as 1906 an article by Christian Brinton entitled "Idols of the Russian Masses" appeared in the April issue of the *Cosmopolitan*. It gave a comprehensive picture of Stanislavsky and the Moscow Art Theatre. Regarding Stanislavsky, Brinton remarks: "He impresses you at once with an absolute reverence for truth and an inherent scorn of sham or artifice."

Brinton praises Olga Knipper in *The Sea Gull, Three Sisters,* and *Uncle Vanya* and speaks of Stanislavsky's wife, "Madame Lilina," as "a dramatic ingenue of richest promise." He also extols the acting ability of Baranov, Veshnevsky, and Moskvin. Of Stanislavsky's method he says:

His methods are the methods of a clear, discriminating mind. Though an inflexible realist, what he demands is not reality, but the illusion of reality; not life but the closest, tensest, most faithful translation of life.[7]

Brinton also showed appreciation of the plays of Chekhov and Gorky. His article contained photographs of Anton Chekhov, Tolstoy, Gorky, Chaliapin—who was the basso at the Imperial Opera in Moscow at the time—Moskvin, Baranov, Stanislavsky, Olga Knipper, and Veshnevsky, as well as Paul Orlenev and Nazimova. Brinton speaks of Nazimova as "an actress of consummate versatility and charm." He says, furthermore: "So plastic is her personality and so supreme are her powers of identification that it would be hazardous to say in what part Mme. Nazimova excels." His comment was in a sense prophetic. The article appeared in America seven months before her English-speaking debut in *Hedda Gabler*.

In 1920, after his visit to Russia, Sayler wrote: "I know from Gordon Craig and others that Moscow and Petrograd had carried the modern theatre to its finest achievement."[8] Writing of his observations in Moscow in 1908, Craig had the highest praise for the acting of Stanislavsky and the Moscow Art Theatre:

The Russian actors of the Künstlerisches Theatre at Moscow give one the impression that they experience a keener intellectual enjoyment during their performances than any other actors in Europe. All their performances are admirable, and whether they touch a play of modern life and modern feelings or a fairy tale, the touch is always sure, always delicate, masterly. Nothing is slipshod. Everything is treated seriously . . . . In England . . . the managers and actors are afraid to be serious. . . . Here in Moscow they risk the blunder and achieve the distinction of being the best set of actors upon the European stage.[9]

Of Stanislavsky himself, Craig declares:

> A simpler technique, a more human result would be difficult to find. A master of psychology, his acting is most realistic, yet he avoids nearly all the brutalities. His performances are remarkable for their grace . . . . In *The Enemy of the People* Stanislavsky shows us how to act Dr. Stockman without being "theatrical" and without being comic or dull.[10]

Two years after Craig's book was printed in Chicago, a book by another English critic, Huntley Carter, appeared in America. Entitled *The New Spirit in Drama and Art,* it gives a careful analysis of the aims and results of the Moscow Art Theatre. Carter comments upon both the mental and the physical organization, describing the theatre as "a university of dramatic art as well as . . . a national theatre." He mentions the excellent stage provided with a revolving center and praises the attempts to solve such problems of stage lighting as the truthful distribution of light and shadow. He declares, "Even the wig maker and the costumer are artists, unlike the London samples, who are merely tradesmen." [11] Commenting on the method of the Moscow Art Theatre, Carter says:

> The actor obedient to the director's will, brought the spectator into the action of the play, united and harmonized everything—action, words, line and color . . . . So the organization grew, guided by the wisdom of its celebrated director, Stanislavsky. Gradually rumors of its extraordinary attempts to reform interpretation and stage setting attracted attention in other parts of Europe. Its new naturalistic methods of acting came as a revelation to a public long accustomed to the old conventions of the declamatory school, and surprised even those persons whom M. Antoine's advanced method had prepared to accept them . . . . Indeed the extraordinary attention paid to the technique of acting, and the over-emphasis on detail and effect came to most playgoers in the nature of a "new thrill." [12]

Carter maintained that the Moscow Art Theatre System was one of the best for training and developing the actor and the director as well as for improving stagecraft and for artistic and scientific experiments in light, sound, and movement. Finally, Carter made a plea for "an aristocracy of brains" to administer the London theatre as was done in Moscow by the wealthy shareholders of the Moscow Art Theatre.

Another English writer, Jean D'Auvergne, reported on artistic achievement in Russia in *The Fortnightly Review* of May, 1914. He speaks of the recent interest in Russian art and literature of English intellectuals but deplores the absence of a repertory theatre in London despite the example of the Moscow Art Theatre. He rejoices over "Mr. Granville-Barker's recent visit to Moscow," which he hopes presages "at least a repertory theatre run on the lines of the Moscow Art Theatre and including some of its most famous productions." He goes so far as to recommend that other English dramatists and producers follow Barker's example, pointing out the warm reception that would await them. D'Auvergne gives a brief history of the founding of the Moscow Art Theatre, including the meeting of Stanislavsky and Danchenko and the summer of rehearsals at the Pushkino barn. He mentions the outstanding productions and agrees with Maurice Baring that "Moscow is well worth visiting for one night, if only to see *The Cherry Garden* (sic)." He goes on to describe the "magnificently equipped" theatre and the wonderful lighting system and praises the cooperative system of management, where the players share not only the artistic honors but the financial returns as well. He also reports on Gordon Craig's production of *Hamlet* with its famous golden screens and praises Kachalov's portrayal of the name role. He mentions the First Studio's "small repertory season which has been no less successful than the mother-theatre." Finally, he declares: "Here is the perfect theatre." [13]

Performances of The Moscow Art Theatre were reviewed in detail by two American writers in 1915 and 1917. The first review was by Gertrude Besse King; it appeared in the *New Republic* of June 26, 1915. It ignores Stanislavsky but praises the overall production of *The Cherry Orchard* of April 30 in Petrograd:

> Here were people behaving in a most human sort of way—not at all as those who exhibit extravagant emotions before the footlights . . . . They were not even attempting, as in our so-called "realistic" drama, the tricks, mannerisms, and telephone verisimilitudes that produce such artificial naturalness.[14]

The second article is by Arthur Ruhl and is more comprehensive. It describes the Moscow Art Theatre as the most original theatre of the modern world, and mentions the spontaneous charm of the First Studio's performance of *A Cricket on the Hearth*. The acting in *Three Sisters* gives the impression "not so much of getting into a play as of getting into Russia. And not merely an instant of Russian life . . . but into the whole stream of influences, inherited and otherwise, which had produced this family, and out of which their lives must flow." He comments on the fact that the performances of the Moscow Art Theatre are always sold out, and this "without advertising or exploitation." Finally he points out that the plays which the Theatre produces "all meet the demand, not necessarily Russian, for something spiritually nourishing, something that does not merely pass over the skin like a cold shower bath, but warms a person inside, stays with him, and broadens the consciousness of life with which he already starts." [15]

During the next few years Americans continued to hear about the Moscow Art Theatre. In February, 1919, an article entitled "The Russian Dramatic Stage" appeared in *Drama,* the popular magazine devoted to news about the theatre. It was actually a brief history first of the Russian theatre and then of the Moscow Art Theatre. It discussed ensemble acting, the relationship between Anton Chekhov and the Moscow Art Theatre, and, finally, the difference between the methods of Stanislavsky and those of Meyerhold.[16]

November, 1921 marked the triumphal return of Chaliapin to the Metropolitan Opera House in New York City. It was through his contact with the great Russian basso that Gest succeeded in bringing Nikita Balieff to this country in January, 1922.[17] Balieff's *Chauve Souris* was the artistic and imaginative potpourri which had originated in Moscow during Lent as the private entertainment of the members of the Moscow Art Theatre players and their friends. Stanislavsky refers to these evenings, originally held in a cellar, as "cabbage parties." [18] The success of the *Chauve Souris* in America lasted for several years, and both Chaliapin and Balieff must be credited with persuading Stanislavsky to accept Gest's offer to the Moscow Art Theatre to visit America. They reached an agreement in September, 1922.[19]

ADVANCE PUBLICITY

The success achieved by the Moscow Art Theatre during its American tours was aided largely by the interest aroused by Oliver Sayler through his articles in the newspapers and magazines and through his book, *The Russian Theatre,* all written as a result of his trip to Russia and his intensive observations of the Moscow Art Theatre.[20]

In two issues of *Theatre Arts Magazine,* July and October, 1920, Sayler's article entitled "Theory and Practice in Russian Theatre" gives a brief history of the Russian theatre of Gogol, Shchepkin, and Ostrovsky, and the subsequent founding of the Moscow Art Theatre by Stanislavsky and Nemirovich-Danchenko. He also writes appreciatively of Chekhov's plays and discusses the interdependence of theatre and playwright. He mentions the innovations of Meyerhold and even speaks of Kommisarzhevsky's objections to Stanislavsky's System. He concludes, however, that this is no threat to the position of the Moscow Art Theatre or of Stanislavsky's theory. The October issue was devoted entirely to Stanislavsky's company. It contained pictures of the leading players and scenes from the plays discussed, and was even called the "Moscow Art Theatre Number." [21]

On September 17, 1922, the Book Review and Magazine section of the *New York Times* carried an article by Sayler entitled "Origins and Progress of the Moscow Art Theatre." [22] One month later, *Theatre Magazine* printed two full pages of pictures of Moscow Art Theatre productions and players, together with an article by Sayler under the title, "Europe's Premier Playhouse in the Offing." Here Sayler recapitulates the story of the founding of the Moscow Art Theatre as a protest against the nineteenth-century Russian theatre; he compares their protest with that of Gordon Craig, Adolph Appia, and Max Reinhardt. Again he mentions Chekhov and likens his association with the Moscow Art Theatre to Synge's relation to The Abbey Theatre. Defining Stanislavsky's method as "the spiritual emphasis on the psychological background of realistic interpretation," Sayler declares:

> By a contagious alchemy of the spirit, which has baffled the descriptive powers of all Russian critics, Stanislavsky implanted in his associates an inner vision of plays and roles and a general method of spiritual and psychological as well as superficially realistic interpretation which distinguishes the theatre's productions from all others.[23]

He also defines it as "a spiritualized realism, a use of the realistic form as a means and not an end, a means to the more vivid interpretation of life." [24]

Writing of his first impressions of the Moscow Art Theatre's per-

formance of *Three Sisters,* Sayler says that out of the very simple
lines that Chekhov has written for the last moment between Masha and
Vershinin, "Stanislavsky and Knipper have constructed the proudest,
most unaffected, most deeply moving farewell of the modern theatre.
To see it is to feel a knife cut clean through the heart." Speaking of
Stanislavsky's performance as Vershinin, he declares, "There is no
actor on the English speaking stage and I doubt if there is one in
the world today who can do what Constantin Stanislavsky does in
these scenes." Remarking that in the first act he didn't remember
"noticing Stanislavsky any more than any of the others in the perfect
ensemble," he continues:

> Then I suddenly awoke to the presence of towering genius in that
> great, unobtrusive scene in the second act. The third and fourth followed
> with the proud anguish of that farewell, and I understood the secret of
> the Moscow Art Theatre. . . . And so to Stanislavsky, producer, and
> Stanislavsky, actor, must be added Stanislavsky, teacher, and probably the
> greatest teacher of acting our generation has known.[25]

America was prepared for appreciation of the Moscow Art Theatre
also by reports of visitors to Europe who were unable to go to Moscow.
In this regard Sayler remarks about the fact that some time after the
revolution of 1917 travelers returning from central and western
Europe had brought back accounts "of the amazing work of a mere
handful of the original staff of the Moscow Art Theatre . . . playing
first in the Balkans, then in Berlin and Vienna and finally in Scandi-
navia." [26] This "mere handful" was a group from the Moscow Art
Theatre on a guest journey to Kharkov. They were prevented from
returning to Moscow by the sudden surprise advance of the White
Army. Stanislavsky mentions this forced division of the company,
which lasted several years and worked much hardship on those at
home as well as on those abroad.[27] At the end of the tour Kachalov
and his wife Litovtseva; Knipper; Baksheiev; Bersenev; Tarassova; the
brother of Moskvin; Tarhanov; Soloviova; and Jilinsky returned to
Moscow, but Boleslavsky, Germanova, and Masselitinov stayed in
western Europe.[28] John D. Crane, writing from Prague to the *New
York Times,* pronounced the productions of the Art Theatre "the
finest dramatic art in the entire world." [29]

When the Moscow Art Theatre accepted Gest's invitation to come
to the United States, it was agreed that the company should visit
Germany and France on its way here. The result of this was more

critical acclaim, which served as advance publicity for the New York opening. Cyril Brown, the foreign correspondent of the *New York Times,* reports the overwhelming welcome tendered to Stanislavsky in Berlin. Of his own reaction to the Moscow Art Theatre's production of *Tsar Fyodor,* which he characterizes as "a dead piece" until "the Muscovites blew into it the life-breath of their art," he writes: "One sat in almost religious awe, although one did not understand the text; this art spoke more eloquently than words." [30] In Paris the special celebration given to Stanislavsky and his company was especially significant. For it was sponsored by Jacques Copeau, founder of the "Vieux Colombier," and André Antoine, the great French champion of realism in the theatre since 1894. Antoine praised Stanislavsky for his reform of the Russian stage, particularly since he himself had been unable to do the same for the stage in France. According to the *New York Tribune*'s Paris correspondent, the success of the Russians overshadowed anything that had ever been known in the French theatre for years.[31]

Barrett H. Clark saw the performances of the Moscow Art Theatre when the company played in Berlin on the way to its American tour. Writing from that city in November, 1922, to the magazine *Drama,* he declares: "The most remarkable thing about the Art Theatre is that it is an all-star company in which no one is starred." Of Stanislavsky he says: "He has learned the lesson of proportion and taught it in turn to every one of his associates"; and of the performance of *Tsar Fyodor* he asserts: "I was left with an abiding sense of human tragedy, though I had not understood a word of what was uttered." Since there was no airmail, Clark's account was not published until January, 1923, just at the time when the famous company was about to arrive in America.[32]

In January, 1923, just before the arrival of the Moscow Art Theatre in New York, three Russian writers published in this country discussions of the art of Stanislavsky and the Moscow Art Theatre. One of these articles by P. Yartsev, entitled "The Quiet Light," had appeared in a magazine called *Russkaia Mysl (Russian Thought).* Discussing the external techniques of the "French" school, where the actor reproduces the gestures and tone of voice he used in rehearsal, he refers to the innovations of Shchepkin, whose precept, "Take your example from nature," was misconstrued for a time, when there arose a so-called school of "simple playing" or "simplicity for the sake of simplicity." This consisted of actors speaking "naturally," often so low as not to be understood, or walking "naturally" with their hands in their pockets. Yartsev declares that the new technique of the Moscow Art Theatre came into being gradually and at the same time spontaneously from Stanislavsky's remarks in training his pupils, which his assistants repeated in rehearsals. Yartsev also lists many of Stanislavsky's sayings:

> A person never knows exactly what he is going to say. It is only actors who know!

> Empty eyes! An actor with empty eyes—how horrible!

> A person always *walks into the room*. It is only actors who *appear upon the stage*.

Yartsev also tells how Stanislavsky gave an exercise in sweeping the floor or dusting a table as a stage task, during which he directed the actor to concentrate on some phase of the task, on the "cool surface" or the color of the table, instead of on the lines he has to speak, as a means of relaxing and avoiding tension.[33]

Another writer, Gregory Zillboorg, wrote an article entitled "The Russian Invasion" in *The Drama*. He himself had seen the Moscow Art Theatre three and a half years before. He emphasized their seriousness and dedication and their great love for the theatre. "They do not bow or play for the sake of cheap popularity," he declares. "People do not talk loudly in the Moscow Art Theatre, nor do they applaud," he explains, and he expresses the hope that applause will not be permitted at the New York performances; but he is fearful of the Russians living in New York who "have acquired all the skill in baseball noise-making so characteristic of the theatre here." He recalls that these same people "spoiled many a beautiful moment at Chaliapin's concerts" by forcing the singer to stop in the middle of a song to reprove them. Describing the effect of the Moscow Art Theatre, he makes a discerning comparison:

> They bring the average man before their footlights and compel him to feel the complex spiritual reality of life so that he accepts the greatness of the theatre and submits to it more willingly and more creatively than, let us say the worst, the mechanistic, logical, commercial theatre of Broadway which is afraid of not being understood by the average man.[34]

The third writer, A. L. Fovitzky, with the title of Lecturer of the Russian Universities, wrote a book *The Moscow Art Theatre and*

Its Distinguishing Characteristics giving the substance of a history of Stanislavsky which had been recently published in Moscow. In addition, Fovitzky gave his own impressions of Stanislavsky's rehearsal techniques and an evaluation of his contribution. Much of this appears here for the first time. Many of the techniques appear later in Stanislavsky's book, *An Actor Prepares,* and in the work of his disciples. Fovitzky mentions Stanislavsky's interest in Hindu teachings and his application of the usefulness of the idea of *prana* to his stage work. According to Vera Soloviova, who was one of Stanislavsky's pupils and a member of the First Studio, the use of *prana* consisted in transferring one's inner feelings or "radiance" to the audience. Another purpose which these teachings served was concentration. Fovitzky explains that Stanislavsky's goal was the expression of depth of feeling for the sake of the depth of truth. "By the time these exercises were finished," he declares, "concentration and sensitiveness had become characteristic of the actors of the Moscow Art Theatre." [35] Fovitzky also mentions Stanislavsky's practice of holding rehearsals first "without words—then with words picked by the actors themselves." This refers to the building of a scene following the line of inner feelings with the actor using different objects as a means of expressing his feelings and then improvising by adding words which correspond in meaning to the author's text of the play. Finally, Fovitzky concludes:

> From very small and wordless portions the actors are led on by Stanislavsky to the great whole. This whole is in artistic images. It is not photography of life. Even in conditional suggestions there must be a real life of the soul, a depth of truth, a profound grasp of the inner meaning of the play. "With Stanislavsky, our work is hard," explained one of the most famous artists of the Moscow Art Theatre, "but without Stanislavsky, our work is futile." [36]

Fovitzky then speaks of Stanislavsky's contributions to the Russian people in continuing the work of Tolstoy and Dostoyevsky "in teaching a whole generation of the Russian intelligentsia to think and feel." He characterizes the Moscow Art Theatre as "a high school of spiritual life," and recounts how people came to Moscow from all over Russia, sometimes standing in line all night to obtain tickets to a performance.[37]

One other statement in the press shortly before the Moscow Art Theatre Company set sail from France on the S.S. "Majestic" was perhaps a stronger force in promoting the advance sale of tickets than all the expensive advertising indulged in by Gest. This consisted of a protest by the Washington division of The American Defense Society against the Moscow Art Theatre, declaring that its members were Soviet spies and would use the receipts from the American performances for the cause of world Communism. The press came to the Moscow Art Theatre's aid and there were apologies in editorials of the *New York Times* and *The New Republic*. Actors Equity Association came to the defense of the Russian company and conferred upon them honorary membership in Equity for their stay in America. A statement in support of the Moscow Art Theatre by Otto H. Kahn was published in the *New York Tribune* of December 27.[38] Stanislavsky's own statement given out in France was published in the American papers. It was simple and straightforward: "It is not so—we have no connection with the Soviet Government. We are interested only in art. It is our art that we have come to bring you, not politics." [39]

THE MOSCOW ART THEATRE IN AMERICA

The reaction to the Moscow Art Theatre's performances in this country may be evaluated from three points of view, those of the theatre-going public, the critics, and American actors and producers. The engagement opened on January 8, 1923 at the Al Jolson Theatre with a performance of *Tsar Fyodor*. This was the play with which the Moscow Art Theatre had begun its career on October 14, 1898.

THE THEATRE-GOING PUBLIC

While the unprecedented public response to the performances of the Moscow Art Theatre, especially in New York City may be in part attributed to the thoroughgoing publicity of Morris Gest and Oliver Sayler, nevertheless certain facts would seem to indicate a very true appreciation of what the Russian players were offering. According to Sayler, the advance sale was the largest on record for any dramatic company, whether playing in English or a foreign language; the announced eight weeks' engagement in New York City was completely sold out before the company set foot in America. Moreover, J. Rankin Towse, the critic of the *New York Evening Post,* remarking on the ovation tendered by the opening night audience, declared that "the public demonstrations were mostly genuine 'this time' and most thoroughly well deserved, and so carried with them a special significance." [40] Also significant is the fact that the engagement was extended to cover an additional four weeks because of the public demand. When this was announced, ticket buyers at the box office of the Al Jolson Theatre stood in a line which extended around the corner.[41] William Lyon Phelps reported that the public was as enthusiastic over Chekhov's plays as over Tolstoy and Gorky and that hundreds stood for each performance.

The tour was to cover Chicago, Boston, and Philadelphia, with a final return engagement in New York. The audiences in Chicago were as appreciative as those in New York and just as articulate, if one judges by the press notices. Mollie Morris of the Chicago *Daily News* characterized the audience reaction as "a violent demonstration unlike anything Chicago has known in the theatre." Butler of the *Chicago Tribune* described another kind of audience:

> The people who count in the theatre—those who go to see rather than to be seen—filled the balconies nightly to their topmost reaches, and here there was rapt attention and discerning admiration.[42]

A drive to raise $100,000 for Russian relief was started with a dinner given by the American Quakers in Stanislavsky's honor. In Philadelphia and Boston, the Moscow Art Theatre met with the same enthusiasm. There was an official greeting by the city of Boston and the offering of bread and salt in the Russian manner. On May 21, the company returned to New York for its farewell engagement of two weeks. At the final performance June 2, 1923, the audience gave Stanislavsky a great ovation, which continued even after he had made a speech in French to express his appreciation and that of the company. Finally he spoke in Russian, and the applause reportedly lasted for nearly half an hour; afterward presents were exchanged backstage. The Moscow Art Theatre sailed for Europe on June 7, 1923. Stanislavsky went to Freiburg, Germany, where he spent the summer with his family and continued to write the reminiscences of his life in the theatre begun in America in March. He had been prevailed upon by Little, Brown and Company to write the account of his life which he called *My Life in Art.*[43]

The second season, which opened on November 9, 1923 in New York with *The Brothers Karamazov,* included several new plays. Two other Chekhov plays not done during the first season were *Uncle Vanya* and *Ivanov.* Also presented were Ibsen's *An Enemy of the People,* Goldoni's *La Locandiera,* and one play each by Knut Hamson and Ostrovsky. Not only was the repertoire greatly increased but the tour was expanded by the addition of seven additional cities. The company played nine weeks in New York, three in Chicago, and one week in each of the following cities: Boston, Philadelphia, Washington, Pittsburgh, Brooklyn, Detroit, and Cleveland (Magarshack calls it Clivedon), and three days each in Hartford and New Haven. However, Gest unfortunately reduced the publicity drastically and had very little advance publicity. Johnston maintains that the reason for this was the impresario's preoccupation at this time with Duse's "farewell engagement" as well as Reinhardt's production of *The Miracle,* both of which Gest was sponsoring in addition to the return engagement of the *Chauve Souris.* Moreover, Sayler was kept busy writing articles for Gest on Duse and Reinhardt and preparing his book, *Max Reinhardt and His Theatre,* which came out in the midst of the Moscow Art Theatre's second season. As a result of these factors the attendance fell off, although the quality of the performance was still high. The productions drew the same appreciation from the audience. For example, at one performance in Chicago, the critic of the *Chicago Daily Journal,* "E.S.," reported:

> A shouting house made outcry until Kachalof appeared upon the stage alone for what is practically an unknown rite in the visiting company, a solo curtain call.[44]

At the final performance in New York on May 11, 1924, both Knipper-Chekhova and Stanislavsky made speeches. Stanislavsky also wrote a letter of farewell and thanks which was published in the newspapers. In it he spoke of David Belasco and the joy he and his fellow actors felt "in discovering in his [Belasco's] theatre the same atmosphere, attention and care, and the same devotion to the theatre which are the heart and soul of our home stage." The official farewell to the American public came from the pen of the manager of the company, Sergei Berthenson, and appeared in the papers under the title "The Moscow Art Theatre Says *'Do Svidaniya.'*" It thanked the Americans for their heartiest and most sincere hospitality and for the example of such amazingly efficient work methods, by which he meant the work of the stagehands in scene shifting, etc. He declared that what the company had learned in this respect would enable them to work nearly twenty-four hours a day.[45]

REACTION OF THE CRITICS

In his searching study of the Moscow Art Theatre's American visit, Johnston demonstrates that most of the criticism in the newspapers and periodicals was highly favorable. The one captious criticism came from the producer William A. Brady, who referred to the silly preference of Americans for foreign drama and music and asserted that he or "any one of six or seven other practical men of the theatre could develop a company as competent in all ways as the Moscow Art Theatre Players." The critic of the *Chicago Sunday Tribune* gave the perfect answer. Agreeing with the possible truth of Mr. Brady's boast, he nevertheless pointed out that no one had yet done so, nor was likely to do so, since the American audiences are "interested in actors rather than in acting," as are the actors themselves.[46]

As for the language acting as a barrier, while a few found it an impediment to a full appreciation of the plays, the majority felt that the acting of the Moscow Art Theatre surmounted even that obstacle. Some of the critical comments which they offered to illustrate this point were:

> The "handicap" was no handicap at all, the Art Theatre's art was all the more effective because of its dependence upon acting alone.
>
> *Christian Science Monitor,*
> January 10, 1923, p. 8.

> Many of us forgot through long stretches that we understood no word of the text.
>
> John Corbin, "Realism of the
> Spirit," the *New York Times,*
> January 14, 1923, Sec. 7, p. 1.

> . . . the Russians are here, speaking, it may be, a language you do not understand, but doing nothing else which is not perfectly clear to all who have eyes to see and a mind to understand.
>
> O. L. Hall, "Gossip of Plays
> and Players," *Chicago Daily
> Journal,* April 12, 1924, p. 5.

> The great drama of the world is not spoken by the characters so much as it is looked and above all, felt by them . . . . If we feel what a

character, through its actor, feels, it is not entirely important that we should know what he thinks.

George Jean Nathan, *Materia Critica* (New York: Alfred A. Knopf, 1924), pp. 33–35.

For the most part the Moscow Art Theatre players were praised for three facets of their acting: their excellent ensemble; the utter natural-ness and lifelike quality of their productions; and the fact that they seemed to be "living" their roles instead of "performing" them.

Stark Young declared the ensemble acting of *Tsar Fyodor* "the highest achievement . . . that the Russian theatre or any other now-adays can boast." Jack Crawford in a review of the same play written for *The Drama* declares: "The greatest merit was its perfect team work. There was not one out of the picture and no one ever stopped acting because there was an interval in which that person had no lines to speak." [47]

The reviewer of the *New York Times* comments upon the "elo-quent vocal coloring" of the "kaleidoscopic crowd":

> Our traditional device of "another general shout" is put to shame. Every actor in the scene is no less an individual than the Tsar himself. The varied voices paint a picture of shifting emotions as if from a tonal palette. The result is a flood of shifting, cumulative passions, a sweep of drama, that must long stand as an example and a shame to the American producer.[48]

Robert Allerton Parker wrote in *The Independent* of February 3, 1923, that "the visit of the Moscow Art Theatre to this country is undoubtedly the most important theatrical event of this decade." He considered *The Cherry Orchard* the best example of ensemble acting. He suggests a slightly different concept of ensemble acting from the one usually held when he says: "Messrs. Stanislavsky, Leonidov, Moskvin and especially Vassily Luzhsky as well as Mesdames Olga Knipper-Chekhova and Maria Ouspenskaya, all contribute full length portraits of the characters they enact; yet they act orchestrally to-gether." Sheppard Butler calls the Moscow Art Theatre Company's performance of *The Lower Depths* "a veritable symphony of acting, each of its parts an elaborate study in itself, but blended cunningly into an harmonious whole . . . . One wonders," he concludes, "how illusion could be more complete." [49]

In the majority of critical comments which the Moscow Art Theatre received for its productions both abroad and in America, following close upon the praise for its fine ensemble and inextricably bound up with this, was the observation that the spectator was looking at a section of life rather than a play on a stage. In his book of theatre criticism, *Glamour,* Stark Young reports this impression very succinctly when he says: "There was that seven-days wonder of stage directing— a complete air of human beings living there in the familiar ways of men." [50] Similarly, Percy Hammond, critic of the *New York Tribune,* remarked: "The most important of them come into a room or leave it without theatrical emphasis. You suddenly discover that they are present or—absent." [51] J. Rankin Towse, in commenting upon the production of *The Cherry Orchard* in the *New York Evening Post* of January 23, 1923, declared that "the mirror had been held squarely up to nature," and in his review of *The Three Sisters* on January 30, he remarked that "to look upon it seemed almost like an unwarrantable intrusion upon privacy." A similar comment was made by the critic of the *New York Call,* Maida Castellun, on the following day:

> Once more the acting of the Russian actors makes a responsive spectator feel that he is committing the indiscretion of looking through the open window and listening to the private affairs of the Prozoroff family and their friends. From their shabby rooms to their unassuming, appropriate clothes they are children of life, not of the stage . . . .[52]

Closely allied to the praise for its fine ensemble and the lifelike impression of the Moscow Art Theatre productions was a third critical evaluation, that the actors seemed to be "living" their parts and not "acting" them. Stanislavsky himself in his praise of David Warfield mentioned this standard:

> Warfield is the best Shylock I have seen . . . . He is a real Russian actor. He lives his part. He doesn't act. That, in our eyes, is the essence of master acting.[53]

The ability to live the part is, of course, one of the fundamentals of Stanislavsky's System of acting. That the members of the Moscow Art Theatre accomplished it is evidenced from the remarks of the critics. William Lyon Phelps said of *The Cherry Orchard,* "The men and women seem to be living rather than acting," and the critic of the *Christian Science Monitor* in his review of *The Three Sisters* declared:

Let it be stated again that the acting is so good that we are convinced that it is not acting. We feel that we are intruding into a room where a most private conversation is taking place. We feel like saying, "I beg your pardon, I made a mistake," and stepping out again.[54]

AMERICAN ACTORS AND PRODUCERS

The *Chicago Daily Journal* of April 4, 1923 observed that those who appreciated the work of the Moscow Art Theatre most were actors or those thoroughly acquainted with "the feel for acting skill." It is a fact that a request from American actors and actresses had come to Stanislavsky while the company was still in Paris, asking him to give matinees on Fridays to permit those engaged in the acting profession to attend. The first such performance was held on January 12, 1923, and according to Johnston, the actors were even more enthusiastic than the general public. John Barrymore, who was present, reportedly wrote a note to Gest declaring this "the most amazing experience I have ever had by a million miles in the theatre." [55] He was playing in *Hamlet* at the time, and according to Ethel Barrymore, John gave a special matinee of *Hamlet* for the Moscow Art Theatre. Her own reaction has been recorded in several places. She herself writes:

> While Jack was playing Hamlet the Moscow Art Theatre came to New York. They played Friday matinees and so I could go to see them and I was at their feet. You didn't need to know Russian to understand every word that was said. They were superb.[56]

Miss Barrymore also tells of her experiences with her brother Jack in taking the Russian players to supper at a Russian restaurant run by a Czarist general, "who in those Prohibition days thoughtfully gave his compatriots vodka in small after-dinner coffee cups." The Barrymores also took the Russians to see Harlem. A further comment of her admiration for the Moscow Art Theatre is contained in a report on the actors' matinees by the critic, Percy Hammond:

> We have yet to hear an American actor who does not say that they are greater than the critics and ourselves have pronounced them to be. So hard-boiled an American artist as Mr. Frank Keen for instance, sits night after night in rapt observation of them, interrupting his rehearsals of *Peter Weston* in order to do so. We have seen Miss Ruth Draper and many others in what we believed were tears of approbation; and Miss Barrymore's large eyes grow larger as they witness the miracles.[57]

Indeed so great was the effect of the Moscow Art Theatre upon Miss Barrymore that less than two months after their opening Arthur Hopkins announced that she planned to do only repertory for the following two seasons and that this would include plays of Shakespeare, O'Neill, Ibsen, and Hauptmann. She was actually unable to break with the star system because of her success in the current play, *The Laughing Lady*. Furthermore, the American public wanted her as a star.[58] As great an actor as Dudley Digges declared that the Moscow Art Theatre made him feel he would be willing to carry a spear.

William Lyon Phelps summed up the effect on the acting profession when he said: "The players of the Moscow Art Theatre made a profound impression in New York—both on the spectators, and, as a normal school, on professional actors." [59] Three lessons for American actors pointed out by Diana Bourbon were "trying to play together instead of competing"; "developing the art of expressive listening"; and "learning the technique of playing spontaneously after long experience with their roles." [60]

Productions of the Moscow Art Theatre made it increasingly clear that repertory offered the best possibility for approaching their standard of performance. Several schemes for organizing repertory groups were announced. The board of directors of the Theatre Guild, headed by Lawrence Langner, held several meetings with Stanislavsky with the idea of his forming a Guild Acting Company. Moreover, they set about planning the building of a new theatre which would be large enough to house the scenery of several productions to enable them to "have more than one play running at the same time, presented by an Acting Company appearing in repertory, and developing ensemble acting performances along the line of the Moscow Art Theatre." [61]

One direct result of the tours was the invitation to the Musical Studio to visit America under the sponsorship of Gest. Another was Alla Tarassova's remaining behind when the Moscow Art Theatre departed in order to play the part of the nun in Reinhardt's *The Miracle*. She gave full credit for her beautiful portrayal to Stanislavsky and his teaching. In this connection Johnston declares that "it was evident from the reviews of her performance that although the Moscow Art Theatre was gone, 'the Stanislavsky Method' of acting should not be allowed to leave."

What the Moscow Art Theatre accomplished with its American

visit has perhaps been best expressed by the critic Edmund Wilson, writing in *The Dial* of March, 1923:

> It constitutes perhaps, the only successful attempt to put on the stage the aesthetic ideal . . . of the school which went beyond notation and merely conveying the impression of life and accepting the convention of plausibility, aimed to produce not merely something real, but something beautiful . . . something valid as art.
>
> It is this extremely difficult formula which the Russians have brought to perfection in the theatre . . . . They present a surface so perfectly convincing as realism that we can scarcely believe when we leave the theatre that we have not been actual visitors in a Russian household and stood watching the family go about its business; but at the same time they bring out a whole set of aesthetic values to which we are not accustomed in the realistic theatre; the beauty and poignance of an atmosphere, of an idea, a person, a moment caught and put before us without emphasis, without that which we recognize as theatrical, but with brightness of the highest art.[62]

Notes

1. Clifford Ashby, "Alla Nazimova and the Advent of the New Acting in America," *Quarterly Journal of Speech*, xlv:2 (April, 1959), pp. 182–83, quoting Owen Johnson, "Mme. Alla Nazimova," *Century Magazine*, LXXIV (June, 1907), p. 219; Mary B. Mullett, "How a Dull, Fat Little Girl Became a Great Actress," *American Magazine*, XLIII (April, 1922), p. 112.
2. Oliver Sayler, *The Russian Theatre* (New York: Brentano, 1922), p. 306; Ashby, p. 185.
3. Ashby, p. 187.
4. Ashby, pp. 186–88.
5. Sayler, *The Russian Theatre*, pp. 308–310.
6. Sayler, *The Russian Theatre*, pp. 310–15.
7. Christian Brinton, "Idols of the Russian Masses," *The Cosmopolitan*, Vol. 40 (April, 1906), pp. 613–20.
8. Sayler, *The Russian Theatre*, p. 2.
9. Edward Gordon Craig, *On the Art of the Theatre* (Chicago: Browne's Bookstore, 1911), pp. 134–35.
10. Craig, pp. 135–36.
11. Huntley Carter, *The New Spirit in Drama and Art* (New York: Mitchell Kennerley, 1913), pp. 200–201.
12. Carter, p. 198.
13. Jean D'Auvergne, "Moscow Art Theatre," in *Fortnightly Review*, Vol. 101 (May, 1914), p. 793.
14. Gertrude Besse King, "The Cherry Orchard," in *The*

New Republic, Vol. 3 (June 26, 1915), p. 207.

15. Arthur Ruhl, "Plays at the Moscow Art Theatre," in *Current Opinion,* Vol. 63 (September, 1917), pp. 170–71.

16. "The Russian Theatre," in *Drama,* Vol. IX (February, 1919), pp. 31–61.

17. Sayler, *The Russian Theatre,* pp. 316–18.

18. Stanislavski, *My Life in Art,* p. 457.

19. Sayler, *The Russian Theatre,* pp. 318–22.

20. Arthur Hornblow, "Olla Podrida," in *Theatre Magazine* (May, 1923), p. 40.

21. Sayler, in *Theatre Arts Magazine,* Vol. 4 (July, 1920), pp. 200–216, and (October, 1920), pp. 290–315.

22. Sayler, "Origins and Progress of the Moscow Art Theatre," in the *New York Times Book Review and Magazine,* September 17, 1923, cited by Robert Albert Johnston, "The Moscow Art Theatre in America" (unpublished doctoral dissertation, Northwestern University, Evanston, 1951), p. 22. Much of the information which follows on the critical reception of the Moscow Art Theatre on its American visits is derived from this most helpful and reliable study.

23. Sayler, "Europe's Premier Playhouse in the Offing," *Theatre Magazine* (October, 1922), pp. 215–18.

24. Sayler, "The Russian Theatre," p. 29.

25. Sayler, "The Russian Theatre," p. 52.

26. Sayler, "When Moscow and New York Negotiate," in the *New York Times,* July 16, 1922, Sec. 6, p. 1.

27. Stanislavski, *My Life in Art,* p. 557.

28. From a conversation with Vera Soloviova, New York, January 10, 1960.

29. John D. Crane, "On the Muscovians," the *New York Times,* December 31, 1922, Sec. 7, p. 1.

30. Cyril Brown, "News of the Russians," the *New York Times,* October 22, 1932, Sec. 7, p. 1.

31. *New York Tribune,* December 25, 1922, p. 8.

32. Barrett H. Clark, "The Moscow Art Theatre in Berlin," in *The Drama* (January, 1923), pp. 136–37.

33. P. Yartsev, "The Quiet Light," in *Living Age,* Vol. 316 (January, 1923), pp. 171–74.

34. Gregory Zillboorg, "The Russian Invasion," in *The Drama,* XIII (January, 1923), pp. 127–30.

35. A. L. Fovitzky, *The Moscow Art Theatre and Its Distinguishing Characteristics* (New York: A. Chernoff

Publishing Company, 1923), p. 42.

36. Fovitzky, p. 45.

37. Fovitzky, pp. 7–8.

38. Oliver M. Sayler, *Inside the Moscow Art Theatre* (New York: Brentano, 1925), pp. 219–20.

39. The *New York Times*, January 5, 1923, p. 12, and the *Christian Science Monitor* (Boston: January 6, 1923), p. 6.

40. J. Rankin Towse, "Triumph for the Moscow Art Theatre," *New York Evening Post*, January 9, 1923, p. 8.

41. The *New York Times*, February 22, 1923, p. 10, and Sheppard Butler, "Mr. Gest Discourses on Miracles from Moscow," *Chicago Sunday Tribune*, April 1, 1923, Sec. 7.

42. Mollie Morris, "Russian Actors Here a Triumphant Band," *Daily News* (Chicago), April 4, 1923, p. 20, and Butler, *Chicago Sunday Tribune*, April 22, 1923, Sec. 7, p. 1.

43. David Magarshack, *Stanislavsky, A Life* (New York: The Chanticleer Press, 1951), p. 367.

44. "News of the Stage," *Chicago Daily Journal*, April 15, 1924, p. 6.

45. Johnston, "The Moscow Art Theatre in America," pp. 131–32.

46. Donaghey, "Some Words About the Returning Russians," *Chicago Sunday Tribune*, April 6, 1924, Sec. 9, p. 1.

47. Jack Crawford, "Moscow to Broadway," in *Drama Magazine*, Vol. 13 (March, 1923), pp. 212, 236.

48. Corbin, "Moscow Players Open to a Throng," the *New York Times*, January 10, 1923, p. 28.

49. Sheppard Butler, "Symphony of Woe is Acted by Russians," *Chicago Daily Tribune*, April 7, 1923, p. 17.

50. Stark Young, "The Moscow Art Theatre," *Glamour* (New York and London: Charles Scribner's Sons, 1925), p. 47.

51. Percy Hammond, "The Theatre," *New York Tribune*, January 30, 1923, p. 6.

52. Johnston, "The Moscow Art Theatre in America," pp. 232–33.

53. "Stanislavsky Told Hullinger," The *New York Times*, January 26, 1923, p. 20.

54. Johnston, "The Moscow Art Theatre in America," p. 232.

55. Sayler, *Inside the Moscow Art Theatre*, p. 27.

56. Ethel Barrymore, *Memories* (New York: Harper and Brothers, 1955), p. 248.

57. Percy Hammond, "Oddments and Remainders," *New York Tribune*, February 7, 1923, p. 8.

58. The *New York Times*, February 25, 1923, Sec. 7, p. 1.

59. Johnston, "The Moscow Art Theatre in America," p. 294

60. Johnston, "The Moscow Art Theatre in America," p. 272.

61. Lawrence Langner, "The Little Theatre Grows Up," in *The Theatre Guild, The First Ten Years*, ed. W. P. Eaton and others (New York: Brentano, 1929), pp. 218–19.

62. Johnston, "The Moscow Art Theatre in America," p. 247.

nine

The Impact of Stanislavsky on the Contemporary American Theatre

THE SECOND GENERATION OF THE MOSCOW ART THEATRE

The lasting effect upon American acting, however, was not accomplished by the performances of the Moscow Art Theatre alone. They served to father the desire, as it were, in the American actor to make his acting more realistic, more truthful, more truly creative, and they prepared the ground for further study of Stanislavsky's System.

Alla Tarassova, one of the Moscow Art Theatre actresses, remained behind to play the nun in Reinhardt's production of *The Miracle*. She received high praise for her performance, but gave all the credit for her accomplishment to Stanislavsky and his teachings.

It was chiefly through members of the First Studio, however, that Americans came to know Stanislavsky's method of working. Some of the actors and actresses remained in America when the Moscow Art Theatre left; others came here later. Richard Boleslavsky, who had directed the First Studio's opening production, *The Good Hope* (see p. 115), left Russia in 1920. He was in New York to greet his former comrades when the Moscow Art Theatre arrived in January, 1923. The week after the opening of the Moscow Art Theatre's New York engagement, Boleslavsky began a series of lectures with the aid of an interpreter. The first was held at the Princess Theatre on January 18, 1923. Among the professional people in his group were Rosalind Fuller, the actress playing Ophelia to John Barrymore's Hamlet; Helen Arthur, the manager of the Neighborhood Playhouse; and the playwright, Sophie Treadwell.[1] In April, *Theatre Magazine* published an article called "The Man and His Methods." Here Boleslavsky described Stanislavsky's dedication to the art of the theatre, his eternal vigilance in the expansion of his theories, which brought about the organization of the Moscow Art Theatre. He declared that the first factor in the success of such an organization is tradition; he asserted that there can be no excellence where there is no permanency; and he pointed to the element of cooperation and unity that went into the founding of the Theatre Antoine, the Comédie Française, and Wallack's and Daly's companies in New York—as well, of course, as the Moscow Art Theatre, most of whose artists had been with the company for fifteen years or longer. He spoke of Stanislavsky's development of certain basic principles which demanded the coordination of elocution, singing, dancing, fencing, scenic art, and lighting. Finally he pointed to the realism which the Art Theatre had achieved and which accounted for a large measure of its success:

> By realism, however, is not meant sordid detail, mechanical cleverness, make-up, nor scenic intricacy. The realism that Stanislavsky preaches is internal, not external. An actor who can stand in an imaginary snowdrift and actually make an audience shiver has mastered the reality of his art.[2]

In July, 1923, Boleslavsky wrote an article for *Theatre Arts Monthly* entitled "The Laboratory Theatre," [3] in which he praised the experimental laboratory where new forms could be developed.

In the summer of 1923 Boleslavsky went to the country with a handful of players, including six staff members of the Neighborhood Playhouse. With this group he rehearsed two plays which he produced at the Neighborhood Playhouse the following fall (see p. 203). In 1924 he founded the American Laboratory Theatre, which was instrumental in shaping the course that American teaching of acting was to follow, to a great extent, in the succeeding years. Among its early members were Stella Adler, Lee Strasberg, and Harold Clurman; [4] these were to be instrumental in the application of the Stanislavsky method to the American theatre. Boleslavsky left New York in 1929 to go to Hollywood, where he directed until his death in 1936, but the Laboratory Theatre carried on until 1932.

Closely associated with Boleslavsky in teaching the Stanislavsky System at the Laboratory Theatre were two former Moscow Art Theatre actresses, Maria Ouspenskaya, who had won theatregoers and critics by her performances with the Moscow Art Theatre in New York, and Germanova, who took over the directorship of the School of the American Laboratory Theatre at the time of Boleslavsky's departure. The success of these disciples of Stanislavsky is attested to by a caption which appeared in the September, 1925 issue of *Theatre Arts Monthly* below a picture of the first play presented by the students at the Laboratory Theatre: "The detailed and devoted method of the Moscow Art Theatre Studios is to be found in the American Laboratory Theatre . . . . His pupils have already caught something of the flux and continuity of Russian ensemble playing." [5]

Ouspenskaya also taught at the Neighborhood Playhouse, and in 1931 she established her own school of acting in New York City. Three years later, she drew an unforgettable portrait of the Baroness in Sidney Howard's adaptation of Sinclair Lewis' novel *Dodsworth*. In 1936 she was called to Hollywood to play the same role in the filmed version. Three years later she opened her school there and was active both in teaching and acting until her tragic death in 1949. [6]

Schools of acting were established by other members of the Moscow Art Theatre who remained here at the conclusion of the American engagement or who came to the United States at a later time. Ivan and Maria Lazariev went to Chicago, where they opened a school called Gorky's Studio. After her husband's death, Mme. Lazariev taught privately for many years. According to Johnston, she was a member of the staff of Hull House as late as 1951.

Leo Bulgakov, another member of the First Studio, who, with his wife, Barbara, played with the Moscow Art Theatre during the American tours, was recalled by Morris Gest to play in *The Miracle*. The Bulgakovs remained in New York, he to achieve success as an American director, she to win praise for her performance of Nina in *The Sea Gull*, which her husband directed. He also produced *The Lower Depths* in an English translation with the title *At the Bottom*. [7] The Bulgakovs established the Westchester Repertory Company in 1931, and in 1939, opened the Bulgakov Studio of Theatre Art in New York City, which continued until 1942.

The following year, Bulgakov played General Golz in the motion picture, *For Whom the Bell Tolls*. A number of other Russian actors appeared in this picture, among them Vladimir Sokoloff and Akim Tamiroff. Bulgakov died in July, 1948. He had taught at the American Theatre Wing the year before, and after his death, his wife took the class. She is still teaching, and during the spring of 1960 she directed a group of Russian actors in a production of *Uncle Vanya* at the Master Institute.

Tamara Daykarhanova, one-time member of the Moscow Art Theatre, came to this country with Balieff's *Chauve Souris* and she received praise for her performance in the revue. She taught for several years with Ouspenskaya at the latter's studio in New York City, and in 1935 she opened the School for the Stage to prepare young actors and actresses in the fundamentals of the Stanislavsky System. Madame Daykarhanova herself has appeared in the ANTA production of *The House of Bernarda Alba* and as the Empress in *Anastasia* in summer stock. She occasionally plays on television. She has been a member of the Actors Studio for some time and won praise from the New York drama critics for her performance of the nurse in the Actors Studio production of Chekhov's *The Three Sisters,* which opened in New York City on June 22, 1964.

Early in 1935, Michael Chekhov, nephew of Anton Chekhov, brought his company of players to this country under the management of Sol Hurok. They played for three months at the Majestic Theatre in New York City as well as in Boston and Philadelphia with great success, as this comment from *The Christian Science Monitor* will show:

> The enthralling effect these players invariably achieve in their joyful custom of so fulfilling the purpose of each play they do . . . as to become its very texture. The names of G. Chamara as Fyodor, V. Soloviova as his wife, Elene, and A. Jilinsky as Chairman of the Committee on Cultural Relations with foreign countries, are featured.

At the end of the American engagement, several members of the company remained in America. Chekhov had been one of Stanislavsky's most gifted pupils, a member of the First Studio, and its director when it became the Moscow Art Theatre Second. After the American tour he went to England at the invitation of Mr. and Mrs. Leonard Elmhirst, founders of Dartington Hall in Devonshire. There he developed the Chekhov Theatre Studio, with Beatrice Straight, actress daughter of Mrs. Elmhirst, as manager. In 1939 the Studio was moved to Ridgefield, Connecticut,[8] and two years later to New York City, where they rehearsed and presented their own production of *Twelfth Night* on Broadway. Yul Brynner, Hurd Hatfield, and Beatrice

Straight were among Chekhov's pupils who appeared in it. The production later went on tour, but was finally abandoned because many of the actors were called into the armed services. In the meantime Chekhov himself had gone to Hollywood, where he opened a studio. He continued to teach there and to play in motion pictures until his death in 1955. Two years before his death, he brought out his book, *To the Actor,* with a preface written by the well-known actor, Yul Brynner, who was his pupil. In it, Chekhov states:

> To the best of my knowledge, theatrical history records the existence of only one method expressly postulated for the actor—that created by Constantin Stanislavsky (and, unfortunately, much misunderstood and often misinterpreted). Let this book, then, be another effort in the direction of a better theatre through better acting . . . . "Organize and write down your thoughts concerning the technique of acting," Stanislavsky said to me, "It is your duty and the duty of everyone who loves the theatre and looks devotedly into its future." [9]

Vera Soloviova was one of the leading players in the visiting company, as she had been in the First Studio's productions of *The Good Hope* and *The Cricket on the Hearth.* Indeed, she often alternated between the parts of Natasha in *Lower Depths* and Princess Mstislavskaya in *Tsar Fyodor* at the Moscow Art Theatre and her roles in the First Studio.

Soloviova's playing of the Queen in *Hamlet* in the Moscow Art Theatre Second had received great critical acclaim, not only in Moscow but also in Lithuania, where she played in Lithuanian. Of her New York appearance the drama critic of the *World-Telegram* wrote:

> Again they revealed brilliant individual performances such as the ones of Soloviova and Pavlov. In spite of the fact that the performances were in a foreign language (Russian) it did not spoil the enjoyment of the remarkable acting of these fine performers. No one can fail to see that the Moscow Art Players are about their work with the highest skill and understanding.[10]

On October 27, 1923, the twenty-fifth anniversary of the founding of the Moscow Art Theatre, Vera Soloviova, Seraphima Birman, and their colleagues received the Moscow Art Theatre Medallion "given to those who had been working no less than ten years in the Moscow Art Theatre," and in the words of Nemirovich-Danchenko, "as an expression of heartfelt gratitude for the deep and valuable work for the sake of our dear theatre." [11]

Andrius Jilinsky, Soloviova's husband was also a member of the First Studio and the Moscow Art Theatre Second, and had been Managing Director of the Lithuanian State Theatre, where he played the leading role of *Hamlet* under Michael Chekhov's direction. He played leading roles in the American engagement of Chekhov's company, as well, and is pictured in the playbill for the New York spring season of 1960 in a scene from *The Days of the Turbins,* in their New York engagement in 1935. This playbill also contains an article by P. Markov, head of a visiting troupe of Soviet actors who visited the United States on the cultural exchange program in 1959. (Markov is the same critic who had reviewed Soloviova's performance of Gertrude in Moscow and who wrote the chronicle of The Moscow Art Theatre Second.) Typical of the reception accorded Jilinsky is the comment of Boston critic Helen Eager concerning his appearance in *The Days of the Turbins:*

> Especially impressive is Andrius Jilinsky's "Colonel." An actor of great power and the possessor of a glorious speaking voice, he dominates the play with the force of his personality.

At the close of the tour, Soloviova and Jilinsky joined Daykarhanova in her School for the Stage and taught there for five years. At the same time Jilinsky organized his own group, the New York Troupe. After working with them for three years, he directed them in a Broadway production of Strindberg's *The Bridal Crown.* In 1938, a group of graduates from the School for the Stage formed the American Actors Company with Jilinsky as their director. In this group were Mary Hunter, Jane Rose, Joseph Anthony, Perry Wilson, William Hansen, and playwright Horton Foote. Jilinsky directed Lynn Riggs' *Sumpin' Like Wings* and Paul Green's *Shroud My Body Down* with this group.

In 1940 Soloviova and Jilinsky opened the Actors' Workshop in the Sutton Hotel's little theatre. In addition to his regular students, Jilinsky taught a class for opera singers at the American Theatre Wing until his death in February, 1948. The great artist Mstislav Dobujinsky, who designed sets for the Moscow Art Theatre, the Lithuanian State Theatre, the Paris Opera, and the Metropolitan, wrote in an obituary for Jilinsky which appeared in the *Novoye Russkoye Slovo* in New York City:

. . . being a very gifted actor himself, he was fascinated by experimental studio work. Even in this he followed the footsteps of Stanislavsky, and it was to this true vocation and pedagogical talent that he gave himself in America, working with his pupils literally to the last day of his life.

Soloviova was asked to continue this work at the Wing, but she was busy with her own pupils. Since 1951 she has been teaching in her own studio, The Vera Soloviova Studio of Acting in New York City.

That the work of these disciples of Stanislavsky has borne fruit is evidenced on many sides. Many of the well-known actors in Hollywood, as well as on Broadway, were students of theirs. To name a few: Hurd Hatfield, Ford Rainey, Beatrice Straight, and Yul Brynner were members of the original Chekhov Players; Franchot Tone studied with Ouspenskaya; Mildred Dunnock, William Prince, and Jane Rose studied with Daykarhanova, Jilinsky, and Soloviova, as did the three well-known directors, Joseph Anthony, Vincent Donehue, and Boris Tumarin.

THE GROUP THEATRE

A second factor in extending the influence of the Stanislavsky System among American actors and directors was the Group Theatre's use of it both in acting and directing. Lee Strasberg, Stella Adler, and Harold Clurman had all been exposed to the technique of acting according to the Moscow Art Theatre at the American Laboratory Theatre.[12] Strasberg himself gives credit to Ouspenskaya and Boleslavsky in a footnote to his chapter on "Actor and Actor Training" in John Gassner's *Producing the Play*.[13] Moreover, the Group Theatre bore many resemblances to the Studios of the Moscow Art Theatre. The members followed the First Studio's experiment in communal living during the summer while rehearsing a production for the following season. They were concerned with finding ways and means of improving creativity. They made use of Chekhov's notes before they were generally available to the American public, and had the notes from Vakhtangov's diary translated for their use.[14]

Finally, Strasberg adopted a method of rehearsal during the first summer at Brookfield (1931) in working on *The House of Connolly*, which emphasized, as Clurman points out, two particular aspects of the System. These were improvisation and affective memory.[15] It was the overpreoccupation with the latter "as a key to that elusive ingredient of the stage, true emotion" which caused so much discussion and dissension and brought adverse criticism not only upon the Group Theatre but, unfortunately, also upon the Stanislavsky System.

Stella Adler and her husband, Harold Clurman, called upon Stanislavsky in the summer of 1934 in Paris, where he was recuperating from a recent illness. When Adler complained that certain aspects of his System had worried her for the past three years and that she no longer found any joy in acting, Stanislavsky said to her, "If the System does not help you, forget it. But perhaps you do not use it properly." This remark of Stanislavsky's has been quoted out of its proper context to suggest that even the master made light of his own method. Instead, Stanislavsky offered to work with Adler on a scene that she had found difficult, and for five weeks she worked daily with him on a scene from a play called *Gentlewoman*. As a result of this the interpretation of Stanislavsky by the Group Theatre suffered a sea change. Clurman describes the result of Adler's report of her work with Stanislavsky:

> To put it bluntly, she had discovered that our [the group's] use of the Stanislavsky system had been incorrect. An undue emphasis on the "exercises" of affective memory had warped our work with the actor. Strasberg's first reaction to this declaration was the charge that Stanislavsky had gone back on himself. Later, however, he decided to take advantage of the suggestions furnished by Stella's report, and to use what he could of the "innovations" in Stanislavsky's method. Stella herself began to give classes that summer.[16]

Adler gives her own account of the change that took place:

> Only in 1934 was the approach to the actor's craft changed very radically. The emphasis which had been put very strongly on the conscious manipulation of the actor's exact emotion was abandoned by most of the actors. The Stanislavsky system was from then on reinterpreted by pressure coming from his own statement. This clarified the ideas in which the Group had misunderstood his theories. From that time on, the emphasis shifted. Now emphasis was put on the circumstances of the play and a much stronger use of the actor's need to find greater justification in the use of these circumstances and a more *conscious* use of them.[17]

The Group's effect upon the American theatre has been pointed out by many writers. The history of its founding and development is clearly traced by Clurman in *The Fervent Years*. Raymond Dominic Gasper, in his "A Study of the Group Theatre and Its Contribution to American Theatre," speaks of the Group Method as "derivative of or an adaptation of the Moscow Art Theatre's Method." Nevertheless, his examples of the techniques used are in some cases identical with those which appear in the writings of Stanislavsky and Vakhtangov and other members of the Moscow Art Theatre and its Studios. Gasper declares, moreover:

> The Group Theatre was the only organization in America which put the system into anything like successful practice and through its efforts at least a portion of the system came into more common use in this country. The Group's adaptation of the Stanislavsky approach—or the Group Method—has become more commonly known on both the professional and amateur stage, the Group having articulated its method successfully through its productions, articles on its rehearsal techniques, statements, lectures, and symposiums by its directors and actors, direct and indirect instruction in its use by members of the Group and their students, and utilization of much of the system in contemporary productions by directors, directly or indirectly trained by the Group.[18]

John Gassner's evaluation of the Group Theatre identifies its significance in propagating the Stanislavsky System. He speaks of the Group as "a memory of the best ensemble acting Broadway had ever known" and an influence through its directors and actors.[19] The greatest influence has been due to the work of the three directors, Harold Clurman, Elia Kazan, and Robert Lewis, all former members of the Group Theatre. The directing methods of all three reveal the use of the Stanislavsky principles.

PUBLICATIONS

The third factor in making the Stanislavsky System available to American students of acting was the publication of the writings of Stanislavsky and others about the System. Before the end of the first season in America Stanislavsky had begun the writing of his autobiography, *My Life in Art*. It was published in 1924 by Little, Brown and Company, and reprinted in 1937 one year before his death. In 1948 Theatre Arts Books brought out another edition to mark the fiftieth anniversary of the founding of the Moscow Art Theatre. Here Stanislavsky gave the merest outline of his System. Nevertheless, for a number of years it was the only guide to the uninitiated except for a series of articles written by Boleslavsky for *Theatre Arts Monthly*. These were entitled "The First Lesson in Acting," October, 1923; "Fundamentals of Acting," February, 1927; "A Second Lesson in Acting," July, 1929; "A Third Lesson in Acting," July, 1931; and

"A Fourth Lesson in Acting," March, 1932; and a three-page article entitled "Direction and Acting," which Stanislavsky wrote for the 1929 edition of the *Encyclopaedia Britannica*.[20] "The First Lesson in Acting" was reprinted in the introduction to *Theatre* by Edith J. R. Isaacs,[21] which was published by Little, Brown and Company in 1927. Boleslavsky's book, *The First Six Lessons in Acting*,[22] did not appear until 1937.

In June, 1932, however, two graduate students of speech and dramatics at Cornell University, Barnard Hewitt and Aristide D'Angelo, discussed "The Stanislavsky System for Actors" in an article under that title in *The Quarterly Journal of Speech*.[23] They mentioned the fact that the Stanislavsky System was often referred to in books and articles on the theatre, but they deplored the lack of an adequate statement of the System. They spoke of the "fragmentary information scattered through *My Life in Art*" and Stanislavsky's "poorly translated article on Direction and Acting" in the *Encyclopaedia*. They declared, however, that the practice and occasional writings of such followers of Stanislavsky in America as Maria Ouspenskaya, Leo Bulgakov, Alla Nazimova, and Lee Strasberg, director of the Group Theatre in New York City, contribute materially to an understanding of the System. The article showed an understanding of the basic principles of the System and it gave the background of its development. The writers referred to Boleslavsky's mention of the five senses as instruments for developing the emotions and to Stanislavsky's emphasis on the importance of imagination in stimulating the emotions which often arise from sensory recall. The article also discussed the actor's search for the fundamental line of action of his role and its organic relation to the main trunk, that is, to the fundamental action of the entire play. They went so far as to explain what Stanislavsky calls the "magical creative *if*" in terms of what Stanislavsky was to label the objective:

> Each moment in the actor's part, each minor line of action will present a special problem, will pose a special question. The actor asks, "If I am this character in these circumstances, what do I want to do?" The answer will come in the form of a verb, for example: "To get a raise in salary." And finally the expression will come in action, all of which springs from the verb which answered the question. This procedure—question, answer in the form of a verb, and expression in action—should be applied to the whole play (the fundamental line of action) and to each of its subsidiary parts (the minor lines of action).

Finally, the authors defined the Stanislavsky System as "an analysis of the process of artistic creation as applied to the art of acting, an analysis so practical that it offers to the ordinary actor a method by which he may approach the results of genius." They looked forward to the publication of Stanislavsky's new book in an English translation by Mrs. Norman Hapgood.

However, *An Actor Prepares* was not published in America until 1936. This was, nevertheless, two years earlier than its Russian edition, which was not published until just after Stanislavsky's death. In 1930, while working on the manuscript in Nice (see p. 105), with the Hapgoods nearby, Stanislavsky had given Mrs. Hapgood, his friend and translator, the American rights to all his writings; and he had agreed then to send her the entire manuscript of *An Actor Prepares* for publication in America as soon as he had completed the revision on which he was then working. Unfortunately, his ill health prevented him from preparing more than the first half of it, which he sent Mrs. Hapgood in 1934. When she visited him in 1937, he promised to send her the rest of the notes on his System shortly. Stanislavsky died the following year and World War II intervened before Stanislavsky's family finally sent the second part of the material which makes up the second volume of the System. It was published under the title *Building a Character* by Theatre Arts Books in 1949. Stanislavsky's final work, "The Method of Physical Actions," which Mrs. Hapgood also translated, was published in 1961 under the title, *Creating a Role.*

An Actor Prepares was well received by the critics. Walter Prichard Eaton, reviewing it in the *New York Herald Tribune,* declared that it should be a required textbook for all dramatic schools.[24] John Mason Brown in his review for the *New York Post* of November 18, 1936, asserted that it ought to find its way into the hands of every serious worker in the theatre in the United States. The actor Morris Carnovsky, writing in the *Brooklyn Daily Eagle* of December 27, 1936, maintained that the laws of the method were fundamental and universal and could be of use to the American actor. He went so far as to proclaim *An Actor Prepares* "the greatest and deepest guide to the laws of acting written in modern times." [25]

Stark Young sounded a dissenting note in the *New Republic* with his statement that the System was inadequate "with regard to the broad field of art, culture, acting style." His objection, however, needs to be viewed in the perspective offered by his basic belief that acting should be every moment designed. Moreover, he declared, "The achievement of more variety and speed [in speech] would help clear away the . . . realistic clutter now so much in the way of the art of the theatre."[26] In "The Prompt Book," an article which he wrote for *Theatre Arts Monthly* in March, 1924, Young defines scenes as statements of an idea in dialogue, and he asserted that attempts to justify the dialogue with realistic movement would only accomplish the childish rubbish of illusion.[27] It is hard to reconcile this statement with his admiration for the acting of Ouspenskaya, who later played in his *The Saint* when it was produced at the Provincetown Playhouse (see p. 206).

In reviewing the performance of *The Lower Depths* for the *New York Times* on September 14, 1924, Young had written, "Ouspensky [Ouspenskaya], when she stepped out of the line of peasants and sang the verse of that song, brought something to the stage that was magnificent and wild, with enough resemblance to make it credible in a realistic method, but with a power and ferocity added that made it not external life but a great and unforgettable idea."[28] Young had used the term "super real" rather than "merely real" in praising Moskvin, Kachalov, and Alla Tarassova. Yet only thirteen years later Young condemned the very system that had helped these players to achieve the results which he had praised.

Young's influence was evidenced as late as 1944 when Edwin Duerr, a teacher at Cornell University, wrote a bitter attack on the Stanislavsky System as a contribution to a book in honor of his former professor, the late Alexander M. Drummond, formerly head of the Department of Speech and Drama at Cornell. He condemned *An Actor Prepares* specifically, declaring categorically that it did not teach the actor "emphatically and always," to hunt for the playwright's idea and then to express it.[29]

Duerr's accusation is, of course, completely unfounded. It amounts, as Hetler points out, to actual misrepresentation by quoting out of context from *An Actor Prepares*. Furthermore, Stanislavsky leaves little room for doubt as to his feeling for the playwright's idea when he says, "You will have to read the play over many times. Only on the rarest occasions can an actor seize the essentials of a new part instantly and be so carried away by it that he can create its whole spirit in one thrust of feeling."[30] Speaking of the super-objective or main purpose of the play he says:

In a play the whole stream of individual, minor objectives, all the imaginative thoughts, feelings, and actions of an actor should converge to carry out the *super-objective* of the plot. . . . If it is human and directed toward the basic purpose of the play it will be like a main artery, providing nourishment and life to both it and the actor.[31]

Again, when asked how an actor can make himself feel the life of the play, Stanislavsky cautioned, "Of course you must study the play and its main theme first." [32] Moreover, had Duerr been familiar with Stanislavsky's original statement of the System, which appeared in the *Encyclopaedia Britannica* in 1929, he could never have made this accusation. For Stanislavsky says here:

. . . but only by profound attention to the artistic individuality of the author and to his ideal of mentality, which have been disclosed as the creative germ of the play, can the theatre realize all its artistic depth and transmit, as in a poetical production, completeness and harmony of composition.[33]

In 1937 *Theatre Arts* printed a symposium on *An Actor Prepares* and the Stanislavsky System with John Gielgud, Robert Sherwood, Harold Clurman, and Norris Houghton participating, in the January and March issues. There was agreement on the value of the method. Gielgud found the book of great value to directors especially. He felt that good actors would have to find something like it. He had only one reservation, that it was not practical for theatrical plays. Sherwood, Clurman, and Houghton thought it useful for any style of theatre. Clurman pointed out that Vakhtangov and Meyerhold had used it. Houghton, however, believed that it would yield the best results if all the actors and the director were familiar with the System.

According to Hetler the influence of *An Actor Prepares* was felt as early as 1939 in American textbooks on acting, starting with Aristide D'Angelo's *The Actor Creates* [34] and, in the following year, Barnard Hewitt's *The Art and Craft of Play Production*.[35] Hewitt acknowledged the influence of Stanislavsky's "theory and practice" in actor training and listed six of his subjective techniques: observation, affective memory or recall of emotions, imagination, improvisation, relaxation, and concentration. Hetler offers the text by Harry Darkes Albright, *Working Up a Part,* as evidence of the profound influence of Stanislavsky's method. Albright includes relaxation, sense memory, observation, and motivation; under the last he takes up the given circumstances, justification, and action: "A good actor seeks the 'why' of an action," Albright explains, adding that the "how" grows out of the "why." [36]

Albright had the advantage of the works of several Stanislavsky interpreters. A number of important publications appeared in the same year as *An Actor Prepares.* Two were especially important in their presentation of the Stanislavsky System. *Moscow Rehearsals* [37] by Norris Houghton was an account of rehearsals at various Soviet theatres. Houghton visited Stanislavsky in 1935 and was privileged to watch him rehearse (see p. 126). In addition to his descriptions of rehearsals at the Moscow Art Theatre, Stanislavsky's Opera Studio, Meyerhold's Theatre, and a number of others, Houghton gave a very clear exposition of the Stanislavsky System; he even included a brief reference to the final method of working: the method of physical and psychological problems of the actor. In 1936, also, Nemirovich-Danchenko's autobiography, *My Life in the Russian Theatre,*[38] made its appearance. While it gave very little information about the Stanislavsky System, it pictured the actual meeting between the two founders of the Moscow Art Theatre in detail, and in explaining what prompted them to their undertaking, it described the traditional acting of nineteenth-century Russia, which, incidentally, was similar to that in America for the same period (see p. 164). Another publication in 1936 was a little magazine called *Theatre Workshop,* the official organ of the New Theatre League. Among its contributing editors were Barrett H. Clark, Mordecai Gorelik, John Howard Lawson, and Lee Strasberg. The October, 1936 number was the first one. It was called the Art of Acting issue. In it appeared an essay of 36 pages called "The Work of the Actor." This was written by I. Rapoport,[39] who was a member of the Third Studio, which became the Vakhtangov Theatre. This article gives the most lucid outline of the Stanislavsky System that has ever been offered. It is in some respects clearer than Stanislavsky's own exposition. Rapoport makes clear the importance of organic attention, the five senses as the organs of attention, freedom from muscular strain through the focusing of attention upon an object, the justification of stage movement by the use of the imagination, the use of creative fantasy to develop a characterization, the ability to regard the fiction and make-believe of the stage as though it were real, and the recollection of physical actions or sense memory. He explains the three elements of what he calls the "stage task": (1) *Action—What* I am doing, (2) *Volition—Why* I am doing it, (3) *Adjustment—How* I am doing it (form, character of action). "The first two elements—*action* and *volition* are consciously determined by the actor and as a result of their performance the third element, adjustment, arises involuntarily." Rapoport illustrates the importance of the will or volition for the actor: "He sets himself his stage task by determining what aim he is pursuing . . . . The fulfilling of his task will be stage action." Rapoport gives many examples and exercises which will be familiar to anyone who has studied with the former members of the First Studio. The same exercises have undoubtedly been adopted by their students. Rapoport also discussed counteraction or obstacles, external or internal, which interfere with the carrying out of the stage action or task and are a factor in strengthening the actor's objective. As in life, the more interference one encounters, the more energetically one attempts to carry his task to fulfillment. Text and subtext, outer and inner characterization, as well as the division of the role into sections are treated simply and succinctly.

This issue of *Theatre Workshop* also included an article, "Case History of a Role," by Giatsintova, one of the members of the Moscow Art Theatre who was with the company in New York.

The next issue of *Theatre Workshop,* January–March, 1937, contained articles by the Soviet director I. Sudakov, who was one of a committee of three directly responsible to Stanislavsky and Nemirovich-Danchenko for the management of the Moscow Art Theatre.[40] Sudakov acknowledged the influence of the leaders of the Moscow Art Theatre. His article also covers several elements of Stanislavsky's System, such as the concentration of attention, the feeling of truth, action, adaptation, and sense memory. His exposition is far less clear than Rapoport's and his treatment of sense memory and the object of the actor's attention is overemphasized. Since this article was translated especially for the Group Theatre, it may have influenced their use of the Stanislavsky System. In the same issue Harold Clurman discussed the two recently-published books, Danchenko's *My Life in the Russian Theatre* and Stanislavsky's *An Actor Prepares.* Clurman asserted that all the developments of the modern theatre spring from Danchenko and Stanislavsky—and from their joint creation, the Moscow Art Theatre.

The third and fourth issues of *Theatre Workshop* for April-July and September–October, 1937, carried articles entitled "Principles of Directing" by B. E. Zakhava, a director of the Vakhtangov Theatre who worked under Vakhtangov in the Third Studio. In the second article Zakhava quotes Stanislavsky several times: "You can't act emotions," says Stanislavsky—"The actor should not worry about emotion. Emotion will come of itself." Zakhava himself warned, "The director should not exact the imitation of emotions from the actor but the execution of specific actions. He must tell the actor what to do, and not how to feel." Like Rapoport, he emphasized the importance of the actor's "doing":

> Doing differs from feeling chiefly in the element of will which is present in it; to persuade, to quiet, to beg, to mock, to bid farewell, to wait, to drive away, to hold back the tears, to hide one's joy or suffering; these are all verbs inferring a will-power (I wish to persuade and I do persuade, I wish to quiet and I do quiet). The actor can undertake to execute such action at any given time provided he understands the motives behind them.[41]

In 1941 John Gassner made a contribution to the knowledge of the Stanislavsky System with his book, *Producing the Play*.[42] Every phase of production was covered and always by a person prominent in his field. Among the contributors were Harold Clurman, Robert Lewis, and Lee Strasberg.

In 1947 the articles of Rapoport, Sudakov, Zakhava, and Giatsintova were reprinted in a collection containing among other essays Stanislavsky on "Direction and Acting" from the *Encyclopaedia,* notes made by Michael Chekhov while he was a member of the First Studio, and an excerpt from Stanislavsky's production plan for *Othello* in *Acting, a Handbook of the Stanislavski Method*.[43]

In 1948 *Stanislavsky Produces Othello* [44] appeared. This was actually compiled from the notes which Stanislavsky made in 1929–1930 in Nice for the production of *Othello,* which he contemplated with Leonidov in the title role.

In 1948, also, to mark the fiftieth anniversary of the founding of the Moscow Art Theatre, Robert MacGregor of Theatre Arts Books brought out an anniversary edition of *My Life in Art* and *An Actor Prepares* as well as Boleslavsky's *The First Six Lessons in Acting.* John Gielgud wrote the Introduction for this edition of *An Actor Prepares.* His praise is particularly interesting in the light of the recent tendency by some teachers of Stanislavsky's technique to regard it as complex.[45] Quite to the contrary, Gielgud declares:

The book is absorbing. One is enthralled by it—one cannot put it down.

In it there is much wonderful understanding and advice—both for those who practice acting and direction, and those who only study it. How to relax, to control the body. How to study a part, to work with imagination, to build a performance from within. How to work with other actors, to give and take, how to regard the audience so that one may control their reactions at certain times and allow them to take control at others. The style of playing in classical and realistic work, the art of concentration. All these matters are discussed and examined with masterly clearness and simplicity.[46]

Gielgud also maintains that there is no reason why Stanislavsky's System should apply only to Russia. His evaluation of the book is, in a sense, a statement of the purpose of the System. He says:

> This book gives some of the reasons why such ambitions are unworthy, why a great artist should seek for truth and dignity and style in acting, why he must have a true appreciation of the quality of the play itself, and try to understand the intentions of his author and director, and help the efforts of his fellow players to work with him to interpret these intentions properly.[47]

Finally Gielgud says: "Stanislavski's book is amazingly modern . . . . He was a true artist in the deepest sense, and when you read his book, you feel how much more he had to give to the theatre than the mere trappings which so often delude its most ardent followers."

In 1949 the long-awaited second part of Stanislavsky's manuscript, called *Building a Character*,[48] was published by Theatre Arts Books. It concerns itself with the externalization or, as Stanislavsky calls it, the "embodying of the role." Those critics who had charged that the Stanislavsky System was subjective and failed to take note of the primary task of an actor, to communicate with the audience, should certainly have been silenced. "Here is the most careful attention to pauses, to the line of inflection, to conservation of energy, to the most calculated increase of pitch by rising five notes and dropping three for each measure, to pushing the climax to the highest and loudest point." [49] So George R. Kernodle wrote in *The Quarterly Journal of Speech* for December, 1949. He asserted finally that Stanislavsky was just as much concerned with the external perspective of the actor as he was with the inner perspective of the role. Henry Schnitzler of the University of California, at Los Angeles, called it a "highly significant book" that should help to clarify various misunderstandings as to the nature of the Stanislavsky System. Cornelia Otis Skinner, who had spoken out sharply against the Stanislavsky System in 1942,[50] now declared: "This is a fine, revealing and inspiringly constructive book . . . a great contribution to the world of the theatre." [51]

While it is true that *Building a Character* shows clearly the wholeness of the Stanislavsky System by giving attention to the external elements of an actor's performance, it must be emphasized that these externals are always related to the inner characterization. In speaking about speech tempo-rhythm, for example, Stanislavsky reminds his students, "tempo-rhythm, whether mechanically, intuitively or consciously created, does act on our inner life, on our feelings, on our inner experiences." He goes on to say, "There is an indissoluble interdependence, interaction, and bond between tempo-rhythm and feeling, and conversely, between feeling and tempo-rhythm." He demonstrates, moreover, that "The correctly established tempo-rhythm of a part or a role, can of itself intuitively (on occasion automatically) take hold of the feelings of an actor and arouse in him a true sense of living his part." [52]

In 1949, also, *Vogue* published an article written by Joshua Logan, "Rehearsal with Stanislavsky," in which he told of the experience which he and his friend, Charles Leatherbee had in 1931 when they left Princeton nine months before graduation to journey to Moscow to learn from Stanislavsky. They were privileged to observe his rehearsals with the Opera Studio [53] (see p. 126).

In the same year another book appeared on the rehearsal techniques which Stanislavsky used in the Opera Studio. This was *Stanislavsky on the Art of the Stage;* it was translated by Magarshack, who, in an introduction, also discussed the ten elements of Stanislavsky's psychotechnique. The second part of the book, entitled "The System and Methods of Creative Art" is a collection of the shorthand notes of Stanislavsky's lectures at the Bolshoi Opera Studio between 1918 and 1922 as taken down by a member of that group.[54]

In the following nine years at least nine books were published, which added significantly to the knowledge and understanding of the Stanislavsky System. In 1951, *Stanislavsky, a Life* [55] by David Magarshack made a contribution in its coverage of the period in Stanislavsky's life from his trip to America until his death. It also made use of certain comments on Stanislavsky's acting by Knipper-Chekhova and Leonidov. In 1952 Theatre Arts Books published the score which Stanislavsky had written for the original production of *The Sea Gull* and a new translation of the play by Magarshack. This volume also contained an informative essay by S. D. Balukhaty, the historian of the Moscow Art Theatre.[56]

A year later, Michael Chekhov's book, *To the Actor*,[57] appeared. Chekhov pays tribute to Stanislavsky, with whom he worked for sixteen years, calling his System the "only method postulated expressly for the actor." (See p. 243.) His own method is really a further means of building a characterization. It differs from Stanislavsky in its emphasis upon the outside environment and its effect upon the actor. If used with Stanislavsky's System as a base, Chekhov's technique can greatly enrich the actor's palette of emotions.

Directing the Play, a source book of directing,[58] was also published in 1953. Among the articles dealing with the work of directors, from the Duke of Saxe-Meiningen and Antoine down to that of contemporary Americans, were Stanislavsky's plan for the fourth scene of the Third Act of *Othello;* transcripts of Meyerhold's notes for rehearsals of *The Inspector-General;* Zakhava's two articles, "Work with the Actor," which had previously appeared in *Theatre Workshop* in 1937; Kazan's notes on his production of *A Streetcar Named Desire;* Clurman's outline of the main actions of the characters in *A Member of the Wedding;* and Joshua Logan's elaboration of the advice given him by Stanislavsky: "Love the art in yourself rather than yourself in the art." Not only is *Directing the Play* of great historical interest, but it reveals Stanislavsky's influence upon the working methods of two leading contemporary American directors, Clurman and Kazan.

Two English actor-directors known to American audiences acknowledge Stanislavsky's influence in their writing. In 1953, Michael Redgrave in *The Actor's Ways and Means* referred to *An Actor Prepares* as "The only successful attempt which has ever been made to come to terms with the fundamentals of the actor's art." [59] The following year, Bernard Miles, the man who recreated the *Mermaid Theatre* on the Exchange several years ago and who is known to American audiences for his film acting, asserted that the attitude toward acting has changed "largely through the influence of Stanislavsky whose three great studies . . . have given to acting its first clear map and the first grammar and syntax of its own special language." [60]

Another very important book appeared in 1954. Nikolai M. Gorchakov, a member of the Third Studio of the Moscow Art Theatre and a director under Stanislavsky, made public his stenographic reports of the rehearsals which Stanislavsky conducted with his group. The book, *Stanislavsky Directs,* was translated by Miriam Goldina, another pupil of Stanislavsky, who has been teaching in California for many years. In the foreword, written expressly for the work, Norris Houghton marvels that Stanislavsky could exert such a powerful influence upon the theatre even under the Soviet regime, which regarded art as a means to an end. He calls the book "an incomparable record of the rehearsal—that is to say, the creative—experiences of one of the modern world's great theatre masters." [61] Included in the reports are the rehearsals of Griboyedov's famous comedy, *Much Love from Wisdom* (*Woe from Wisdom*); a dramatization of a Dickens story, *The Battle of Life;* the writer Bulgakov's play, *Molière;* a French melodrama, *The Sisters Gérard,* an adaptation of *The Two Orphans;* and a modern French satire *Merchants of Glory* by Marcel Pagnol. The book is an invaluable addition to *An Actor Prepares.* In *The Battle of Life,* Stanislavsky illustrates step by step how the actor creates the "inner monologue," that is, the thoughts and mental reactions of the character. It demonstrates the working out of many elements in the System which had already been introduced in *An Actor Prepares* and *Building a Character.* For instance, Stanislavsky explains *scenic rhythm:* "The scenic rhythm is not the acceleration or diminishing of tempo, but the acceleration or diminishing of the *inner intensity*— the desire to realize the problem and to execute the inner or outer physical action."

Luzhsky, a fine actor of the Moscow Art Theatre, complained to Stanislavsky of one student's wrong application of the inner monologue, saying that his gesticulating and muttering were disturbing the rest of the company. Stanislavsky displayed his common sense and understanding in his reply:

Any fool can act that way. This amusing example is typical of applying the method of the inner technique in a general way, taking the terminology literally. Besides the method, actors must have all the qualities that constitute a real artist: inspiration, intelligence, taste, the ability to communicate, charm, temperament, fine speech and movement, quick excitability and an expressive appearance. One cannot go very far with just the method.[62]

The number of books that appeared in the ten years following the publication of Stanislavsky's *Building a Character* is evidence of the growing influence of his System. It is significant that two textbooks on acting predicated on the Stanislavsky method were published in 1954 and 1955. The first was *An Introduction to the Theatre*.[63] Its author, Frank Whiting, director of the University of Minnesota Theatre, maintained that the Stanislavsky System was particularly appropriate for university or educational theatre because it demands that the student create for himself and thus permits him to develop for himself. In an earlier volume, *Rehearsal Techniques*,[64] Whiting had asserted that the creative approach as developed by Stanislavsky was of greater value to beginners than the technical method. The second text, *Acting Is Believing*,[65] was written by Charles McGaw of Ohio State University—"A practical, informative and inspirational presentation of the Stanislavski method of acting which will enable the young actor to work toward creating believable characters in the theatre" is the statement on the jacket. The writer describes the book as an attempt "to draw upon some aspects of the system which have proved to be practical in helping beginning actors to develop an effective technique for bringing a character into existence on the stage." The back jacket credits McGaw with having studied directing with Lee Strasberg, and acting with Joseph Anthony, both at the American Theatre Wing. Since Anthony is a pupil of Daykarhanova, Jilinsky, and Soloviova, the book is an example of the continuity of the teaching of these disciples of Stanislavsky.

More information on the activities of Stanislavsky was furnished in Nikolai A. Gorchakov's *The Theatre in Soviet Russia*,[66] which appeared late in 1957. Norris Houghton, reviewing this book for the *New York Times*, praised its "excellent exposition of Stanislavsky's system of acting" and its "emphasis on Stanislavsky's flexibility of mind as he sought changing ways of discovering artistic truth." [67] Most valuable, however, is the light it throws on the activities of Stanislavsky's last years. It also makes frequent references to his most recent way of working, the method of physical actions. Gorchakov now lives in Munich. He should not be confused with Nikolai M. Gorchakov (*Stanislavsky Directs*), who is still in Moscow.

Two other books in this period are significant in the body of literature on Stanislavsky and his System. *Stanislavski's Legacy* [68] is a collection of essays, letters, and speeches chosen by Mrs. Hapgood from Stanislavsky's papers and translated by her. It was published by Theatre Arts Books in celebration of the "triple Stanislavsky anniversary," the twentieth following his death, the ninety-fifth of his birth, and the sixtieth anniversary of the founding of the Moscow Art Theatre. The selections show the breadth of Stanislavsky's interests and knowledge. "A Letter to a Young Student" in 1901 spoke of the duties and obligations of an actor, of his need for culture and education. In 1935, in "Talks with Opera and Acting Students," he wrote: "You are lucky. You have a studio into which you can bring the very best that is in you. When you enter, along with your rubbers, leave all that is petty and mean outside, bring inside only your very best feelings and share them with your friends." In 1937, in "Back to Study—Talks with Established Actors," he spoke of his desire to turn over to his actors the bases of his technique, that they might "spread it and inevitably develop it further." He reminded them of the need for "every great and meticulous actor at certain intervals . . . to return to his studies."

One other book in the field, Robert Lewis' *Method—or Madness,* remains. However, its significance depends not only upon the extent to which it illustrates the objectivity of Stanislavsky's System, but, to a greater degree, upon the circumstances which inspired it. For this reason it belongs to the succeeding section of this chapter.

OTHER FACTORS

Two other factors played an important part in spreading the Stanislavsky System. The first of these was the Neighborhood Playhouse School of the Theatre, which was established in 1928 (see p. 204) and has ever since continued to instruct young actors in the knowledge and practice of the Stanislavsky System at first under the guidance of Sanford Meisner and later under David Pressman.

The other factor was the founding of the Actors Studio in 1947 by Elia Kazan, Cheryl Crawford, and Robert Lewis. Here actors who are accepted have the opportunity to act in selected scenes and receive criticism by the teacher and the other pupils. The idea that prompted the formation of the Studio was an admirable one, for here would be a kind of laboratory where the actor could come to keep his instrument in tune. It is undoubtedly true, as Seymour Peck pointed out in his article in the *New York Times* of May 16, 1956, that Kazan has been responsible for the prestige of the Actors Studio. Peck also pointed out that Kazan has used a great many Studio actors in his films *On the Water Front* and *East of Eden,* and in his play, *Cat on a Hot Tin Roof.*[69]

After a year or two, Lewis disassociated himself from the Actors Studio and Lee Strasberg took over the direction of its classes instead of Kazan. The Stanislavsky System had often drawn criticism from the uninitiated, both in Moscow and in America. Some of its critics insisted that it was too subjective, that Stanislavsky had no concern with communication or the "externalizing" of a role. Such comments, of course, showed an utter disregard for *Building a Character* and Stanislavsky's many other writings about voice, speech, body movement, and rhythm.

Now, however, another kind of criticism arose as a result of certain practices which were ascribed to the Actors Studio. For one thing, instead of the Stanislavsky System, the Studio began to call the technique which they used merely "the Method." This was an unfortunate choice, for disparagers of the Actors Studio began calling it "The Method," and the talk was about "Method" and "non-Method" actors. Such a division is, of course, untenable, and implies a division between those with a vested interest and the outsiders. The use of the word Method, however, arose from the most irreproachable motives, as Lee Strasberg himself explained in a letter to the author:

I do not believe that anyone but Stanislavsky himself has a right to talk of the Stanislavsky System. I have therefore stressed the use of the word "Method" as against "System" to suggest that while we obviously are influenced by Stanislavsky's ideas and practices, we used it within the limitations of our own knowledge and experience. . . .

By saying that the Group Theatre used an adaptation of the Stanislavsky Method, we mean that we emphasized elements that he had not emphasized and disregarded elements which he might have considered of greater importance. Also, that in experimenting with some of the ideas propounded by Stanislavsky, we came to conclusions and practices of our own which he might not have agreed with. Personally, I am critical of the way in which Stanislavsky used his own work in some of his own productions, and therefore, I could not subscribe to many of the basic essentials of the ideas which he made use of. . . . In other words, while it would be true to say that we try to make use of the basic ideas of the Stanislavsky System, we do not feel it necessary to be limited just to those ideas or procedures that Stanislavsky himself used, nor would he necessarily agree with whatever is done in his name.

I therefore feel it both theoretically wise and practically sound to talk of the work done by the Group Theatre and the Actors Studio as being an "Adaptation of the Stanislavsky System." The "Method" is therefore our version of the System.[70]

Mr. Strasberg's letter is very illuminating. It could be of tremendous assistance in clarifying the discussion so prevalent over "Method versus non-Method" acting. If, for instance, the term "Group-Method" were used instead of "The Method," critics of the Actors Studio would be less likely to equate it with the Stanislavsky System and they would not lay at Stanislavsky's door whatever faults they might ascribe to "The Method."

By 1956 it was apparent that there was confusion in the minds of many people between the Stanislavsky System and "The Method" as practiced in the Actors Studio. Moreover, in their zealous attempts to play realistically, some actors began to bring adverse criticism upon the Studio. Lee Strasberg explained the basic tenets of the Actors Studio in a Sunday article for the *New York Times*.[71] He spoke of "the methods used in the studio, or . . . those of Stanislavsky from which they derive." He mentioned Gary Cooper, John Wayne, and Spencer Tracy as examples of Stanislavsky's ideas, since these actors try to be themselves rather than to act, and he asserted that they refuse to say or do anything they feel not to be consonant with their own characters.

The article aroused some sharp responses several Sundays later. Howard Lindsay took exception to Strasberg's implied praise of an actor's refusal to do anything he "didn't feel." Beaufort, the drama critic of the *Christian Science Monitor*, published an article entitled "Back to Stanislavski." He declared: "For some time, the 'Stanislavski Method' has been popularly associated with a kind of 'garbage can' school of acting. But this association merely proves again how a many-faceted artistic concept can become obscured." After a brief mention of the purposes of the Moscow Art Theatre, Beaufort pointed out by direct quotations from *Building a Character* Stanislavsky's dedication to art, his admonitions to Logan and Leatherbee and others, "to love the art in yourself, rather than yourself in the art," to let the theatre "ennoble you, make you a better person." He called attention to Stanislavsky's emphasis upon the importance of good speech, and his question: "Of what use will all the subtleties of emotion be if they are expressed in poor speech?" He stated that "few, if any, of the directors prominently identified with The Method have ever directed a classic drama." [72]

The controversy continued. Finally Robert Lewis, one-time member of the Group Theatre and the director of such widely different kinds of theatre as *Teahouse of the August Moon* and *Witness for the*

Prosecution, attempted to clear the air. Accordingly, he secured the Playhouse Theatre and offered eight consecutive Monday night after-theatre talks, calling the series "Method—or Madness." Some of the most prominent persons in the theatre world were present. After each lecture there was a question and answer period.[73] At the close of the series, Lewis wrote the leading Sunday article [74] on the drama page of the *New York Times,* in which he outlined his purpose and the content of his talks. At the outset he declared that the Group Theatre in the 1930s and its offshoots in the next two decades had popularized the phrase, "Stanislavsky Method of Acting," and this in turn had revived the ancient theatre dispute over the question, "Should an actor really 'live his part' or merely impersonate the character?"

On the basis of their letters requesting tickets to his talks, Lewis divided the audience into the "true believers, an insular group that felt part of a 'holy order'; the angry knockers who used the word 'method' as an abusive epithet; the giddy misconceivers who had attended one session conducted by a friend of a former student of someone who was thrown out of a class held in the summer by Mme. Ouspenskaya; and those with a normal, objective interest in *all* theatre techniques."

While Lewis never once mentioned the Actors Studio, he made definite reference to the criticism that had been leveled against its members. Everything he spoke of as being part of the Method he documented from Stanislavsky's books, *An Actor Prepares* and *Building a Character.* He asserted that the trouble over the Method began when the followers became more dogmatic than the creator, when certain aspects of the theory became fetishes. As an example, he pointed to the overemphasis on a kind of digging or straining for emotion, plus a seemingly wild disregard for the means of expressing that emotion. In elaboration of this idea he declared:

> One senses that the actor is really feeling *something,* but that the emo-
> tion is a personal one, not necessarily related to the character or the
> particular play. Also, one is disturbed by an absence of such elements as
> rhythm, appropriate speech, a sense of movement, or even the ability to
> execute small, seemingly unimportant, problems easily and unobtrusively.[75]

Lewis suggests, as one reason that so many exponents of the Method are neglecting the external aspects of characterization, the fact that the "complete Stanislavsky method is embodied in two books," which while conceived together were published thirteen years apart; "they are still placing more emphasis on the problems in the first volume to the neglect of the all-important elements in the second."

Lewis touched upon recurrent criticism when he asked:

> Are these 100 per cent "living the part" folks really living the part, or are they living themselves and adding the author's words to that life? When they speak of "psychological truth" do they mean their psychology, or the truth of art which includes, in addition to true feeling, all the circumstances of the character, the situation, the style of the play, etc.? [76]

A little over a year later, Samuel French published the lectures in a book by the same name, *Method—or Madness.*[77] It is a lucid statement of the principles underlying the Stanislavsky System and should certainly silence the carpers who accuse Stanislavsky of neglecting the external elements of characterization. On the other hand, the book should serve as a form of catharsis for those bastardizers of Stanislavsky's theories whose chief concern is with their own emotional involvement rather than those of the character. Lewis discussed the elements of the System in colloquial terms, thus clearing the air of the mystery that had obscured them. He also demonstrated that actors who "have no interest in anything like Stanislavsky" use the elements unconsciously. The reader cannot fail to note that Lewis' definition of the Method is at some variance with that given by Strasberg (see p. 261). After pointing out that there are many methods, Lewis says, "We must presume, however, that what is meant by 'The Method' as it is being discussed around Downey's (Note: An Actor's restaurant on Eighth Ave. in N.Y.C.) [parentheses by Mr. Lewis] is the system set down by Constantin Stanislavsky, or more probably, some derivative of that system."

One of the aspects of tradition which Lewis deplored was that the original ideas of an innovator get sifted through his followers and often run the danger of being diluted, or even warped. This may be the basis for the flagrant misinterpretations of Stanislavsky that continued to appear in the press, even after Lewis' brilliant exposition of the true Stanislavsky System. The seriousness of the matter is compounded by the prominence and prestige of the perpetrators. A separate volume could be devoted to these twistings of the System, but an examination of two or three will serve.

Before the publication of Lewis' book, but not more than three months after his report of the lectures in the *New York Times,* the eminent British director, Tyrone Guthrie, wrote an article for the *New York Times Magazine* called "Is There Madness in 'The Method' ?" Printed immediately below the title is what might well be assumed to be the answer: "Not really, says a prominent director— but many actors who follow it have gone too far in the direction of self-analysis and away from a sensible pursuit of craftmanship." This apparently harmless statement, however, is not Mr. Guthrie's answer. Indeed there is more madness in his article than in anything of which the most criticized Studio actor ever has been accused. Admitting that he has no "first-hand experience of the Method," although he has "met and worked with zealous Method-ists," Guthrie goes on to make assumptions and to state—as facts—half-truths and even complete misrepresentations. Apparently he is equally unfamiliar with the basic teachings of Stanislavsky and with the literature on the Moscow Art Theatre. His explanation of the basis of the teachings of Stanislavsky is a case in point:

> . . . the basis of this is that the actor must derive his characterization from his own personal experience. He must imagine a given situation so strongly that he can "feel" himself in it. His own experience being necessarily limited, he must also feel it legitimate to derive at second-hand from the real experience of other people, but not from other acting.
> With little of this could any sensible person disagree. My own disagreement with the Method is limited, and under two heads; theoretically, it is in rebellion against conditions which have ceased to exist and, consequently, is out of date. Practically, it places too much emphasis upon self-analysis and too little upon technique.[78]

While admitting that the Moscow Art Theatre was the "most powerful influence on the stage of its time," Guthrie asserts that it was never of any great popular or commercial account—that the theatre was tiny and by no means always full.[79] Actually, it has a seating capacity of 1350 according to Mr. Prokofyev, Historian of the Moscow Art Theatre.

Guthrie gives no mention of his source for this assertion, which is nothing short of ridiculous in the face of the facts as reported by reliable eyewitnesses. In September, 1917, Arthur Ruhl reported in *Current Opinion* that "performances at the Moscow Art Theatre are always sold out without advertising or exploitation." (See p. 220.) In 1923 Fovitzky in his book *The Moscow Art Theatre and its Distinguishing Characteristics* commented on the fact that people came to Moscow from all over Russia, sometimes standing in line all night to obtain tickets to a performance (see p. 225), and in 1936 Norris Houghton wrote in *Moscow Rehearsals,* "I looked about and scanned the balcony and the orchestra. Not a single empty seat! I was to go to the theatre ninety times in Russia and not more than a dozen times was I to see a vacant chair." [80] Mr. Guthrie is too good a director to be so uninformed about a matter so pertinent to his subject.

Guthrie expressed satisfaction over Strasberg's announcement that more time was being spent on voice production and diction, but his next remark furnished another example of the way in which the true elements of Stanislavsky's System can be misinterpreted. In *Building a Character,* Stanislavsky says: "The actor must not only be pleased himself by the sound of his own speech but he must also make it possible for the public present in the theatre to hear and understand whatever merits its attention. Words and their intonation should reach their ears without effort." [81] A little farther on we find: "But what recourse have you in the theatre when actors pronounce the text in a fashion comparable to your badly printed book, when they drop out whole letters, words, phrases, which are often of cardinal importance to the basic structure of the play?" Again he warns: ". . . whereas distortion of our conversational speech may be half way condoned in the surroundings of our home, any coarse grained way of talking carried on to the stage, and used to pronounce melodious verse on exalted topics, on freedom, ideals, pure love—is offensive and ridiculous." Again he remarks, "How good it would be if the teachers of singing simultaneously taught diction, and teachers of diction taught singing! But since this is impossible, let us have specialists in the two fields working with each other." [82] In addition to the chapter on "Diction and Singing," from which these excerpts are taken, Stanislavsky also devotes a chapter to "Intonation and Pause," to "Accentuation: the Expressive Word," and to "Speech Tempo—Rhythm." Surely Mr. Guthrie has never even glanced at a copy of *Building a Character* or he could not have written:

> Also it is a radically new idea that anything so self-conscious and artificial as Vocal Technique, so unspontaneous, so remote from the animal life of the individual, or the social life of the group, should be admissible as part of the Method. And so influential has the Method become in the contemporary theatre that it is going to be very hard to eradicate the notion that any cultivation of this Craft can only be to the detriment, not only of an actor's Art, but of his Psyche. [83]

Guthrie characterizes as "just middle-class sentimentality" the very "superior" attitude which he implies belongs to adherents of the Method, of imagining "that it is more 'real' to be rough than genteel, more 'real' to wear blue jeans, than a neat Ivy League number, more 'real' to look like a whore than a Junior Miss." Perhaps Mr. Guthrie is being just a little superior himself when he says:

> Surely it is not more real, but less expensive. The proletariat does not dress and speak and behave as it does, not live where it does, from choice, but because it cannot afford to do otherwise. In America today it is only eccentric "intellectuals" who are "prole" by choice.[84]

Guthrie traces the proletarian fad to the influence of the Group Theatre, which he asserts was an all-important influence in the evolution of the Method.

Certainly some of the criticisms of the Actors Studio have been deserved. As "proletarian" a writer as Paddy Chayefsky, while praising the Method as "one of the finest approaches to acting," and Method actors as being "after the inner truth of their roles, that is to say, the deeper motivations of the character," nevertheless was prompted to declare: "So it is a continual shock to me to see how shallow is the result of their intellectualizing and probing. They still read the simplest improvised lines of dialogue as if they were epic statements." [85] It is regrettable, however, that the critics do not disassociate "The Method," which has now become synonymous with the technique of the Actors Studio, from the System evolved by Stanislavsky and still taught by a number of his artistic heirs.

Arthur Gelb shed some light on this confusion with his article, "Two and Two are Five," in the *New York Times* of Sunday, February 2, 1958. This was actually an interview with Mme. Barbara Bulgakov on the "Imaginative Truths of the Method." After remarking that the talk about the Method is becoming "about as heated as, in fashion circles, talk about the pros and cons of the sack," he makes this statement:

> More and more in recent years, the Method—which is, of course, the Stanislavsky Method of training actors—has been held up for mocking public scrutiny, often by people who have only a foggy idea of what it aims to achieve and what, in this country, it has actually accomplished in the hands of qualified proponents.[86]

Gelb lists the five people now in this country who acted with Stanislavsky's Moscow Art Theatre: Barbara Bulgakov, Akim Tamiroff, Tamara Daykarhanova, Vera Soloviova, and Olga Baklanova. Mme. Bulgakov makes clear that Stanislavsky never claimed that the Method could create a talent. She compares the process to the polishing and processing of a diamond.

"This . . . is a question of awakening the actor's imagination," says Mme. Bulgakov, "of leading him to discover and interpret large truths in a large, theatrical way." She asserted that Stanislavsky deplored preoccupation with such small truths as how to shake hands realistically or button one's overcoat naturally. She pointed out that discipline was another facet of Stanislavsky's method which is "sometimes ignored by contemporary actors."

"No one would have dreamed of coming to a rehearsal" she declared, "or even to an acting class, sloppily dressed or haggard from a night's carousing." She declared also that Stanislavsky's emphasis on discipline extended to the perfection of expressiveness in body and speech.[87]

One possible reason for the adverse criticism of certain aspects of the Method as allegedly practiced at the Actors Studio or by individual so-called "Method actors" is the understandable fact that various practitioners are apt to emphasize different aspects of the System. Harold Clurman offers an explanation of where the fault lies, and the reason for it, in an article written for the *New York Times* of Sunday, January 12, 1964, entitled "There's a Method in British Acting." After a discussion of the differences in environment, upbringing, general conditioning, and culture between English and American actors, and the lack of opportunity here for playing the classics, Clurman has this to say:

When the Group Theatre (1931–41) made the "System" part of its way of work, the fact was of comparatively little interest to its audience. . . .

Only since the fifties, when the "System" was transfigured and dubbed "The Method" has so much public attention been accorded to a purely professional or "inside" matter in the theatre.

How is this to be explained? Ever since the end of the Second World War, the young American has more than ever begun to seek himself as a person. . . . the young folk of the fifties felt the need to throw off the constrictions of "conformism"—the affliction of a too highly organized industrial society devoted to mass production. The young began an anxious search for their individual reality, their true identity. . . . "The

Method" has a particular appeal to the young American actor, who, like every other member of the community, is subject to its moral climate, because while *not the whole of the Stanislavsky System,* it emphasizes the inner nature of the actor's self, the truth of his private emotion as the prime source of artistic creativity. This disclosure of self strikes the actor as a veritable revelation—in both the personal and professional sense. Too frequently he tends to make a cult of it, a sort of therapy akin to the benefits of psychoanalysis. When this occurs—and a lack of cultural background conspires to make it occur—it becomes a distortion of art in general and of Stanislavsky's teachings in particular.[88]

The significance of Clurman's explanation can be more fully appreciated if two facets of Stanislavsky's teaching are reviewed. In the first place, Stanislavsky makes it very clear that while the actor's personal experience may be used as a springboard for arousing the emotions required in the part, the emotions sought should be those demanded by the role, in other words, those of the character, and therefore not necessarily those which the actor would experience at that moment. Furthermore, Stanislavsky was always discovering new means for the actor to use in portraying the role. Toward the end of his life, as Gorchakov reminds us, he expanded his "method of physical actions" which depended upon the discovery of the correct physical and psychological actions and no longer led his actors to be "absorbed in delving within their own experiences" as the source of their emotions. (See p. 106.)

One of the chief controversial points is concerned with the difference between the Method and the Stanislavsky System. In addition, enlightenment is desirable in relation to the existing variations among different teachers of the Stanislavsky approach. Considerable clarification of these questions is provided by a comparison of the answers given to the same question by four prominent teachers of acting in New York City, all adherents directly or indirectly of the Stanislavsky System. Their replies appeared in the *Tulane Drama Review* for September, 1964.

Question: Is affective memory useful only for training or is it useful in rehearsal and performance, too?

Strasberg: Affective memory is a basic element of the actor's reality. . . . The basic idea of affective memory is not emotional recall but that the actor's emotion on the stage should never be really real. It always should be only *remembered* emotion. An emotion that happens right now spontaneously is out of control—you don't know what's going to happen from it, and the actor can't always maintain and repeat it. Remembered emotion is something that the actor can create and repeat, without that the thing is hectic.

. . . Therefore, Vakhtangov stressed the idea of affective memory as the central expression with which the actor works . . . for high moments on the stage, shock moments. For these the affective memory is the only thing that I know of that will work.[89]

The question put to Soloviova, Adler, and Meisner was: What is your concept of "emotion recall" and how are your students trained to practice it?

Soloviova: "Emotional recall" or "affective memory" as it is often called, is the remembrance or recall of any experience or incident that "affected" you emotionally. It need not necessarily have happened to you as Stanislavsky pointed out. It can be something that you witnessed, as an accident or even something that you read about which affected you deeply. In the last two cases, the actor has to recall how he felt when he saw somebody suffer or read about it.

In the motion picture, "Maternelle" a little girl of nine years old had to cry over her dead mother. When she was asked if her own mother was dead, she said, "No, she is sitting out there in the auditorium." "How can you cry, then?" they asked her. She answered, "My dog just died and when I think of that, I cry."

Affective memory or emotion recall starts from sense memory. I recall how hot my glass of tea was. I recall what I did to cool my hand. I recall how cold it was when I was walking to the studio.

Boleslavsky, like Stanislavsky, mentioned how our memory is awakened when any of the five senses is stimulated. Boleslavsky used to say that when he smelled cucumbers, he felt like Spring. I had "lily of the valley" perfume many years ago in London, and long afterwards whenever I smelled that scent, I saw London.

In practice I never permit my students to recall events that are so to speak "luke warm." I start always from something very sharp, very important. Actors have a tendency to start to recall "luke warm" events and this does not "turn the switch" of their emotions. . . .

We use "emotional recall" or "affective memory" when our inspiration or, in Stanislavsky's expression, when "Apollo" does not answer readily. But if your intuition gives you what you need, you don't have to use affective memory. Stanislavsky used to say, "If the part comes to you spontaneously, you don't have to go through affective memory. Just thank Apollo and act!" I always tell my students to pay attention to the first impression the role makes upon them when they read it or hear it read. I never knew what key would open the door to the heart of the part for me. Would it be through affective memory or would I feel the part from the first reading of the play? Seeing myself in the same situation would I have the same feelings, understanding and response to it as the character I was to portray—finding the same feelings in my heart? Or would I visualize it so clearly that it would awaken in me the necessary feelings? [90]

Soloviova's reply to this question is quite different from Strasberg's and this is understandable considering her background. She started at the Moscow Art Theatre and First Studio under Stanislavsky's training and later in the Moscow Art Theatre Second, which was the First Studio grown up, she worked with Michael Chekhov. The greatest difference between the latter and Stanislavsky was in Chekhov's preference for the imagination over affective memory. (See page 122.) Soloviova, then, can be said to combine the methods of Stanislavsky and Chekhov.

Adler reveals a similarity to Chekhov's point of view, while at the same time she is close to Stanislavsky's method of physical actions:

> . . . in teaching I do not require a student ever to go to the emotion itself or ask the student to use emotion as a source. As a teacher I discourage the student from reaching out for any emotion, conscious or unconscious. If a student needs to use his conscious memory it is only as a frame of reference for the action itself. All emotion is contained in the action. The action can be a personal or an imaginative one.
>
> The question of imagination can be touched on here as a source for the actor's craft. I have never come in contact with any student or actor who could not use his imagination. The teacher can use many means to provoke and develop this essential source for the craft of acting. This imaginative source is very rich—much richer than the conscious and unconscious experience which is contained within it. A student is encouraged to respect his creative, imaginative life as a source for his acting craft. To go back to a feeling or emotion of one's own experience I believe to be unhealthy. It tends to separate you from the play, from the action of the play, from the circumstances of the play, and from the author's intention. All this has to be embodied in the action. [91]

Meisner: The problem of the deliberate stimulation of emotion is to me the most delicate and dangerous element in the actor's craft. Emotion without which a performance can be effective but not affective, is a most elusive element. It works best when it is permitted to come into

272 THE STANISLAVSKY HERITAGE

play spontaneously, and has a perverse inclination to slither away when consciously wooed. Lionel Trilling, in differentiating between the seemingly accidental and arbitrary fantasizing in life and creative fantasy, defines the latter as "controlled fantasy." It is a form of day dreaming, too, but on an essential theme extracted from the text—a kind of auto-suggestion, if you will. I prefer this approach rather than the more direct probing into our life experiences. The inventions in fantasy, if they are truly stimulating, have been selected because they already mean something to the actor. He is in close contact with himself, but by potent suggestion rather than direct probing. For example, an actor entering a scene has just come from a producer's office where he signed a contract for the best part of his career. We may assume he is in exceptionally "high spirits." One can for the purpose of future clarification call the "high spirits" the emotional theme or essence of what characterizes the inner life of the role at that moment. It supplies the springboard for the day dream. In "preparing" for this scene he may "day-dream" or "fantasize" along the lines of all the by-products of this contract: the applause, the financial rewards, the praise, the fame—in short, the world at his feet. *Or* any other private wish which produces the same condition.[92]

Meisner's use of "controlled fantasy" or "auto-suggestion" bears little resemblance to either Stanislavsky's "emotional memory" or the Actors Studio use of "affective memory."

Strasberg's remarks would seem to point up a marked difference between the Actors Studio method and the Stanislavsky System. One of the primary tenets of Stanislavsky is that the actor must learn to control his emotion on stage. As to the question of whether or not the actor ever feels things on the stage for the first time—and whether or not it is good for him to have original, fresh, feelings—Stanislavsky says: "It depends upon the kind." Here he discussed how undesirable a sudden lust for blood would be if it should arise within the actor playing Hamlet as he throws himself upon Claudius. However, when the questioner pursued the point and asked, "Does that mean that they are never desirable?" Stanislavsky replied, "On the contrary, they are extremely desirable."

He then explains that "direct, powerful and vivid emotions" do not last for long periods on stage but rather "flash out in short episodes, individual moments."

"In that form," he continues, "they are highly welcome. We can only hope that they will appear often, and help to sharpen the sincerity of our emotions, which is one of the most valuable elements in creative work. The unexpected quality of these spontaneous eruptions of feeling is an irresistible and moving force." [93] With regard to Strasberg's reliance only upon Vakhtangov, it should be remembered that Vakhtangov, beloved student of Stanislavsky, took what he had learned from Stanislavsky as the foundation for all his work. This has been attested to by all who worked with him. He would undoubtedly have followed the later developments of the System if he had not died so early. It seems fair to assume, therefore, that the Method is equivalent to "early Stanislavsky."

Perhaps the most startling instance of the confusion between the Method and the Stanislavsky System is offered by an article that appeared in the *Columbia University Forum* nearly two years later. In the Winter 1960 issue, no less a person than Theodore Hoffman, then head of the drama department of Carnegie Institute of Technology, offered what purported to be a defense of Stanislavsky in his article entitled "At the Grave of Stanislavsky or How to Dig the Method." [94]

There can be no quarrel with Mr. Hoffman's castigation of actors who indulge in long pauses before speaking or who overemphasize the use of articles (cigarettes, cups, and glasses). The drama critic of the *Journal American*, Jack O'Brien, criticized Ben Gazzara in a "Playhouse 90" television role, saying that he "overacts his underplaying." The fault lies in confusing the weaknesses of the "Method," in the context of Actors Studio technique, with the "System" of Stanislavsky. From his statements it is apparent, however, that Mr. Hoffman intends his indictment for the Stanislavsky System as well.

For one thing, he condemns certain elements such as exercises on sense memory, communion, concentration, and animal characterizations. While Stanislavsky used the last merely to stimulate the imagination, some of his followers seem to make much of this phase. However, such a non-Method production as the Hollywood movie of *The Women* made use of what was thought to be a novel device: it showed a picture of an animal symbolic of each woman in the cast of characters.

Although Hoffman praised the second book on the System, *Building a Character,* he gives little evidence of having read it, since he declares: "His aim, of course, is to feel this character." Moreover, it would be difficult to present a more contrary picture of the training outlined in *Building a Character* than his assertion that the whole training involves "trying different characters like so many suits of clothes . . . to achieve a shamanistic ability to create a second, coexistent identity for oneself . . . with or without recourse to the play." Stanislavsky continually emphasizes the need for studying the play in *Building a Character*. "It is only when we study a play as a whole and can appreciate its overall perspective," he writes, "that we are able to fit the various planes correctly together, make a beautiful arrangement of the component parts, mold them into harmonious and well-rounded forms in terms of words." [95] In the same chapter on "Perspective in Character Building," he speaks of some who play the part of Luka in Gorky's *The Lower Depths* and do not even read the last act because they do not appear in it. "As a result," Stanislavsky declares, "they cannot possibly have a true perspective and are unable to play their role correctly."

Hoffman is apparently distrustful of the value of improvisation as a rehearsal technique. He maintains that it is hard to conceive any old-style actor learning to understand Hamlet by changing his words to "Man, what a s.o.b. and peasant slave I turned out to be!" Possibly the actor Louis Calvert is too modern to use as an example, though he lived more than a quarter century ago—Mr. Hoffman's yardstick for change in acting style—nevertheless, Calvert illustrates an improvisation involving just such a transference into the vernacular for an actor playing Bassanio in *The Merchant of Venice* (see p. 179).

Hoffman shows a complete misconception of the use of "actions" when he states: "Since basic character in the Method is a relatively static affair, the action of the play is conceived as a matter of goals for which the word 'objectives' is used." What can be less static than an objective, whether it is thought of in military terms or merely as goals in life? Moreover, have not all good actors in all ages of the theatre concerned themselves with the motives for their actions as called for in the play? Doesn't the term acting imply exactly that? Is Joan of Arc "static" when she *defies* the Grand Inquisitor—for that is the action which she plays.

On the other hand any director, Method or non-Method, who could possibly take, as the main objective for Hamlet, "to save Denmark," is not worth the time it would take to discuss him.

It is difficult to know whether Mr. Hoffman's indictment of the Method and the Stanislavsky System stems from his observation of inept educational productions or of those on the Broadway stage, or whether it is not, after all, the consequence of his allegiance to Brechtian philosophy.

Regardless of what one may think of his point of view on the much-argued question of Hamlet's *antic disposition*, is not Mr. Hoffman guilty of the very practice which he condemned earlier, that is, of creating a personality *without recourse to the play,* when he states: "If we want to understand and act Shakespeare's Hamlet we had better simply take the fact of his madness for granted and not try to find the answers in the play, lest we risk missing the rest of what is there."

There are, however, more serious indictments of Hoffman's article than those already discussed. For one thing, the last quotation of Stanislavsky "If the system does not help you, forget it," is incomplete as well as out of context. The remark was made to Stella Adler in the summer of 1934 when she and Clurman called upon Stanislavsky in Paris. Adler complained that the interpretation of his System with which she had been working in the Group Theatre was confusing her. Stanislavsky said: "If the system doesn't help you, forget it. But perhaps you do not use it properly." Mr. Hoffman is undoubtedly familiar with Clurman's account of the change in the Group's method which resulted from Stanislavsky's clarification given to Miss Adler (see p. 246).

It is regrettable that Mr. Hoffman did not check the source of the quotation from which he extracted the following statement: "The foundation of The Method rests on one book, *An Actor Prepares,* published here in 1938 [1936], of which Stanislavsky said: 'Don't mention this book to me; and never give it to a student.'"

This is a direct quotation from an article written by Henry Schnitzler which appeared in *The Quarterly Journal of Speech* for April, 1954. It was entitled "Truth or Consequences, or Stanislavsky Misinterpreted." [96]

Schnitzler starts out with the apparent purpose of defending Stanislavsky against interpreters. This is a laudable impulse but misdirected. For one thing, it is hard to believe that Stanislavsky, with his fine sense of humor could take offense, as Mr. Schnitzler does, at the four-line jingle sung by Danny Kaye at a New York nightclub to poke fun at the Stanislavsky System, according to Mr. Schnitzler:

> *Be a tree, be a sled,*
> *Be a purple spool of thread,*
> *Be a storm, a piece of lace,*
> *A subway train, an empty space. . . .*

Moreover, there is nothing pernicious [Mr. Schnitzler's word] in suggesting that students' creative fantasy might be prodded by resorting to such practices as imagining themselves even to be a "glacier."

There are numerous examples of misinterpretations of Stanislavsky's theories, such as that of the girl in an acting class who missed the point in attempting to portray Lady Macbeth and defended her bad performance on the grounds that she "felt" it. However, even if the example of misguided students and directors were multiplied many times, it could hardly be construed as a repudiation of the Stanislavsky System, nor can Stanislavsky be held accountable.

Schnitzler gives the complete statement of Stanislavsky to Adler. The lack of documentation, however, in the most significant portions of the article is evident. To begin with, Schnitzler makes the statement that *An Actor Prepares* is a "mere fragment" of the original and that the Russian version is almost three times as extensive. The facts are these: In the third Russian edition of *My Life in Art*, published in 1954, there is a note left by Stanislavsky in which he tells of his plans for two parts of a book on the work of the actor, the first to be devoted to living the role and the second to embodying the role or putting it into physical form: "But when I counted the pages, about 1200 by that time, I got frightened and decided to make two books. Now after tremendous cutting, it looks as though I will be able to get out my second book. My third book would be the work on the role." [97]

There were plans for fourth, fifth, sixth, and seventh books; the fourth was to be on a particular part, the fifth on three types of art, the sixth on the work of the regisseur, and the seventh on opera. Then a note by Stanislavsky appears in which he says, "And I forgot something very important, an eighth book in which I wish to talk about revolutionary art."

The Russian edition of *My Life in Art* has been enlarged by the addition of notes and variations of certain events, such as five lines on Andreyev's *Life of Man* and two and a half pages on *The Cherry Orchard* and Chekhov's philosophy, four pages on the production of Byron's *Cain*, copious footnotes identifying people mentioned in the text, and the lists of Stanislavsky's productions, including his work with the Bolshoi Opera Studio and his own Opera Studio.

The Russian edition of *An Actor Prepares, Rabota Aktyora Nad Soboy,* has been made longer in the same way. There is an introduction of 38 pages about Stanislavsky by G. Kristi, who prepared the text and the notes, 8 pages of notes on the chapter on "Action," 8⅔ pages on "Communion," 3 pages on the "Interrelation Between Actor and Public," which is translated in *Stanislavsky's Legacy*, 6 pages of a talk between two students called "Naivete," and 15 pages of footnotes.

Schnitzler's most flagrant misrepresentation, however, is the quotation the last lines of which Hoffman extracted and repeated in his indictment of the Method and Stanislavsky in his article, "At the Grave of Stanislavsky":

> After the book *An Actor Prepares* had been published, he was shocked to realize that it had apparently made things worse. Vladimir Sokoloff, the noted actor, told me of a discussion he once had with Stanislavsky on the problems involved in training for the stage. At one point, Sokoloff referred to the book we know under the title *An Actor Prepares*. Stanislavsky reacted with a start and said: "Don't mention this book to me; and never give it to a student." [98]

In the first place, Stanislavsky saw only the page proofs for his book during his last illness. Magarshack recounts that one of his editors brought Stanislavsky the proofs and found him looking very ill: "He asked her a few questions about the paper and the binding (he was very anxious that the cover of the book should not be expensive as he wanted everybody to be able to afford to buy it)." Magarshack reports that Stanislavsky asked her suddenly, "May I take the book and just turn a few pages?" Magarshack adds, "She gave him the book and, as he took it, his face colored and his fingers trembled. At that moment he seemed to be sure that he would live to see it published. But the book only came out after his death." [99]

This hardly seems to be the attitude of a man who did not want his book put into the hands of a student. The following excerpts from a letter from Vladimir Sokoloff to Mrs. Hapgood, dated January 14, 1959, will offer unimpeachable proof of this. After recounting Stanislavsky's instructions for the use of his book with American students, Sokoloff continued:

> (2) "Sokoloff referred to the book we know under the title 'An Actor Prepares' "—Sokoloff did not *"refer"* to the book; K.S. was reading to me excerpts from it. (In manuscript evidently, it was not published in any language until two years later, 1936, when it was issued by Theatre Arts).
> (3) "Stanislavsky reacted with a *start*."—This is not only a misquotation, this is a stupid invention of Mr. Schnitzler.
> (4) "Don't mention this book to me and never give it to a student."—Of course Konstantin Sergeievich could *never* have said such a silly thing,

and naturally I could never have invented such an idiocy, even using Schnitzler's clumsy perverse faculty of imagination. . . .

By the way, what I told you in a short version about my interesting conversation with K.S. in the summer, 1934, I describe more explicitly and reverently in my coming book, commenting also on the fact how right was K.S., when I see now how young American actors and aspirants are bedevilled by the so-called "Method," thanks to the unholy, harmful heritage of the Theatre Group—or is it Group Theatre? (I forget the name of the organization.)

It is sad and disappointing to watch those "Methodists" acting. Every individuality has been levelled by the cliche—"Method" to an inarticulate performance in speech and expression. See one, see all. As one very intelligent author said, "What they need is a method not to discipline them but to *galvanize* them."

The Stanislavsky System was not advanced merely through such controversy. There were many testaments to its effectiveness from persons respected in the theatre in America and England. For one thing, Edward G. Robinson, while playing in Paddy Chayefsky's *Middle of the Night,* recalled the Moscow Art Theatre's actor Kachalov as the best example of an actor with a sense of balance.

"When he was subordinate to the scene, you wouldn't know he was on stage," Robinson told dramatic columnist Tom Donnelly. "When the character he was interpreting had something to do, he'd come forward and dominate the action, effortlessly. And then he'd merge into the background again, as gracefully as you please." [100] In 1957 also, Fordham University advertised a "Basic Course in Acting Techniques of the Stanislavsky Method" as preparation for the theatre.[101]

Joshua Logan visited Moscow again in 1958, the year of the Moscow Art Theatre Centennial. Upon his return he wrote the feature article for the Sunday *New York Times,* "Russia Revisited." [102] In February, 1958, Brooks Atkinson's feature article in the Sunday *New York Times* discussed the production of Gorky's first play, *The Courageous One.*[103] It was directed by Miriam Goldina, one-time pupil of Stanislavsky, who came to this country with the Habima Theatre, which was founded in Moscow by her late husband. She herself has been a teacher of the Stanislavsky System both in New York and in Hollywood. In the fall of 1959, she played in Dore Schary's play, *The Highest Tree.*

In this article Atkinson calls attention to the discussion of the Stanislavsky acting method between Arthur Gelb and Barbara Bulgakov, on the same page (see p. 268). He declares, "The Method, as it is dubbed in the vernacular, is still the most explosive subject in theatre esthetics." He says also:

> Strange how the pre-revolution Russian theatre still haunts us. It is constantly in the news. We are still drawing dividends from the artistic investment that Russians made a half century and more ago . . . . What the Russians were doing at the turn of the century is still of absorbing interest to us today.[104]

As recently as March, 1959, Brooks Atkinson's feature article called "Amazing Paradox—America is Steeped in the Art of the Nation that Gives Us Anxiety" made some positive statements about the System:

> In 1898 Stanislavsky produced Chekhov's *The Sea Gull* at the Moscow Art Theatre; and that event has had the most enduring influence on our theatre . . . . And Stanislavsky's principles of acting are the primer of the method.[105]

Michael Redgrave, the English actor, who had spoken highly of Stanislavsky in his first book, *The Actor's Ways and Means* (see p. 257), brought out a second book, *Mask or Face*, in 1958. In it he reprinted a section originally published in 1946, called "Echos De Constantin, the Stanislavski Myth." After mentioning the fact that certain of the actors who worked with Stanislavsky, like Akim Tamiroff and Michael Chekhov, are occasionally glimpsed in Hollywood films, he says, "But even had not Stanislavski and Nemirovich-Danchenko's Moscow Art Theatre survived to this day as a living tradition and a contemporary force, we should still receive Stanislavski's influence through the pages of his book *An Actor Prepares*." He has more to say of this book:

> Certainly no book can teach anyone to act. But no one would deny for a moment that to come in close contact with a great actor working at his craft must be illuminating, and to read *An Actor Prepares* is to be privileged to be in close contact with a great actor-director not in "a fiction and a dream of passion" but in the great evening of his life, still in active contact with what is probably the greatest of living theatres, telling us again and again, with all the clarity of a great intellect, the simple truths of our art.[106]

Redgrave compares reading *An Actor Prepares* to going on a trip abroad, but he adds: "A man can receive from either experience only in proportion to what qualities he brings with him."

Finally, another English actor, Sir John Gielgud, who is also a brilliant director, wrote what may be termed a valentine for Stanislavsky. On February 14, 1960, in his article written for the *New York Times Magazine*, "The Urge to Act—An Incurable Fever," Sir John declared:

> Stanislavsky came closest to giving expression on paper to the creative processes of the actor, but even his advice can be very easily misapplied by a young player who is hoping to find a quick answer to the problems that beset him. . . .
>
> Technique must sustain and discipline the actor, but technique is useless without true feeling and intention. . . . The truest test an actor must pass in sustaining a role over a long period of consecutive performances is that he is continually discarding every unnecessary gesture, simplifying every movement and inflection, so that he may eventually achieve the most truthful expression of his role at every moment of his creation, however often he has to repeat it.[107]

When the Moscow Art Theatre returned to Russia in the spring of 1924, it left behind memories of its performances which influenced the work of many American actors in the succeeding years. It seems fair to assume that the Moscow Art Theatre and the methods of its director, Constantin Stanislavsky, affected the American theatre to a greater extent than any other single group, native or foreign, to whom American actors have been exposed. Their performance remained as a criterion for later critical evaluation.

Four of the foremost American directors were definitely influenced by Stanislavsky. Clurman, Kazan, and Lewis came from the ranks of the Group Theatre, whose ten years of existence was a factor in popularizing the Stanislavsky System for the actor and the director. The fourth, Joshua Logan, visited Stanislavsky in 1931, and in an article written for *Look Magazine* [108] remarked, "The great Russian Stanislavski has influenced everything I've done." Three other prominent American directors, Joseph Anthony, Vincent J. Donehue, and Boris Tumarin, as well as some of the leading American actors and actresses, among them Yul Brynner, Mildred Dunnock, Hurd Hatfield, Ford Rainey, Jane Rose, and Perry Wilson are pupils of the second generation of Moscow Art Theatre artists who made their home in America.

There are, furthermore, several other factors which show the continuing vitality of the Stanislavsky influence. A great many publications directly concerned with his System of acting appeared in the thirty-five years following the American visits of the Moscow Art Theatre. An increasing number of studios admittedly use his System in their teaching. Finally, the spirited articles in the American press and theatrical magazines from time to time and the heated discussions that go on among theatre people testify to the continuing interest which the System arouses in American actors and students of the theatre.

An interesting example of the latter appeared on January 6, 1965 in a three column article in the 59th Anniversary number of *Variety*. Written by Lee Norvelle, head of the Department of Speech and Theatre at Indiana University, it purported to answer the article by Theodore Hoffman, "How to Dig the Method" which had appeared in the January 4, 1961 Anniversary issue of *Variety*. Actually, this had originally been printed in the *Columbia University Forum* in the Winter of 1960 (see p. 273). The complete title then had been "At the Grave of Stanislavsky, or How to Dig the Method."

Norvelle takes particular exception to the closing paragraph which ends ". . . perhaps [it is] time to bury the poor man." Referring to two recent books, Theresa Helburn's *A Wayward Quest* (1960) and *Actors Talk About Acting* (1961) by Lewis Funke and John E. Booth, Norvelle says:

> These are only two of the many recent references indicating that the most alive figure in the field of acting and directing thus far in the 20th Century is Constantin Stanislavski. His influence, whether for good or bad, according to the individual point of view, has been greater than that of any of his contemporaries, hence we are forced to favor a delay of the ritual.

Norvelle goes on to give a very searching review of how Stanislavsky evolved his System, the chief elements in it, and its importance to people of the theatre.

Far from being outmoded, the Stanislavsky System continues to extend its influence. Its power to stimulate the thinking of persons connected with the theatre was demonstrated by the cordial reception extended to a group of artists from the Moscow Art Theatre in November, 1964. The four members who conducted seminars for two weeks in New York City were invited by the Institute of International Education with the cooperation of the American Council of Learned Societies and the State Department as part of the educational and cultural exchange program. Victor Manyukov, a leading director and teacher at the Moscow Art Theatre School, Vladimir Prokofyev, historian, Angelina Stepanova and Vasily Toporkov, both actors of the Moscow Art Theatre and Honored People's Artists of the U.S.S.R., conducted 14 seminars for two weeks in New York City for the purpose of sharing their experiences in working in the Stanislavsky System and explaining its principles. The two artists had actually worked with Stanislavsky and so could speak from their own experience. Toporkov had played leading roles in Stanislavsky's last productions and so spoke authoritatively about Stanislavsky's latest element in his System, the theory of physical actions. The group had come at Stella Adler's suggestion. Leading persons of the New York theatre, writers, directors, actors, came again and again to learn more about Stanislavsky and the working out of his famous System.

In addition to the seminars, which were limited to thirty-five persons each because of the number of earphones available, there were two large sessions at the New York State Theatre for four hundred members of Actors Equity, and at the Kaufman Auditorium of the YMHA for specially invited students. At this last session, an audience of eight hundred heard the panel and saw a movie of Stanislavsky's life which had been made in Russia on the one hundredth anniversary of his birth.

The group also went to Tulane University. After that, Stepanova had to return to Moscow for rehearsals, but the other three members went on to the University of Michigan at Ann Arbor and to Yale University.

This was followed by a four weeks' appearance of the acting company of the Moscow Art Theatre at the New York City Center. Forty-one years after their first visit to America under the brilliant leadership of their founder, Constantin Stanislavsky, the Moscow Art Theatre returned for a four weeks' engagement from February 4 to February 25, 1965. The previous May and June, they had played a short repertory season of 3 plays in London: Gogol's *Dead Souls,* Chekhov's *The Cherry Orchard,* and a modern Soviet play, *Kremlin Chimes,* by Pogodin. The reviews were extremely favorable. For example, *The Stage and Television Today* for June 4, 1964, declared, "The Moscow Art Theatre production of Chekhov's *The Cherry Orchard* is so renowned it comes as a shock to find that, in performance, it actually lives up to its reputation." Harold Hobson of the *Sunday Times* on May 31, said, "If there is inspiration in the London Theatre it is to be found in the Moscow Art Theatre's 'Cherry Orchard'." And W. A. Darlington of the *Daily Telegraph* in a column entitled "Moscow Art Company's Perfect Control" wrote: "There is no greater delight to be experienced in a theatre than that caused by a really magnificent exhibition of ensemble acting. This rare delight was ours last night at the Aldwych, when the Moscow Art Theatre opened in Gogol's *Dead Souls.*"

The New York engagement added *The Three Sisters* to the repertory. Two days before their opening at the City Center (on February 4, 1965), five members of the Artistic board of directors of the Moscow Art Theatre and S. Hurok were interviewed by the press. According to a report of the conference which appeared in the *New York Times* of February 3, 1965, the director of the Company declared that they have taken great steps forward. They now have added five or six new plays to the yearly repertory of thirty-two plays.

The visiting troupe consisted of fifty-nine actors and with the addition of back-stage helpers totaled seventy-five. The entire staff of the Moscow Art Theatre is 740. This includes 140 actors who perform on two stages. Salaries range from 100 to 200 rubles ($111 to $222) a month.[109]

For their four-week engagement in New York, the repertory consisted of Gogol's *Dead Souls,* Chekhov's *The Cherry Orchard* and *The Three Sisters,* and two performances of *Kremlin Chimes,* a play by Nikolai Pogodin. Of all the company, only Tarassova had played here during the prior visit under Stanislavsky in 1923–24.

The first play, *Dead Souls,* evoked surprise from some of the critics that the Moscow Art Theatre should depart from the realistic style for which it had always been famous to present a production that at times bordered on the burlesque. Nevertheless, there was praise from most for the vitality of the acting and the humorous portraits presented.

The final production, *Kremlin Chimes,* most of the critics felt was more or less a propaganda play. Norman Nadel writing in the *New York World-Telegram and Sun,* asked:

> Do they believe so implicitly in this play and its trumpeted message, or are they so superbly schooled that they perform anything superlatively well? Whatever the answer, they treat their audience to a display of dramatic arts far beyond the value of the play itself. . . . It is the ensemble acting that earns our admiration. . . . most of the time we are watch-

ing a beggar woman, an old clock maker, an excited child, a doll peddler, or the girl with the lace. These are the small but memorable wonders of *Kremlin Chimes*.[110]

It was, however, for the two Chekhov plays, and rightly so, that the actors of the Moscow Art Theatre received their greatest accolade. Walter Kerr offered high praise for *The Cherry Orchard*:

> It is precisely because the present acting company refuses to acknowledge that there are such things as unimportant matters that this *Cherry Orchard* seems played in an infinite perspective. Behind every room lies another room, and behind every onstage life lurks a hidden one, furtively or wistfully waiting to assert itself.[111]

Again and again individual actors were mentioned for their outstanding performances. Angelina Stepanova's Charlotta won from Edith Oliver in *The New Yorker* the following :

> . . . as Charlotta, the lanky, nutty governess and amateur conjurer, Angelina Stepanova gives the only legitimate performance of this part I've ever seen, making this mysterious woman's loneliness as important as her freakishness, and at the same time retaining all the comedy of the role.[112]

Speaking of Gribov in the part of Firs, in *The Cherry Orchard,* Edith Oliver reminded us that Chekhov wrote the part expecially for Artem, an old actor of the Moscow Art Theatre whom he loved very much, but she felt that Chekhov would have approved of the Firs of Mr. Gribov.

Finally, she concluded her review with this comment:

> So much of *The Cherry Orchard* has gone almost unnoticed in other productions of it. In this vigorous, thorough, and subtle one, under Victor Stanitsyn's direction, the details are all brought to light—the nuances of feeling, the bits of high and low comedy, the clues to personality, the quirks of social behavior and the ways in which social distinctions are made clear. And the details are the play. The Moscow Art Theatre has succeeded in transporting a masterpiece and the manner of life it portrays.[113]

After the opening of *The Three Sisters,* the New York newspaper critics burst into superlatives. Of the subtlety of the acting of these performers, Nadel said:

> But each of the three sisters (as well as the men and women about them) contains more passion than she overtly expends, and the expres-

sion of this is the most subtle kind of acting. . . . For all the spoken dialogue, there is as much communication among the sisters (and with the audience) that is unspoken.

Of course, that is the beauty of Chekhov. In one sense, he tells you all you need to know in the dialogue and action. In another, the dialogue and action only show where you are to look for the deeper and more poignant truths.

This is the way the Moscow Art Theatre plays *The Three Sisters*. The performances are exquisitely controlled—eloquent music within a small octave.[114]

The comments of the critics make very clear what Stanislavsky meant when he said: "Chekhov gave that inner truth to the art of the stage which served as the foundation for what was later called the Stanislavsky System, which must be approached through Chekhov, or which serves as a bridge to the approach to Chekhov." [115]

The review by Walter Kerr in the *New York Herald Tribune*, was perhaps the most penetrating:

This company epitomizes ensemble playing; it is not easy to select the outstanding performers, for each performance seems almost a group accomplishment. Thus Alexei Gribov's Chebutykin is far more than an aging army doctor; he is a man who loves and is loved by a family and whose sorrows are theirs. Anastasia Zueva's Anfissa is a woman who knows her prerogatives as a Nannie of thirty years' standing: but age and servility overpower her before the vulgar rages of the shrewish newcomer to the family. The merest visitor to the house stands clearly defined as an individual and as part of the texture of the family's daily life.

The three women who portray the sisters are impeccable and each has moments of brilliance. Kira Golovka, as Olga, by the firm aversion of her head and the almost furtive wiping of a tear, conveys the inner horror of her final appraisal of the vulgarian her brother has married. Raissa Maximova's Irina glows with the impatient passions and frustrations of youth, and Marguerita Yureva, a beautiful and graceful Masha, tells us with a sudden smile all we need know of a woman in love.

There is a striking subtlety about the performances that carries the strongest emotional impact. The love affair between Masha and Vershinin (played with sophisticated understatement by Pavel Massalsky) is deeply affecting and yet it is conducted with a glance, a pause in conversation; the devotion of the Baron to Irina becomes heartbreakingly apparent in his quick return to kiss her hand before the duel. The deepest felings are exposed—and unspoken.

And this is the art of the Moscow Art Theatre. You owe it to yourself—

and to your understanding of Chekhov—to see *The Three Sisters,* and, of course, *The Cherry Orchard.*[116]

Only a few critics had reservations about the excellence of the performances, and these few seem to have been motivated by a desire to display their loyalty to highly talented Americans who have never had the opportunity to work under the conditions enjoyed by the Moscow Art Theatre.

On the whole, however, the reception given the Moscow Art Theatre Company was warm and appreciative. Actors Equity Association conferred honorary membership upon the Russian players. The public greeted them with full houses and standing ovations and audiences at other theatres read articles in the *Playbill* entitled "The Poverty and Wealth of Soviet Theatre" by Norris Houghton, "A Morning at the Moscow Art Theatre School," by Carol Lynn Wright and "Entertainment in Moscow" by Theodore Shabad, all written especially as a gesture to the visiting Russian actors. In addition to the reviews there were Sunday articles, and several feature stories by Harrison E. Salisbury about Stanislavsky and Chekhov, an appreciation of Stanislavsky's work in his Opera Studio by Kurt Adler in *Opera News* of February 6, and a two-page summary in *The Reporter* for March 25, a magazine not generally devoted to dramatic criticism. Its critic, Gordon Rogoff, entitled his comments, "The Moscow Art Theatre: Surprises after Stanislavski," and he made mention of two surprises. The first of them he characterized as "the gaiety, the delight in caricature, the obvious pleasure in acting as, first of all, a performing art." [117]

Mr. Rogoff explained his second surprise by reference to the acting of Boris Peker's watchmaker in *The Kremlin Chimes:*

> . . . he was speaking of his humble craft while attracting attention not to his words but to the strange, almost feline wanderings of his hand on the table. These quietly anxious motions were more emblematic of his need for work than all the hollow phrases placed on his tongue.[118]

This, then, is the surprise, the Moscow Art Theatre's "aggressive awareness of everything physical." He gave other examples of this quality, among them, ". . . a somewhat younger Angelina Stepanova, plays the isolated, wishful, aging governess in *The Cherry Orchard,* Charlotta Ivanovna, with a drooping bounciness that constantly betrays how prim and finished she really is." [119]

"Behind these gestures," he continued, "lies yet another tale to add to the Stanislavski legacy." This he explained in terms of what Mikail Kedrov and Josef Raevsky, once students of Stanislavsky and now director-actors with the company, explain as two facets of their inheritance from the master, namely, the method of physical actions and the fact that the work must not remain static but continue to advance. These goals the Company seem to have succeeded in achieving.

Certainly the visit of the Moscow Art Theatre was one of the most important dramatic events that has occurred in many years—a worthy follow-up of the original visit under Stanislavsky in 1923–1924. Beyond a doubt, the Moscow Art Theatre is still a living testament to its founders, Constantin Stanislavsky and Nemirovich-Danchenko.

❧

Notes

1. Robert Johnston, "The Moscow Art Theatre in America" (unpublished doctoral dissertation, Northwestern University, July, 1951).
2. Richard Boleslavsky, "The Man and His Methods," *Theatre Magazine*, Vol. 37 (April, 1923), p. 27.
3. Richard Boleslavsky, "The Laboratory Theatre," *Theatre Arts Monthly*, Vol. 7 (July, 1923), pp. 244–50.
4. Harold Clurman, *The Fervent Years* (New York: Alfred A. Knopf, 1945), p. 16.
5. Louis Hetler, "The Influence of the Stanislavsky Theories of Acting on the Teaching of Acting in the United States" (unpublished doctoral dissertation, University of Denver, June, 1957), pp. 99, 106. (Most of the information about books concerned with the Stanislavsky influence in American teaching is derived from this very valuable study.)
6. "Obituary," the *New York Times*, Vol. 54, December 4, 1949, p. 108.
7. Robert Littell, "Tchekov and April Fools," *Theatre Arts Monthly*, Vol. 13 (June, 1929), pp. 401–402 and John Hutchins, "The Theatre of Imagination," *Theatre Arts Monthly*, Vol. 14 (March, 1930), p. 190, cited by Hetler, pp. 101–102.
8. Obituary of Michael Chekhov, *New York Times*, October 2, 1955, p. 86.
9. Michael Chekhov, *To the*

288

Actor (New York: Harper and Brothers, 1953), p. 178.

10. George Ross, "The Moscow Art Players," *World-Telegram*, February 21, 1935, p. 13.

11. Seraphima G. Birman, *Poot Aktricy* (*The Path of an Actress*, Moscow, 1962), p. 75.

12. Clurman, p. 11.

13. John Gassner ed., *Producing the Play* (New York: The Dryden Press, Inc., 1941), p. 162.

14. B. E. Zakhava, "Principles of Directing," *Acting, A Handbook of the Stanislavski Method*, compiled by Toby Cole (New York: Crown Publishers, 1955), pp. 208–209.

15. Clurman, pp. 42–44.

16. Clurman, p. 139.

17. Stella Adler, "The Actor in the Group Theatre," in Toby Cole and Helen Krich Chinoy, eds., *Actors on Acting* (New York: Crown Publishers, 1949), pp. 538–39.

18. Raymond Dominic Gasper, "A Study of the Group Theatre and Its Contributions to Theatrical Production in America" (unpublished doctoral dissertation, Ohio State University, 1955), p. 133.

19. John Gassner, *The Theatre in Our Times* (New York: Crown Publishers, 1954), pp. 299–300.

20. Toby Cole, ed., *Acting, A Handbook of the Stanislavski Method* (New York: Crown Publishers, 1955), pp. 22–32.

21. Edith J. R. Isaacs, *Theatre* (Boston: Little, Brown and Company, 1927).

22. Richard Boleslavsky, *The First Six Lessons in Acting* (New York: Theatre Arts Books, 1933).

23. Barnard Hewitt and Aristide D'Angelo, "The Stanislavsky System for Actors," *The Quarterly Journal of Speech*, Vol. 18, No. 3 (June, 1932), pp. 440, 446.

24. Walter Prichard Eaton, *New York Herald Tribune, Books*, December 20, 1936, p. 14.

25. Morris Carnovsky, "The Actor's Mystery," *Brooklyn Daily Eagle*, December 27, 1936.

26. Stark Young, *Theatre Practice* (New York: Charles Scribner's Sons, 1926), p. 33.

27. Stark Young, "The Prompt Book," *Theatre Arts Monthly*, Vol. 8 (March, 1924), pp. 159–68.

28. Johnston, pp. 225–36.

29. Edwin Duerr, *Studies in Speech and Drama, in Honor of Alexander M. Drummond* (Ithaca, New York: Cornell University Press, 1944), pp. 34–36, 44–50.

30. Stanislavski, *An Actor Prepares,* translated by Elizabeth

Reynolds Hapgood (New York: Theatre Arts Books, 1936), p. 237.

31. Stanislavski, *An Actor Prepares,* p. 256.

32. Stanislavski, *An Actor Prepares,* p. 286.

33. Stanislavski, "Direction and Acting," *Acting, A Handbook of the Stanislavski Method* (New York: Crown Publishers, 1955), p. 23.

34. Aristide D'Angelo, *The Actor Creates* (New York: Samuel French, 1939).

35. Barnard Hewitt, *The Art and Craft of Play Production* (New York: J. B. Lippincott Company, 1940), p. 186.

36. Harry Darkes Albright, *Working Up a Part* (Boston: Houghton Mifflin Company, 1947), p. 221.

37. Norris Houghton, *Moscow Rehearsals* (New York: Harcourt, Brace and Company, Inc., 1936).

38. Vladimir Nemirovich-Danchenko, *My Life in the Russian Theatre,* translated from the Russian by John Cournos (Boston: Little, Brown and Company, 1936).

39. I. Rapoport, "The Work of the Actor," *Theatre Workshop,* Vol. I, No. 1 (October, 1936), pp. 5–40; Toby Cole, ed., *Acting, A Handbook of the Stanislavski Method,* pp. 33–68.

40. *Theatre Workshop,* Vol. I, No. 2 (January–March, 1937), p. 2.

41. B. E. Zakhava, "Principles of Directing," *Theatre Workshop,* Vol. I, No. 4, (September–October, 1937), pp. 18–19; Toby Cole, ed., *Acting, A Handbook of the Stanislavski Method,* pp. 182–217.

42. John Gassner, ed., *Producing the Play* (New York: The Dryden Press, 1941, rev. ed., 1953).

43. *Acting, A Handbook of the Stanislavski Method,* Toby Cole, ed. (New York: Crown Publishers, 1955).

44. *Stanislavski Produces Othello* (New York: Theatre Arts Books, 1948).

45. Stella Adler, "The Art of Acting," *The Theatre,* Vol. 2, No. 4 (April, 1960), p. 17.

46. John Gielgud, Introduction (London, April 30, 1948), *An Actor Prepares,* p. xiv.

47. Gielgud, p. xix.

48. Constantin Stanislavski, *Building a Character,* translated by Elizabeth Reynolds Hapgood, Introduction by Joshua Logan (Theatre Arts Books, 1949).

49. George R. Kernodle, "Building a Character," *The Quarterly Journal of Speech,* Vol. 35 (December, 1949), p. 533, cited by Hetler, p. 232.

50. Cornelia Otis Skinner,

"Actors Just Act—or No 'Pear-shaped' Tones," the *New York Times Magazine,* December 13, 1942.

51. Quoted on the dust jacket of *Building a Character.*

52. Stanislavski, *Building a Character,* pp. 235–36.

53. Joshua Logan, "Rehearsal with Stanislavsky," *Vogue* Vol. 113, No. 10 (June, 1949), p. 78.

54. *Stanislavsky on the Art of the Stage,* translated with an introductory essay on Stanislavsky's System, by David Magarshack (London: Faber and Faber, Limited, 1950), p. 78.

55. David Magarshack, *Stanislavsky, A Life* (New York: The Chanticleer Press, 1951).

56. *The Sea Gull Produced by Stanislavski,* edited with an introduction by Prof. S. D. Balukhaty, translated by David Magarshack (New York: Theatre Arts Books, 1952), pp. 9–10.

57. Michael Chekhov, *To the Actor* (New York: Harper and Brothers, 1953), p. 178.

58. *Directing the Play,* Toby Cole and Helen Krich Chinoy, eds. (Indianapolis and New York: The Bobbs-Merrill Company, Inc., 1953).

59. Michael Redgrave, *The Actor's Ways and Means* (New York: Theatre Arts Books, 1953), p. 50.

60. Bernard Miles, "The Acting Art," *Films in Review,* Vol. V, No. 6 (June–July, 1954), p. 267.

61. Nikolai M. Gorchakov, *Stanislavsky Directs,* translated by Miriam Goldina (New York: Funk and Wagnalls Company, 1954), Foreword, p. vi.

62. N. M. Gorchakov, *Stanislavsky Directs,* p. 52.

63. Frank Whiting, *An Introduction to the Theatre* (New York: Harper Brothers, 1954), p. 138.

64. Frank Whiting, *Rehearsal Techniques* (Cincinnati: The National Thespian Society, 1948), pp. 227–28.

65. Charles McGaw, *Acting Is Believing* (New York: Rinehart and Company, Inc., 1955).

66. Nikolai A. Gorchakov, *The Theatre in Soviet Russia,* translated by Edgar Lehrman (New York: Columbia University Press, 1957).

67. Norris Houghton, "Exit Greatness, Enter the Party Line," the *New York Times Book Review,* January 5, 1958, p. 3.

68. *Stanislavski's Legacy,* edited and translated by Elizabeth Reynolds Hapgood (New

York: Theatre Arts Books, 1958).

69. Seymour Peck, "The Temple of 'The Method,'" the *New York Times Magazine* (May 6, 1956), p. 24.

70. From a letter of Lee Strasberg to the writer dated April 1, 1960.

71. Lee Strasberg, "View From the Studio," the *New York Times,* September 2, 1956, Sec. 2, p. 1.

72. John Beaufort, "On and Off Broadway; Back to Stanislavski," *Christian Science Monitor* (Boston), September 26, 1956.

73. The writer was present at all but the first two.

74. Robert Lewis, "Method—or Madness?" the *New York Times,* June 23, 1957, Sec. 2, p. 1.

75. Lewis, p. 1.

76. Lewis, p. 1.

77. Robert Lewis, *Method—or Madness* (New York: Samuel French, Inc., 1958).

78. Tyrone Guthrie, "Is There Madness in 'The Method'?" the *New York Times Magazine,* September 15, 1957, pp. 23, 82–83.

79. Tyrone Guthrie, p. 23.

80. Norris Houghton, *Moscow Rehearsals,* p. 6.

81. Stanislavski, *Building a Character,* p. 78.

82. Stanislavski, *Building a Character,* pp, 83, 89.

83. Guthrie, p. 83.

84. Guthrie, p. 82.

85. Paddy Chayefsky, *Television Plays* (New York: Simon and Schuster, 1955), p. 265.

86. Arthur Gelb, the *New York Times,* February 2, 1958, Sec. 2, Part 1, pp. 1, 3.

87. Gelb, pp. 1–3.

88. Harold Clurman, "There's A Method in British Acting," the *New York Times Magazine,* January 12, 1964, Sec. 6, p. 62.

89. Lee Strasberg, interview with Richard Schechner and Theodore Hoffman, in *Tulane Drama Review,* Vol. 9, No. 1 (Fall, 1964), pp. 131–32.

90. Vera Soloviova, *Tulane Drama Review,* Vol. 9, No. 1 (Fall, 1964), p. 142.

91. Stella Adler, *Tulane Drama Review,* Vol. 9, No. 1 (Fall, 1964), p. 143.

92. Sanford Meisner, *Tulane Drama Review,* Vol. 9, No. 1 (Fall, 1964), p. 144.

93. Stanislavski, *An Actor Prepares,* p. 165.

94. Theodore Hoffman, "At the Grave of Stanislavsky," *Columbia University Forum,* Vol. III, No. 1 (Winter, 1960), pp. 31–37.

95. Stanislavski, *Building a Character,* pp. 170–71.

96. Henry Schnitzler, "Truth or Consequences, or Stanislavsky Misinterpreted," *The*

Quarterly Journal of Speech (April, 1954), pp. 152–64.

97. Mrs. Hapgood went through the entire four volumes of Stanislavsky's works in their Russian edition with the writer, as well as a fifth volume composed of articles, speeches, notes, and memoirs of Stanislavsky from 1877 to 1917, *Theatrical Legacy of Stanislavsky.* One more volume is contemplated, probably covering the period after 1917.

98. Schnitzler, p. 153.

99. Magarshack, *Stanislavsky, A Life,* p. 400.

100. Tom Donnelly, "All Right, Louie, Don't Upstage Me," *New York World-Telegram,* February 1, 1957, p. 18.

101. *Show Business,* Monday, September 23, 1957.

102. Joshua Logan, "Russia Revisited," the *New York Times,* August 3, 1958, Sec. 1, p. 1.

103. Brooks Atkinson, "Gorky's First Play," the *New York Times,* February 2, 1958, Sec. 2, Part 1, p. 1.

104. Atkinson, the *New York Times,* February 2, 1958, Sec. 2, Part 1, p. 1.

105. Brooks Atkinson, "Amazing Paradox," the *New York Times,* March 8, 1959, Sec. 2, p. 1.

106. Michael Redgrave, *Mask or Face* (London: William Heinemann, Ltd., 1958), p. 176.

107. John Gielgud, "The Urge to Act—an Incurable Fever," the *New York Times Magazine,* February 14, 1960, p. 47.

108. Joshua Logan, "My Greatest Crisis," *Look Magazine* (August 5, 1958), p. 60.

109. Richard F. Shepard, the *New York Times,* February 3, 1965, p. 28.

110. Norman Nadel, *New York World-Telegram,* February 25, 1965, p. 10.

111. Walter Kerr, *New York Herald Tribune,* February 10, 1965, p. 16.

112. Edith Oliver, *The New Yorker,* February 20, 1965, p. 54.

113. Edith Oliver, *The New Yorker,* February 20, 1965.

114. Norman Nadel, *New York World-Telegram and Sun,* February 12, 1965.

115. Stanislavski, *My Life in Art,* p. 351.

116. Walter Kerr, *New York Herald Tribune,* February 12, 1965, p. 9.

117. Gordon Rogoff, *The Reporter,* March 25, 1965, p. 49.

118. Gordon Rogoff, *The Reporter,* p. 50.

119. Gordon Rogoff, *The Reporter,* p. 50.

❧

ten

The Stanislavsky Heritage

Any one who is familiar with the writings of men of the theatre from the earliest times will see how very close to these are the beliefs and precepts of Stanislavsky. There is, moreover, nothing of the mysterious or occult about the System which he developed. It has its roots firmly grounded in the teachings of the most respected practitioners of theatre art.

Stanislavsky believed, first of all, that the actor must experience real emotion, that he must identify with the character he is portraying, that he may use his own past emotional experiences, and above all, that he must learn to speak and behave naturally, as a human being in life. The Roman orator Quintilian said:

The great secret . . . for moving the passions is to be moved ourselves. . . . But how shall we be affected, our emotions not being at our command? . . . What the Greeks call φαντασίας we call *visiones,* whereby the image of things absent are so represented to the mind that we seem to see them with our eyes . . . . Whoever shall have conceived these thoroughly will have complete power over his emotions." (See p. 150.)

The French actor Talma believed the actor must have "that faculty . . . which enables him to enter into the most tragic situations and the most terrible of the passions as if they were his own." (See p. 133.) Moreover he disdained the unnatural method of declamation that was current at his time "in almost all theatres of Europe" and gave careful directions to the actor for speaking his lines in a natural, lifelike manner. Talma, too, recommended that the actor make use of his own emotional experience in playing his role.

Sir Henry Irving believed that the actor should be *affected* by the emotion of the character but not mastered by it, and he believed in the actor's identifying himself with the character he was playing. He referred to Flecknoe's praise of Burbage for so completely becoming the character and never returning to himself, even in his dressing room, until the end of the play. It will be remembered that the same praise was given to Richard Mansfield.

The English critic George Henry Lewes, over half a century before Stanislavsky, wrote: "It is from the memory of past feelings that he [the actor] draws the beautiful image with which he delights us." (See p. 144.)

In short, most of the great actors and critics had offered suggestions as to what the actor should strive to accomplish, what goals he should set for himself, but few if any gave precise directions for their realization. Stanislavsky studied the advice of his predecessors and carefully observed his own acting and that of his contemporaries who had achieved success and then, like Shakespeare's "learned apothecary," he compounded seemingly magic formulas. For as long as the theatre endures those who are eager and willing to learn may share the riches of his wisdom. In his writings, which include *My Life in Art, An Actor Prepares, Building a Character, Stanislavski's Legacy,* and *Creating a Role;* and in *Stanislavsky Directs,* the stenographic notes taken down by Gorchakov during actual rehearsals and lessons, Stanislavsky makes his prescriptions to the actor crystal clear. No point is too small to engage his attention. He says again and again that his system is "not a recipe for becoming a great actor." It is a way of working, a way to achieve the creative state on the stage.

How can the many contributions which Stanislavsky made to the study of acting be measured? It is necessary first to agree upon what constitutes a contribution. The question was referred to five [1] leading representatives of different fields in theatre. They agreed that anything which clarifies the playwright's intention for the actor, the director, and the audience; which assists the actor in interpreting and executing his role; and which is a means of helping the director in understanding the actor's problems and in offering assistance in their solution is a valuable contribution. They came to close agreement also that anything which stimulates an emotional or intellectual response on the part of the audience or which will stimulate interest in theatre as an art and as a craft can be called a valuable contribution.

How has Stanislavsky contributed to clarification of the playwright's intention for the actor, the director, and the audience? He has, first of all, emphasized the need for the actor (and of course the director) to study the play and the role in order to discover the playwright's meaning. He has given abundant examples of the importance of this in his writings. In the chapter on "Perspective" in *Building a Character* he says:

> If you do not feel the whole impact of the shock Hamlet receives from what the ghost tells him . . . there will be no understanding his doubts, his painful efforts to uncover the meaning of life, his break with his beloved, and all the strange conduct which makes him appear abnormal in the eyes of others.[2]

Stanislavsky warns the actor against making up his mind too soon about the author's meaning. He must keep an open mind while reading the play and guard against prejudice; he must "come to no false opinions upon the first acquaintance." [3] Many authors need to be reread as Ibsen, Maeterlinck, and others whose work lies in the direction of stylization or the grotesque, Stanislavsky explains.[4]

He gives an example of how to find the skeleton of a play by answering the question, "Without what thing, what circumstances, events, experiences, would there be no play?" Using *Othello* as an example, Stanislavsky takes five different circumstances which could answer the question and then analyzes each one, showing a "whole series of firmly grounded conditions as signals" on the way to the author's meaning. The five circumstances chosen are: Othello's love for Desdemona; the cleavage between the two races; Iago's wicked tongue; his diabolical slyness, vengeance, ambition, and resentment; and the truthfulness of the barbarian, Othello. If we examine two of these circumstances, we see how skillfully Stanislavsky develops them:

> Now let us examine each of the answers separately. Without what would there be no love between Othello and Desdemona?
> Without the romantic ecstasy of a beautiful young woman, without the fascinating, legendary stories of the Moor about his military exploits, without the innumerable obstacles to their unequal marriage which arouse the emotions of a visionary young girl-revolutionary, without the sudden war, which forces the recognition of the marriage of an aristocratic girl with the Moor in order to save the country.

And without what would there be no cleavage between the two races? Without the snobbery of the Venetians, the honor of the aristocracy, their scorn of conquered peoples (including Othello), without the sincere belief in the disgrace of mixture of black and white blood.[5]

With such careful analysis Stanislavsky charts the course for the discovery of the playwright's intention. If the actor follows the theme of the play, Stanislavsky maintains that its plot and idea will be clear to the audience.[6]

How has Stanislavsky assisted the actor in interpreting and executing his role?

Stanislavsky's contribution on this score is very clear. He says, however, again and again that his method is not a recipe for becoming a great actor or for playing a particular part, but rather a way for the actor to find the "correct state of being on the stage, . . . the normal state of a human being in life." He suggests certain prerequisites for the creative state:

He must be physically free, must control his muscles, and must have limitless attention. He must be able to hear and see on the stage the same as he does in life. He must be able to communicate with his partner and to accept the given circumstances of the play completely.

I suggest a series of exercises to develop these qualities. You must do these exercises every day, just as a singer or pianist does his scales and arpeggios.[7]

The way in which Stanislavsky helped the actor in the interpretation of his role can be appreciated from an examination of his directions to apprentices playing in the crowd scene of *Othello*. "What are the physical and psychological objectives and actions which go to make up this scene of nocturnal alarm and pursuit?" Stanislavsky asks, and then enumerates: "To understand while still [half] asleep what has happened; to clarify something no one can make head or tail of; to question each other; to argue back, quarrel; and if answers do not satisfy, to voice one's own ideas; to come to agreement; to test or prove whatever is not well founded." [8]

Notice that Stanislavsky refers to the *actions,* both physical and psychological, of the actors in the crowd scene, and that he uses infinitives or active verbs to express them. This is what is known as the playing of actions, and it is one of the fundamental elements of the Stanislavsky System and one which is of great assistance to the actor, both in the interpretation and in the execution of his role.

Stanislavsky's contribution here is the concept of the actor as a person who *does* something such as cherishes, shares, destroys, accuses, rather than one who *is* kind, unselfish, mean, suspicious, as the case may be. The first gives a picture of a character in "actable" terms which an actor can readily understand and translate into action on the stage; the second is merely a list of qualities such as a member of the audience might use in describing the character on stage. In life there is a tendency among some people to make judgments of chance acquaintances, friends, and even of characters in a book or play because of their actions without attempting to understand the motives for those actions. The people so characterized, however, never think of themselves in these terms.

In the same way, the actor should think of his character in *active*, actable terms, best expressed by the active verb. Stanislavsky calls this playing "the correct actions in the progressive unfolding of the play." [9] He recommends that the actor put himself into the given circumstances by saying to himself, "What would I do *if* all that happens to this character happened to me?" This is what Stanislavsky called the magic *if*. He himself describes it in this way: "I believe this *if* . . . helps an actor to begin to *do* on the stage." [10] However, the actor must be sure to find all the reasons and justifications for the character's actions; these motives are the objective—because they tell what the character wants to achieve. *Acting,* then, is *doing* what is necessary to fulfill the objective.

Stanislavsky stated the principle of outer physical actions and inner psychological actions very simply and succinctly in *Stanislavsky Directs:*

> Every physical action has an inner psychological action which gives rise to it and in every psychological inner action there is always a physical action which expresses its psychic nature; the unity between these two is organic action on the stage.[11]

The relation of inner (psychological) actions to outer (physical) actions may be clearer if we consider a specific character. Let us take St. Joan in Shaw's play by the same name. What is the main objective of the character? Is it not to save France? What then, does she *do* in order to accomplish this objective? We may say that her main action is to *reveal.* She has, of course, many minor actions in each scene. Take, for instance, the scene before the Grand Inquisitor. Here she definitely *defies,* and her accompanying physical action is to *destroy:* "Give me that paper!" She *destroys* in order to *defy.*

The execution of the correct actions, inner plus outer, will bring about the correct feelings or emotions in the actor. Thus the combination of these three principles, correct state of being, actions, and feelings, Stanislavsky maintains will give organic life to the character and will lead to what Stanislavsky terms *metamorphosis.* It is well to bear in mind, however, the proviso that Stanislavsky offers at this point:

> Of course this takes for granted that you have understood the play correctly—its idea and its theme—and that you have analyzed the character accurately. And beyond all this, the actor must have a good appearance, clear and energetic diction, plastic movement, a sense of rhythm, temperament, taste, and the infectious quality we often call charm.[12]

From his own experience he gives the advice once given to him: "Don't think about the feeling itself, but set your mind to work on what makes it grow, what the conditions were that brought about the experience." [13] In other words, by recalling the stimulus, the actor can reproduce the emotion.

Another means of arousing feeling or emotion is through an object which the actor uses. An ash tray that holds cigarette butts and the end of a cigar can engender a feeling of disgust, while a rare old piece of china or a fine piece of antique furniture can fill us with reverence and even awe. Objects on stage are also a means of revealing the actor's inner state and of helping him to play an action. We saw how St. Joan defied the Grand Inquisitor with the help of the paper which she destroyed. Similarly an actor can express the idea of cherishing in his playing, and the audience will realize how precious certain objects are to him by the way he handles them.

An editorial by Norman Cousins in *The Saturday Review of Literature* for December 12, 1959 illustrates how in life we show our feelings through our use of objects. Cousins is recalling a recent interview he had with the great cellist Pablo Casals, who was speaking of a visit he had made after World War II to his old friend, Wilhelm Kuchs, owner of one of the most valuable collections of music manuscripts in the world. When Casals expressed concern for their safety, and in particular, for the B Flat Quartet of Brahms, Casals' favorite composition, Kuchs put the original Brahms manucript on the table. Casals says of this moment:

I could hardly believe my eyes. I stood transfixed. I suppose every musician feels that there is one piece that speaks to him alone, one which he feels seems to involve every molecule of his being. This was the way I had felt about the B Flat Quartet ever since I played it for the first time. And always I felt it was mine. Mr. Kuchs could see that when I held the B Flat Quartet manuscript in my hands, it was a very special and powerful emotional experience.

Not only the sense of touch but all the other four senses are of great importance for the actor. The chapter entitled "Concentration of Attention" in *An Actor Prepares* takes up the development of awareness in the five senses. The concentration of attention upon something on the stage is the best means of overcoming fear or overconsciousness of the audience. Stanislavsky points out the importance of learning "how to look at and see things on the stage. It is essential to look and see, on the stage," he tells his pupils, "to listen and to hear." [14] Exercises for the five senses as the organs of attention are developed in Rapoport's essay, "The Work of the Actor." [15] The five senses may be considered a bridge between the actor and the audience. Through them the actor reveals to the audience his inner state and his relation to the objects which he uses. The writer has contributed a chapter called "Training the Actor in the Use of Objects" to John Gassner's revised edition of *Producing the Play,*[16] which treats this topic in detail.

This direction of attention to material objects on the stage Stanislavsky calls external attention. He suggests that the actor strengthen this by means of his creative imagination in endowing the objects which surround him "with an imaginary life." For example, he takes the antique chandelier hanging in the studio and says it "may have been in the house of some Field Marshal when he received Napoleon." This he calls the attention based on feeling.

There is, however, inner attention which he considers just as important for the actor because so much of the life on the stage "takes place in the realm of imaginary circumstances." He declares, "The objects of your 'inner' attention are scattered through the whole range of your five senses."

Stanislavsky reminds his students that such imaginary objects demand an even more disciplined power of concentration than the material things that surround the actor on stage. In order to strengthen this inner attention he suggests that the actor exercise his powers of sensory recall by going over the events of the day after going to bed at night, trying to recreate "every possible concrete detail," such as the dishes on which food was served, the various places where he went for a walk, the people he met. "Bring back all the thoughts and inner emotions," he adds, "which were touched by your conversation at the meal."

He illustrates the need for sensory recall by an example where an actor's part might call for him to look out to sea after a departing vessel, when all he can see is the rear wall of the auditorium. He must remember how his eyes focused to see it at an actual moment in life and then fix his attention at a point even beyond the rear wall.[17] Lee Strasberg gives much attention to training the actor in the use of imaginary objects or sense memory, and he credits Boleslavsky and Ouspenskaya in having taught him their use.[18]

Another source of emotion or feeling pointed out by Stanislavsky and his pupils is the use of counteraction or the overcoming of obstacles that get in the way of the actor's fulfilling his objective. It is a common trait of human nature for a person to attack a project even more strongly when he meets with opposition. So, too, on the stage, any interference with smoothly carrying out an objective will actually give the actor greater impetus for fulfilling his stage task.

To take an illustration which Mr. Jilinsky used to give his students: the simple action of crossing the street presents no problem; but if the street is icy or if oil has been spilled upon it, the problem is complicated and will require a greater degree of concentration and effort. In the same way, the simple act of looking out of a window to distinguish someone in the street is made much more difficult in a fog or if the person is one of a crowd and is at times obscured by other figures. Exercises in listening for sounds outside a room or in a house on a still night, and again when there is the noise of a passing car or plane, reveal the same principle: the greater the interference, the more concentration required to perform a given action or task.

The actor can create obstacles to make his acting more interesting. The simplest example is well known and commonly resorted to. The actor is called upon to search for something which he or another person has lost. The more difficult the search, the more interest it arouses in the audience. These are, of course, elementary examples but they can be multiplied and their difficulty increased. Inner psychological problems or objectives are made more interesting in the face of counteraction. The more facile the actor's imagination, the more interesting obstacles he will be able to discover in the role and the more readily will he seize upon the counteraction. Often an unforeseen event, even an accident, will serve as counteraction. Stanislavsky mentions this in another respect in *An Actor Prepares:* "Often a simple *external* occurrence, having nothing at all to do with the play, or the part, or the peculiar circumstances of the actor, suddenly injects a bit of real life into the theatre and instantly sweeps us into a state of subconscious creativeness." His elaboration of this idea is very informative:

Anything. Even the dropping of a handkerchief, or the overturning of a chair. A live incident in the conditioned atmosphere of the stage is like a breath of fresh air in a stuffy room. The actor must pick up the handkerchief, or the chair, spontaneously, because that wasn't rehearsed in the play. He doesn't do it as an actor but in an ordinary, human way and creates a bit of truth that he must believe in. . . .

If he can really believe in the spontaneous occurrence and use it in his part, it will help him. . . .

Therefore, learn to appreciate any such occurrences. Don't let them slip by. Learn to use them wisely when they happen of their own accord. They are an excellent means of drawing you closer to the subconscious.[19]

Rapoport speaks of feelings as resulting from the conflict between the task (action) and the counteracting circumstances.[20] For example, a man about to catch a plane is ready to leave his home when he suddenly discovers that his plane ticket is not in his wallet. As he searches through his luggage, a great many different feelings will arise, depending, of course, upon the given circumstances. The more important they are, the stronger and more intense will be the feeling.

I. Sudakov, at one time a director under Stanislavsky and Danchenko, says this:

No sooner does the actor come out upon the stage to enact a part that is packed with intense feeling than he seizes upon those feelings, trying to act them out, and thus foredooms himself to cliches which inevitably distort the nature of his acting . . . . What I [the actor] might feel—this should not even be answered. To think of what I might have thought, said or done in such a case—that is the best way of making oneself have that inner experience. To think of how I might feel in any given situation is the surest way of falling into the beaten track of affected acting. Try to act, *to meet obstacles* and *to overcome them* and you will come to feel as you should in the given case.[21] (Italics supplied.)

Stanislavsky offers still another source of emotion or feelings. He points out that everyone has within him "the elements of all human characteristics, good and bad." The actor, therefore, must learn to use his art and his technique to find out which of these elements to develop for the given part. Stanislavsky asserts that often powerful and vivid emotions flash upon the actor unexpectedly and that from them springs inspiration or the truly creative state. Sometimes they are less powerful. "If you learn how to be receptive to these recurring memories," says Stanislavsky, "then the new ones as they form will be more capable of stirring your feelings repeatedly." [22]

Regarding the use of these emotion (affective) memories Stanislavsky is very explicit:

> Another reason why you should cherish those repeated emotions is, that an artist does not build his role out of the first thing at hand. He chooses very carefully from among his memories and culls out of his living experiences the ones that are most enticing. He weaves the soul of the person he is to portray out of emotions that are dearer to him than his everyday sensations. Can you imagine a more fertile field for inspiration? An artist takes the best that is in him and carries it over on the stage. The form will vary, according to the necessities of the play, but the human emotions of the artist will remain alive, and they cannot be replaced by anything else.

Stanislavsky emphasizes that in order for the actor to develop sensitivity and response to beauty and human feeling, he "must lead a full, interesting, beautiful, varied, exacting and inspiring life." [23] He adds to this, "He should study the life and psychology of the people around him, of various other parts of the population at home and abroad." Nowhere, however, does he suggest that the actor should sit at home and delve into his past experience after the fashion of the psychoanalyst. In complete agreement with the many actors whose emotional reactions Archer studied (see pages 151–156), Stanislavsky declares:

> We use not only our own past emotions as creative material but we use feelings that we have had in sympathizing with the emotions of others. . . . So we must study other people, and get as close to them emotionally as we can, until sympathy for them is transformed into feelings of our own.[24]

Stanislavsky warns the actor, however, that he must never lose himself on the stage: "Always and forever, when you are on the stage, you must play yourself. But it will be in an infinite variety of combinations of objectives, and given circumstances which you have prepared for your part, and which have been smelted in the furnace of your emotion memory." [25] It is clear that Stanislavsky does not wish the actor to relive an experience in all its original and often painful details, for he declares: "Time is a splendid filter for our remembered feelings—besides it is a great artist. It not only purifies, it also transmutes even painfully realistic memories into poetry." [26]

Stanislavsky never approved of naturalistic details merely for the sake of themselves, as can be seen from his criticism of a student's improvisation:

> Why do you exaggerate truth to such an undesirable degree in the death scene? You have cramps, nausea, groans, horrible grimaces, and gradual paralysis. You seem, at this point, to be indulging in naturalism for its own sake. You were more interested in external, visual memories of the dissolution of a human body.[27]

Instead, he asserts that on the stage truth is transformed into a poetical equivalent by creative imagination.

Stanislavsky makes a point of the "difference between 'telling' about feelings, thoughts, the plot, and the idea of the play, and finding hidden in the text and situation the deep, inner life of human beings which is familiar to us all." [28] He demonstrates how the actor can bring this inner life of the character to the audience by means of the inner monologue. In his work on the dramatization of Dickens' *The Battle of Life*, Stanislavsky illustrates this in an exercise, with the two students playing the parts of the two sisters Marion and Grace. He required each one to speak her reactions to the words of the other in a lower tone, although loud enough to be understood. Next he asked them merely to whisper these reactions, then to pronounce them soundlessly, and finally to express them only with the eyes. Gorchakov reports on the success of this experiment:

> The actors couldn't help listening to their partners, answering what they said, and reacting correctly to all that was happening. And suddenly all the roles became colorful, and the speeches were filled with new expression.[29]

The inner monologue is made up of ideas and images which are the reactions to the partner's words. Stanislavsky emphasized continually the need for an actor to allow images to form in his mind in response to the thoughts of his own part. This is one of the chief contributions which the system makes toward giving life to the text.

In all his work the actor must develop his imagination and creative fantasy, to give life not only to the words he speaks but to fascinate himself, as it were, with the given circumstances of the play.

Stanislavsky fully understood the problems that confronted the director as well, and gave concrete suggestions for their solution. When Gorchakov asked what principles the director needed to know, Stanislavsky answered, "All those I mentioned for the actor, plus three more." It stands to reason that the director cannot really help the actor if he does not understand his problems. It is essential, therefore, that he realize what it is that the actor is trying to accomplish. In addition Stanislavsky insisted that the director must know how to work on the play with the author, if he is alive, or without him, if he is dead; this means that he must be able to "make a complete and profound analysis of the play." He must also work with the actor, the scene designer, the costumer, the composer, if there is one, as well as with the production crew. Stanislavsky asserts that the director must work on himself ten times as hard as the actors do, since he must teach not only himself but them.[30]

B. E. Zakhava, director of the Vakhtangov Studio and co-worker of Vakhtangov during his work with the Third Studio, wrote two illuminating articles called "Principles of Directing." They originally appeared in the two issues of *Theatre Workshop*, April–July, 1937, and September–October, 1937, and they have been reprinted in Toby Cole's *Handbook*. Zakhava writes: *"The material of the director's creativeness is the creativeness of the actor."* [italics in the text] Under "Creative Reciprocity" he enumerates three possible actor-director situations. The first two are equally bad: in the first the director is weak through lack of creativeness; in the second he does not occupy the leading position by reason of lack of knowledge. The third situation is, of course, one of collaborative activity in creativeness. Zakhava often refers to Vakhtangov. He declares, "I know of no director who penetrated more closely into the inner life of the actor." [31] Zakhava also mentions Stanislavsky often, and Vakhtangov's relation to his master:

In his diary Vakhtangov wrote: "Stanislavski has the perfect comprehension of the actor. He knows him from head to foot, from his guts to his skin, from his thoughts to his spirit." It was this science Vakhtangov absorbed from Stanislavski and it is a science which should be acquired by every director. Without it a true reciprocity between actor and director can never be realized.[32]

Zakhava lists six common impediments for an actor. These are: lack of attention, muscular tension, absence of justification, the lack of creative "food," the attempts of the actor to enact emotion, and the entrance of falsehood. Zakhava points out the necessity of the director's being able to diagnose the actor's trouble correctly before he can correct it. His final statement reflects Stanislavsky's relationship to his actors:

> From all this it is clear how carefully the director must treasure the actor as the material of his art; what understanding, what keenness and discernment he must apply to him. All these qualities will evolve naturally if the director loves and values the actor; if he forces nothing mechanically onto the scene; if he remains unsatisfied up to the perfection point where the expression of the actor attains inner and artistic truth.[33]

A measure of Stanislavsky's contribution to the director can be seen from an examination of the notes of two directors who acknowledge his influence, Harold Clurman and Elia Kazan.[34] These two directors list the main actions or spines for each of the leading characters of *The Member of the Wedding,* and *A Streetcar Named Desire.* Clurman explains all the incidents in the play in active, actable terms. Kazan in his method of theatricality shows a kinship with Vakhtangov. How firmly based it is upon Stanislavsky's principles can be seen from an interview in the *Tulane Drama Review* in the winter issue of December, 1964. In discussing his method of working with Richard Schechner, the editor, Kazan says:

> I put terrific stress on what the person wants and why he wants it. What makes it meaningful for him. I don't start on *how* he goes about getting it until I get him wanting it. And then I make clear the circumstances under which he behaves; what happens just before, and so on. Then I try to find the physical behavior without preconception on my part if possible, but from what the actor does to achieve his objective under the circumstances.[35]

Stanislavsky believed that the audience should be involved in the play—that, in fact, they should forget that they were present in the theatre. Since Stanislavsky's System of acting succeeds in accomplishing this, it can be said to stimulate an emotional response on the part of the audience. There are many reports of performances by the Moscow Art Theatre testifying to the fact that the audience felt as though they were looking through the windows of a private home, "eavesdropping" in fact. (See p. 231.)

There are innumerable evidences of Stanislavsky's next contribution, namely, stimulating interest in theatre as an art and as a craft. For one thing, the number of books and articles about Stanislavsky or the Stanislavsky System written in America in the last twenty years seems to be increasing steadily. The authors are some of the leading actors and directors in the American theatre, such as Clurman, Kazan, Lewis, and Gielgud. As noted earlier Brooks Atkinson said on February 2, 1958, "The method, as it is dubbed in the vernacular, is still the most explosive subject in theatre esthetics." (See p. 279.) In the Sunday *New York Times,* Arthur Gelb said that talk about the pros and cons of the "Method" was becoming as heated in theatre circles as the talk of the "sack" in fashion circles. (See p. 267.) Moreover, Brooks Atkinson and Gelb state that the "Method" is the Stanislavsky System of training actors. Regardless of one's viewpoint on the extent of influence of the Actors Studio, Stanislavsky's stimulation of interest in theatre art must surely be admitted.

Another indication of the effectiveness of Stanislavsky in this respect is the number of acting courses given by his spiritual descendants, "even to the third and fourth generation." One advertisement of a West Coast studio has a drawing of Stanislavsky in its copy.

Further evidence of Stanislavsky's influence was given in the form of an invitation extended by IASTA (Institute for Advanced Studies in the Theatre Arts) in the spring of 1960. This organization was formed in 1959 and has a Board of Directors composed of leading theatre people, among them Marc Connelly, Mildred Dunnock, George Freedley, Rosamond Gilder, Norris Houghton, Donald Oenslager, Michel Saint-Denis, Margaret Webster, and Robert Whitehead. The aim of the organization was to subsidize foreign directors of representative schools of acting for a six weeks' program in New York City, at which time a company of American actors and actresses, all members of Actors Equity, among them Jessica Tandy and Kent

Smith, would play without remuneration under the visiting director. The first director was Willi Schmidt from the Schiller State Theatre in West Germany, who presented Schiller's *Kabale und Liebe* (*Love and Intrigue*); the second was Jacques Charon of the Comédie Française, who directed Molière's *Misanthrope;* the third was Yuri Zavadsky, Director of the Mossoviet Theatre of Moscow, a former pupil of Vakhtangov and a member of the Third Studio of the Moscow Art Theatre.

In his youth Zavadsky had played the part of St. Anthony in Vakhtangov's spectacular success, *The Miracle of St. Anthony*, and that of Prince Calaf in his famous production of *Turandot*. Under Stanislavsky's direction, he had played Chatsky in *Woe from Wisdom* and Count Almaviva in *The Marriage of Figaro* in 1927. In connection with the latter Zavadsky said, "Stanislavsky experimented with different rhythms for different characters and that is the school of Stanislavsky." Zavadsky is perhaps the one person accessible to us who had the latest contact with Stanislavsky, and therefore his comments are of especial interest. I, myself, was privileged to be at his rehearsals of *The Cherry Orchard* and for a time acted as his assistant.

In his talks to the actors he continually referred to Stanislavsky and made constant use of his method of working on a play. Since he was a pupil of Vakhtangov before joining the Moscow Art Theatre, his remarks reveal also how firmly grounded Vakhtangov was in the Stanislavsky System. Following are a few of Zavadsky's words to the actors during rehearsals:

> The actor must play his inner thoughts, desires, actions, but not feelings; however, the moment he tries to do so, the real feelings disappear. But if he makes the thoughts and actions of the character his own, then he awakens the real feelings of the character. . . . Each character is a succession of actions. Stanislavsky said, "In our work, *to know* is to be able *to do*."
> Stanislavsky spoke of *living through* a part.
> A person only says part of what he thinks, and each speech therefore, is only part of the thoughts [of the character]. In Chekhov the actor must create an uninterrupted line of thought. During the last years of his life Stanislavsky worked a great deal on this inner monologue. The inner monologue combines thoughts and feelings.
> When you pronounce one thought, at the same time, another is in your mind. The first thought prepares for the arrival of the second. The *subtext* [the thoughts under the words or "between the lines"] must permeate the part.
> Stanislavsky himself played Dr. Astrof in *Uncle Vanya* originally, and

many years later, when he was seventy, he played the same part. I met him in the corridor the day before the performance—he was very old and feeble. When he came on stage, he had tossed off thirty or forty years. He had no make-up but he was young. That is the art of Stanislavsky—the transformation of a person because "I am in a new world with every character."

The Stanislavsky System above all is not an acting style. It is a living, vibrant way of life on the stage, whether the actor is called upon to play classical or contemporary comedy, drama, or tragedy. It has been kept alive in Moscow by Stanislavsky's pupils who were actors in the Moscow Art Theatre or its Studios. I visited Moscow in 1962 and had the pleasure of meeting Stanislavsky's son, Igor Alexeiev, as well as several friends of Vera Soloviova, who with her had been members of the First Studio. One of these, Seraphima Ghermanovna Birman, was playing the part of the nurse, Miss Porter, in the production of Tennessee Williams' *Orpheus Descending* at the Mossoviet (Zavadsky's) Theatre. She has also been a very successful director and has written a book describing her experiences in the theatre, *The Journey of an Actress,* dedicated to Stanislavsky, "inspired artist and teacher." Lida Daykun and her husband are teachers at the Dramatic School connected with the Maly Theatre. I also visited Vera Orlova, who played Mytyl in the *Blue Bird.* I attended several rehearsals of a new play which Yuri Zavadsky was directing.

Further proof of the vitality of Stanislavsky's System is the continuity of the very institution which Stanislavsky founded, the Moscow Art Theatre, and the fact that its repertoire still includes many of the plays which he himself directed. I attended performances of two of these. The first, *Goryacheye Serdtze* (*The Ardent Heart*) was originally staged by Stanislavsky in 1926 and marked a distinct departure from his customary realistic style. It is still played very broadly, approaching farce.

The second production, Maeterlinck's *Blue Bird,* is given as originally staged by Stanislavsky every Sunday morning at eleven just as when he lived. The audience is composed for the most part of children under twelve. Looking about in the darkened house and seeing the rapt faces, one half expects to see the huge figure of the Director, with his great head of white hair, sitting in his accustomed place behind the transverse aisle, the first seat on the right of the center aisle. Danchenko's seat was the second seat on the left of the center aisle. I had been invited to this performance by Deema Kachalov, son of the

renowned actor of the original Moscow Art Theatre Company, colleague of Stanislavsky and Olga Knipper-Chekhova.

He also invited me to the final performance of second year students
of the School of the Moscow Art Theatre where he teaches stage management. The play was an old Russian classic and the young student
actors played the parts of mature men and women convincingly. They
also succeeded in evoking a mood which drew the audience into participation with the players. Kachalov also escorted me to the Museum
of the Moscow Art Theatre. Here I met Fedya Mikhalsky, its director, a
friend of Vera Soloviova. He took us through the Museum, where there
are many pictures of the productions of the original Moscow Art Theatre Company and of the First Studio. Mikhalsky pointed out to me
with pride the life preserver used in the Studio's twentieth anniversary production of *The Good Hope* in which Soloviova repeated the
part of Jo which she had created for the first performance. Turning
it over, with a twinkle in his eye, he showed me that it had been used
also on the fiftieth anniversary in 1958.

The house where Stanislavsky lived for the last seventeen years of
his life, and where he held his last classes in acting and opera, has
been made into the Stanislavsky Museum, and here I was taken by
Stanislavsky's son, Igor Alexeiev.

On the hundredth anniversary of Stanislavsky's birth, in 1963, there
were several books published in Moscow in his honor. One of these is
a collection of letters to him and writings about him by famous actors
and writers such as Gorky, Birman, Block, Kachalov, Leonidov,
Vakhtangov, Afinogenov, Charles Chaplin, and others. And so he
lives on in the practice of his System by his former pupils and the
present generation of actors at the Moscow Art Theatre and other
theatres in Moscow and Leningrad. His books have been translated
into twenty different languages, including Japanese.

In America, in 1958, the sixtieth anniversary of the founding of the
Moscow Art Theatre was marked by an exhibit at the Forty-Second
Street Library, arranged by George Freedley, and the publication of
thus far unpublished writings and addresses of Stanislavsky translated
by Mrs. Hapgood and entitled *Stanislavski's Legacy*. Mrs. Hapgood
also translated the last work of Stanislavsky, *Creating a Role* which
was published three years later.

All of his works have been published by Theatre Arts Books, Inc.
of which Robert MacGregor is the editor. All are now easily accessible
to American actors and students of acting. According to Hetler, in

American college and university classes the System is perhaps the dominant method used, or at least it is combined with the mechanical or external method. The effect of Stanislavsky's teachings is evident in the interest in his writings, in the work of contemporary American performers and directors, and in the many theatre workshops and acting studios admittedly adhering to the Stanislavsky System, where a new generation of American students of acting are learning their first steps along the road which he charted.

Stanislavsky's greatest contribution appears to have been in *assisting the actor in interpreting and executing his role.* Among the most valuable aids to this end are the discovery of the trunk line of the play, and the superobjective, and the main actions and objectives of the character; the playing of actions; the use of counteraction; the use of the five senses to express actions and inner states; the use of emotion (affective) memory; the inner monologue and the actor's creation of images in response to the thoughts of his own part and the lines of his partner. A further contribution in this area is his emphasis upon the use of so-called external techniques such as intonation, inflection, pause, tempo-rhythm, and body movement in relation to the inner scheme of the play and the character.

Most of the actors from Talma to those of the present day set up remarkably similar goals. Most of them believed that the actor should experience real feelings while on the stage; that he should use his own experiences to create those feelings; and that the actor and the character should be fused into a single personality. No one, however, except Stanislavsky, has given such workable directions for accomplishing these objectives. The Stanislavsky System offers the actor a means for understanding his role and for fulfilling the goal of interpreting and executing it in such a way as to present *the life of a human being on the stage.*

In the year following Stanislavsky's death, Olga Knipper-Chekhova, beloved actress of the Moscow Art Theatre from its beginning and widow of Anton Chekhov, wrote of the man who had been her director all her life:

> Konstantin Stanislavsky! This name should sound like a clarion call not only to those who knew and loved him and had worked with him. That is how it should sound to the younger generation and to posterity summoning us all to be scrupulous and honest in our approach and understanding of art.
>
> His name is our conscience.

❀

Notes

1. The five were the actress, Mildred Dunnock; the director, Vincent Donehue; the critic, John Gassner; the producer, Norris Houghton; and the teacher, Vera Soloviova.

2. Constantin Stanislavski, *Building a Character,* translated by Elizabeth Reynolds Hapgood, introduction by Joshua Logan (New York: Theatre Arts Books, 1949), p. 173.

3. K. S. Stanislavski, *Die Arbeit des Schauspielers an der Rolle,* zusammengestellt von J. N. Semjanowskaja, redigiert, kommentiert und eingeleitet von G. W. Kristi (Berlin: Henschelverlag, 1955), p. 28.

4. Constantin Stanislavski, *Creating a Role,* translated by Elizabeth Reynolds Hapgood (New York: Theatre Arts Books, 1961), p. 116.

5. Stanislavski, *Creating a Role,* p. 129.

6. Nikolai M. Gorchakov, *Stanislavsky Directs,* translated by Miriam Goldina (New York: Funk and Wagnalls Company, 1954), p. 39.

7. N. M. Gorchakov, *Stanislavsky Directs,* p. 119.

8. Stanislavski, *Creating a Role,* p. 144.

9. N. M. Gorchakov, *Stanislavsky Directs,* p. 119.

10. N. M. Gorchakov, *Stanislavsky Directs,* p. 120.

11. N. M. Gorchakov, *Stanislavsky Directs,* p. 119.

12. N. M. Gorchakov, *Stanislavsky Directs,* p. 120.

13. Constantin Stanislavski, *An Actor Prepares,* translated by

Elizabeth Reynolds Hapgood (New York: Theatre Arts Books, 1936), p. 175.

14. Stanislavski, *An Actor Prepares*, pp. 72–73.

15. I. Rapoport, "The Work of the Actor," in Toby Cole, ed., *Acting, A Handbook of the Stanislavski Method* (New York: Crown Publishers, 1955), pp. 35–39.

16. Christine Edwards, "Training the Actor in the Use of Objects," in John Gassner, ed., *Producing the Play* (revised ed., New York: The Dryden Press, 1953), pp. 163–71.

17. Stanislavski, *An Actor Prepares*, pp. 82–85.

18. Lee Strasberg, "Acting and Actor Training," in John Gassner, ed., *Producing the Play* (New York: The Dryden Press, 1941), p. 162n.

19. Stanislavski, *An Actor Prepares*, p. 270.

20. Rapoport, "The Work of the Actor," p. 54.

21. I. Sudakov, "The Actor's Creative Work," in *Theatre Workshop*, Vol. 1, No. 2 (January–March, 1937), Second Acting Issue, pp. 10–11; and Toby Cole, ed., *Acting, A Handbook of the Stanislavski Method*, pp. 72–73.

22. Stanislavski, *An Actor Prepares*, pp. 164–68.

23. Stanislavski, *An Actor Prepares*, p. 166.

24. Stanislavski, *An Actor Prepares*, p. 179.

25. Stanislavski, *An Actor Prepares*, p. 167.

26. Stanislavski, *An Actor Prepares*, p. 163.

27. Stanislavski, *An Actor Prepares*, p. 150.

28. N. M. Gorchakov, *Stanislavsky Directs*, p. 43.

29. N. M. Gorchakov, *Stanislavsky Directs*, p. 57.

30. N. M. Gorchakov, *Stanislavsky Directs*, p. 121.

31. Cole, *Acting, A Handbook of the Stanislavski Method*, p. 208.

32. Cole, *Acting, A Handbook*, p. 209.

33. Cole, *Acting, A Handbook*, p. 217.

34. Elia Kazan, "Notebook for *A Streetcar Named Desire*," pp. 296–310, and Harold Clurman, "Some Preliminary Notes for *A Member of the Wedding*," pp. 311–320, in Toby Cole and Helen Krich Chinoy, eds., *Directing The Play* (Indianapolis: The Bobbs-Merrill Company, Inc.).

35. Elia Kazan, interview with Richard Schechner and Theodore Hoffman, *Tulane Drama Review*, Vol. 9, No. 2 (Winter Issue, December, 1964), p. 73.

❊

Bibliography

A. *BOOKS*

Albright, H. D. *Working Up a Part*. Cambridge, Mass.: The Riverside Press, Houghton Mifflin Company, 1947.

Archer, William. "Masks or Faces," in Denis Diderot, *The Paradox of Acting*, and William Archer, *Masks or Faces*. New York: Hill and Wang, Inc., 1957. Pp. 75–226.

Bakshy, Alexander. *The Path of the Modern Russian Stage*. Boston: John W. Luce and Company, 1918.

Baring, Maurice. *An Outline of Russian Literature*. New York: Henry Holt, n.d.

Baron, Michel, in Toby Cole and Helen Krich Chinoy (eds.), *Actors on Acting*. New York: Crown Publishers, 1949. Pp. 158–59.

Barrymore, Ethel. *Memories*. New York: Harper and Brothers, 1955.

Belasco, David. *The Theatre Through Its Stage Door*, ed. Louis V. Defoe. New York and London: Harper Brothers, 1919.

Blanchard, Fred C. "Professional Theatre Schools in the Early Twentieth Century" in Karl R. Wallace (ed.), *History of Speech Education in America*. New York: Appleton-Century-Crofts, Inc., 1954. Pp. 617–40.

Boleslavsky, Richard. *Acting—the First Six Lessons*. New York: Theatre Arts Books, 1933.

Boucicault, Dion. "The Art of Acting" in Brander Matthews, ed., *Papers on Acting*. New York: Hill and Wang, 1958. Pp. 137–160.

Bradshaw, Martha (ed.). *Soviet Theatres 1917–1941*. New York: Research Program on the U.S.S.R., Ann Arbor, Michigan, Edwards Brothers, Inc., 1954.

Calvert, Louis. *Problems of the Actor*. London: Simpkin, Marshall, Hamilton, Kent and Company, Ltd., 1918.

Carter, Huntley. *The New Spirit in Drama and Art*. New York: Mitchell Kennerley, 1913.

————. *The New Spirit in the Russian Theatre*. London: Brentano's Ltd., 1929.

Chayefsky, Paddy. *Television Plays*. New York: Simon and Schuster, 1955.

Chekhov, Michael. *To the Actor*. New York: Harper and Brothers, 1953.

Cheney, Sheldon. *The Art Theatre*. New York: Alfred A. Knopf, 1925 (first published 1917).

Clapp, Henry A. *Reminiscences of a Dramatic Critic*. Boston: Houghton Mifflin and Company; Cambridge: The Riverside Press, 1902.

Clurman, Harold. *The Fervent Years*. New York: Alfred A. Knopf, 1945.

Coad, Oral Sumner, and Mims, Edwin, Jr. *The American Stage: The Pageant of America*, Vol. XIV, ed. Ralph Henry Gabriel. New Haven: Yale University Press, 1929.

Cole, Toby (comp.). *Acting, A Handbook of the Stanislavski Method*. New York: Crown Publishers, 1955.

————, and Chinoy, Helen Krich (eds.). *Directing the Play*. Indianapolis and New York: The Bobbs-Merrill Company, Inc., 1953.

————. *Actors on Acting*. New York: Crown Publishers, 1949.

Coquelin, Constant. "Art and the Actor," in Brander Matthews (ed.), *Papers on Acting*. New York: Hill and Wang, 1958. Pp. 1–40.

Craig, Edward Gordon. *On the Art of the Theatre*. Chicago: Browne's Bookstore, 1911.

————. *Towards a New Theatre*. London: J. M. Dent and Sons, Ltd., 1913.

Crowley, Alice Lewisohn. *The Neighborhood Playhouse, Leaves from a Theatre Scrapbook*. New York: Theatre Arts Books, 1959.

D'Angelo, Aristide. *The Actor Creates*. New York: Samuel French, 1939.

Dean, Alexander. *Fundamentals of Play Production*, rev. ed. New York: Farrar and Rinehart, Inc., 1941.

Deutsch, Helen, and Hanau, Stella, *The Provincetown*, New York: Farrar and Rinehart, Inc.

Dickinson, Thomas H. *The Insurgent Theatre*. New York: B. W. Huebsch, 1917.

———. *The Theatre in a Changing Europe.* New York: Henry Holt and Company, 1937.

Diderot, Denis. "The Paradox of Acting," in Denis Diderot, *The Paradox of Acting,* and William Archer, *Masks or Faces.* New York: Hill and Wang, Inc., 1957. Pp. 5–74.

Dolman, John. *The Art of Play Production.* New York: Harper Brothers, 1928.

Drew, John. *My Years On the Stage.* New York: E. P. Dutton and Company, 1921.

———. *My Years on the New York Stage.* New York: E. P. Dutton and Company, 1922.

Duerr, Edwin. "Stanislavsky and the Idea" in *Studies in Speech and Drama, in Honor of Alexander M. Drummond.* Ithaca, New York: Cornell University Press, 1944.

Dumesnil, Marie Françoise. "A Reply to 'Reflection on Dramatic Art' of Clairon" in Toby Cole and Helen Krich Chinoy (eds.), *Actors on Acting.* New York: Crown Publishers, 1949. Pp. 174–176.

Eaton, W. P. *The Actor's Heritage.* Boston: The Atlantic Monthly Press, 1924.

Evreinoff, Nicolas. *Histoire du Théâtre Russe.* Paris: Edition Du Chêne, 1947.

Felheim, Marvin. *The Theatre of Augustin Daly.* Cambridge: Harvard University Press, 1956.

Fovitzky, A. L. *The Moscow Art Theatre and Its Distinguishing Characteristics.* New York: A. Chernoff Publishing Company, 1923.

Franklin, Miriam A. *Rehearsal,* rev. ed. New York: Prentice-Hall, 1942.

Freedley, George, and Reeves, John A. *A History of the Theatre.* New York: Crown Publishers, 1941.

Frohman, Daniel. *Daniel Frohman Presents.* New York: Claude Kendall and Willoughby Sharp, 1935.

Fülöp-Miller, René, and Gregor, Joseph. *The Russian Theatre.* Translated by Paul England. Philadelphia: J. B. Lippincott Company, 1930.

Fyles, Franklin. *The Theatre and Its People.* New York: Doubleday, Page and Company, 1900.

Gassner, John. *Form and Idea in the Modern Theatre.* New York: The Dryden Press, 1956.

———. *Masters of the Drama.* New York: Dover Publications, 1945.

———. *Producing the Play.* New York: The Dryden Press, Inc., 1941. Rev. ed., 1953.

———. *The Theatre in Our Times.* New York: Crown Publishers, 1954.

Gielgud, John. Introduction (London, April 30, 1948), in Constantin Stanislavski, *An Actor Prepares,* anniversary ed. New York: Theatre Arts Books, 1948. Pp. xiii–xx.

Gilbert, A. H. (Mrs. G. H.). *The Stage Reminiscences of Mrs. Gilbert.* New York: Charles Scribner's Sons, 1901.

Gillette, William. "The Illusion of the First Time in Acting," in Brander Matthews (ed.), *Papers on Acting.* Notes. New York: Dramatic Museum of Columbia University, 1915. Pp. 115–136.

Gorchakov, Nikolai A. *The Theatre in Soviet Russia.* Translated by Edgar Lehrman. New York: Columbia University Press, 1957.

Gorchakov, Nikolai M. *Stanislavsky Directs.* Translated by Miriam Goldina. New York: Funk and Wagnalls Company, 1954.

Gorky, Maxim. *Reminiscences.* New York: Dover Publications, 1946.

Hale, Lester L. "Dr. James Rush," in Karl R. Wallace (ed.), *History of Speech Education in America.* New York: Appleton-Century-Crofts, Inc., 1954. Pp. 219–237.

Hapgood, Norman. *The Stage in America, 1897–1900.* New York: Macmillan, 1901.

Hewitt, Barnard, Foster, J. F., and Wolle, Muriel Sibell. *Play Production, Theory and Practice.* New York: J. B. Lippincott Company, 1952.

Hornblow, Arthur. *A History of the Theatre in America,* Vol. 2. Philadelphia: J. B. Lippincott, 1919.

Houghton, Norris. *But Not Forgotten.* New York: William Sloane Associates, 1951.

———. *Moscow Rehearsals.* New York: Harcourt, Brace and Company, 1936.

Hughes, Glenn. *A History of the American Theatre.* New York: Samuel French, 1951.

Irving, Henry. Introduction, "Reflections on Acting" in Brander Matthews (ed.), *Papers on Acting.* New York: Hill and Wang, 1958. Pp. 42–43.

Isaacs, Edith. *Theatre.* Boston: Little, Brown and Company, 1927.

Jefferson, Joseph. *Rip Van Winkle: The Autobiography of Joseph Jefferson.* New York: Appleton-Century-Crofts, Inc., n.d.

Kjerbuhl-Peterson, Lorenz. *Psychology of Acting.* Translated by Sarah T. Burrows. Boston: The Expression Company, 1935.

Kommisarzhevsky, Theodore. *Myself and the Theatre.* New York: E. P. Dutton and Company, 1930.

Langner, Lawrence. "The Little Theatre Grows Up," in W. P. Eaton and others (eds.), *The Theatre Guild, The First Ten Years*. New York: Brentano, 1929.

Lewes, George Henry. *On Actors and the Art of Acting*. New York: Grove Press, n.d.

Lewis, Robert. *Method—or Madness*. New York: Samuel French, 1958.

Macgowan, Kenneth, and Melinitz, William. *The Living Stage*. New York: Prentice-Hall, Inc., 1955.

Mackay, F. F. *The Art of Acting*. New York: F. F. Mackay, 1913.

Macleod, Joseph. *Actors Cross the Volga*. London: George Allen and Unwin, Ltd., 1946.

Magarshack, David. *Stanislavsky, A Life*. New York: The Chanticleer Press, 1951.

Markov, P. *Moskovsky Khudozhestvenny Teatr, Vtoroi (Moscow Art Theatre Second)*. Moscow, 1925.

Matthews, Brander. Introduction to "Actors on Acting, A Discussion by Constant Coquelin, Sir Henry Irving, and Dion Boucicault" in *Papers on Acting*. New York: Hill and Wang, 1958. Pp. 161–200.

McGaw, Charles. *Acting Is Believing*. New York: Rinehart and Company, Inc., 1955. Second printing, 1956.

Mirsky, D. S. *A History of Russian Literature*. New York: Alfred A. Knopf, 1949.

Moody, Richard. *America Takes the Stage*. Bloomington, Ind.: Indiana University Press, 1955.

Morris, Clara. *Life on the Stage*. New York: McClure, Phillips and Company, 1901.

———. *Life of a Star*. New York: McClure, Phillips and Company, 1906.

Moses, Montrose J., and Brown, John Mason. *The American Theatre as Seen by Its Critics*. New York: W. W. Norton and Company, 1934.

Nemirovich-Danchenko, Vladimir. *My Life in the Russian Theatre*. Translated by John Cournos. Boston: Little, Brown and Company, 1936.

Oenslager, Donald. *Scenery, Then and Now*. New York: W. W. Norton Company, Inc., 1936.

Orlovsky, Serge. "Moscow Theatres 1917–1940" in Martha Bradshaw (ed.) *Soviet Theatres 1917–1941*. New York: Research Program on the U.S.S.R., Ann Arbor, Michigan: Edwards Brothers, Inc., 1954. Pp. 1–127.

Redgrave, Michael. *The Actor's Ways and Means*. New York: Theatre Arts Books, 1953.

————. *Mask or Face.* London: Heineman, 1958.

Rosenstein, Sophie, Haydon, Larrae A., and Sparrow, Wilbur. *Modern Acting.* New York: Samuel French, 1936.

Sayler, Oliver M. *The Russian Theatre.* New York: Little, Brown and Company, 1920.

————. *Inside the Moscow Art Theatre.* New York: Brentano, 1925.

Selden, Samuel. *First Steps in Acting.* New York: F. S. Crofts and Company, 1947.

Shaver, Claude L. "Steele MacKaye and the Delsartian Tradition" in Karl R. Wallace (ed.), *History of Speech Education in America.* New York: Appleton-Century-Crofts, Inc., 1954. Pp. 202–218.

Short, Ernest. *Introducing the Theatre.* London: Eyre and Spotteswood, 1949.

Simonson, Lee. *The Stage is Set.* New York: Dover Publications, 1932.

Skinner, Otis. *Footlights and Spotlights.* Indianapolis: Bobbs-Merrill Company, 1923.

Stanislavski, Constantin. *An Actor Prepares.* Translated by Elizabeth Reynolds Hapgood, New York: Theatre Arts Books, 1936.

————. *Building a Character.* Translated by Elizabeth Reynolds Hapgood. Introduction by Joshua Logan. New York: Theatre Arts Books, 1949.

————. *My Life in Art.* Translated by J. J. Robbins. New York: Theatre Arts Books, 1948. P. 351.

————. *Stanislavski Produces Othello.* Translated from the Russian by Dr. Helen Nowak. London: Geoffrey Bles, 1948.

————. *The Sea Gull Produced by Stanislavski.* Edited with an introduction by Prof. S. D. Balukhaty, translated by David Magarshack. New York: Theatre Arts Books, 1952.

————. *Stanislavski's Legacy.* Translated by Elizabeth Reynolds Hapgood. New York: Theatre Arts Books, 1958.

————. *Creating a Role.* Translated by Elizabeth Reynolds Hapgood. Foreword by Robert Lewis. New York: Theatre Arts Books, 1961.

Stanislavsky, K. S. *Die Arbeit des Schauspielers an der Rolle,* zusammengestellt von J. N. Semjanowskaja, redigiert, kommentiert und eingeleitet von G. W. Kristi. Berlin: Henschelverlag, 1955.

Stanislavsky on the Art of the Stage. Translated, with an Introductory Essay on Stanislavsky's System by David Magarshack. London: Faber and Faber, Ltd., n.d.

Talma. "Reflections on Acting," in Brander Matthews (ed.), *Papers on Acting.* New York: Hill and Wang, 1958.

Timberlake, Craig. *The Bishop of Broadway.* New York: Library Publishers, 1954.

Toporkov. *Stanislavskii na Repetitsii* (Stanislavsky at Rehearsal). As cited by N. A. Gorchakov in *The Theatre in Soviet Russia.*

Towse, J. Rankin. *Sixty Years in the Theatre.* New York: Funk and Wagnalls Company, 1916.

Van Gyseghem, Andre. *Theatre in Soviet Russia.* London: Faber & Faber, Ltd., 1943.

Varneke, B. V. *History of the Russian Theatre, Seventeenth Through Nineteenth Century.* Original translation by Boris Brasol. New York: The Macmillan Company, 1951.

Whiting, Frank. *Rehearsal Techniques.* Cincinnati: The National Thespian Society, 1948.

———. *An Introduction to the Theatre.* New York: Harper Brothers, 1954.

Wilson, Francis. *Joseph Jefferson, Reminiscences of a Fellow Player.* New York: Charles Scribner's Sons, 1906.

Wilstach, Paul. *Richard Mansfield.* New York: Charles Scribner's Sons, 1909.

Winter, William. *Ada Rehan: A Study.* New York: 1891.

———. *Other Days.* New York: Moffat, Yard and Company, 1908.

———. *The Wallet of Time.* New York: Moffat, Yard and Company, 1913.

———. *Vagrant Memories.* New York: George H. Doran and Company, 1915.

Woollcott, Alexander (ed.). *Mrs. Fiske, Her Views on Actors, Acting, and the Problems of Production.* New York: The Century Company, 1917.

Young, Stark. "The Moscow Art Theatre," *Glamour.* New York and London: Charles Scribner's Sons, 1925.

Zakhava, B. E. "Principles of Directing," in *Acting, A Handbook of the Stanislavski Method,* compiled by Toby Cole. New York: Crown Publishers, 1955. Pp. 182–217.

B. *PERIODICALS*

Adler, Stella. "The Art of Acting," *The Theatre,* II, No. 4 (April, 1960), 17.

———. "The Reality of Doing," *Tulane Drama Review,* IX, No. 1, Fall 1964, p. 143.

Ashby, Clifford. "Alla Nazimova and the Advent of the New Acting in America," *Quarterly Journal of Speech,* XLV, No. 2 (April, 1959), 182–83, citing Owen Johnson, "Mme. Alla Nazimova," *Century Magazine,* LXXIV (June, 1907), 219; Mary B. Mullett, "How a Dull, Fat Little Girl Became a Great Actress," *American Magazine,* XLIII (April, 1922), 112.

Ben-Ari, R. "Four Directors and the Actor," *Theatre Workshop,* I, No. 2 (January–March, 1937), 65–74.

Boleslavsky, Richard. "The Laboratory Theatre," *Theatre Arts Monthly,* VII (July, 1923), 244–50.

———. "Stanislavsky—the Man and His Methods," *Theatre Magazine,* XXXVII (April, 1923), 27.

Brinton, Christian. "Idols of the Russian Masses," *The Cosmopolitan,* XL (April, 1906), 613–20.

Carter, Huntley. "The New Age of the Moscow Art Theatre—Ten Years under Soviet Power," *Fortnightly Review,* CXXIII, New Series (January–June, 1928), 58–71.

Clark, Barrett H. "The Moscow Art Theatre in Berlin," *The Drama* XIII, No. 4 (January, 1923), 136–37.

Clurman, Harold. "Founders of the Modern Theatre," *Theatre Workshop,* I, No. 2 (January–March, 1937), 75–81.

———. "Stanislavsky in America," *New Republic,* CXXI (August 22, 1949), 20–21.

Crawford, Jack. "Moscow to Broadway," *The Drama* XIII, No. 6 (March, 1923), 212, 236.

D'Auvergne, Jean. "Moscow Art Theatre," *Fortnightly Review,* CI (May, 1914), 793.

Giatsintova, A. S. "Case History of a Role," *Theatre Workshop,* I, No. 1, Acting Issue (October, 1936), 68–72.

Gielgud, John. "An Actor Prepares: A Comment on the Stanislavsky Method," *Theatre Arts Monthly,* XXI (January, 1937), 30–34.

Guthrie, Tyrone. An interview, *Equity* (September, 1957).

Hewitt, Barnard, and Aristide D'Angelo. "The Stanislavsky System for Actors," *The Quarterly Journal of Speech,* XVII, No. 3 (June, 1932), 440.

Hoffman, Theodore. "At the Grave of Stanislavsky," *Columbia University Forum,* III, No. 1 (Winter, 1960), 31–37.

Hornblow, Arthur, "Olla Podrida," *Theatre Magazine* (May, 1923), 40.

Kazan, Elia. An interview, *Equity* (December, 1957).

———. "Interview with Richard Schechner," *Tulane Drama Review,* IX, No. 2 (Winter, 1964), 73.

King, Gertrude Besse. "The Cherry Orchard," *New Republic,* III (June 26, 1915), 207.

Lathrop, George Parsons. "The Inside Working of the Theatre," *Century Magazine,* LVI (June, 1898), 271–72.

Lewisohn, Ludwig. "Players from Moscow," *The Nation,* CXVI (March 14, 1923), 312.

Lindsay, Howard. "Professional Courtesy," *Equity* (March, 1958).

Logan, Joshua. "My Greatest Crisis," *Look Magazine,* XXII, No. 16 (August 5, 1958), 54, 56, 58, 60, 61.

―――. "Rehearsal with Stanislavsky," *Vogue,* CXIII, No. 10 (June, 1949), 78, 137, 139.

Meisner, Sanford, "The Reality of Doing," *Tulane Drama Review,* IX, No. 1, Fall 1964, p. 144.

Miles, Bernard. "The Acting Art," *Films in Review,* V, No. 6 (June–July, 1954), 267.

Nemirovich-Danchenko, Vladimir. "The Staging of a Novel," *Theatre Workshop,* I, No. 4 (September–October, 1937), 7.

Oliver, Edith. "The Theatre—Off Broadway," *The New Yorker,* February 20, 1965, p. 54.

Patterson, Ada. "David Belasco Reviews His Life Work" (Chats with American Dramatists, No. 6), *Theatre,* VI (September, 1906), 248.

Rapoport, I. "The Work of the Actor," *Theatre Workshop,* I, No. 1 (October, 1936), 5–40.

Rogoff, Gordon. "The Moscow Art Theatre: Surprises After Stanislavski," *The Reporter,* March 25, 1965, pp. 49–50.

Ruhl, Arthur. "Plays at the Moscow Art Theatre," *Current Opinion,* III (September, 1917), 170–71.

"The Russian Theatre," *Drama,* IX (February, 1919), 31–61.

Sayler, Oliver M. "Europe's Premier Playhouse in the Offing," *Theatre Magazine* (October, 1922), 215–18.

―――. "Theory and Practice in Russian Theatre," *Theatre Arts Magazine,* IV (July, 1920), 200–216, and "The Moscow Art Theatre," (October, 1920), 290–315.

Schmidt, Willi. "The American Actor," *Equity,* XLV, No. 4 (April, 1960), 6.

Schnitzler, Henry. "Truth or Consequences, or Stanislavsky Misinterpreted," *The Quarterly Journal of Speech* (April, 1954), 152–64.

Sherwood, Robert, Clurman, Harold, and Houghton, Norris. "An Actor Prepares: A Comment on the Stanislavsky Method," *Theatre Arts Monthly,* XXI (March, 1937), 148.

Soloviova, Vera. "The Reality of Doing," *Tulane Drama Review,* IX, No. 1, Fall 1964, p. 142.

Strasberg, Lee. "Interview with Richard Schechner," *Tulane Drama Review,* IX, No. 1, Fall 1964, pp. 131–32.

Towse, J. Rankin. "A Critical Review of Daly's Theatre," *Century Magazine* (June, 1898).

Tynan, Kenneth. "The Director as Critic," criticisms of "Lies Like Truth," a compilation of articles on the theatre written by Harold Clurman, and "Method—or Madness" by Robert Lewis, *The New Yorker* (January 31, 1959), 90–93.

Welch, Deshler. "Some Reminiscences by Deshler Welch," *The Book-Lover's Magazine,* III (April, 1904), 496.

Yartsev, P. "The Quiet Light," *Living Age,* CCCXVI (January, 1923), 171–74.

Zakhava, B. M. "Principles of Directing," *Theatre Workshop,* I, No. 3 (April–July, 1937), 43–58.

———. "Principles of Directing, Part II," *Theatre Workshop,* I, No. 4 (September–October, 1937), 14–33.

Zavadsky, Yuri. "Conversation with a Young Regisseur," *Theatre Arts Monthly,* XX (September, 1936), 726–30.

Zillboorg, Gregory. "The Russian Invasion," *The Drama,* XIII (January, 1923), 127–30.

Zolotow, Maurice. "The Stars Rise," *The Saturday Evening Post* (May 18, 1957), 44–45, 83–84, 86.

C. NEWSPAPERS

Announcement—"Library Exhibition Honors Stanislavski," *New York Herald Tribune,* October 27, 1958.

Atkinson, Brooks. "Amazing Paradox—America is Steeped in the Art of the Nation that Gives Us Anxiety," *New York Times,* March 8, 1959, Sec. 2, p. 1.

———. "Chekhov Centennial in Moscow," *New York Times,* January 10, 1960, Sec. 2, pp. 1–3.

Beaufort, John. "On and Off Broadway: Back to Stanislavski," *Christian Science Monitor* (Boston) September 26, 1956.

Darlington, W. A. "London Letter—A Visit by the Moscow Art Theatre and Some Home Grown Products," *New York Times,* Sunday, June 8, 1958, Sec. 3, p. 5.

Donnelly, Tom. "All Right, Louie, Don't Upstage Me," *New York World-Telegram,* February 1, 1957, p. 18.

Fordham University. "Basic Course in Acting Techniques of the Stanislavsky Method," advertisement, *Show Business,* September 23, 1957.

Gelb, Arthur. "An Actress Prepares," *New York Times,* April 12, 1959, Sec. 2, pp. 1–3.

———. "Two and Two Are Five," *New York Times,* February 2, 1958, Sec. 2, Part 1, pp. 1, 3.

Gielgud, John. "The Urge to Act—an Incurable Fever," *New York Times Magazine,* February 14, 1960, pp. 42, 47, 50.

Guthrie, Tyrone. "Is There Madness in 'The Method'?" *New York Times Magazine,* September 15, 1957, pp. 23, 82–83.

Houghton, Norris. "Exit Greatness, Enter the Party Line," a review of *The Theatre in Soviet Russia* by Nikolai A. Gorchakov, translated from the Russian by Edgar Lehrman, *New York Times Book Review*, January 5, 1958, p. 3.

————. "Lines Spoken off Stage," a review of *Mask or Face* by Michael Redgrave, *New York Times Book Review*, September 28, 1958.

Kerr, Walter. "Kerr Reviews Moscow Art Theatre's 'Cherry Orchard,' " *New York Herald Tribune*, February 10, 1965, p. 16.

————. " 'Three Sisters'—Moscow's Group Accomplishment," *New York Herald Tribune*, February 12, 1965, p. 9.

Lewis, Robert. "Method—or Madness?" *New York Times*, June 23, 1957, Sec. 2, p. 1.

Lindsay, Howard. Drama Mailbag, letter to the *New York Times* answering Strasberg's "View from the Studio," September 23, 1956.

Locke, Robinson. Robinson Locke Collection, Scrapbooks (press clippings on Daly, Otis Skinner, and Mrs. Gilbert).

Logan, Joshua. "The Method is the Means," a review of *Stanislavsky Directs* by Nikolai M. Gorchakov, translated by Miriam Goldina, *New York Times Book Review*, January 23, 1956.

————. "Russia Revisited," *New York Times*, August 3, 1958, Sec. 1, p. 1.

Moore, Sonia. Drama Mailbag, from a former student of Stanislavsky. She writes that Anthony Perkins should not be afraid to acquaint himself with "the Method." *New York Times*, December 29, 1957.

Nadel, Norman. "Soviet Play Artistically Done," *New York World-Telegram and Sun*, February 25, p. 17.

————. "Three Sisters Admirable at City Center," *New York World-Telegram and Sun*, February 12, 1965, p. 9.

"The New Logans and Kazans," *New York Times Magazine*, December 9, 1956, p. 26.

"News and Gossip of the Rialto," *New York Times*, May 25, 1958, Sec. 2, Part 1, p. 1.

Obituary of Maria Ouspenskaya, *New York Times*, December 4, 1949, p. 108.

Obituary of Michael Chekhov, *New York Times*, October 2, 1955, p. 86.

Peck, Seymour. "The Temple of 'The Method,' " *New York Times Magazine*, May 6, 1956, pp. 26, 27, 42, 47–48.

Ross, George, "The Moscow Art Players," *New York World-Telegram*, February 21, 1935, p. 13.

Sayler, Oliver M. "Origins and Progress of the Moscow Art Theatre," *New York Times Book Review* and *Magazine*, September 17, 1923, Sec. 3, p. 8, cited by Robert Albert Johnston, "The Moscow Art Theatre in America" (unpublished doctoral dissertation, Northwestern University, Chicago, 1951), p. 22.

Shepherd, Richard F. "Moscow Troupe Back After 40 Years," *New York Times,* February 3, 1965, p. 28.

Skinner, Cornelia Otis. "Actors Just Act—or No 'Pear-Shaped Tones,' " *New York Times Magazine,* December 13, 1942.

Strasberg, Lee. "Renaissance," *New York Times,* July 30, 1958, Sec. 2, p. 1.

————. "View from the Studio," *New York Times,* September 2, 1956, Sec. 2, p. 1.

Tallmer, Jerry. "Worst Foot Forward," *Village Voice,* November 26, 1958, p. 9.

Zolotow, Maurice. "The Olivier Method," the *New York Times,* February 7, 1960, Sec. 2, pp. 1–3.

D. *UNPUBLISHED MATERIALS*

Coffee, Mrs. Joe E. "The Practicability of the Stanislavsky System for General Use." Unpublished Master's thesis, West Texas State College, 1941.

Coger, Leslie Irene. "A Comparison for the Oral Interpreter of the Teaching Methods of Curry and Stanislavsky." Unpublished Doctoral dissertation, Northwestern University, 1952.

Engers, Kathleen Maria. "A Study of the Theories of Acting Proposed by the Actors and Actresses of Tragedy." Unpublished Master's thesis, Catholic University, 1949.

Gasper, Raymond Dominic. "A Study of the Group Theatre and Its Contributions to Theatrical Production in America." Unpublished Doctoral dissertation, The Ohio State University, 1955.

Grimes, Edith L. "The Method of Ensemble Acting in Russia and America." Unpublished Master's thesis, Hardin-Simmons University, 1948.

Hetler, Louis. "The Influence of the Stanislavsky Theories of Acting on the Teaching of Acting in the United States." Unpublished Doctoral dissertation, University of Denver, June, 1957.

Johnston, Robert Albert. "The Moscow Art Theatre in America." Unpublished Doctoral dissertation, Northwestern University, July, 1951.

Kramer, Sister Mary Angelita. "A Description and Comparison of the Backgrounds, Working Methods and Influences of Constantin Stanislavsky and Max Reinhardt." Unpublished Master's thesis, Marquette University, 1949.

Soloviova, Vera. "Memories of the Moscow Art Theatre." Unpublished manuscript.

Wagner, Arthur. "A Comparison Between Organic Acting and Organic Architecture." Unpublished Master's thesis, Smith College, 1948.

❊

Appendix

January 14, 1959

Dear Mrs. Hapgood:

Thank you for your interesting letter of January 9th, 1959. I certainly am very glad to be able to throw some light on Mr. Schnitzler's article, which I haven't had an opportunity to read—otherwise I would have immediately and categorically objected in writing and in publication to this coarse misleading misquotation.

You quote this paragraph from Mr. Schnitzler's article in The Quarterly Journal of Speech *(April, 1954) as follows:*

> *Vladimir Sokoloff, the noted actor, told me of a discussion he once had with Stanislavsky on the problems involved in training for the stage. At one point, Sokoloff referred to the book we know under the title* An Actor Prepares. *Stanislavsky reacted with a start and said: "Don't mention this book to me; and never give it to a student."*

I remember I saw Mr. Schnitzler in 1937 in Berkeley and had a conversation with him about the training of young American aspirants for the stage. During this conversation I told Mr. Schnitzler about the interesting talk which I had with Konstantin Sergeievich.

Evidently Mr. Schnitzler either didn't get at all the gist of my talk, or, using his clumsy, unbridled fantasy, distorted and maimed Stanislavsky's words.

These are the facts:

(1) I did not have a "discussion" with Konstantin Sergeievich "on the problems involved in training for the stage." When I saw Konstantin Sergeievich for the last time, we were sitting in the Bois de Bologne

326

in Paris and K.S. was reading to me a few chapters from the script of
An Actor Prepares. *In the ensuing conversation with K.S., to whom
I told how I had been working with my students in the school at
"Théâtre Montmartre—Charles Dullin," and that I might go to America, K.S. said to me approximately this: "Sokoloff, if and when you
go to America and work with young students and actors there, you
have to make considerable adjustments in using my book and our
'system.' The upbringing, education, speech, language, schooling, mentality, historical and social heritage, the economic system, all the way
of life there, are so entirely different from what you and other young
students had in Russia, that many of the principles, rules, advice,
methods in our 'system' are not applicable, not necessarily useful and
practicable for the human material that you'll have to do with over
there. The young people there are more free than the youngsters used
to be in Russia, they are more extrovert, which is the essential symp-
tom and characteristic of an actor; they don't have so many inhibitions
as our youngsters used to have; they don't suffer so much shyness,
stage fright, etc., they are used to a democratic way of life. So don't
copy our system, adapt it, don't insist rigorously on some of the exercises; they don't need them, and it will only bring harm, only be confusing to them, will kill the spontaneity of their reactions and acting
and make them introverts; they will be afraid to make a single step
or inward gesture, constantly spying on themselves, being in doubt
whether they are 'feeling' anything, or not."*

*(2) "Sokoloff referred to the book we know under the title 'An Actor
Prepares' "—Sokoloff did not* refer *to the book; K.S. was reading
to me excerpts from it. (In manuscript evidently, it was not published
in any language until two years later, 1936, when it was issued by
Theatre Arts.)*

(3) "Stanislavsky reacted with a start.*"—This is not only a misquotation, this is a stupid invention of Mr. Schnitzler.*

*(4) "Don't mention this book to me and never give it to a student."
—Of course Konstantin Sergeievich could* never *have said such a silly
thing, and naturally I could never have invented such an idiocy, even
using Schnitzler's clumsy perverse faculty of imagination.*

I hope I have been able to tell you exactly *the circumstances of where
and when I had the opportunity to talk with K.S. after he was kind
enough to read to me excerpts from his book, knowing very well that
I always cherished every happy occasion to see him and listen to him
when he was in Berlin, where I used to be a German actor with Max
Reinhardt and in Paris, where I used to be a French actor with
Copeau, Jouvet, Dullin.*

By the way, what I told you in a short version about my interesting conversation with K.S. in the summer, 1934, I describe more explicitly and reverently in my coming book, commenting also on the fact how right was K.S., when I see now how young American actors and aspirants are bedevilled by the so-called "Method," thanks to the unholy, harmful heritage of the Theatre Group—or is it Group Theatre? (I forget the name of the organization.)

It is sad and disappointing to watch those "Methodists" acting: Every individuality has been levelled by the cliché—"Method" to an inarticulate performance in speech and expression. See one, see all. As one very intelligent author said, "What they need is a method not to discipline them but to galvanize them."

The "System" was originally devised to counter the style of acting which used to be known as "ham," but trying to destroy the "ham" the distorted "System" under the name of "Method" is destroying the theatre—using a Russian saying:

("They throw out the child together with the water.")
(I know you understand and speak Russian perfectly.)

I'll be happy to present you with a copy of my coming book with my respect and admiration for your splendid work in translating Stanislavsky's books.

With my very best wishes,

Very sincerely yours,
(signed) Vladimir Sokoloff

Criteria for Judging a Contribution to Theatre Art and Practice as Submitted to a Jury of Practitioners

	Essential	Desirable	Unnecessary
1. A contribution will clarify the playwright's intention for the actor, the director, and the audience.			
2. A contribution will assist the actor in interpreting and executing his role.			
3. A contribution will be a means of helping the director in understanding the actor's problems and of offering assistance in their solution.			
4. A contribution will assist the designer in making environment an integral and supporting factor of the actor's presentation.			
5. A contribution will stimulate an emotional and/or intellectual response on the part of the audience.			
6. A contribution will stimulate interest in theatre as an art and as a craft.			
7. A contribution will stand the test of time.			

Signature: _____

329

Index

Abbey Theatre, 208, 221
Achurch, Janet, 154
Acting: Belasco "quiet style," 195–96; Bouci-cault definition, 140; by-play, 168; Chekhov (Michael) method, 257; classical, 41–42; concentration in, 87, 100, 141–42 (*See also* Concentration); copying, 29, 30, 32, 36, 41, 42, 44, 49; Delsarte System, 156–58, 165; dual consciousness in, 144, 147–56, 159, 181, 304; emotion and, 130–59 (*See also* Emotion); improvisation in, 94, 116–17, 179, 182, 225, 245, 251, 274, 304–305; "Method" *vs.* "non-Method," 261–65; realism in (*See* Realism); Stanislavsky early practice, 29–31, 34–35, 39; Stanislavsky System (*See* Stanislavsky System); technical influences in America, 130–59, 252; technique changes (1900–1925), 164–82; through-action, 92, 106, 108. *See also* Actors; Characterization; Direction; *and see* specific aspects of acting.
Acting Is Believing (McGaw), 259
Acting, A Handbook of the Stanislavsky Method (Cole), 125, 305
Actor Creates, The (D'Angelo), 251
Actor Prepares, An (Stanislavsky), 105, 177, 258, 263, 295; on the accidental, 302; American publication, 249–54, 275; on concentration, 300; on entrances, 175; Gielgud on, 254–55; Redgrave on, 257, 279; on rehearsal, 225; Russian edition, 276–77
Actors: American culture and, 268–69; American response to the Moscow Art theatre, 232–34; communal living and, 117, 205–206, 245; communion on-stage, 38, 60, 90, 100, 168, 255, 297, 304–305; director relationships, 305–306; historical records of, 176–77; nineteenth-century favorites, 14–17; non-professionals, 84; "permanent companies," 24; per-

sonality *vs.* dramatic interpretation, 41, 52, 134, 176, 178, 229, 262, 269; private conduct of, 11, 12–13, 48, 66, 69, 90; qualifications, 177, 258, 299, 303; salaries, 68, 116, 189, 202, 208, 210, 283; serf, 8, 9–13; "spiritual order" of, 117; Stanislavsky System response, 70–71, 91, 116, 239–87, 295, 311; star system, 71, 191–93, 200, 233. *See also* individual names.
"Actors and Acting" (Coquelin), 138
Actors Equity Association, 210, 226, 282, 286, 307
Actors Studio, 242; "Method" and, 260–62, 263, 267, 268, 272, 273, 307
Actors Talk About Acting (Funke and Booth), 281
Actor's Ways and Means, The (Redgrave), 257, 279
Actors' Workshop, 244
Adams, Maude, 192, 193
Adasheff School, 114. *See also* First Studio.
Adler, Stella, 240, 245–46, 275, 276; on affective memory, 270, 271; seminars (1964), 282
Adrienne Lecouvreur, 138–39
Affective memory, *see* Emotion
Afinogenov, 310
Aglavaine and Selysette (Maeterlinck), 208
Albright, Harry Darkes, 251–52
Aldwych Theatre, London, 283
Alexander I, tsar of Russia, 7, 8, 11
Alexander II, tsar of Russia, 21, 22
Alexander III, tsar of Russia, 58
Alexandrinsky Theatre, 59, 73, 77
Alexeiev Circle, 29–39, 50, 58; *Mikado* of, 35, 97
Alexeiev (Stanislavsky's father), 27, 29, 32, 39, 40

Patterson, Ada, 194
Paul I, tsar of Russia, 10
Pavlova, Anna Matveyeva, 216, 243
Payne, B. Iden, 202
Peabody, Josephine Preston, 200
Peck, Seymour, 260
Peer Gynt (Ibsen), 169
Peker, Boris, 286
Perevoschikova, Marie, *see* Lilina
Perkins, Osgood, 200
Peter I (The Great), tsar of Russia, 6
Peter III, tsar of Russia, 7, 8
Peter Weston, 232
Peters, Rollo, 209
Phelps, William Lyon, 227; quoted, 231, 233
Philadelphia Museum, 186
Philanderer, The (Shaw), 200
Philharmonic Dramatic School, 58, 59, 60, 93; Moscow Art Theatre and, 65, 67, 215
Philosophical Institution, Edinburgh, 142
Philosophy of the Human Voice (Rush), 159
Pickford, Mary, 193
Pigeon, The (Galsworthy), 200
Piper, The (Peabody), 200
Pissemsky, 23, 43–44, 53
Playbill (periodical), 286
Playhouse Theatre, 200–201, 263
Plays, *see* Drama; *and see* specific works.
Plymouth Theatre, New York City, 205
Poel, William, 202
Pogodin, Nikolai, *Kremlin Chimes*, 282, 283–84, 286
Polish Jew, The, see *Bells (The)*, or *The Polish Jew* (Erckmann and Chatrian)
Polus, 150
Potekhin, *Practical Man*, 31, 32, 58
Povarskaya Street Studio, 85, 93
"Poverty and Wealth of Soviet Theatre, The" (Houghton), 286
Power of Darkness, The (Tolstoy), 83, 84
Powers, Leland, 157
Practical Man, The (Potekhin), 31, 32, 58
Press, The, 70, 71, 217, 281; on *Days of the Turbins*, 102; on the First Studio, 116, 118, 119, 120, 220; foreign, 85–86; on the Moscow Art Theatre American tour, 226–34; Russian culture and, 214, 220–21; on *The Sea Gull*, 78; on the star system, 188; on *Winter Bound*, 207. *See also* specific journals.
Pressman, David, 260
Prince, William, 245
Princess Theatre, New York City, 205, 239
Princess Turandot (Gozzi), 98, 121, 124–25, 206, 308
Princeton University, 256
"Principles of Directing" (Zakhava), 253–54, 305–306
Problems of the Actor, The (Calvert), 177, 182
Producing the Play (Gassner), 245, 254, 300
Production: experimental techniques of, 88–89, 97–108, 119–20, 121, 123, 124, 125; little theatre, 201–10; Nemirovich-Danchenko techniques, 58, 60, 64–65, 67–68; nineteenth century decline in standards, 22–23, 24; Povarskaya Street Studio, 85; Soviet techniques,

99; Stanislavsky authority in, 65–66; Stanislavsky early practice in, 28–29, 31–39, 50–57, 65. *See also* Staging.
Programs, 66
Prokofyev, Vladimir, 265, 282
"Prompt Book, The" (Young), 250
Properties, 76, 108; imagination and, 80, 299
Province of Expression, The (Curry), 158
Provincetown Playhouse, New York City, 202, 204–207, 210, 250
Prunella (Housman and Granville-Barker), 200
Pulitzer Prize, 207
Pushkin, Alexander S., 7, 18, 40, 92, 95
Pushkin Theatre, 21
Pushkino rehearsal group, 68, 69, 219

Quakers, 227
Quarterly Journal of Speech, 248, 255, 275
Queen of Spades, The (Pushkin), 95
"Quiet Light, The" (Yartsev), 223
Quintilian, on emotion, 150, 156, 294

Rachel (Elizabeth Felix), 138–39, 144, 152
Racine, Jean, 7
Radcliffe College, 202
Raevsky, Joseph, 287
Raikh, Zinaida, 96, 97
Rainey, Ford, 245, 280
Rapoport, I., 252–53, 254, 300, 302
Raubicheck, Letitia, 183 nn. 10–11
Ravinia Park, Chicago, 201
Realism, 1, 102, 230, 231–32, 250; the accidental and, 302; of Antoine, 218, 223; "artistic maximalism," 99; Chekhov and, 59, 72–79; Diderot and, 131; Griboyedov, 17–18; Guthrie on, 267; Meyerhold rejection of, 93–95, 96–97; "natural school of acting" and, 139–47; Shchepkin and, 16, 19–21, 23, 24, 223; "Socialist," 122; Stanislavsky view of, 47, 56, 60, 71, 84, 87–88, 106, 108, 215, 217, 219, 221, 234, 240, 304; "theatrical," 125; Vakhtangov, 116, 121
"Realism of the Spirit" (Corbin), 229
Realistic Theatre, 126
Redemption (The Living Corpse—Tolstoy), 91, 114
Redgrave, Michael, quoted, 257, 279
Reeves, John A., cited, 4 n. 2
"Reflections on Acting" (Talma), 130, 132–36, 143
Rehan, Ada, 187, 190, 191
Rehearsal, 1–2, 13–14, 83, 87, 91, 225; Belasco and, 194; characterization exercises, 179; direction at, 67, 101, 268; emotion and, 181; First Studio, 115–16; Houghton on, 252; improvisation and, 274; Nemirovich-Danchenko dress-rehearsals, 59, 60; Opera Studio, 256; pre-rehearsal phase, 58, 66, 68; Pushkin Theatre, 21–22; at Pushkino, 69, 219; *Sea Gull*, 73; *Snow Maiden*, 80; Solodovnikov Theatre, 51; Stanislavsky family practice, 31, 32, 33, 35–36; Stanislavsky on value of,

❋

Erratum

In the caption for Illustration 2 (following page 88), *Chekov* appears as *Tchekov*.